THE
OLIVE ROUTE

the
Olive Route

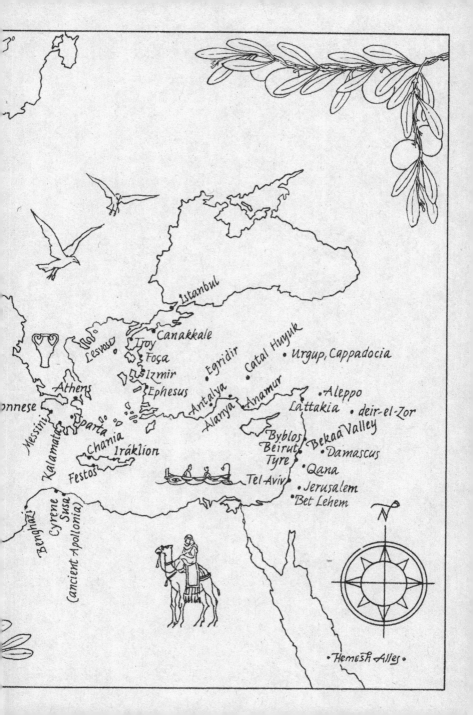

Praise for the Olive series

'Drinkwater has a sharp eye for character, and the people who populate *The Olive Route* will not disappoint her fans'

Independent on Sunday

'A storyteller of great economy and deftness and one who, in telling tales, captures the Midi effectively. There are few better portraits of the different worlds – farmers and water-diviners, crooks and Euro-trash, Algerians and wearying officialdom – that intersect to create the Côte d'Azur' *Daily Telegraph*

'Drinkwater is a rare writer who tackles other people brilliantly . . . Vibrant, intoxicating and heart-warming'

Sunday Express

'The new leader of the pack' *The Times*

'Charming and well written. As the olives ripen to a luscious, dark-purply black, the reader is drawn into the peculiarities and joys of Provençal life' *Daily Mail*

'A spellbinding memoir and a must for anyone who dreams of moving to a kinder climate and starting a new life' *Choice*

Carol Drinkwater is a multi-award-winning actress, who is best known for her portrayal of Helen Herriot in the BBC Television series *All Creatures Great and Small*. She is also the author of over twenty books, both fiction and non-fiction. Her quartet of memoirs set on her olive farm in the South of France has sold more than a million copies worldwide, and her solo journey round the Mediterranean in search of the olive tree's mythical secrets inspired two books – *The Olive Route* and *The Olive Tree* – and a five-part documentary film series, *The Olive Route*. She is also the author of several novels including *The Forgotten Summer, The Lost Girl, The House on the Edge of the Cliff* and *An Act of Love*.

Carol lives in the South of France where she is writing her next novel.

By the same author

NON-FICTION

Crossing the Line: Young
Women and the Law
The Olive Farm
The Olive Season
The Olive Harvest
Return to the Olive Farm
The Illustrated Olive Farm
The Olive Route
The Olive Tree

FICTION

An Abundance of Rain
Akin to Love
Mapping the Heart
Because You're Mine
The Forgotten Summer
The Lost Girl
The House on the Edge of the
Cliff

FICTION FOR YA

The Haunted School
Molly
Molly on the Run
The Hunger
Twentieth-Century Girl
Suffragette
Nowhere to Run
The Only Girl in the World

KINDLE SINGLES
(e-book novellas
for Amazon)

The Girl in Room Fourteen
Hotel Paradise
A Simple Act of Kindness
The Love of a Stranger

Best known for her role as Helen Herriot in BBC Television's *All Creatures Great and Small* (for which she was awarded The Variety Club Television Personality of the Year Award), Carol Drinkwater has enjoyed a long and distinguished career as both an actress and writer. During her acting career she has worked in film, television and theatre. Her credits include being a member of Laurence Olivier's National Theatre, working with Stanley Kubrick on *A Clockwork Orange*, and with Max Von Sydow, whom she played opposite in the film *Father*, for which she won the Critics Circle Award for Best Film Actress. Her bestselling children's novel, *The Haunted School*, has sold over 150,000 copies and was made into a film and television series which won the Chicago Film Festival Award for children's films. Carol Drinkwater continues to write for both youngsters and adults. Her memoirs *The Olive Farm*, *The Olive Season* and *The Olive Harvest* are international bestsellers. Carol is working with UNESCO to help found an Olive Heritage Trail around the Mediterranean Basin. The aim is to create peace within the region and honour the heritage of this sacred tree.

Visit her website at www.caroldrinkwater.com.

THE
OLIVE ROUTE

A Personal Journey to the
Heart of the Mediterranean

CAROL DRINKWATER

WEIDENFELD & NICOLSON

A W&N PAPERBACK

First published in Great Britain in 2006
by Weidenfeld & Nicolson
This paperback edition published in 2007
by Weidenfeld & Nicolson,

an imprint of The Orion Publishing Group Ltd,
Carmelite House, 50 Victoria Embankment,
London EC4Y 0DZ

An Hachette UK company

19 20

A CIP catalogue record for this book
is available from the British Library.

ISBN 978-0-7528-8139-3

Typeset by Input Data Services Ltd, Frome

Printed and bound at Clays Ltd, Elcograf S.p.A.

The Orion Publishing Group's policy is to use papers that
are natural, renewable and recyclable products and made
from wood grown in sustainable forests. The logging and
manufacturing processes are expected to conform to the
environmental regulations of the country of origin.

www.orionbooks.co.uk

For Linda,
don't let us look back,
but onwards, arm in arm

Acknowledgements

There are so many to thank for this book, generous people I met throughout my travels who assisted me, showed me warmth or pointed me in a good direction, that I hardly know where to begin. They are written in no particular order: Matty Cremona, Sammy Cremona, Stuart Anderson, Dominic Conner, Uri Avnery, Frank Barrett, Wendy Driver, Cleopatra Taliani, Vicky Gonidellis, Professor Kiourellis, Soheila Hayek, Alexandre Hayek, George Kiniklis, Professor Striapolis, Dierk Schaaf, the Nassar family, Daphne Caruana Galizia, Susie de Cataret, Natalino Fenech, Adam Keller, Salah Hayek, Esaaf Hayek and Iris Hornick.

Back at base, there is a fabulous team at my publisher's looking after me, headed by my treasured editor and friend Alan Samson for Weidenfeld & Nicolson, and Susan Lamb for Orion. Enormous thanks to all, including my publicists, marketing team, designers, sales teams, Alice Walker for the loan of her very wise words, and of course the booksellers.

Thank you also to my splendid and great fun agent Jonathan Lloyd at Curtis Brown and his two assistants, Camilla Goslett and Alice Lutyens, to Hitesh Shah, Chris Brown and Hilary Heath, and to my stalwart and loyal mother, Phyllis McCormack, Dennis Drinkwater, and my husband, Michel, for supporting me throughout this long and sometimes scary journey.

We will simply not let the writers of history claim we did not exist. Why should the killers of the world be 'the future' and not us?

ALICE WALKER, *The Way Forward Is With a Broken Heart*

Marseille

2005

Glasses of cloudy yellow Ricard pastis between our fingers, a half-emptied bottle of mineral water on the table in front of us, Michel and I gazed at the oil-slicked water slapping the hulls of docked vessels. It was not a particularly inviting sight, rainbowed and sludged with diesel and debris emitted by the constant flow of maritime traffic within this ancient harbour.

'It should have been a carafe of tap water, not San Pellegrino,' I grinned at my husband, 'then this moment would have been intrinsically French Mediterranean.' I sipped my aniseed drink, whose tint was of the fine yellow dust that blankets the Côte d'Azur in spring; pollen blown off the pine trees by accommodating winds.

It was creeping towards July. Early evening. We were in Marseille to mark the 'embarkation' of my journey, though my flight for Beirut did not leave for another week.

Along the waterfront to left and right, the restaurants and bistros were busy with preparations for the arrival of diners. The outdoor tables of the quayside bars were milling with animated folk of all ages and nationalities, blistered by the sun, quaffing *apéritifs*. This was the Mediterranean, after all, where life has been lived out of doors since time immemorial.

Michel turned to me and smiled. 'It's been a long while in gestation, this journey of yours, and we'll celebrate it this evening with a delicious bouillabaisse.'

I had originally set off in search of the historical roots of the olive tree in the autumn of 2001. At that time, my marriage was hanging together by the slenderest of threads and I had intended that the journey put some distance between me and the solitary experience life on our French olive farm had become for me. I had flown to what I had hoped would be the ideal base, the Levant, nudging the cradle of Western civilisation, to a strip of Mediterranean coast divided today into Lebanon and Syria. It was September 2001. Needless to say, I never reached my destinations.

Back in Europe, the world in shock, I set my project aside, and as events unfolded and the Middle East grew less stable, all plans for those travels were stuffed into a file I might have entitled 'Trips I will never take'. It disappointed me. I had grown excited by the idea of tracing the olive and its culture back to its inception, to see how the trading of it had influenced the personality, the topography of the Mediterranean. My Mediterranean. Our Mediterranean. But it was not to be. War was imminent. I am neither correspondent nor political journalist. The Middle East was no place for me, or so I had decided.

But fate had tricks in store.

When Tony Blair stood alongside George W. Bush and declared his intention to take British troops into Iraq, I flew to London and marched in protest. I remember that Saturday afternoon clearly. Friends and I were nudging the nib of the rally and so arrived early at the finishing stage in Hyde Park. Deed done, my pals drove home while I retraced my steps, walking the line of protestors, stopping at the Royal Academy in Piccadilly to tour an exhibition. When I emerged into the afternoon sunlight a couple of hours later, the procession was still taxiing forward in upbeat spirits towards the park. The numbers were impressive. I was optimistic, but the Sunday papers the following day reported the figures of attendance short of the reality, diminishing in the eyes of

Britain an opposition that had spoken out resoundingly yet peacefully. I was dismayed. A considerable proportion of city windows were flying anti-war stickers, but the protests went unheard. The weapons of mass destruction argument had won the day. War on Iraq was declared. The history books tell the rest.

I returned to France, to the farm. Nonetheless, the reportage coming in from the Middle East troubled me, as much as it did everyone else who had resisted the intervention, and I began to feel depressed by the destruction and my impotence.

On a personal level, the marital challenges Michel and I had confronted were resolving themselves. I felt no need to flee my life, but I felt an urgent need to return to the eastern Mediterranean, to learn the secrets of the olive tree. The project I had shelved remained in my mind; a terrific adventure; a once-in-a-lifetime opportunity I had given up on. And then, quite out of the blue, I received a letter from a complete stranger living in Australia. The sender had read of my passion for olives and had sent a photograph that portrayed him standing within a hollowed-out olive tree in Lebanon. What really grabbed my attention was that he claimed the tree was six thousand years old. If I had been without commitments, I would have jumped on a plane to Beirut that very morning. Instead, I pulled down my boxes, rummaged through the paperwork and reconsidered my route in earnest. I searched everywhere to find out the whereabouts of that Lebanese old-timer, but without success. If such a specimen really existed, it would take the history of olive cultivation further back than I had imagined. I resolved to go in search of it, and once discovered, I intended to continue on around the Mediterranean basin, seeking clues, marking what remained. I ordered obscure tomes on the Internet, I made contact with

3

universities, publishers working with material in languages that had not been spoken for thousands of years. I visited UNESCO in Paris. I understood they had been debating a World Heritage status for the olive trail, perceiving it as cultural landscape, a shared legacy. The Greek lady I met up with was firmly behind the project, 'But,' she said, 'it is difficult to define such a trail. Where does it begin, or end?'

That was precisely what excited me about the quest. The trails, the routes had not been identified; they were uncharted. This was virgin territory. I would start with the Lebanese tree, if I could find it, and from there I would go wherever the next clue took me. Michel, friends judged my plan too vague, but I knew that I had to get going, not in books, but across the water. I knew I had to be there, at the foot of that old Lebanese master, breathing the scents of the Mediterranean, meeting its people, listening to its winds, giving myself up to its locations and taking my botanical sleuthing any which way.

Michel signalled the waiter. '*L'addition, s'il vous plaît.*'

Someone called, '*Bonsoir!*' It was a grinning African, skin impenetrably black, in leaf-green *galabiya*. He was covered in satchels bursting with sunglasses and attempted to interest us in a 'designer wristwatch' or fishing tackle. I said I'd take the fishing tackle if it was Gucci. He laughed, dallied a while, gazing about, smiled *bonne soirée* and plodded off along his way. This teeming city of Marseille is France's largest, busiest port. It also represents the nation's most colourful melting pot; in that sense, Marseille is quintessentially Mediterranean.

'So why Marseille, why begin the journey here?' asked Michel.

'Aside from the pleasure of a night in a hotel with you, there are two reasons,' I replied.

'And they are?'

'Until 600 BC, this was little more than a well-situated inlet, a deep creek with a backdrop of mountains to protect it. Its history was born when Greek sailors from Phocaea, on the Aegean coast of Asia Minor, modern-day Turkey, landed here, founded a settlement and christened it Massalia.'

Steps from where Michel and I were sitting was the original creek of Lacydon. It was to here those pioneering, salt-blasted, pre-Christian Greeks sailed in after their long and hazardous crossing from the eastern shores of the Mediterranean. They discovered a well-sheltered estuary, between mountains and sea, ideal for the docking of their boats and the establishment of a portside colony.

'Quite a navigational feat to have plied this sea from east to west in their wooden galleys. Did they chance upon this coast, do you think, or had they been told of it?'

I shook my head. I had no idea. 'But what is highly probable is that aboard those vessels were olive saplings. Those sea-faring Phocaeans introduced olive trees to this coast. Here, in Marseille, steps from where we are sitting, the French olive story began.'

Who had spotted their approach? Were they made welcome? Were the olive trees received as peace offerings? Who planted them?

According to the Greek historian Herodotus, those Phocaeans were the first long-distance sailors. But, I wondered, were they really the first on the scene here? Or might it have been the Phoenicians who lived in city-states along the coast of Phoenicia, better known today as Lebanon and Syria? Massalia is a Phoenician word, not Greek.

Michel glanced at his watch. 'If you really want to stay over, we should find a hotel, *non*?'

I nodded.

'We'll come back later and eat bouillabaisse.'

'Ah, good Turkish cuisine,' I jested.

We left a few euros on the table and set off, wandering through the narrow, winding, souk-like lanes of the market behind the port, where two languages, French and Arabic, were being shouted, high-pitched strains across grimy streets, where down-at-heel Arabs in hats milled to and fro, where dark-skinned men with moustaches in black leather jackets brushed close against one another, looking furtively about them before swift exchanges of some illicit substance, where the butchers advertised their wares as authentic halal, Arabic for 'lawful', 'permissible', as opposed to *'haram'* which is 'not permitted'. (From *'haram'* comes 'harem' – wives and concubines owned by one male are forbidden to others.) The streets were litter-strewn and cramped. Everywhere the sweet-stale odour of exposed meat. Here and there at kerbsides, scruffy men, all warped bones and stiffness, stretched out crow-fingers for a euro. Crossing over the main thoroughfare, La Canebière, from the market, we faced a series of deteriorating blocks of flats. *Ashelems* is the French nickname for them, HLMs or *habitations à loyer modéré*: state-subsidised high-rises occupied predominantly by Arab families and African blacks, the most underprivileged sectors of French society. From where we were standing, displays of washing and satellite dishes dominated the meagre terraces. Carried across the evening air, we heard the cries of fraught women and the bawling of agitated babies. Everywhere gypsies, Arabs or squatting whiskery buskers with guitars, few white faces in the *centre ville*. The *vieux* port was more European in this season of tourists, more expensive. The police presence around the streets of the gritty city was disquieting. Their cars screeched round corners as though driven by stuntmen in action movies. Their pedestrian profile seemed to be equally imposing, patrolling in packs of four.

Pausing outside the Espace Culture, violet-blue eyes looked down upon us from a calm, smiling, well-fed face. A giant poster of Florence Aubenas alongside her Iraqi interpreter, Hussein Hanoun al-Saadi, hung from the façade. Photos taken before they were kidnapped in Baghdad on 5 January. Six months of incarceration. In this Muslim-dominated city, it was reassuring to see the Belgium-born journalist and her colleague remembered. The organisation Reporters Sans Frontières had joined forces with the daily newspaper *Libération*, which Aubenas wrote for, and together they were working tirelessly for her release.

Michel wrapped an arm over my shoulder. 'Promise you'll be careful,' he whispered.

I had intended to visit both Iran and Iraq. Even if olive culture had not originated there, they might contain traces of its venerable past, but a woman travelling alone in war zones without professional credentials would have been irresponsible. Lebanon, though risky, was perfectly accessible and I had friends there. I was going to begin my journey with them, jumping off in search of trees from a secure springboard.

We found a hotel offering the smallest but cosiest of rooms; inexpensive and a step from the port. The lift stopped at the fifth floor. Our room was on the sixth. M carried our bag up the remaining flight and from there we climbed to the roof, to a view the desk clerk insisted was unmissable. We found ourselves gazing down upon red rooftops and all the way along the port past the Fort St-Jean to the lighthouse, the sea, to distant invisible locations where, in future weeks, I would find myself.

Over the bay to the east was the towering Notre-Dame de

la Garde basilica. It shone in the evening sunlight like an overgrown Christmas decoration. We toyed with the idea of climbing to it after dinner, but knew that we would not.

'And the second reason for commencing the journey in Marseille?' asked Michel.

'It was from here that I set off on my first travel adventure. My maiden voyage,' I laughed. 'I had recently turned twenty-two. It was late May. I had taken a high-speed train from Paris intending to change here and continue directly to Antibes, where actor friends awaited me. Unfortunately, the express arrived after sunset and the last train towards Italy had already departed. I had split London a week earlier with £100 in my purse, scrimped and scratched during a poorly paid year as an actress at the Citizens' Theatre in Glasgow. Descending into the deep-blue world of olive groves, mauve mountains and Judas trees, I doubt I even noticed them. I was set on a course for Greece. My funds were precious. They had to be eked out over an entire summer, transporting me to Hellenic isles and back. I had no return ticket. A hotel in Marseille was beyond my slender means, so I settled for a wooden bench in the St-Charles railway station, only to be woken by a porter giving me my marching orders. My protestations in minimal French achieved no results and I found myself turfed out, staring into a darkened sky beyond the cityscape. I descended the sweep of steps lugging my unwieldy case, clueless as to where I might pass what remained of the night.

'Of Marseille it is said all roads lead to its ancient harbour. Instinctively, I traced that path and descended seawards, ending up at the head of the Quai du Port.' I pointed a finger to a spot not far from where we had enjoyed our pastis.

'Once at the harbour, perched on my upturned case, I inhaled the stench of diesel and discarded fish and innocently awaited the dawn. So naïve was I that it never occurred to me I had installed myself in the red-light district.' Michel laughed. 'In fact, *so* naïve was I that even once there, facing the swell of boats and stinking sludge of sea, engaged by the comings and goings of the night, bemused by the number of males who approached me, I still did not cotton on to the delicacy of my situation. It took one of the women whose beat I was obviously trespassing on to shift me. With a raised fist, she growled at me. Although I did not comprehend her street French, the message was perfectly clear. I passed the remaining dark and lonely hours wandering aimlessly about the streets, dreaming of the distant shores I was bound for, in search of deep, southern skies, exotic perfumes and ancient civilisations whose stories were scored in stone. I knew nothing of primeval olive groves weathered by time.'

'Well, we can afford our cramped little room, and dinner, too. Let's go.'

'There are no drugs in this city any more,' the waiter was assuring a party of five middle-aged American women at a neighbouring table. '*Chères mesdames*, happily life here is not like the film *The French Connection*.'

Marseille's municipality was keen to promote its benign Marcel Pagnol image and leave the vice and drug traffic behind, but having watched exchanges up in the market earlier in the afternoon, in spite of the very active police presence, Michel and I both agreed that the seedy portside underworld was alive and kicking, as it had probably been for two and a half thousand years.

We had chosen a restaurant, plastic tables and chairs, checked cloth adorned with spluttering candle, and ordered a bottle of wine. Dinner was to be the traditional Marseillaise bouillabaisse. The warm night air reeked of cooked fish and cigarette smoke.

The waiter, balding, black-waistcoated, large white apron, returned with our wine, eager to strike up conversation. It was relatively early. There were only the English-speaking Americans or us.

'Is it true that the origins of bouillabaisse are in Asia Minor and that here the dish is as old as Marseille itself?' I enquired.

He shook his head, hotly denying any such notion. 'The Greeks founded the city, yes, but we Provençals created the fish soup. *"Boui-abaisso"* is a Provençal word. A pot for boiling is a *"boui"* in the local dialect. Boiled liquid, that was the basis of it. It was born out of the fishing community working this coast. The lesser-known fishes were given to the families as well as leftovers and unsold catch. All taken home and boiled up in a solid iron pan. It was a working man's soup, but it was the Catalonians who contributed the saffron, the addition of which gives it its distinct colour and flavour. The dish, like the city of Marseille, is a melting pot. A *mélange*. Every race is here.'

The tourists called for our waiter's attention. He chatted with them for a few minutes and then returned to regale us with the story of how the entire port made a killing out of cheating a local insurance company. A small fishing trawler returning from a night out at sea broke the lines of coastal fishing nets and, unwittingly, hauled everyone's overnight catch into port. The world of the harbour woke the next morning to schools of large fish swimming in between the boats. Everyone claimed damages: fishermen, boat owners, the restaurants for lack of produce, even the trawler. Each stood witness for the rest and the insurance company was obliged to pay up. 'The harbour population relive it as a tale of triumph.'

I wondered from which peoples had the traits of trickiness, wiliness, such caricature-drawn characteristics of the Provençals, been inherited. Our bouillabaisse arrived and we tucked into it with gusto. Unfortunately, it was not the best we had eaten and the sum paid was more costly than our hotel room, but the waiter's tales compensated for the disappointment.

After an early breakfast, we took a leisurely stroll to the lighthouse, past the Fort St-Jean, undergoing renovations. From the farthest point, I spotted, round the quayside, the dock used for ferries and cruise ships, where several mighty vessels bound for North Africa awaited embarkation. If I had intended to begin my journey in Tunisia, it would have been on one of those ships I would have ploughed the sea.

'That's where Quashia boards his ferry for Algeria.' Quashia was our Algerian Arab gardener.

A trio of retired, salty-faced fellows, amateur fishermen in check shirts and flat caps, were seated on canvas stools on the jetty, alongside their rods, baguette sandwiches in hand, calling out to one another, talking recipes and intricate, varied preparations for food. Locals in shorts and canvas shoes sat about reading *La Provence*, smoking, drinking beer. It was not yet 10 a.m., but it was not uncommon to see the diehards in the bars downing their first brandy at six or seven in the morning. Visitors licking ice creams watched on fascinated as the ruddy-faced *pêcheurs* in blue berets, bow-legged, varicose-veined, repainted the hulls of their striped fishing boats.

'The work they are engaged in has been lived out around this basin since the beginning. I will come across it everywhere.'

A couple of boats were for sale. The going rate seemed to be €2,000 apiece, which struck us as precious little for a vessel that served a man's occupation and his stomach and had done so for millennia. Church bells chimed the hour. It was time to leave. I slipped my hand into Michel's. An empty Fanta bottle bobbed aimlessly in the water, which had a fishy and rank odour, yet I felt its pull. Christened *'mare nostrum'* by the Romans, 'our sea'. I heard its sirens.

'That night on my upturned case, all those years back, my first solo outing, this city was threatening to me,' I said to Michel.

'In what way?'

'The pimps, whores, sailors, the Arabs, the foreignness of their speech, their manners. I feared I would be raped, robbed, harmed in some way. It was the alienness I mistrusted, the unknown. This same city is, today, even grimier, seedier, more hard-nosed than it was then, but what it embodies is no longer alien to me and I don't fear it. Quite the opposite, I embrace it. It is intrinsic to our French Mediterranean, to a way of life that began in this very harbour. Don't look so fearful,' I said, brushing Michel's cheek. 'I won't be staying away for ever, and I will have to return every now and then to help Quashia when you are not around.'

'I don't know why you can't wait until the war in Iraq is over.'

'It is because of the war, don't you see, that I must go now. When the peoples living round this big pond began to look beyond their own patch, to climb into boats, cross the waters, find harbours, ports, trading posts, they commenced the weaving of a Mediterranean tapestry. Our Mediterranean. Our sea. And wherever they landed, the olive tree with its branch of peace seems to have been a calling card. Yet nobody knows from where this mythical tree originally hailed, or who the visionaries were who first fell upon the brilliant idea of domesticating it and turning its products into one of the cornerstones of our diet. We have an olive farm. I am itching to know its trees' secrets. Before fanatics spread their wars into our sea, before they destroy everything, I have to find what's out there.'

One of life's remarkable twists was my chance encounter with Maryam in August 2001 on a flight departing Nice for London. Seated alongside one another, we struck up conversation. I was travelling onwards to Beirut, towards my aborted Middle Eastern trip. Exotic, dark-haired Maryam was married to a Lebanese. It seemed a fortuitous coincidence as she scribbled lists of places I should visit. She was Persian. In 1979, at the outset of the Iranian revolution, she and her family had fled as exiles to the States, where she had met Paul, also an exile. After their studies, they had married and moved to London.

To the surprise of us both, our plane passage blossomed into a cherished friendship. Four years on, I was now returning to Beirut and Maryam was there, holidaying with Paul. She had invited me to spend the first days of my journey with them in Beit-Shabeb, a mountainous village inland of the capital, where her in-laws had built their home after their return in 1990 at the end of the Lebanese Civil War. I was grateful for that offer. It provided me with a safe base from where I could step out and start my searching.

I cleared customs and was greeted not by the warm-hearted Maryam I knew, but by a pale, anxious sketch of that woman. London had been hit by a series of suicide-bomb attacks. There were casualties. Numbers dead. The news was shocking and not without a twisted irony, given that others had been concerned for my safety in the Middle East. Maryam, quite naturally, was desperate to reach her daughter, but neither of our phones would connect to England. All lines were jammed, or down.

Her in-laws' chauffeur, Hani, awaited us and Maryam begged to return directly to Beit-Shabeb. As the city of Beirut fell away behind us, we drove through one suburban jungle after another, followed by a series of steep, snaking roads running through zones that resembled concrete landslides. During the fifteen long years of civil war, Beiruti citizens desperate to distance themselves from the daily bombardment of mortar shells or to live amongst those of their own faith had hastily built anew out of harm's way, in safer areas, which explained the high-density construction ranging all about us, but even once the war had ended, the urban sprawl had continued. Without planning regulations, people purchased plots and threw up whatever they fancied. Fortunately, according to Hani, restrictions were now in place.

Maryam's phone rang. It was Paul. He had spoken to their daughter; she was safe in her Camden Town flat in north London. Now lighter of spirit, Maryam pointed out to me an imposing statue of the Virgin Mother, Our Lady of Lebanon, perched on a distant cliff's edge, gazing benignly down upon capital and coast from the town of Harissa. This larger-than-life, perpendicular Mary was the first of many extravagant religious icons and places of worship I was to encounter in this country; power statements in a jostle for religious supremacy where, I learned during our drive, seventeen creeds contrived to cohabit. Beit-Shabeb was a sprawling mountain community that boasted thirteen churches. The home of Paul's parents, some distance outside the village, was an airy six-storey house, unfussily furnished. Its tranquil location, along an unmade track on a pine-clad, barely asphalted hillside, gave a temporary, recently moved-in feel to the place. I deposited my case on the tiled floor in my room on the fourth level and wandered out on to the balcony. The air was crisp, fragrant, alpine clean. Two workmen were hammering within a newly constructed shell 20 metres higher up the hillside. I picked up the distant, insistent saw of cicadas, reminding me of home. I had crossed the Mediterranean, was looking back from an opposite seaboard, and the views sweeping down past valleys and woods to the water were stupendous. I had managed to contact loved ones in London and I, like Maryam, had been reassured. I gazed gratefully upon the cedars and pines – were we too high for olives? – before descending to the second storey, where the females of the family were employed in elaborate culinary preparations. I had rarely seen a kitchen so massed with mouth-watering ingredients. My friend's mother-in-law, Elizabeth, a warm-eyed woman full of nervous energy, assisted by a tall and solid maid, Leyla, who lived one storey below with husband Hani, the chauffeur, were engaged in food preservation.

Maryam, also lending a hand, while I hovered in the background observing, was decanting freshly made jams, jellies, pickles, bottled fruits and other concoctions I did not recognise. This was *mouneh*, the custom of stocking up on wholesome seasonal crops for the ensuing months. In this way, families were never lacking home-grown produce. No fast-food mentality here. Everything in the garden – nuts, seeds, fruits, leaves – contributed to one dish or another.

'These vegetables are packed with every nutrient you could wish for,' I was informed by Maryam's father-in-law, Emile, our host, whose beloved garden it was. 'Go and see for yourself,' he invited proudly. 'Food storage was essential during the civil-war years and even beyond it.'

Emile, soft-spoken, a result of poor health rather than a character trait, was watching me constantly, puzzled by my presence in this family scene.

'Maryam says you met on a plane?' Before I could acknowledge the fact, the power went off. It was the second cut since
I had arrived. Emile blasphemed under his breath and then
continued in English, 'Once, we were a great nation. Now,
we have difficulties supplying our people with water and
electricity. Shortages, power cuts are the norm here. Cor-
ruption is the problem. The only commodities you'll have
easy access to are hashish and opium poppies. It wears me
down, makes me older than my years.'

A vague memory returned from drama-school days of
fellow students eulogising the delights of Lebanese Gold hash.

'In the Beqaa Valley, three thousand hectares of land have
been culled for cannabis cultivation. The government offered
grants to farmers to switch crops, but when the cash fizzled
out or was syphoned off elsewhere, the agriculturists returned
to illicit harvests. "We have to eat," was their argument.'

'Don't listen to his griping. That was a long time ago.' His
wife, Elizabeth, shaking her head, was lighting a cigarette and
bidding us to the table. No one seemed ready to expound on
Emile's reference to drugs and, more importantly, lunch was
being served.

Paul came through from his office, greeting me. Maryam
bowed her head and said grace, while I marvelled at the
selection of *mezze* dishes on offer: houmous, tabbouleh, raw
carrots sliced and, moistened with lemon juice from Emile's
garden, *fattoush* salad of lettuce, tomatoes, onion, mint and
fried morsels of pitta bread seasoned with a dark mauve spice
crushed from sumac berries, bowls of black Lebanese olives
and a platter of fried chicken.

'Maryam says you are keen on olives. Here, two different
varieties.' Elizabeth pushed the bowls towards me. 'Both
grown along the Mount Lebanon range. Try.'

Both were delicious, but she could not supply me with

names of varieties. The meal was accompanied by generous portions of *manaeesh*, a warm, strongly scented bread that resembled a fat, floppy oven glove.

'Are you familiar with the herb the *manaeesh* has been stuffed with?' quizzed Maryam.

It was a perfume I recognised, but could not immediately place.

'*Zaatar.*'

I was none the wiser until Maryam confirmed it as thyme, which I should have known.

Moujaddara, a dish of lentils, garlic and rice cooked to a creamy texture and topped with lightly fried onions followed, along with *batinjan makdous*, aubergines stuffed with walnuts and garlic. I was wilting by the time Elizabeth called to Leyla for coffee, French chocolates I had brought and swags of dampened mint leaves accompanying black cherries the size and shape of small hearts.

'We eat well because we fear that tomorrow our tables will be empty, our food supplies discontinued again.' This was Emile, who had swallowed barely a mouthful, watching me consume my lunch. 'Are you a journalist?'

Mouth full, I shook my head.

'What do you know of our history?'

'Politics again!' Elizabeth abandoned the table to smoke out on the terrace.

'A brief résumé?' offered Paul.

'Why not?' I bit into a cherry that bled wine-red juice.

'At the end of World War I, after the collapse of the Ottoman Empire, Syria and the coastal regions of the Levant went under French control. At that stage, there was no Lebanon. The Republic of Greater Lebanon came about through an unhappy merger between the country's two dominant religious communities: Maronite Christians and Sunni

Muslims. The Maronites, founded in sixth-century Syria, had managed to secure their survival in the Middle East throughout centuries of Muslim rule by allying themselves with Western Christian powers and by concentrating their population in one area, here, where we are right now, Mount Lebanon, a rugged bone of land running the length of the country. Here, on these sunburned, chalky slopes, we Maronites were always the dominant faith. Our only neighbours were Druze Muslims. After decison-making fell to the French, the Christians let it be known they wanted their independence. Unfortunately, independence for so small a group inhabiting such an insignificant spine of land, short of fertile uplands, was not economically viable, so the Maronites persuaded France to throw in the coastal plains and create a larger state, Greater Lebanon. The major stumbling block was that the coastal areas were inhabited by Muslims, not Christians. Sunnis controlled the cities of Beirut, Tripoli and Sidon, while Tyre and the exceptionally fecund Beqaa Valley are Shi'ite. Nonetheless, France backed the Christians and the Republic of Greater Lebanon was born, giving the Maronites majority control.'

'By a tiny percentage,' interrupted Emile. 'And the Muslims were not pleased.'

Paul nodded. 'If alliances were necessary, the Muslims would have preferred to be linked to Syria, an Islamic state.'

'In 1943 we gained independence and our conflicts are still not resolved. Our war was an escalation of religious differences. Over a hundred and thirty thousand people were killed, mostly civilians, and a million fled the country. And with the Israel–Arab conflict on our doorstep, our hopes for peace are not bright.'

'Hezbollah, a radical organisation principally funded by Iran and Syria, is sitting in the South playing border control and denying Israel's right of existence while Israel is just waiting for Hezbollah to overstep the mark so that they can come back in here all guns blazing, to hammer us with their military might. Our country is their chessboard,' sighed Paul.

The gathering went quiet. We folded our napkins and joined Elizabeth on the terrace for coffee. The family's attention turned to preparations of the pipe. It was late afternoon. While the glass-bowled *narguileh* was being made ready by beautiful, squatting Maryam, I leaned out over the balcony and surveyed the well-maintained, generous-sized garden packed tight with fruit trees and vegetables, reflecting upon the seeds of dissension that had spawned so much violence within this starkly attractive Mediterranean country. It was fifteen years since the civil war had ended; I had not expected people, even in this fractured land, to be quite so raw. Hosepipes wound like snakes in between bushes and young olive trees. Behind me, the scent of apple tobacco began to seep into the settling day. I turned back towards the family, a bonded unit, engaged in conversation in Arabic, laughing loudly in frequent outbursts. The pipe was alight and Paul was drawing on it. The water within it was bubbling and gurgling like the damaged lungs of an octogenarian. Elizabeth rocked back and forth on the shaded lounger, *allegro tempo*. She had dispensed with her cigarette and was cradling the pipe, sucking hard before passing it across to Maryam. Emile, who suffered from a heart condition, was excluded from the ritual, as was I. I did not smoke and would have declined, but I was puzzled as to why, in an environment as hospitable as this, I had not been invited to try. Were there customs about the sharing of hubble-bubble pipes I had yet to acquire? Instead, I inhaled the pure air, cooler here than at the coast, perfumed with fragrances of the *garrigue*: sage and thyme, or *zaatar*. Quintessentially Mediterranean. The lackadaisical mood suggested time suspended, stomachs replete. Dead-lines, schedules, even politics had been shelved. The evening was unfurling at its own leisurely pace. Life was about the moment, though I was silently pondering my olive-tree quest, until the conversation – now in English for my benefit – returned to the recent past, current events. These ardent Christians abhorred the crime committed earlier in the year against their prime minister, Rafiq al-Hariri. 'He was a Muslim, but he was loved and respected by all Lebanese people,' explained Elizabeth. Hariri had been murdered in a car-bomb explosion on St Valentine's Day and in the after-math of the assassination his government had crumbled.

'He believed in a united Lebanon.'

'Lebanese people crave peace. We are bone-wearied from fighting and from the stranglehold of the Syrians, who involved themselves during the war and, when it was over, stayed,' said Emile.

The family, jumping between languages, was hotly debat-ing the still-undetected ownership of a van, registered abroad, employed for and destroyed in the assassination of their prime minister. 'Syrians,' was their unanimous decision before they relapsed into subdued silence.

Maryam and I took an evening stroll around Emile's garden, munching Lebanese cucumbers, which were smaller and crunchier than their European cousins, as we sauntered up and down the red-earthed alleyways. She picked us tart-sweet offerings from a black mulberry tree, insisting that I consume only the very darkest to avoid 'gut ache'. We guzzled greedily, staining and stickying our hands and chins.

'The Phoenicians spread this plant around the Medi-terranean,' she told me, before remembering that we were supposed to be feeding the chickens.

When I glanced back towards the house, I caught her

father-in-law watching us from the terrace high above. He and Elizabeth had fled Lebanon soon after the outbreak of civil war, taking Paul and his baby brother with them. They had travelled as cargo with goats on a boat to Cyprus and from there had bought passage on a ship bound for Marseille. From France, they had emigrated to Mexico, winding up in the United States. They returned from exile two years after the war had ended.

Emile was fascinated, Maryam confided, to know what I was doing – a woman travelling unaccompanied in a land as troubled as this one. 'It won't be easy for you here alone,' she warned me.

Back on the terrace, sitting with the family, when Emile quizzed me again about my presence in their country, I explained that I was embarking on a journey round the Mediterranean.

'What's in Lebanon?'

'An olive grove, or a single tree —'

'This country boasts thirteen million olive trees!'

'And more than five hundred mills!' they cried.

I had not known that. 'I'm looking for a particular grove where there is at least one noble tree believed to be six thousand years old.'

All eyes widened. No member of the family had heard of such an antique beast.

'It doesn't exist!'

'Where is it?'

I confessed that I had failed to find out. 'In the northern hills behind Tripoli, I suspect.' I had organised a rendezvous with an olive farmer inland of Zgharta, who I was hoping would point me in the right direction.

'What do you want with the old trees?'

'To know their story. To seek out the earliest traces of

olive culture, discover where it all began, reconnect with it,' I mumbled.

'Why?'

Why? I had spent so long alone during the difficult years of my marriage, running the farm, battling for its existence, that I felt a need to strike out for myself. I was not leaving home. Quite the contrary. I believed this journey could deepen my understanding of olive farming, of nature, the Mediterranean. If I could find the earliest ancestors of the olive tree or the reasons for the reverence bestowed upon it, I believed there might be something I could take from it. I had no idea what.

I remained silent.

'But why?' Emile frowned.

I didn't have the answer to his question, nor would I until I had fallen upon it and perhaps not even then, but all eyes were upon me; I felt obliged to respond. 'It's similar to researching a family history, attempting to learn where one comes from. I have an olive farm. That first dribble of oil, when it drizzles from the press, is always so exhilarating. I try to imagine how it must have been during those first moments when man discovered the oil. What did it mean to him?'

From across the coffee table, from sofas with neatly pressed cushions, they stared at me.

'How are you intending to travel about?' Emile wanted to know. 'There's no public transport. Our rail system was destroyed during the war.'

'Service taxis,' was my immediate response, but they strongly advised against this form of shared transport, warning that I would be unsafe, that the vehicles were seldom insured and were unfit for the roads.

'Find yourself a private driver,' advised Emile, which was what I had hoped to avoid.

Leyla came through from the kitchen, rubber shoes flip-flopping against marble, with yet another pot of coffee and sweet replenishments. She lit an oil lamp and smiled at me in a way that I did not understand and then returned to the dirty plates and the *mouneh*.

'You're wasting your time. No such grove exists.' Heartening words offered by Emile.

When I arrived for breakfast the following morning, only the men were at the table. Paul was devouring *manaeesh* that Emile had walked to a bakery in Beit-Shabeb to collect. He always rose early; he could not sleep. His son tore off triangular slabs of the flat bread and curled them into a trowel. On to these he ladled helpings of olive oil and *labneh*, a tart cheese, which he gorged on shamelessly. The white cheese lipsticked his mouth. His face was moon-round with mobile perky features and he grew handsomely boyish when his tobacco-wizened mother hovered over him, delighted by his appetite, disregarding of her son's expanding waistline. Elizabeth pushed a plate groaning with freshly baked breads towards me. Alongside them were fruits and a dish of oil. I helped myself to a handful of olives and cherries.

They had prodigious news for me, grinned white-lipped Paul. 'Leyla was born in the village of Bechealeh.' This meant nothing to me, until Emile elucidated. The olive grove I had spoken of was growing in Bechealeh.

I was astounded.

Hani had been instructed to prepare the car. Before my departure, Emile took me aside, clasping my hands in his. 'Our war was an ecological disaster; water was contaminated, natural habitats destroyed, our lives crushed. Talk to farmers, hear why they have returned to drug cultivation, but please be careful. If you need help, call us.'

Directly after breakfast, Paul, Maryam and I set off on a pilgrimage to 'Carol's trees'. I had pictured this assignment as a private undertaking, a personal quest that might have cost me several days. Part of the pleasure was to have been the challenge of tracking the grove down, but I shrugged my shoulders and flowed with yet another serendipitous card life had thrown my way.

An hour later, we spiralled into the hot, silent hinterland village of Bechealeh, nestling within the alpine curves of Mount Lebanon. Hani, eating a spray of green chickpeas while driving, was steaming along at such a pace that we shot right by the trees.

'That was the grove!' I yelled.

The car screeched to a halt and we reversed at the same breakneck speed.

'Are you sure? How do you know?' quizzed my friends.

'The girth of their trunks,' I muttered.

In fact, once parked, we discovered a sign, directly beneath the Methuselahs, confirming the longevity of the grove. I grabbed my camera and we progressed up the steep bank on to the drystone terraces where half a dozen olive trees planted in 4000 BC were thriving. Silent masters over time. Behind them were dozens of younger examples, possibly a century old. Juniors. I turned my attention back to the tortile giants I had traversed the Mediterranean to pay homage to.

I had found them, or they had found me, these ancestors of our fellows back at the farm. Half a dozen six-thousand-year-old cultivated olive trees. It was difficult to appreciate what I was in the presence of.

In the bygone years of prehistory, after the last great Ice Age, when the Mediterranean and its surrounding shores began to hot up again, when forests regained ground and flourished, there was the wild olive. *Olea sylvestris* was one of the earliest trees to take root around the baking coastal plains of the Mediterranean, wetter in those days. The fellows I was standing alongside were a mere eight thousand years younger than the last Ice Age, which was remarkable, but even more remarkable was the fact that these were not wild trees, they were of the genus *Olea europaea*, cultivated olive trees. Somebody had planted these six-thousand-year-old compelling beauties and somebody had farmed them.

We were high in the ridged hills of chalky Mount Lebanon in Christian territory. These terraces were owned by the Church. Today, the fruits were harvested by pietists, yet the trees were older than Christ – four thousand years his senior. They pre-dated not only Christianity, but Islam and Judaism, too.

I took a good long look at them. They were growing in an aligned row. Each possessed a collection of five to eight trunks fanning out on either side of the original, now a shell, and from each grew silvered, feathery young branches. Every one of the spawned extensions dwarfed us and their height was exaggerated by banyan-like roots, perforated, knitted, honeycombed. The trees appeared half-human. Awesome, prehistoric creatures on tiptoe caught in a frenzied dance, pushing against gravity or tearing themselves out of the ground. It was a marked affirmation of energy, of life force.

I began to pace their stretch, to step in and out of their hollowed central trunks. I stroked my palms against their ridged surfaces, pressed against their empty vertical husks, peered inside chambers scarred by the centuries. I clambered over metre after metre of the rising, buckled roots. I ducked beneath pendulous branches, slid in between their silvery extensions bearing young, pellet-hard drupes, keen to cajole a story out of these living monuments.

From the interior of a trunk cavity, I looked out upon

the world and attempted to visualise this tree's inception, its adolescence, its first blush. Whose bare or shod foot was alongside it, pressing its sapling form firmly down into the pebbled earth, keeping it upright, securing its lodgement on this hillside, never imagining that their humble yet precious act might prove a testimony of its time six millennia later? Which sex had been the planter? Had he or she owned this seedling, or were they in the employment of another? Were they engaged in planting up the entire grove? Did they sing as they lowered the roots earthwards? An act of work, love, worship, or a combination of all? I was peering into the lens of an inverted telescope, looking backwards across a sweep of time, immeasurable, inconceivable. When this tree was dug into the ground – the soil would have been richer then, less damaged – civilisations were in the fog of prehistory; it was an age before an alphabet had existed, before writing had been learned. Six thousand years ago, no young couples were canoodling after dark beneath this tree, carving their names into its tender trunk to mark their first kiss, to crystallise a moment of passion. They could love, but they had not the means to write. But what, I asked myself, if this elephantine survivor could recount its tale? *Sixty centuries*, what had that immense lifespan borne witness to?

The greater part of Mediterranean history, was the answer.

Paul and Maryam were calling. Beside the grove was a presbytery where a servant of the Church had informed Paul of other mettlesome survivors from a second ancient grove a few yards further down the street, on a lower hillside.

We descended a kibbled goat trail flanked by terraced cherry orchards. So gravid were the clusters of shiny, scarlet fruits they dragged their straining boughs earthwards. In between them, elbowing for space with every extended root and limb, were another half a dozen *oliviers*. They were equally impressive, but they were difficult to access. We returned to the road.

Alongside the presbytery was a store, the only one as far as I could see serving this invisible highland community, where we, the sole customers, poked about inside its two fusty rooms; a gallimaufry of dusty everything from farming utensils, chilled soft drinks, shrivelled notepads more gnarled than the olive trees to insecticides and curious-tasting sweets. In the window was a yellowed Arabic newspaper article in a wooden frame. Paul said it was a report from a French archaeobotanist who had stayed in Bechealeh and had radio-carbon-dated the trees at seven thousand years old. 'I will settle for six thousand,' I joked. 'The seventh millennium I might call upon later.'

I scaled the sloping granulated earth once again, returning to the grove, unable to keep distance from it, drawn to its menhir-ness.

If the trees had survived on this hillside for six thousand years, who had been inhabiting this region then? I estimated that the village was approximately ninety kilometres inland of Beirut. What was Beirut in that bygone era? When the Phoenicians arrived here, in 1500 BC, Beirut was a lesser port, lacking the power and status of Tripoli, Byblos, Sidon or Tyre. But the germ I was fossicking was way before the Phoenicians. Hani told me later that we were closer to Byblos. Byblos was an active harbour-city before Beirut, trading far beyond its own coast. Was it possible that I had fallen upon the origin of olive production?

The trees in these two remaining groves were growing on terraces, drystone-walled, fashioned in the same *en restanque* method as ours back at the farm, which suggested that this method of agricultural irrigation pre-dated Christ. Had the drystone walls been added later? From where I was standing,

I could not actually see the Mediterranean, though I knew that, as the crow flies, it lay in front of me. I attempted to imagine activity around this sea at the time the farmers – a farmer, family, young couple embarking upon married life? – were bent digging holes in preparation for their saplings.

On the island of Crete, a short boat crossing from here, where I would travel later, had lived the Minoans, a mysterious people. According to scientists, they were pressing oil from sacred olive groves in around 3500 BC, five centuries after our anonymous farmer here was hard at work. The Phoenicians who traded along this coast, today Lebanon, and founded several of the bustling port-cities I was soon to visit, were intrepid seafarers who, it is believed, transported the cultivated olive tree west across the Mediterranean, yet their presence on this coastal strip dates back a mere two and a half thousand years after this grove had been planted. What of Palestine, the ancient land of Israelites and Canaanites, a short hop from here? I was intending to find out for myself later along my route. Further north lay the Syrian coast and, beyond, Turkey. In Turkey, or rather central Anatolia, at Çatal Hüyük, had existed a civilisation that mysteriously disappeared around 5800 BC. They had been an agricultural and trading people living almost two thousand years before these trees alongside me had been planted. In the fields surrounding their Neolithic settlement, they cultivated pistachio, almond and cherry trees and 'oil was pressed'.

Is it conceivable that the very first cultivated olives came from central Anatolia and that these giants around me had arrived here as striplings on caravans or from across the seas? Or might I argue that the labourers from here, about whom history tells us nothing, took cuttings and crossed the water to teach others how to farm olives?

The Minoans, Phoenicians, Çatal Hüyük, Anatolians, the

planters of these groves, all had vanished, but these grizzled trees live on, guarding their secrets, still bearing fruit. The olive tree is so ancient no one knows who first thought of preserving its fruit or mashing its flesh to extract the oil, but someone did. Stone Age man – it must have been! – took a bitter, inedible drupe, cured it and discovered it was edible. He ground its flesh and out flowed olive oil: liquid gold, exquisite to taste, rich in medicinal properties, a beauty product and combustible. Man had learned to master fire. Then he discovered he could produce an oil that provided him with fuel for light. He was capable of mastering darkness.

Who first picked a fruit and ground it to release that precious liquid? When? Was it during prehistory from trees that grew wild?

I was contemplating my lack of answers, and the adventures that lay ahead, as I stepped out into the sunlight from the tree's semicircular husk, when Maryam, laughing, pushed me back inside and, from the terrace of the presbytery, Paul snapped our photograph, setting the moment in time.

At the end of our day, Maryam and Paul unloaded my bag outside a hotel next to a bombed-out lot, now a jungle of weeds, in west Beirut. My friends were returning on a dawn flight to London, where their student daughter, mercifully unscathed by the recent violence, awaited them. I was off to ancient port-cities in search of olive clues.

'Bissalama.' Paul smiled, kissing my cheeks.

'You too, travel safely.' I waved as they sped off to spend their last evening with Emile and Elizabeth. Along with my friends' departure went my access to conversation; I lacked all skills in Arabic. I was truly alone.

In the hotel lobby, the bases of the makeshift glass tables were outmoded Singer sewing machines. A brief encounter in the lift introduced me to a clean-cut, thirty-something Lebanese Christian who remarked that he had never before set foot in west Beirut, having fled with his parents as a child and been reared in the States.

'When I was tiny,' he smiled, exposing terrific white American teeth, 'this side of the city was Muslim. We never came here.' He was employed by a US 'special security operation' in Iraq and was earning in excess of $30,000 a month, he boasted. 'I speak Arabic, know the territory.' When I pressed him about the precise nature of his work, he grew cagey, speeding away as soon as the lift doors opened. (I spotted him the following day in the lobby, but he avoided me.)

I set off to explore Beirut. Rambling without direction, it was close to 10 p.m. when I reached downtown, where the partygoers, unlike me, were awakening. The night was young; the cafés were throbbing, and everywhere the abiding scent of fruit tobaccos rose in smoke plumes from the *narguilehs*. I sat next to a bunch of American students as I sipped my Ksara *blanc de blancs* and rested my feet, observing them as they sucked their bubbling pipes and paid 7,000 Lebanese pounds, or £4.50, apiece for the pleasure. From there, I descended to the water. Unable to approach directly I found myself, quite by chance, at the cordoned-off crime site of the St Valentine's Day massacre. I skirted its perimeter, peering into a deep crater, from where the car transporting Prime Minister Hariri had been blown skywards, taking the ground beneath with it. Army youths were sitting casually on stone steps in twos and threes, cradling rifles, mounting guard over the lifeless chasm. Evidence, I supposed.

The night sounds I heard were soft conversations, distant waves, the incessant honking of city horns, a cricket or two, a ringing phone and a woman's strident laughter from an apartment on high. I fell into conversation with a chef from a neighbouring seafood restaurant. Its windows remained jagged apertures patched over with newspaper and Sellotape. He was young, smoking heavily, had shares in the venture, was losing money hand over fist.

'No one will come near the joint,' he moaned.

'What's on offer?' I stepped inside. The menu was pricey, but the fresh catches looked mouth-watering. I accepted his recommendation of red *dorade* Lebanese-style, served with vegetables.

While Chafeek, the chef, hurried to the kitchen with my order, I passed through one sombre inner room to another where half the space had been boarded up, blasted to charcoaled ruins. I settled at an underlit table by a beachside window. Two tables away, a middle-aged couple sat close, whispering, smoking, kissing. Otherwise, the premises were deserted. It was uninspiring, *triste*. Maybe it always had been, even before the wreckage. I gazed out to sea, black as ink and impenetrable. Chafeek made conversation while dinner was underway.

'At Hariri's funeral both Muslims and Christians wept,' he said. The man was a true Lebanese. He cared for his country and his people. 'It is always the good who are massacred,' he sighed.

'Who was responsible?' My half-bottle of white wine appeared along with a dish of tabbouleh. I was surprised that no one touched upon the financial jiggery-pokery that had been associated with the prime minister during his lifetime.

'Syrians, of course, but we want names. We want to see the criminals decried in the newspapers.'

I listened to Chafeek's woeful insurance problems; without reimbursement, he was unable to begin repairs, and without a decent-looking eatery tourists avoided the venue; then I settled my bill – the equivalent of £4.50 – and ambled along the seafront. It was close to one in the morning when I chanced upon the celebrated, arabesquely chic Café d'Orient. It was heaving with young lovelies, all conversing in French, as though they hadn't a care in the world. I sat alone, feeling alone, at a wooden table right on the beach, lit by a guttering candle, spume almost lapping my toes, hair teased by a gentle wind, looking out across the moonlit strip of violet-navy sea towards home, downing spoonfuls of rose-water sorbet while attempting to get to grips with the complexities of this ravaged, broken-hearted city and asking myself what, if any, olive history I might unearth here.

I had designated three days to Beirut. The 'Paris of the eastern Mediterranean' had been its reputation during its golden era before the civil war, and the following day I walked. I walked until my feet screamed and then I hung out in cafés along the Corniche, nattering with locals, watching their games of backgammon.

The Levantine metropolis exposed radically different faces to me, two sides to its bankrupted coin. Downtown was an ambitiously reconstructed district – assassinated multi-millionaire property developer Rafiq Hariri's project – with arcades of art galleries, cafés, designer boutiques alongside blocks of freshly plastered units, sterile and unoccupied; many Beirutis could not afford the rents in this neighbourhood.

A fascinating or tragic aside to so much downtown redevelopment was the discovery by archaeologists of ancient sites buried beneath the city; findings that shunted the history of Beirut much further back in time. Nothing much of Phoenician Beirut had really existed before, but jars dating back to the Canaanites, in 3000 BC, were revealed. Unfortunately, this was the business district, zillions of dollars were being poured into its build-up and the archaeologists were getting in the way. Several incidents were recounted to me, by a group of students in a café and, down at the waterfront, by a henna-haired Armenian teacher, of foundations excavated for reconstruction that had thrown up antique treasures, but as soon as the historians tried to call a halt to proceedings, the work was achieved in the dead of night. The city woke up to find that potentially rich archaeological zones had been concreted over while they slept. If there were olive stories for the picking, they lay sealed beneath the marble floors of international banks and ornate jewellery emporiums.

Large sections of the inhabited city remained war-damaged. There were abandoned *quartiers*, bombed-out plots, shells of buildings where the exterior façades had been fenes-trated, dismantled by gunfire – a daily reminder, a twenty-first-century cuneiform, clocking up scores after fifteen years of bloodshed, religious intolerance and atrocities. Then there were the shabby neighbourhoods where baggy-eyed women queued in rubbled streets with plastic bags, where wooden barrows offered breads for sale, where men with bare torsos, wearing only pyjama bottoms, smoking, stared dolefully out of tall windows, slipping from sight when they caught me peering, where battered cars exposed cavities that had once been head- or rear-lights, blown or shot out during the war and never replaced.

The next morning, I visited the National Museum, situated in what had been the Green Line district. In 1975, at the outset of the war, Beirut had been divided into two. A designated strip of no-man's-land, the Green Line, had demarcated the Christian districts of the city to the east from the Muslim quarters in the west. Christians living in the western districts and Muslims in the eastern were anxious to move, to settle in zones with others of their own religious affinity. Those with the means left town. Many fled their homeland altogether, not easy for Christians because the airport lay in the Muslim west. This had left them with the choice of escaping by boat, as Emile and Elizabeth with small children had done, or paying handsomely to be smuggled across the Green Line and on to a plane. Those without adequate resources struggled on, attempting normality, while facing the daily horrors of war.

Even within the Green Line district, many buildings had been seriously damaged, including the National Museum. Fortunately, the curator, working all hours with his wife and staff members, had encased all the national treasures in concrete and buried them in the cellars, hidden beneath earth. Tragically, during the years of strife, water swamped the basements and every item required airing and dehumidifying when eventually removed from storage, but the majority of the pieces had been preserved.

Almost the first exhibit I encountered upon entering was not an exquisitely carved sarcophagus, of which there were many, but a broad-girthed log from a cedar tree. The cedar tree is a potent symbol of Lebanon's history and the emblem on its flag. In ancient times, this emerald conifer, the *Cedrus libani*, was much sought after for the quality of its wood and its perfume. Egyptians, Assyrians, Babylonians used it to build their ships and palaces. The shipyards of ancient Byblos grew wealthy from its exportation. Solomon requested the King of Tyre provide him with the finest of its timbers for the construction of the Temple of Jerusalem. Such intensive logging, deforestation and, consequently, the loss of topsoils eventually left the hillsides eroded, chalky, barren. The topography was changed for ever. So serious was the loss of the cedars that the Roman emperor Hadrian created reserves and forbade by imperial edict the felling of the forests. Did this make Hadrian one of our earliest ecologists? Many centuries later, Queen Victoria ordered a mighty wall to be built around the cedar forests in an attempt to protect what little remained of this nation's heritage. Alas, to no avail. The twenty-first-century cedar stands were a sorry sight when I visited them during my previous trip; the experience had put me in mind of a zoo displaying a handful of decrepit elephants and toothless tigers. The few strong and healthy trees that remained were spectacular, some averaging two thousand years, but the maturity and splendour of those few mighty fellows had been turned into a tacky tourist attraction.

Fortunately, the olive groves in Bechealeh, three times the age of the most senior surviving cedars, had not been discovered by tourist operators; no touts hung about selling keyrings and tickets. But what was remarkable to me, after a tour of the museum, was that there was no mention of the olive tree, no log to honour it, nothing to track the role it had played and the wealth it had brought to this Levantine coast.

It was early in the morning, the sun was rising above the urban skyline. Dust, too, was lifting off the melting tarmac streets as cars sped by. Rucksack at my feet, feeling the swell of heat, I hailed a service taxi at a crossroads a short walk from my hotel. Several jalopies pulled into the kerb, but only one driver understood I was requesting a ride to Sour, ancient Tyre, for the local rate, not private-hire fees. During my days alone in Beirut, I had grown quite accustomed to this transport system. I enjoyed piling in with strangers – women off to shop, men escorting children to school. Most wanted to talk, to hear who I was, but unless they spoke English or French or understood my sign language, we managed little besides *shukran* and *insha'allah*. I had commenced Arabic lessons back in France, but my teacher, a Lebanese restaurant owner in Cannes, had turned out to be a crook, his restaurant a front for some underhand dealings, and he had disappeared without trace, leaving me with less than an alphabet.

Now I tried with Anglo-Saxon accent to speak words I had learned parrot-fashion: '*Sabah alkhair. Kaifhalek?*'

The heavily moustached, big-boned driver nodded. '*Sabah alnur. Ana bekhair.*' He was wishing me good morning, assuring me he was well, appreciative of my conversational skills, which had now been thoroughly exhausted. He handed me his card with telephone number. I assumed this was to prove that he was a bona fide driver, though I was not sure. 'Name Naji. Speech leetle Engleesh.'

'Tyre,' I told him. He was confused, so I added, 'South to Sour,' the modern name for the ancient port, a journey of 83 kilometres. He quoted me a reasonable price, confirmed his assent at making the trip, but warned I must be patient if he picked up others.

'All the better.' I grinned, pitching my rucksack across to the neighbouring rear seat, relieved that Naji's minimal command of Engleesh would see us through. He fired the engine and I felt a surge of excitement wash through me; I was on the road.

Our route followed the coast for much of the way, passing through dusty, chaotic industrial towns. A swift passage through Saida, ancient Sidon, offered a glimpse of the sandstone Château de la Mer perched at the water's edge.

'Ancient jewel in sow's ear,' joked Naji of the waterside castle. The city itself displayed heaps of discarded rubber tyres, broken-down buildings, urban desolation.

I was fascinated to learn that Naji was a Druze Muslim, Duruz in Arabic. Aside from the fact that this Islamic offshoot was established in Egypt in the eleventh century, I knew nothing about these people. Few did. They guarded the doctrines of their faith assiduously. I thought I had fallen upon the exception because Naji talked quite openly about Allah and life after death, but what he said was fundamental to all monotheistic religions. It was not unusual in this finger-length of land to find oneself debating theology. In a country that had been torn apart by religious intolerance, such schisms were part of the daily unfathomables. In his broken English, he attempted to differentiate between Druze and orthodox Muslims.

'A letter was sent to the world,' he began.

'To Muslims worldwide?' I butted in rudely.

'No, to the world,' he repeated emphatically. 'Those who heard the call, heard it. For the rest, we attempted no converts. Unlike Christians, we don't desire to augment our numbers.'

I remembered that the Druze allied themselves with other Muslim sects against Christians during the civil war, operating out of their base in Mount Lebanon, which was where my driver lived, in a house built by his father, where he had been born. Beyond that, he confided nothing and most of the journey passed in companionable silence.

Only when Naji's car had passed through streets stacked with more old tyres and rusted vehicles and drew up beneath a cluster of fig trees so dusty they looked as though they had been dipped in coarsely grained oats, and turned, saying, 'Telephone when to go,' did I understand we had arrived. I nodded as he swung the car towards Beirut, having deposited me south of Sour city, in the middle of Shi'ite territory and a short drive north of the Lebanon–Israeli border. The address I had been given turned out to be a rather scruffy resort. How had I beached up here? Who would choose this for a holiday?

In need of shampoo, I took an early-evening hike to the esplanade. At a boutique, a young sun-wild, sea-wild Arab, bare torso, sporting green Aussie-surfer Bermudas, attempted to palm me off with a free sample of hair conditioner for $3 (£1.65). Crowding the curvature of coastline were Shi'ite families on holiday, indulging in ordinary beach activities, except these women waded and doggy-paddled in the Mediterranean in their billowing black chadors like pods of drowning seals. Chugging the beach with their children, their sodden full-length clothes encumbered by sand, seated in groups on squares of flimsy towels, squashed tight, slick-wet, nibbling roasted corn like lollies while their men jogged about in bathing trunks or tracksuit bottoms. Music, Arab and Western, poured from the sound systems of every vehicle, mobile or stationary. Aural onslaught. I passed corn-vendors who had piled the singed yellow cobs in hummocks between kerb and multicoloured trucks with Lebanese cedars painted on the bodywork. The odour turned my stomach, but what struck me most was how filthy Sour was.

Once upon a time, nine centuries before Christ, in the heyday of Phoenician civilisation, Tyre was the greatest maritime metropolis of the ancient world, a seafaring emirate. The famous purple dye so coveted by aristocrats for their robes and togas was extracted from a sea snail's shell, found in proliferation along this coastal stretch. The Phoenicians traded it everywhere around the eastern Med basin. It was worth its weight in gold and delivered them fortunes. Alas, the murex sea creature was exploited to extinction. Herodotus, the father of history, writing of the Phoenicians from Tyre, claimed that they originated from the Red Sea and that as soon as they had settled on the Mediterranean coast, they took to making long trading voyages. It would appear that reliable Herodotus, who visited Tyre in the fifth century BC, was incorrect. Archaeology has proven that the Phoenicians were Canaanites, who spoke a Semitic language and wrote using an alphabet without vowels, closely related to early Hebrew.

I paused on the palm-tree-lined esplanade. An Arab in a

wheelchair was attempting to negotiate the merciless traffic.
I offered assistance, but he waved me impatiently away. I only
half-registered the cries of children, of mothers, the sea mews
swooping, scudding the benign evening waves, as I looked
south down the coast towards Israel, towards a border I could
not penetrate but that I intended to visit further along my
route. That land so urgently fought over today, Israel, was
once Canaan, the land of the forefathers of the Phoenicians.
Once upon a time, Hiram, King of Tyre, was such an ally of the
Israeli monarchs David and Solomon that he sent stonecutters
and carpenters to assist with the construction of David's
palace and cedar to Solomon for his temple in Jerusalem.
From this great seaport, felled timbers were exported not
only to Jerusalem but to cities circumnavigating the eastern
Mediterranean, for use in the construction of ships and
temples.

It was from Tyre that Cadmus set sail in search of his
beloved sister, Europa, who gave her name to our continent,
after she had been kidnapped by Greeks. Whilst on his
voyages, Cadmus spread the Phoenician alphabet. With
twenty-two consonants, it was unpronounceable to the
Greeks, who added five vowels, thus giving us the foundation
of our written language. The Greeks called their writing
'Phoenikas' after those who had delivered it to them.

Those Tyrian-Phoenicians ruled the seas, founding colonies as distant and prosperous as Carthage and Gades
(Cadiz), and they transported the olive tree and its culture
with them in their fifty-oar galleys, trading its oil everywhere
around the Mediterranean basin. Malta, from the Phoenician
word *maleth*, meaning 'hidden harbour', afforded them an
ideal base, a secure station and a break in their arduous journeys westwards to the Iberian Peninsula. Somewhere around
700 BC the Tyrians sailed beyond the two portals they had

christened the Pillars of Hercules, out into the 'further beyond', testing their formidable navigational skills in the merciless Atlantic while founding trading centres and settlements along the coast of modern-day Portugal.

Eventually, the Assyrians enslaved Tyre. However, by that stage, many of the population were emigrating to their glorious new harbour-city of Carthage in modern-day Tunisia, where they planted up kingdoms of olive groves. Those who were left behind were besieged by a succession of conquerors, including Alexander the Great and, later, the Romans.

Contemplating this border city now, which offered little besides its historical sites, boarded-up cafés bearing names such as Cadmus, hillocks of debris and dust-faded memories, it seemed impossible to conceive that such a glorious past had ever existed. I was approaching the al-Mina Roman ruins and was obliged to circle by a crematorium on the waterfront. Alongside it were several lit pyres. The sweet, sickly stench of burning flesh hung in the unclean air. Or might I have been sniffing whiffs of the charred remains of a lost civilisation?

A century before the triumphant Romans arrived here, further along the North African coast, their nascent armies razed Carthage to the ground, giving their empire control of the lucrative olive farms. The Phoenicians fought fearlessly until no hope remained, while the flagship city of their civilisation burned for seventeen days, depriving them for ever of their historical role as the most intrepid of merchants, pioneers of navigation throughout these Mediterranean waters and, possibly, the first international traders of olive oil.

I felt grateful to the oleanders, coral, *cramoisi*, wine-red, growing amongst the bleached stones and mosaics, jollying up the excavations on what had once been an island city, joined by a causeway to the mainland by Alexander the Great. As I passed along the colonnaded Roman road towards the sea, there was not a soul in sight and I sat and gazed out upon the waves slapping against a series of semi-submerged boulders, the remnants of Phoenician jetties and breakwaters. From those jetties, saplings would have been loaded for the groves of Ifriqa surrounding Carthage. And possibly skilled agriculturists to husband them? Might there have been waiting lists of families, young hopefuls jostling for berths, unemployed and skilled land labourers queuing to emigrate to Carthage, to the new country, dreaming of better prospects? Carthage BC, the land of tomorrow. Burned to cinders by Rome.

From nowhere, a limping man appeared approaching along a winding trail. He was waving, as though flagging me down, but I was stationary. Even as he drew near, he attempted to sell 'antiky' treasures plundered, he claimed, from the bottom of the sea, out beyond the bay.

'Where are you from?' he quizzed. 'Eenland, where's that? Close to Finland?'

His artefacts were packed in a Cuban cigar box. I was more curious to know how he had come by his container than about the fake figurines he boasted were from the 'Phinikons' and 'Ottomens'. He must have read my incredulity because he slapped shut the lid on his wares and hobbled off back the way he had come. I was alone for sunset at the waterside. A few dozen columns and capitals lay about the jumbled ground; two mongrel dogs copulating and a ginger cat prowling around the relics were my companions.

Tyre, Queen of the Seas, buzzing with sailors, wealthy merchants, noblemen, navigators, royalty, travellers. So prosperous had it been, so supreme that every power-hungry empire had nurtured grand designs on this mooring. And what had I so far found? A filthy city surviving at the ragged, bloodstained edges of enemy territory. Invaded in 1982 by

Israel, today Sour was crawling with white UN vans flying their sky-blue flags; a city of ruins, in ruins, funded by Hezbollah, a guerilla force branded as terrorists by the West.

According to Madame Sahia, a handsome Maronite Christian originally from Beirut, now proprietress of a rather eccentrically ramshackle *auberge* alongside the lighthouse, *al-fanar*, on the waterfront, life in Sour had changed dramatically. Until recently, the Shi'ite women had not worn their religious adherence so publicly; they had been more casual. Also, the Shi'ites had become more numerous than before and fewer Christians remained; most had packed up and departed. 'We are sorely outnumbered,' she lamented.

I thought of the ancient city when the boats were disembarking for Carthage. Those of the population who'd had the means had also upped sticks and sailed away.

While I and Madame engaged in conversation – she with her strong chiselled bones and accomplished French (educated Lebanese pride themselves on the fact that French, not Arabic, is their first language. A minority carry French passports), numerous bats, reminiscent of the Shi'ite women in the sand, swooped round the lighthouse. The waves two floors below swirled and licked at the foot of the flashing pharos, while the water's consistent rhythms seemed to belie the undercurrents, the precarious political architecture operating within this area. Madame and I were alone in the dining room; I was the sole guest. She was speaking now of Hezbollah, whose title meant 'Party of God', likening them to resistance fighters in Occupied France during World War II, enumerating their generous social acts: construction of schools, hospitals, orphanages, care and protection of the Christians of Sour. Their purpose, she confirmed, was to safeguard the south, to keep the Israelis out. Sour lay twenty minutes from the border.

'Hezbollah is misunderstood internationally,' she empha-
sised. 'Branded as Islamic terrorists by the United States and
Britain, this is a gross misrepresentation of these people. The
West does not understand what they are about.'

'Who, then, are they?'

'A legitimate if militant Shi'ite political party, nothing to do
with al-Qaeda, which, in any case, is a Sunni organisation.'

'But, *madame, excusez-moi*, Hezbollah kidnapped foreigners, holding them captive for several years: Terry Waite, a
Christian emissary, John McCarthy and Brian Keenan, British
and Irish journalists. They grabbed the attention of the international media by such kidnappings. In what way are they
misunderstood?' I insisted.

She sighed and shrugged her shoulders in a manner that
was quintessentially French. 'How to explain? They were
founded in 1982, during our civil war, to keep Israel, who
had backed our Christian groups against the Muslims, out of
Lebanon. It is why they continue to exist, to keep Israel at
bay.'

'They are funded by Shi'ite Iran, is that correct?'

'Syria also donated finance, but substantial sums have been
raised in Lebanon through charitable organisations and commercial activities. They are exceedingly wealthy and have their
own radio and television stations.'

'Might one of those activities be drug trafficking?'

'Drugs are one of their sources of income, yes, but it is for
a good cause. These are good people.'

I was bemused, lost within the political complexities and
entanglements growing like weeds along this strip of land.

Later, well after night had fallen, on the drive to my hotel,
I spotted lines of UN trucks parked along the beachfront.
Half a dozen or more were stationed outside the hotel bar
when I returned after midnight. At the poolside the following

morning, I noticed that the predominance of bathers were UN staff members who had dropped by to swim and drink cold beer. What took me by surprise, though, in a region dominated by chador-clad Shi'ites, was that the majority of the Western women – wives, friends or UN staff – were topless. I was curious as to how these manners were perceived by the Muslim population.

After a hot, sticky but fascinating tramp around the UNESCO World Heritage site inland of the coast – predominantly Roman ruins that included a spectacular hippodrome furnished with seating for 20,000 spectators, where I found a multitude of crumbling bones but no olive presses – I hailed a service taxi to take me into the mountains to the biblical village of Qana, where Christ, a guest at a marriage feast, transformed water into wine. I did not expect to find olive clues, but I could not resist the haunts of the Marriage of Cana.

The service taxis of Sour were the most clapped-out transport in town, belching pollutants while their drivers rarely shifted out of second gear, but I enjoyed them. I enjoyed my attempts at conversation with the Shi'ites, who were constantly curious about my presence in their town and regularly invited me to their homes to drink tea. To avoid misunderstandings, I carried bits of paper scribbled upon which were my destinations. In this instance, the driver who responded to my hail was a dark, rather striking Palestinian who spoke English. I learned that he was living in a 'base camp' with his family and 12,000 other Palestinian refugees an hour's drive outside the city. Originally, he had been a farmer, afterwards a captain with the PLO, where he had trained as a diver whose job it had been to detonate or dismantle submerged explosives. Now, he drove a cab. Each morning he, Aziz, set out from the camp for Sour, where he found fares, and each evening he returned by the same road.

'Don't you dream of escape?' I asked, when the other passengers, a trio of Shi'ite women, had left us.

'Where would I go? I cannot pass border control into Israel. My wife and children are here; they would be in jeopardy and I would find no work in the Palestinian territories. Palestinians are struggling to survive. Our camp is relatively clean. We are not mistreated . . . What I miss is toiling the land.'

Aziz had not intended to drive me all the way up to Qana – I am not certain that he was allowed to stray so far from the city limits – but we pulled over at the tomb of one of the ancient kings of Tyre, little more than rubbled stones painted with graffiti, but offering biblical views across hectares of olive groves that led to Israel, where we stood beneath the burning sun, where the breeze was insufficient, where we inhaled Mediterranean scents of the *garrigue*, engaged in conversation, and I learned he had once owned olive trees, and, before we knew it, we were in the central square of Qana. I gave my Palestinian driver five times the requested fare, still less expensive than a Central London Tube ticket, and we shook hands. I felt sad as he drove off because there was nothing I could do for him or his family.

The heat was obliterating. I had expected some respite given the altitude, but there was none. Still, I was glad to be out of Sour, to be amongst trees and nature, though my first impression of this scruffy town was of artillery and bomb sites. I was leaning against a disused tank – its metal scalded my flesh – in the ruins of what had been a UN camp, alongside a marble monolith, a commemoration of April 1996, when, during an Israeli air strike, 107 unarmed refugees had lost their lives. Unnecessary to describe the reported horrors of lost limbs and decapitations; witnesses described the attack as a massacre.

Beyond the turreted cement terrace, with its display of tank carcasses and husks of burned-out living quarters, were rows upon rows of olive trees, many contorted, growing in the calcified plains where cicadas stridulated and the heat scorched with the force of a bush fire. A short, hunched man in plimsolls, denims and baseball cap hovered at my side. In spite of adamant refusals, requests to be left to my reflections, he pushed his services as guide. Behind us, a dark hirsute Arab with fierce eyes and head turbaned with a striped towel, who could not have been attempting repairs because the shelled UN building was beyond redemption, stepped like a stork across distorted roof beams. The nuisance at my side yelled to his fellow townsman, engaging him in animated conversation, and while their voices echoed across the limey, sunburned uplands, I slipped away, in search of the spot where Christ performed his miracle.

Outside a launderette, a family of Shi'ites called to me. I handed them my scrap of paper, requesting directions, but they could not read it and hollered to a plump boy descending a hill, drinking Coke through a straw.

'Jesus water, yes?'

I nodded.

The boy beckoned me to follow. We wound down lanes and backstreets, without communication, until he stopped outside a hairdressing salon, where he deposited his empty bottle and another lad, taller, lankier, joined us.

'Christian?' he enquired of me.

'Yes.'

'I'm Carmel and he's Mohammed. This way.'

We climbed and descended for some considerable time. Every so often, as though to encourage this puffing foreigner who could not breathe due to dust spores and heat, they paused and pointed to a church on the summit of a distant hill. 'Christian,' they confirmed. I was perspiring, struggling to keep pace. Eventually, we reached Qana's Christian quarter, where small chapels nestled down untidy lanes, where chickens, mopeds and old wheels cluttered the winding cobbled passages, but not a person in sight and nowhere a sign to direct us.

'Relations between Muslim and Christian very good,' Carmel assured me. 'Christian not the enemy.' These boys had been babes in arms when the UN camp had been decimated so I chose not to pick up on Carmel's remark. I knew, though, that numbers of children had died in that Israeli raid as well as in the strikes preceding it.

Finally, we reached the distant church, dominating a vast vacant plaza. The wooden doors were bolted; the boys seemed baffled. I began to wonder what on earth I was doing, clambering about in ferocious heat, looking for traces of a two-thousand-year-old miracle unrelated to olives, with a pair of Arab adolescents whom I had never set eyes on before and probably never would again and I was overcome by an acute sense of futility. Carmel and Mohammed must have picked up on my gloom. Certainly, they slouched as we began our hike back to town, passing once more into the Muslim district. My downheartedness lifted a little when we crossed paths with two rotund biddies crouching on the ground out of the sun. Shi'ite grannies in full chador, more reminiscent of Greek widows than Muslims. Between them was a creased cloth piled with twigs. They were stripping the minuscule leaves off thyme sprigs. I stopped to observe.

'Zaatar.' I grinned proudly.

The women nodded, dexterous fingers toiling with industry. Carmel explained that I had been searching for the location of Christ's miracle. The grandmothers shook their heads, all the while picking. One did all the talking, an Arabic rasp like sandpaper in her throat. I asked about their chore. She, the older, with one tooth, semi-marbled eyes and more hair on her chin than could be seen on her head, boasted that she was famous. She rose at dawn and trekked with her olive-wood staff and empty swagbag to the hilltops to collect wild thyme. There, she worked until midday, after which she descended the hillside with her harvest loaded on her back. To ease the transmission of her burden, she had attached a strap to her homemade bag, which she wrapped round her brow. She pointed with curled tortoiseshell fingers to a thin impression lining her forehead. The strap secured her freight and facilitated the descent in the heat. Back at home, she and her neighbour – the woman at her side nodded and hooted – squatted in the street, as they were doing now, and passed their afternoons engaged in the separation of the heavily scented wild herb leaves from their stems. In the evenings, she ground the thyme by hand, using a stone pestle and mortar to release its flavours and separate it from any rogue stalks. To the crushed thyme she added sumac – the quantity was her secret, she grinned triumphantly – and sold this powder to local bakers or to housewives who travelled from Sour to purchase from her. On rare occasions, customers had journeyed from Beirut. With it, they baked the famous *manaeesh* bread. I knew it, I nodded. A kilogram of her grain earned her the equivalent of £4.50. The old woman's eyes gleamed with a lifetime's pride as her scored, leathered face broke into a whiskery cackle.

'She is eighty-eight,' Carmel whispered, 'and still climbing hills.'

Not quite a miracle but still remarkable.

I took a service taxi to Sidon, made the shortest of stops and then hailed another to Byblos. Byblos, along with Damascus and Jericho, claims to be the world's oldest continually inhabited town. Around 5000 BC, a thousand years before my Bechealeh *oliviers* were planted, a community of fishermen settled along the rocky promontory known today as Byblos – 'Jbeil' in Arabic. They were early farmers whose diet was based upon cereals, legumes and their stocks of lamb and goats, as well as fish caught from the Mediterranean. This nascent village community of Byblos, with its lovely twin bays, had trading exchanges with, at least, Turkey. This has been attested by local tools fashioned out of obsidian, a green rock produced by the volcanic mountains near Cappadocia in central Anatolia. I intended to visit Turkey a little later, fascinated to discover where and how those earliest trade exchanges took place and whether they included olives and olive oil.

I found no evidence of olive culture entering the lives of those earliest Byblos fishing peoples, but records to prove the trading of olive oil from this port have been found from 3000 BC, a thousand years after the Bechealeh plantations were first cultivated. Might oil from the Mount Lebanon range have supplied the harbour markets?

Around this same period, a partnership was established with Egypt. It was of paramount importance to the wealth of this fishing port. The Egyptians were purchasing wine, olive oil and cedar logs felled from hinterland forests. Thanks to those forestry resources, Byblos assumed the role of an essential trading partner to Egypt as well as to other, lesser powers in the Near East. This small port became a focus, a meeting point, a marketplace for many cultures and peoples. Into these natural bays were imported jewellery from Mesopotamia, metals and obsidian from Anatolia; linen, wheat and papyrus rolls from the Nile Valley; and gold from Nubia. In exchange, logs and olive oil were valuable commodities.

The seafaring vessels used for the exportation of the oil, wine and timber were constructed in the yards of Byblos, whose shipbuilding skills had become renowned throughout the ancient world. They felled the cedar to supply their ship-yards or they sold the wood abroad to others for the same purpose. It would seem that deforestation was of no concern to these early peoples and the ravages caused by logging were not yet apparent.

It was the Greeks who gave this fishing port the appellation Byblos. They sailed here to purchase Egyptian papyrus from the Phoenicians – *bublos*, writing paper. A sheaf of sheets they called *biblion*, and from that word we inherited 'Bible', the Book.

Surely, during these early stages, it was also from Byblos that the Greeks first discovered the art of olive cultivation? Nowhere along this coast have earlier oil-trading records been discovered. If the Greeks were doing business with the locals, then oil must have been a part of those exchanges. I wondered if it might not have been from here that the Cretans – before the Greeks – first discovered their fascination with the olive tree, but I had no answers yet.

By the time the Phoenicians were populating this coast and ruling the seas, Byblos, Tyre and Sidon were the influential ports of the eastern Mediterranean, shipping the edible genus of the olive tree in fleets to destinations as far afield as southern Spain.

None of that ancient bustle was apparent when I arrived late on a summer afternoon. The curving streets that led down the hillside to the port were sleepy, offering a glorious riot of blossoming frangipani, oleander, jacaranda, hibiscus. Lying north of Beirut, up the coast from hip Jounié, Byblos was Christian territory. In Sour, plastic bottles, squashed drinks cans and cigarette packets had been strewn everywhere. Byblos, by contrast, was spotless. I had passed through here previously on a couple of occasions. It was a location I might have chosen to settle in had we not found our olive farm. It had a French feel to it and photographs I had seen from the 1950s displayed a pretty fishing village such as St Tropez had once been.

But it was late July. Down by the harbour with its fortified tower, Byblos was in the throes of stage construction for its annual Mediterranean Festival. Brad Mehldau, one of my favourite jazz pianists, was to be the star attraction. Last time I had been here the honour had belonged to Demis Roussos. Tickets were on sale for the equivalent of £55–80, which put the event well beyond the range of the average Lebanese. I would have liked to stay on for a few days, enjoy the music and the ambiance, but time was knocking at my door. I checked into a hotel right on the waterfront and set off for the ruins also *au bord de la mer*, where I discovered elegantly carved stone olive vats that dated back to the Phoenicians. They must have required several men to lift them, even when empty. How were they transported across the seas, or were they used exclusively for storage? I spotted no olive clues from earlier periods, but learned the town's earlier olive history at the local museum.

I had promised Paul and Maryam that I would visit their sister-in-law, Marie, who owned a boutique in a trendy neighbourhood by the quay. She had been expecting to hear from me and invited me to her magpie-nest shop, where the walls were hung with coloured feathers, metal necklaces and rings. When I arrived she was in the company of another woman. As she washed mint leaves, Marie, who reminded me of an ageing hippie with her flowing, floral skirt and long amber beads, instructed me to take my pick from a saucer containing triangular shards of glass collected from a beach near Sour. 'They are usually bits of smashed bottles, never tidied up, of course, and are washed by many waves and polished by the sand.'

I chose a green fragment that had probably come from a

beer bottle, and while we were nattering, Marie fiddled with the glass, twisting a length of fine wire round it.

Her friend, Lena, who struck me as rather more formal and less at ease with herself, was also a Christian, hailing originally from Sophia, Bulgaria, where she had trained as a civil engineer. The two women had met in Montreal during their years as exiles. Mint tea was served and we raised our cups to three females from diverse backgrounds: Irish, Bulgarian, Lebanese. With no coercion from me, the conversation, jumping between French and English, shifted to the identity of the Mediterranean. What did it mean to be Mediterranean? 'We are not going to discuss politics, though,' they both cried. All the while tugging and weaving, Marie recalled that during her temporary residence in Canada what she had been haunted by was the absence of the sea itself and the perfumed nights of the Orient with their scents of jasmine and joss sticks. Jasmine was her favourite; a floret lay between us on the table. She had plucked it that morning from her walled garden, as she did every morning, to carry throughout the day. When jasmine was out of season, she bought one, which was not quite the same, but she could not bear to be denied the satisfaction of its sweet perfume. For Marie, being Mediterranean meant the end of alienation, to be reunited with perfumes, rose waters, almond oil and a way of life that was closer to nature, to the soil. Although jasmine was her preferred scent, it was orange blossom she had pined for during exile. She recalled how, when she had been a child in Beirut, her mother had spread bedding at the feet of the orange trees during the blossom season and a local boy had been employed to climb up and shake the white blooms from their boughs; white flowers tumbling towards white sheets as their scents wafted through every open window.

Her mother steeped the flowers, heating them in a large

beaked pot used for the extraction of essential oils. Throughout the year, she added two drops of the oil to water and gave it to the children to drink as a tonic for heart and organs.

'It tasted so bitter,' laughed Marie, pulling a face.

'We wait for the fruits and distil with alcohol to make *vin d'orange*. Your mother had smarter ideas.' I smiled.

The women asked me about our olive trees, why the *olivier* meant so much to me. I admitted that I felt pacified by its stillness, its longevity, the rustling and swaying of its pendulous silver branches; its poetry and history offered me faith. About my relationship with Michel, they marvelled at the trust involved in living such independent lives. I confessed that it wasn't always easy.

Being Mediterranean for Lena was 'the foolish heart of love'. She had met a Lebanese Muslim, also studying civil engineering, whilst at university in Bulgaria, fallen in love and married him without pausing to question a life committed to Islam. She had known nothing about the faith. 'To create children without considering the circumstances was rash,' she sighed.

To Lena, the Mediterranean, or more particularly Lebanon, was the force of two opposing energies that could never be united.

'I wedded a culture, a religious doctrine, and once my sons were born I became chained to it. Yet I remained and will for ever be a foreigner here,' she said. 'I spoke no French, little English and certainly no Arabic when I first set foot on this narrow limestone land. I was obliged to renounce my career when my babies were born. I faced motherhood under alien circumstances, was forced to reinvent myself, to take on a Lebanese-Mediterranean identity and live the life of a submissive Muslim woman, and a convert.'

When the war broke out, she, with husband and small children, fled to Montreal, where there was yet another adjustment to make. She was a Christian who had renounced her faith in favour of Islam and now found herself in a Catholic society and, once more, an outsider. It was Marie who befriended her.

After the war, like so many other Lebanese families, Lena returned to Beirut, but she had since chosen to settle in Canada, where her sons, who were grown men now, had their careers. Only brief periods were spent with her husband in Beirut. Gone was the duty of accompanying him to overseas postings in Muslim countries. In Saudi, where she was forced to wear the veil, she made good friends with other expat women enduring the same subjugations. 'The hardest,' she sighed, 'was Libya.'

Libya was scheduled for further along my route.

'Be warned: it is austere and you might not be safe.'

The distant evening call of the *muezzin* sounded beyond the Christian hills. I rose to be on my way. Marie had fashioned the glass into a ring, and once mounted, it had very evidently taken the form of a hard green olive, we all agreed.

'It was meant for you.' She smiled. 'Let it be your talisman. From here, you are going to the Beqaa Valley, a Hezbollah stronghold, and then Syria. Libya awaits you and, later, Israel. A woman alone. Travel prudently.'

The following morning, I rose early to the hot summer wind, the *gharbi*, blowing in off the sea. I swam amongst cresting waves agitated by this southwester, mastery of which must have been paramount to summer seafarers approaching this port in their wooden sailing vessels. After breakfast, I found a service taxi that transported me to the city of Tripoli, 85 kilometres north of Beirut, another of the Phoenicians' ancient trading ports, where I checked into the craziest hotel I had ever set foot in. Within the entrance hall stood a larger-than-life medieval suit of arms. Such greeting was followed by the strains of proprietress Nadia cooing across two salons, 'Hue are in ze Ooriendul sveet, darlink.' The 'Oriental suite' at the back of the house was a capacious room, lacking hot water and offering intermittent bursts of electricity. An overhead bulb flashed on and off like a spot in the middle of the night.

I had chosen this sanctuary for its name, the Olive Castle. Castle it was not – more a salmon-pink winged house. Nor did it, as promised, dwell within hills mantled by olive groves behind the harbour city, but it was run by a unique character. Nadia was a pyramid of a woman, a Lebanese Christian who lounged from dawn to dusk on one of several opulent Ottoman sofas, all the while guzzling chocolates, dressed in loud printed kaftans that hung from her ample bosom in cascades. She spoke with an accent that resembled the many times married Austrian beauty queen Zsa Zsa Gabor, repeatedly calling me 'darlink', while she sat at my side during dinner in the jungled garden, refusing food because she was on a diet, but later, while we gossiped by candlelight on rocking chairs alongside an empty swimming pool, she consumed an entire box of 'sinful' Tripolitan sweets.

Nadia's posada was a movie set, but whether for Gloria Swanson, the Marx Brothers or a Gothic *Arabian Nights*, I was bewildered. It did, at least, possess a fax machine and I was able to receive news from Michel. I was glad of it. I knew that where I was headed was not going to be easy.

The following morning, I was collected by Fareed, a professor at the University of Beirut moonlighting as a driver due to financial constraints. I had one more visit before the Beqaa Valley. Together we travelled inland until we reached the olive groves of Zgharta and from there the farmhouse of Mr Dibdib, an olive farmer. 'Dibdib' means 'wolf' in Arabic.

We were seated on an outdoor terrace, looking across the groves to the mountains, Fareed, myself, Dibdib, his wife and three wholesome beauties, his teenage daughters. Dibdib had begun his working life at fourteen as a blacksmith, to which his horny hands bore witness, in a location where the bulk of his commissions had been the firing of olive presses and vats for local farmers. His labours had kept him indoors. He had grown restless, claustrophobic, jealous of the outdoor environment and the passion with which his customers eulogised their trees. When his father died, he inherited a modest sum and gambled every penny on the purchase of this olive farm. I laughed. We had that risk in common. His holding, though, unlike our modest affair, boasted over two thousand well-established *oliviers*. I turned my head beyond the terrace towards the undulating, powdery-white limestone mountains. The climate and terrain were ideal for the propagation of olive trees. He had created himself an idyllic milieu. His wife was laying out cups, while his three girls bunched around us, leaning close to follow our exchanges, feeding me olives and fresh pistachios harvested from their trees that morning. How they shrieked unashamedly when I popped a nut still clothed in its soft red skin into my mouth. I had not known to peel off the outer covering because I had never come across pistachios served in their natural state before. We drank coffee followed by a bottle of Lebanese white wine. Since they were Maronite Christians, alcohol was a celebrated component of their diet. We talked of harvests, of trees, and then we returned to olives. There were five principal varieties in this country, Dibdib told me. Most farmers grew several. Close to 40 per cent of all olive orchards were over fifty years of age. Most of his trees were younger. It was generally agreed here that at seventy they started degenerating. I hotly disagreed, citing the Provençal farmers who judge a hundred-year-old just a baby. I told him that many of our own trees were over four hundred. He lifted his bushy eyebrows in surprise. He had beautiful eyes, the colour of caramel.

'Where did the olive tree originate?'

'*Here*, of course,' he claimed without a second's hesitation.

'What do you know of its origins?'

'When oil was first extracted from the drupe of the *zeytun*, Arab for "olive", it was used only as seasoning on foods, such as a primitive form of pasta, with fish or vegetables. It was also used for burning to create light, and as perfume. The earliest oils were extracted by placing the drupes on a hard surface and crushing them with a cylindrical stone. The arrival of mills was a Godsend, a revolution!'

This was all solid information, but it was not evidence that Lebanon was the location of the first cultivators, I countered. When I told him of the groves in Bechealeh, he was impressed. That was proof enough, he said, although he had not known of their existence.

'Tradition tells us that it was the Phoenicians who improved the quality of olive fruits by grafting the *Olea europaea* on to wild olive trees. Certainly, it was due to the Phoenicians, with a little help from the Greeks later, that olive plantations grew up round the Med perimeter.'

I requested a *dégustation* of their home-pressed oil and we trooped down interior stairs to the garage, a sombre space that housed no vehicles. Instead, it was cluttered with stacks of *scourtins*, the old-fashioned coconut-fibre mats used for pressing the oil from the paste. The European Union had outlawed their use from our side of the sea due to hygiene risks, but I did not mention this. It was a traditional method of oil extraction. Pride of place was given to the press that Dibdib had spent six months constructing for himself. He stroked it as though it were a pet. Madame Dibdib, careful not to spill a droplet, poured a thimbleful of oil into a liqueur glass she had brought from the dining room and handed it to me. The entire family as well as Fareed, the puffy-eyed professor, smoking constantly, watched on as I sipped their oil, more golden than ours because we press the drupes when they are greenish, waiting for my opinion. Here, the fruits must have been harvested riper, offering a fruity, fragrant flavour, a subtle aroma. The oil was very good, as smooth as a Sauternes wine.

After a tour of a few of his noble trees, during which he confided that his favourite moment of the year was the arrival of the delicate, lacy, white flowers, we returned to the terrace upstairs. I wondered how easy life was here for an olive producer. Handsome, weather-worn Mr Dibdib shared his uncertainties. Had I known that Lebanese farmers had taken to the streets to give their produce away? I shook my head. The Syrians had set up a smuggling network, using closed military roads to bring contraband agricultural products into Lebanon, selling them through street vendors at prices that were bankrupting the local communities. Lebanon, in spite of its fertile agricultural lands, was now one of the least self-sufficient economies on the planet. Lebanese farmers had lined the coastal highways, offering their produce free to all passing cars, begging the occupants to support local agriculture. Their banners had read, 'Drugs out, fresh food in.'

His wife chipped in. Local companies 'in cahoots' with Syria had been purchasing oil from their imposing neighbour at up to 40 per cent less than it could be found in Lebanon and were packaging it as Lebanese.

Dibdib and his neighbours were having difficulties selling

their golden liquid; it cost them more to produce than the fraudulent bottles were marketed at.

'The government was taken aback by the farmers' anger. They made us promises, offered aid programmes, but we'll see,' he sighed.

His trio of daughters, leaning on elbows at the far end of the table, in T-shirts and jeans, almond-eyed, broadly smiling, pubescent – putting me in mind of Michel's lovely twin girls when they were teenagers – were more interested in hearing about Paris than listening to their parents' woes. It was refreshing to be in their vibrant, carefree company after all that I had witnessed in recent days, and, for one exquisite moment, as I turned my head and saw the glow of light, saw the framboised sun slipping west, I felt the fifteen-year war and the political abrasions Mr Dibdib and his wife and all Lebanon had been speaking about, had been scarred by, must have taken place elsewhere. Anywhere except here, within the quietude of these glorious chalk-white shoulders of olive-groved hills.

Syria

After a second night of Nadia's hospitality, I was up early and back on the olive trail. Syria was Beqaaning! With Fareed at the wheel, we ascended into the high plateaux of the Mount Lebanon range, passing through semi-nomadic hamlets, hugging narrow passes that in winter would be snowbound, looking down upon scenery that fed faith, before beginning our easterly descent. At one of the highest summits, Fareed pulled over so I could better appreciate the view down into the vast open plain, one of the most fertile I had ever seen, the breathtaking Beqaa Valley, 'the breadbasket of the Roman empire'.

'Everything required for our cuisine was produced here. With the exception of olive oil,' smiled my driver.

In antiquity, these glorious plains had been part of the Fertile Crescent, a swathe of rich agricultural land that had reached across Syria to present-day Iraq, south to Jordan and north into what is now Turkey. This heartland possibly witnessed the birth of agriculture, the revolution that took man from hunter-gatherer to farmer, some twelve thousand years ago. Here, man was tilling and toiling before the first olives were cracked open.

What I was gazing upon was a fragment of that crescent, that veritable Garden of Eden. The Beqaa Valley, close to 200 kilometres in length and 30 kilometres wide, was situated between two mountain ranges, Mount Lebanon to the west and Anti-Lebanon to the east, beyond which lay Syria, my next destination.

'Today, Beqaa is the poorest region in Lebanon,' sighed Fareed, lighting another cigarette. He had such a weary air about him, I wondered what burdened him.

As we descended into the flatland, with mauve mountains in the background and earth the colour of rust, a series of military checkpoints awaited us. I had not expected this. Syria had policed Lebanon for twenty-nine years until April, which was another reason they were so despised here, but due to international and Lebanese pressure, sparked by the assassination of Hariri, they were forced to make an unprepared withdrawal even if much of their intelligence apparatus remained.

'The checkpoints haven't been dismantled,' explained Fareed, fumbling in the glove compartment for papers.

'Who mans them now?'

'Our soldiers.'

'I was surprised by their formidable presence in this agricultural paradise and concluded it was due to the proximity of the Syrian border, until we approached the first hoarding, rising up out of the countryside as unexpectedly as a man pulling a gun. We had entered Hezbollah country. The Beqaa Valley, their stronghold, their training ground.

Everywhere now, posters with images of guns, tanks, domination. I recalled my evening with Madame Sahia in Sour, how she had praised their good works. Damned by the West as terrorists, they were respected and admired by the Lebanese, she had said. This region was where kidnapped Westerners such as Terry Waite had been held prisoner. Several of the billboards were the height of two-storey buildings. A tight fist brandishing high a Kalashnikov was one of their better-known symbols. It was shocking, and shocking to behold in these verdant plains where farming families dwelled, where Shi'ites were labouring fields and all Lebanon's wine was grown. Posters affixed to every pole, every pylon, displayed the zealous faces of ayatollahs and mullahs. Minarets towered like missiles over orchards and gardens as ancient as agriculture itself, but many were no longer producing fruit or vegetables. Flooded by Syrian contraband, those markets had fallen through the floor, leaving opportunities for drug cultivation wide open. Brazenly, within leafy green holdings, Hezbollah recruitment and training camps thrived. So, too, the drugs to fund them. I found it profoundly disturbing.

At each checkpoint bar one, we were waved directly through. On the other occasion, a young man in uniform rapped vigorously against Fareed's window, closed to protect us against dust. His papers were checked with surly suspicion. I spotted the tremble in his academic's hand as he lit another cigarette. Who was I, and what was I doing with him? The boy officer eyed me uncertainly, then, bored with us, waved us impatiently onwards. Once we were clear, I asked Fareed how this situation within the valley had arisen. His explanation echoed Emile's words.

During the war, the area had produced alarming quantities of hashish and opium. The country was on its knees and a blind eye had been turned to these illicit sources of finance. Hezbollah had smuggled out the illegal produce using channels set up by Syrians. With the funds earned from drugs, weapons had been brought in via a network of military routes to arm Hezbollah against the Israelis. After the war, the Lebanese government attempted to halt the drug production by offering alternative crop subsidies. The farmers complied and discontinued hashish and opium-poppy growing. Unfortunately, little or no compensation was forthcoming. Some said the Syrians blocked the reconstruction programme. Angry bellies howled with hunger. Cannabis had fed them so they replanted their fields and today clashes with the State continued.

I recalled a line of Grahame Greene's about the futility of discussing politics with a hungry man.

As we penetrated the valley, flanking the roadsides were shanty encampments, tents slung with goat- and sheepskin. Families of dark-skinned people milled about the scruffy abodes. Donkeys were tethered to ropes that pegged the tents. Untrusting faces with sullen ebony-black eyes monitored our passage. They never waved, never returned my smiles. Tired young women transporting aluminium pots remarked but never acknowledged us.

'They descend like migrating flocks from Syria,' explained Fareed, pre-empting my question. 'Gypsies working as fruit-pickers, land labourers.'

'They look like Bedouins.'

'No, they're gypsies.'

We lunched at an open-air restaurant overlooking the Bardaouni river, where Fareed, a professor in archaeology, explained that Beqaa, this vast corridor of fecundity, was once a great thoroughfare for commerce. It had been a meeting point, a monumental market place, connecting the city of Damascus with the Mediterranean coast and the Arabian peninsula to Anatolia. It was a true crossroads for many of the civilisations who had occupied this eastern Mediterranean cradle for millennia. Without doubt, olive oil was traded here. Vats of it, but purchased from where? From those unidentified farmers who had planted up Bechealeh in the Mount Lebanon range? From Palestine? Exchanged, bartered for other produce, the jars would have been transported to Damascus, Mesopotamia, Egypt.

Transported on donkeys and asses in the days before camels.

I interrupted to enquire about the donkey. Where had it come from, what was its history?

'Originally bred by the Egyptians, the earliest known remains of a domestic donkey come from a site at Ma'adi in Lower Egypt and have been dated to the fourth millennium BC,' he said.

'The same period as the Bechealeh olives.'

'The wild ass probably originated in Nubia.'

In the long story of the domestication of beasts, the donkey was a latecomer. Sheep and cattle had been part of man's agricultural life for four thousand years before the donkey plodded on to the scene.

I poured the wine. Fareed waved fingers over his glass. He was driving.

'The cultivation of wine in Beqaa,' he told me, lighting yet another cigarette, bursting into a fit of coughing, 'began four thousand years ago.'

It would have been sold to Egypt and Greece and then, later, the Romans took up the subtle arts of the vineyard. By now we were back on the road moving towards Baalbek, where the Romans built some of their most magnificent temples.

After our lunch, before my crossing into Syria, we strolled around the city's ruins; Baalbek, where the limestone rock glowed rose-pink in the glare of the sun and six remaining, remarkably well-preserved colonnades from its Temple of Jupiter soared above the earthquaked city towards a cobalt sky. Baalbek, today a city of bats and owls, was unforgettable and I had to be dragged away, not least because I was anxious about what lay ahead.

Back on the road, confronted once more by the yellow-and-green flags of Hezbollah, I bid farewell to Fareed.

'One piece of advice, if I may. Keep your counsel, give no opinions, never utter the family name of Assad. The *mukhabarat* will be listening. God help you in Syria.' *Mukhabarat*, secret police.

Surrounded by fields where distant mountains the colour of bruised grapes rose like pyramids of smoke, we shook hands. I was genuinely sorry to see him go, with his gentle manners and his worried demeanour. I ran across the country byway, bags flapping at my side, to a waiting white car that did not look fit for the pound. Fareed had no papers to cross the border, which was why he could ferry me no further. This chap did, though I doubted the reliability of his vehicle. Might he be secret police? I climbed aboard and we hit a busy highway at a speed that nearly gave me a heart attack, ascending to a mountain pass where we drove head on at the approaching lorries, who were playing the same Russian roulette with us. Pebbles and shale stones rose, spun and rained upon the windscreen and I truly believed this was where I would meet my end. As I prepared my documents with fumbling fingers in readiness for passport control, hurtling towards the border, I learned that the French journalist from *Libération*, Florence Aubenas, and her Iraqi interpreter, held hostage since January, had been released. She was already on her way back to France. The news was a few days old but it was heartening. It brought tears of relief to my eyes, particularly as the long lines of stationary motors ahead warned me that the iron hand of Syria was beckoning. I was still trembling. Our penetration into the heart of Hezbollah territory with its latent verdant menace had woken me up to the dangers surrounding me, but I knew this time I would not turn back. We slowed to a halt and joined the queue. It promised to be a long sticky wait. I opened the door, feet out, and began riffling through notes and papers.

In spite of international concerns over Syria's policies within Lebanon, their support of terrorism and alleged involvement in drug trafficking, President Bashar al-Assad had maintained control of his country, a substantial dominion that stretched from the Mediterranean coast, bordered with Turkey at its north-western tip, across deserts, over the mighty river Euphrates east to Iraq, while its southern tenures frontiered Jordan and the heavily disputed Golan Heights. It was in 1967, under the dictatorship of Bashar's father, Hafez al-Assad, that Syria lost the Golan Heights to Israel, during the Six Day War.

Bashar, second son to Hafez, landed the presidency through a stroke of family misfortune. The position had been destined for his older and favoured brother, but Syrian history changed dramatically overnight, when, in 1994, Basil, the heir apparent, was killed, James Dean-style, in a high-speed car accident and Bashar was whisked away from his ophthalmology studies at St Mary's Hospital in London to begin a hasty, unanticipated political apprenticeship. Rushed through Syria's Military Academy that same year, promoted to the rank of major in the Presidential Guards, elevated to lieutenant colonel, and almost before he had drawn breath after the death of his father in 2000, he was officially invested with the presidential crown.

'Passport and visa.' My recollections on the Assad dynasty had been interrupted by a black-haired, moustached Syrian border-patrol officer. I glanced at my watch. I had been queuing for more than an hour.

I handed over my documents with a nervous smile.

'What's your profession?'

Aside from Fareed's warnings about never offering opinions on any subject concerning Assad or his Syrian dictatorship, he had also counselled against declaring myself as a writer or actress. Syrians mistrusted writers, feared bad press, and given the role of women in the world of Islam, 'actress' could create the wrong impression.

'Olive farmer,' I replied.

'Why you want in hospitable Syria?' the black-eyed bureaucrat demanded.

'To learn about your olives.' I had read claims that olive farming began in Syria. After the thrill of the Bechealeh groves, I was hoping that luck might remain with me, that I might find a clue, a tree, of the same period or even earlier.

He lit a cigarette, dragged on it, stared mistrustingly, studied my passport and disappeared. I waited for a further thirty-five minutes, observing others queuing in this border office where the floor was strewn with cigarette ends and photos of Assad stared down upon us from every wall. I was the sole female. The rest were shuffling threadbare Arabs in worn-out footwear. Syrians or Lebanese, I could not tell. Outside, their black-clad women waited in battered cars in the heat, squashed against suitcases bursting at the seams. An Arab habit, I noticed here: they sat with their bare feet resting on their shoes or slippers, as though airing them.

Finally, the bureaucrat returned and handed me my passport: 'You are welcome in hospitable Syria.'

It was late evening by the time we arrived in Damascus and my lunatic driver, shirt drenched with sweat, bid me farewell outside the hotel I had stayed at four years earlier when world events had forced me home. Bags in room, I descended to the lobby, feeling unsettled by the change of destination, a little lost, and decided upon a glass of wine before addressing the question of where an unaccompanied woman finds dinner in Damascus. But I had reached the cradle of the Islamic world, an alcohol-free zone. I saw a sign to a bar and crossed to the crepuscular lounge. A blast of arctic air hit me, overactive air-conditioning. Hovering by the entrance, I clocked the fact that I was the only female in sight. Men glared and turned their heads away in disgust. A Western woman alone in a bar in a Muslim enclave, their judgement was written across their faces. I found a table and sat down. The menu offered beer or white wine, both at inflated, tourist prices. The waiter nodded curtly and disappeared. Suddenly a stab of loneliness took hold and I wished that I was back in Lebanon, anywhere but embarking upon this solitary leg into the unknown, frustrated by the confines laid upon my sex. The wine arrived in a thimble-sized glass, had the tint of Lucozade and was corked. I left dollars on the table and set out into the bustling scruffy streets, attempting to cross roads, to negotiate demen-ted traffic. Imposing images of Assad at every crossroads and corner bore down upon me and every passer-by. The rear window of every second vehicle sported photos of him or, more frequently, his deceased brother, Basil, moodily captured in chunky Elvis Presley sunglasses. Everywhere mosques. The *muezzin* was echoing through a dozen loudspeakers all at once, beckoning the faithful from all corners of the city, old and new. On that first evening, those male criers sounded like jackals howling, drawing close from the desert, warning me off.

Unlike the Shi'ites in Lebanon, the majority of black-clad women here were also facially veiled, save for rectangular slits revealing their eyes. Some wore headdresses and robes that concealed them entirely, burqas. All expression of femininity denied. They reminded me of giant chess pieces – pawns in someone's game! I longed to hear their voices, to learn their stories, particularly given the advertisements displayed every-where in the teeming thoroughfares, presenting a very differ-ent image of woman. Whatever the product – shampoos, toothpaste, television sets – the lighter-skinned models with grimacing ruby lips, heavy make-up, perfectly formed snowy teeth, swathes of forties Hollywood hair were leaning into the camera offering a promise of their fully fleshed breasts, décolleté. It struck me as an insulting contradiction in this ultra-strict Sunni society where wives, mothers, girls were shuffling about in the stifling heat in shapeless tents. Who were the advertisers appealing to? Men with wallets, or women who silently begged to cast off those unwieldy garments?

I attempted to put my indignation aside; I had distances to travel, Muslim countries to pass through and some of these females, undoubtedly, submitted willingly to these man-made laws. Certainly, within the roaringly chaotic maze of rubbled streets, in the city that also claimed to be the oldest continuously inhabited, I suffered steely-eyed discrimination from both sexes for the fashion of my clothes, though, in slacks and baggy, long-sleeved shirt, I had taken care to cover myself. Men brushed up against me and whispered in my ear, words I could not understand, but the lascivious intent was clear. I began to feel awkward, uncomfortable about my physical self, *pas bien dans ma peau*, but more than anything I felt affronted. After having traipsed to and fro, staring into shopfronts displaying plastic shoes or women's underwear, unable to brush off my discomfort and brewing anger, I returned to the hotel and ate a tasteless, overpriced meal in its bland 'coffee bar', where only the lonely or those in transit sat at solitary tables, staring into space with bored expressions.

After a night's sleep, I struck out with renewed resolve in search of olive history. The sun was shining, the heat seemed tolerable, statues and fountains (mostly dry) adorned squares. I crossed through a small park with willows, where the gentle tinkling of falling water and the noisy chatter of Arab families picnicking on parched grass resonated and where, from beyond the gates, giant photos of their president kept a watchful eye.

Passing through its vast open courtyard cluttered with beggars, women, mullahs, tourists, guides, raggedy freaks, where I was obliged to don one of those black tents that covered every inch of me save my face and, due to its bulkiness and weight, restricted my movements, I made a tour of Omayyad Mosque, an ornate cavernous place. Once the Cathedral of St John the Baptist, who is revered as a prophet by Muslims, it was rebuilt as a mosque 1,300 years ago and is considered the fourth-holiest shrine in Islam. Bemused by parties of black-clad women (I was one, too!) bunched in corners wailing, I noticed another puzzling activity at play. A continuous procession of males in socked feet were entering from outside. Shiftily, guiltily, they approached a quartet of old men, two of whom were blind, in robes and white caps, cross-legged on woven rugs, praying vigorously. The lay visitors bent low, whispered in the ear of one or other of the prayers, then pressed sums of money into his clasped hands before hotfooting it back outside. I requested of a tallow-faced, bespectacled man who was peering into the shrine of John the Baptist, where his head is allegedly kept, to know what the financial exchanges were about. The men on mats were professional prayers. They observed on behalf of others. 'It is not allowed in the Koran, but it gives these men a living,' he told me.

'Why don't people do their own praying?'

'They're too busy,' he said.

I was making for the street called Straight in the Christian quarter of the old city. In Roman times, it was Via Recta, and my impression was of yet another run-down thoroughfare lined with tacky shops. Clogged with debris in the gutters, choked with browsing pedestrians, ringing bicycles, clapped-out cars, crumbling archways, with dozens of alleyways feeding off to right and left, I found it difficult to negotiate a path. Billboards hung to left and right offering yet another round of movie-star lookalikes in low-cut blouses with smiles you only see in advertisements, while the Assad brothers' portraits, pinned up in shop windows, clocked every move. I was on the hunt for a khan, an ancient caravanserai, situated somewhere along this far-reaching street. As I wound an almost indiscernible kink or two, I remembered Mark Twain's observation, taken from the Acts of the Apostles, that no one claimed the street *was* straight, only that it was *called* straight.

History abounded here. I was walking in the footsteps of Mark Antony, who, in the grip of mid-life or marital crisis, offered this city as a gift to his Egyptian mistress, Cleopatra, much to the chagrin of its inhabitants as well as the powers back in Rome (and possibly his wife). Saul, later St Paul, originally from Tarsus (in modern-day Turkey), found haven at the nearby house of Ananias. An ardent Jew, Saul feared the burgeoning faith was a threat to Judaism and set out to hunt down its devotees, followers of 'the Way', to return them in chains to Jerusalem for execution. His journey to Damascus probably led him through what today is the disputed West Bank and alongside the Sea of Galilee. Outside the city, he was blinded by a force of light and fell from his horse. In Damascus, his sight was restored by Ananias and he was baptised Paul. The house of Ananias, a Christian meeting place, is believed to have been one of the first Judaeo-Christian communities outside Palestine.

I was lost. All signs in Arabic. Some kind stranger near St Paul's Chapel, assuming I was on a Christian pilgrimage, pointed me to the spot where Paul, hidden within a basket, had been lowered down the exterior wall of the city to make his escape. This place was awash with potent biblical and historical images, but these were not what I was after. I was hunting the Khan al-Zait, the olive-oil caravanserai.

A caravanserai had originally been an enclosure that protected a well or water source, where weary travellers paused during their long journeys to take refreshment and fodder their exhausted beasts. From there, they developed into complexes with courtyards used as hostelries for travelling merchants. The noun 'caravanserai' is derived from two Persian words, *karwan*, which describes a troupe or caravan of travellers, and *serai*, a large inn. The caravanserai I had searched all morning for, with its vaulted arcades, dated back to the sixteenth century and was said to have been a vibrant centre in a humming business district, specialising exclusively in the sale and purchase of olive oil. Freya Stark once visited. When I eventually tracked it down, I was disappointed. Its courtyard was certainly a calm respite after the clamour, fumes and grit of the city beyond, and I was relieved to pause a moment beneath fragrant citrus trees, to ease swelling limbs too long in stifling heat, to observe the Damascenes dawdling, consuming gallons of fizzy drinks, before I wandered inside to stroll the parade of artisans at work, heads covered in *kaffiyehs*, cross-legged on the ground, where I found it well presented but antiseptic, as though I had fallen upon a puppet show for tourists. In bygone days, this caravanserai had been a well-known watering hole, an overnight city break for out-of-town olive merchants arriving on sweating camels, laden with crops and produce from all points east and west. Their aching bodies might have been doused by the refreshing fall of water from a central fountain. Here, stinking, sweating beasts hot from journeying were groomed; sacks of olive drupes being unloaded would have released their pungent odour; producers and distributors gathered in the courtyard, laughing, arguing, wheeler-dealing, trading oils, weighing olives, calling for refreshments; the clink of coins; the slapping of slippered feet;

boys running to and fro boiling tea or sweeping away camel turds; a lamb roasting; a few whores or pretty youths prancing to and fro. That, for me, was a more animated, whiffier picture.

Travelling in this land as an unaccompanied woman without knowledge of Arabic was proving problematic. In Lebanon, I had Christianity and French; here, Islam dominated. I was losing courage about setting off into the desert alone. So, the hotel put me in touch with a bearded, muscular agent who looked as though the creases in his flat moon-face had been carved. He invited me for a drink in the lobby. He ordered water, I, chilled beer. All the while we talked, he clasped and stroked his hands as though drying them. It left me uneasy, wary that he might belong to the *mukhabarat*, but he promised to set me up with a driver, and as business was bad due to 'wars in neighbouring lands', he offered to throw in an interpreter for the same fee. He assumed I was sightseeing, but when he learned my quest, his face cracked into a great wrinkled beam.

'My family have olive trees. Olive cultivation began in Syria, did you know that?'

'When?'

'Six thousand years ago.'

The same date as the Bechealeh groves.

'Are there still trees in existence from that period?'

He looked at me as though I was crazy and shook his big, baggy head. He reminded me of Bluto from the animation series *Popeye* (who had a crush on Olive Oyl, I remembered later).

'Go up to Aleppo,' he said. 'In Ebla, jars from that period were found. There's not much at the site, but the surrounding olive hills – ah, you'll praise Allah.'

It was precisely where I had set my sights.

He stood to shake my hand. 'A spoonful of olive oil to start the day. A tradition since generations in my family, and there has never been a single case of cancer. Praise Allah, it's the olive oil. Travel safely, *insha'allah*.'

After he left, the waiter came scurrying after me to settle the bill.

I apologised profusely. 'Sorry, I thought my companion —'

'But you took beer. If you take alcohol, you must pay.' It was a lesson I learned then. In Syria, no practising Muslim buys an alcoholic drink, even for another.

The following morning, my team arrived. Driver and interpreter, both answering to the name of Muhammad. One as tall and silently eloquent as a whispering willow, the other a squinting man of many judgements. Setting off a little later than we had intended, observing beauty spots disfigured by mountains of plastic bottles and fizzy-drink cans, we arrived at our first port of call. The village of Ma'alula, or 'the Entrance', in Aramaic, perched like an eagle's nest in the stark heights of the al-Qalamoon Mountains; it had not been on my itinerary, but interpreter Muhammad, a guide before the loss of tourism, recommended it. Its rocks were honeycombed with caves where many early Christians had hidden from their persecutors. Several had been captured, executed and had risen to martyr status. Muhammad could not recall their names. We wound up and around narrow stone stairwells chiselled out of the rocky altitude until we reached a stone church, dark within and strangely spooky, where a hunched priest, also dark and strange, with several large knobs on his bearded face, rattled off the Lord's Prayer, a party piece for me in Aramaic, the language of Christ. Today, Aramaic is only spoken by Syrian Christians, except in Ma'alula, where it remains the lingua franca. Once, it had been the Semitic tongue of Syria and biblical Palestine.

It was chilly in the church and chilling to be in the presence of Christ's mother tongue. Every naïve picture conjured up in childhood, fed by parables recounted to me at an age when the characters to whom my imagination gave life were as alien to me as the heavens, fell away. Palms, olives, Christ travelling by donkey beneath the shade of olive trees. I had never seen an olive tree nor a waving palm frond and I had assumed Jesus spoke English.

Back in the car, travelling towards Palmyra in the blasting heat – we had faulty air-conditioning – I began recalling some of those childhood images of Christ riding into Bethlehem, followers perched upon branches of fig and olive trees in the hope of a glimpse of him, and I suddenly remembered that when I was a child, olive oil had represented misery. It lived in white screw-capped bottles, expensively purchased from the chemist and stored in our medicine chest. I loathed its acrid odour and dreaded its name because, in our home, its function was to dislodge wax from ears. How could I have known, as I struggled to resist the heated liquid seeping into the clogged orifice, barely able to hear my mother's words – 'It's good for you' – that one day in a distant adult future, I would husband its trees and that very same juice would become the source of journeys, of inspiration?

Palmyra loomed up out of the desert like a shimmering golden mirage, once seen never forgotten. Deep in the heart of baking sands, in the centre of nowhere, 150 kilometres west to the Orontes river and 200 kilometres to the mighty Euphrates in the east, Palmyra, or Tadmor, its original name, had grown up as a caravan stop, a terminus on routes to and from the Far East. Its fabulous wealth and reputation had come from its position, a lush oasis fed by springs of crystal water stationed in the middle of a baking sand-sea of nothingness, mid-point between the Mediterranean and Mesopotamia. Such desert cities lived or perished by the existence of their natural springs. Although those of Palmyra dried up centuries ago, thanks to technology, a miserably underprivileged modern settlement with its inevitable posters of the leader, ripped and fluttering in the desert winds, survived, alongside the golden ruins, irrigated by hundreds of miles of pipes fed from coast and metropolis.

We approached the ancient sandstone city in the early afternoon, toured its perimeter and stopped to buy clusters of sticky, amber dates, the first of the season, picked that morning by an Arab now on his haunches at the roadside selling from his bicycle. There were lines of vendors, all squatting, all offering swags of fruit hanging from donkeys or cycles. On their heads, they wore *kaffiyehs*, while their faces were covered with coloured rags to protect against wind and sand. I bit into the fruit handed to me by Muhammad and licked my fingers – mmm, sweeter, more succulent than toffee, or, in the words of the early twentieth-century archaeologist and Arabist Gertrude Bell, 'The fresh date is a thing apart.' I suddenly pictured Quashia, our Arab gardener back at the farm. He frequently returned from his home in Algeria loaded with plastic bags of dates. Michel adored them, but this was the first time I had tasted one direct from a palm grove.

In the distance were khaki hills from where came the clanking of aluminium pots strapped to the flanks of slow-moving beasts of burden. Camels loped by and donkeys laden with bulging bags. Sand swam up in chiffony whorls.

I made a solo visit to the ruined city while the Muhammads slept. 'Too hot.' Syria claimed ten Roman theatres. One was located at Palmyra. I pranced its stage and tested its acoustics with the opening lines of Cleopatra's death speech. Cleopatra, it was claimed, was an ancestor of Zenobia, the feisty and beautiful widowed Queen of Palmyra. I photographed haughty-faced camels tethered to broken capitals and peddlers of postcards in white *galabiyas* leaning against fluted columns, gazing with sultry eyes. The sun pressed against my flesh like a heated iron. My head began to swim. Shade was essential, but not easy to locate. I slipped beyond the mud walls of a palm grove, where tattooed and bejewelled harvesting Bedouin women in brilliantly coloured dresses beckoned me over, giggling at my clothes. Outstretched painted hands touched me, followed the contours of my features and marvelled at my burned skin.

As the day began to die, I climbed to a hilltop fortress to watch evening unfold in the desert, to await the sunset. A symphony of gold and buff boded well. The distant cry of the *muezzin* from the desultory city beneath echoed across the empty hills and sandy plains. The brown tents of Bedouin encampments, like expiring insects, dotted the undulating corrugated dunes. The gentle breeze at this altitude, as evening drew in, was an exquisite respite. Released from the inferno of flat, blistering heat, Bedouin boys came running to play football among the silent ruins bronzed by the rouging light. Their cries carried across the dunes as the sinking sun turned this isolated oasis into a flaming Blake-like vision. As I picked my way back down to the city, stars appeared, perforating a tar-black sky.

The next morning, I was at the antiquities as day broke, to beat the sun, to avoid tourists and the endless facts, figures and Syrian propaganda reeled off by Muhammad. I found spots where the buildings had been reconstructed, cemented together, which, to my eye, did not enhance their beauty; it diminished their mystery. I tried to picture it as it must have been: around springs of drinking water sprang up a city of sand, golden, bleached by sunlight; a lush, green oasis bustling with merchants of every creed, strangers from all corners of the ancient world, speaking many tongues. It had been a stop-over along the Silk Route; it had linked the Romans with China, India and Persia. Egyptians traded here, Greeks too. Oil was bartered, arriving on packhorses from the north, where I was going, or from Mount Lebanon, surely, and perhaps, also, Palestine, transported in clay amphorae. Exchanged for what? Obsidian, the green volcanic glass from Anatolia? Bronze from Egypt? Gold? Chinese silks, dried figs, Phoenician dyes and glassware, wines, perfumed and scented olive oils, all changed hands here. Most merchandise from the coast passed through Palmyra and it became one of the richest cities in the Near East. Once the Romans arrived on the scene, products, vendibles were shuttled as far as the western coast of England.

So, what happened to this glorious desert city? Queen Zenobia ambitiously challenged Rome by snatching at its eastern empire. In response, the Romans trounced her army, sundered her city's structures and dragged the legendary royal beauty to their capital in chains. Palmyra served as one of their garrison outposts from there on. Its trading activities diminished, it never rediscovered its former glory. The golden sandstone city of bubbling streams became a ghost town. Lizards, creatures of the baking nights, became its occupants as, slowly, over the next two thousand years, sandstorms whipped and whistled at its carcass, burying its secrets. Palmyra was gone, interned beneath the desert it had gloriously risen out of.

After several overnight detours, we took the road to Deir al-Zor, towards the Iraqi border, where we spotted eagles soaring overhead, sailing silently on the slipstreams, hunting desert prey, of which there was plenty, I was surprised to learn. The interminably empty land was the colour of pastry, of unleavened bread. Nature baked in the oven. Its silence was like the sweet lure of a siren. And then the oceans of desert began to break up. To the east, the majestic dun sands continued, while to the west was rough, scratchy scrub with occasional clumps of ankle-high vegetation. There were squat, distant hills, crumbling riverbanks, desiccated ravines. My journeys were silent, private musings. Muhammad the guide slept, while Muhammad at the wheel, who spoke no English, smoked and twiddled with the radio, which produced nothing but high-pitched whirrings. We were beyond all range. Not a soul aside from these two Arabs knew my whereabouts. Although I longed to share this beauty, I also found it liberating to be so distanced from the responsibilities of daily life, to be so entirely my own person, to know that choices were mine. I pitied the women of this land, who, under Islam, could not know such freedom. Yet there was an undercurrent that fed the country as if by subterranean voltage, and the two men guiding me were possibly reporting back to some Damascene headquarters. The accusations I had heard voiced so frequently in Lebanon haunted me. Even when there was nothing but desert and half a dozen huts, there seemed to be strategically placed posters and statues of dictatorship. Recalling the advice of Fareed, I did not risk broaching the subject with my interpreter. I concentrated my mind on olive history.

When I opened the window, desperate for air, the wind whistled, giving off a rustling, tinny sound, and blew sand in my face. It settled between the pages of my books, coated my skin, insinuated itself between my teeth and lashes.

Travelling through Syria was like waking up in the Bible or the New Testament. The heat on the empty roads waved and danced with mystical promise like translucent, corrugated apparitions. I regularly expected a tall, bearded, thirty-something bloke, soft-spoken, drop-dead gorgeous in white robes to walk towards me out of the shimmering void. Not Peter O'Toole, not Lawrence of Arabia, but Christ. My Irish Catholicism squatted in deserted Islamic spaces, rewriting the landscape.

The city of Deir al-Zor, whose name, according to Muhammad, meant 'holy place surrounded by fertile flora', appeared from out of nowhere after endless hours of flatness, after the beige monotony that I found soothing and mesmerising. Deir al-Zor, like Beqaa, had also existed within the palm of the Fertile Crescent. Scaling the banks of the mighty Euphrates river, within the Euphrates Valley, this was the heartland of the cradle of Western civilisation. What we were approaching was a sprawling city surrounded by cotton fields. Lacking the romanticism or poetic grandeur of ancient Palmyra, it had developed into a twenty-first-century trans-desert stopover, a noisy, rather vulgar boom town fired by the discovery of high-grade oil in the vicinity.

My sole reason for this longish detour east, away from the Mediterranean, away from the birth of olives, was to brush up close to the Iraqi border. To make a point, to demarcate the line beyond which I could not travel, the point beyond which I was effectively barred safe passage across the earth. I strode on to the impressive suspension bridge that straddled the river of antiquity, traversed it to its eastern bank and stood facing Iraq. Not long after I received the letter informing me of the existence of the six-thousand-year-old Lebanese trees, I learned of an agricultural tragedy. Before the outbreak of the war, there had been thousands of date farms in Iraq. In 2003, the country lost its entire crop, a sizeable source of income for its farmers, particularly down in the south. It was due to the deployment of US weapons using DU, depleted uranium. Due to fears of toxic pollution, the farmers were unable to wind-pollinate their palm trees. Without pollination, there were no fruits. In a situation where deaths were being reported on a daily basis, the destiny of date palms might seem small fry, but it had added to my growing frustrations about the long-term mismanagement, destruction of our planet. The Fertile Crescent, in the middle of which I was now standing, where agriculture was possibly born, included large acreages of what today is Iraq. There are sites or clues there that, once obliterated, will deny us for ever the opportunities to learn from our past, to understand our ancient history, to know who we, within the developing story of nature, really are and what our role could be. Imagine, I said to myself, if there were trees still surviving over there that could claim a six-thousand-year-old heritage. Every bomb that fell, every explosion, was putting all that further at risk.

At that moment I wanted to continue onwards, east into Iraq, but I had other plans, so I turned and headed back across the bridge, pausing midway to look down upon that mighty river that had irrigated civilisations, that had contributed to the change of direction of our history. Such quantities of water after days of golden desiccation were intoxicating. I returned over the suspension bridge and then I traversed it again, back and forth, several times, growing dizzy, light-headed, looking down upon the splashing liquid glinting in the reflecting sunlight, listening to that rush and flow. Men squatted on its steep banks, fishing. Fishing in the heart of the desert! Children were throwing themselves from the bridge, plunging into the great winding river, shrieking with joy. Young women in black, with bare faces, out perambulating, arms linked in twos and threes, smiled shyly, then giggled at the sight of me, whispering like naughty children. I hopped off the bridge and strolled its western bank, where I found pots of brilliantly coloured flowers and terraced cafés, a hint of Europe. What

I did not discover till later was that this 'holy place surrounded by fertile flora' had recently planted up olive groves numbering over one hundred thousand trees. Olive groves deep in the baking heart of the desert!

I loved the waving Bedouins. At various stops, as we progressed towards the olive-growing regions of what had once upon a time been northern Mesopotamia, they invited me into their tents, but Muhammad always refused. During a break to stretch our legs, I crossed the sand and narrow tarmacked road towards a family who were beckoning me. The woman, strong, broad-faced, made us thick, sweet tea while I sat cross-legged. The two sons had copper skin, black matted hair, coarse as mattress filling, and startlingly brilliant eyes. They were filthy.

The family stared at me, smiling, frowning, trying to fathom me, talking to one another, all the while looking at me, talking about me. They were eager to communicate, to exchange stories with snippets of mine. I called Muhammad over to translate.

'Where are you from?' I asked.

'Here,' they said.

They wanted to know why I was travelling alone, and where my husband was. I was heading towards the border and on to Turkey, I explained, to visit olive farms, to learn traditions. They found this curious, incomprehensible. Olive oil was not part of their diet. They cooked with goat fat and camel lard. The camel humps are giant mounds of fat, I learned. I could smell burned grease in the brown-black tent made out of woven goat-hair, an acrid stench, and on their skins. Muhammad refused to enter. He hovered a distance from the opening, translating when obliged, dismissing them.

'Gypsies,' he hissed in English, looking at his watch. He would not look them in the face. 'We must leave,' he insisted.

I wanted to argue that these people didn't resemble the gypsies I had seen in Beqaa, and even if they were gypsies, so what? But I left well alone.

'Let's go. They are *nawar, dom,* gypsies. You are a *gurbet,* you don't understand.'

Muhammad's left eye closed when he was tense or cross and he squinted at me now with his good one.

'What is a *"gurbet"?'*

I never discovered.

'Let's go.'

The language of these gypsies, I learned later, was Domari, but I could find out next to nothing about them except that they were Muslims and nomadic desert peoples, probably originally Turkumani, Kurdish or Persian. They had gained their livelihood in past times by their music and their jewellery-making. Nowadays, the women were sometimes sent to the cities to work as prostitutes to feed their families, which was possibly the reason for Muhammad's attitude, his refusal to enter their tents.

The density of night. The vast expanse of crystal stars glimmering in a flat black sky, like a tarpaulin drawn over us. I loved the desert, its ineluctable immensity, its silence, save for the wind and the flicking of beasts' tails. But I did not love the pumping frustration I felt towards Muhammad and his intractability. Some of the towns we passed through were squalid. The air was almost brittle. I could grind it between my teeth. Diesel belched from lorries and buses. Butchered meat hung in the heat, blackened by flies. In ancient Mesopotamia and Persia, sesame oil was used as an antibacterial agent. I wondered if that meant anything here. Or were they immune to the filth? I had eaten no meat since Lebanon. Occasionally, I called out that I would like to stop, to walk about, take photographs, but Muhammad grew impatient and told his colleague to keep moving. Onwards, penetrating the desert, travelling the roads in the solid old Mercedes, similar to Michel's dusty, blue 1972 model back at the farm. The similarity of the car helped me feel closer to my husband, whom I had not spoken to in days due to impossible tele-communication access. I felt so far from him, so far from my life and all that I held dear. I pined for him, but I was not unhappy. Quite the reverse.

Whenever it was possible, I kept the window open and I felt the wind burning me, drying me up, shrivelling my skin to an old prune. I lived in my thoughts, staring out at the sea of sand. Nothing on the roads until a lorry rattled by, then emptiness again. Occasionally, we drove by a small group squatting in the middle of nowhere. If I waved, they did too. What were they doing? How had they arrived there? Then we would encounter their goats and a donkey or three sorry-looking, flea-bitten creatures, flicking sandflies away from their ears, wearied by the journeys they trod.

A monumental statue of Assad, the father, demised dic-tator, greeted us in a square in Raqqa, staring like an ogre down upon his people. We passed through another desert town, I never found out its name, where hummocks of water-melon were for sale at the roadsides, where donkeys, cars, carts with long-bearded gnome-like men transporting every-thing from fruits to fridges jostled for passage, where the streams of women purposefully treading the streets were enfolded in black. Head to foot, nothing exposed, not so much as an eyelash. Muhammad said it would be risky for me to get out of the car. When I pressed for an explanation, he refused.

'Please can we pull over?'

'No.' Low-voiced instructions to the man at his side, as though I understood. We inched forward negotiating the shambolic flow of traffic. I was itching to jump from the car.

'What's the name of this town?'

'I don't remember,' he lied.

I still think of it as Black City.

Eventually, Aleppo. Such a city! One of the great metropolises of the Ottoman Empire. A crossroads in so many ways. Between East and West, ancient and modern cultures, Turkey, Syria, Arabs, Christians, Mediterraneans. The covered souk, the longest in the Middle East, was a firework display of colours and pizzazz. Each trade was designated its corner, as is the custom in these eastern bazaars: silver, gold, perfumes. Broker instincts throbbed like a pulse, ran through veins, displaying the timelessness of commerce, of traditions, transcending geography. I might have been walking through an Oriental Breugel: pots, pans, costumes, rude life lived at the edge, pockets of wit, humour, a keen sense of rivalry and survival, sleight of hand and jiggery-pokery; it was human, rough, sweet-smelling and putrid, and had probably not altered since time immemorial.

In the olden days, the early travelling salesmen who descended upon this grand market of Aleppo, carrying their produce from far and wide, would have checked in at their designated khan, refreshed themselves, completed their business, done a little shopping themselves and then journeyed on towards Turkey or east across the desert towards Iraq or south to Palestine. Certain of the traders would have been making for the coast, where Phoenician ships attended the transport of merchandise bound for Cyprus, Greece, Carthage, Egypt, Libya, Spain, even France. After agriculture, commerce was a time-honoured pursuit.

In and around the bumpy, stained and cobbled lanes, I shoved and pushed my way, past donkeys laden with cucumbers, plunging down into the crowded labyrinthine quarters of gold, glass, copperware, spices, the maze of the souk, once the most important trading centre in Syria and, undoubtedly, the busiest outlet for Syrian olive oil and its renowned Aleppo olive soap. In spite of being hideously rooked by a tradesman over five flimsy lengths of silk, for which I miscalculated and paid the equivalent of £44, and spat at by a faceless black-hooded woman outside a male-only filigreed marble hammam, into which I was peering in an attempt to admire the architecture, not the naked flesh, I was left dazed, amazed, bowled over, by the fabulous variety of life and goods on offer. T. E. Lawrence described Aleppo citizens as fighters, fanatical and vicious and yet creators of beautiful objects. After days in the desert, this was a psychedelic injection of edge, technicolour, aromas, buzz, competition, and interchange where the souk was its beating heart.

Muhammad, wishing to purchase a scarf for his wife, accompanied me during one of my expeditions. We stopped to drink tea at a stall selling bolts of silk. All around us, the younger hawkers were flighty, extrovert, screechingly camp. Adolescent boys waited upon our lithe, wavy-haired vendor, who rested his hand upon their heads caressingly. Although he flirted with me, I observed his proclivity. He eulogised 'gay Paris' and yearned to see the Bois de Boulogne. Afterwards, I commented upon his refreshingly open gayness to Muhammad, who grew surly. 'There is no homosexuality in Syria,' he snapped. 'It is against Islam.'

'How I longed for Michel to be with me, to sip a sundowner or two on the unashamedly colonial terrace at the Baron Hotel, where I drank iced lime juice and soda, where Agatha Christie and her husband, archaeologist Max Mallowan, had stayed and she had penned *Murder on the Orient Express*, and from where, according to the barman, who never stopped polishing glasses, T. E. Lawrence had skipped town without settling his account. Strolling through the raucous evening streets, I recalled Marie's yearning for the perfumed nights of the Orient with their scents of jasmine and joss sticks. Exotic scents were redolent here. Since before Roman times, this northern city of Aleppo had been a trading crossroads between Asia and the Mediterranean; spices, silks, luxuries, perfumes, oils, all for the paying.

I stayed in a converted sixteenth-century palace in the Jdeida quarter of the old city, backed up against a mosque. From the outside, it gave nothing away: a doorway in a narrow, winding descent, like a mysteriously beckoning path in a dream, but once inside, I was in the Levant. Arabesque woodwork, lemon trees, inner courtyards, marble floors, exotic birds, fountains, soulful music. The women's quarters during its Ottoman incarnation had been converted into the simplest of guest bedrooms, while the men's rooms had become the dining and reception areas.

Olives steeped in pomegranate juice were served to us among half a dozen *mezze* dishes, followed by cherry lamb kebabs, surely one of the most delicious meals I had ever eaten. Aleppo was the only stop where the Muhammads ate with me. On every other evening, they had disappeared and I had been left to fend for myself. The driver, though gentle and gracious, spoke so little English that communication between us was impossible, which left my dry-as-a-biscuit guide and I struggling to find conversation. We nearly came to blows when I broached the subject of women's rights, returning to our passage through Black City. Such strict dress codes were for women's protection and their happiness, he explained, which nearly sent me through the ceiling.

In a society in which a man could cast off his wife simply by repeating 'I divorce you' three times and where, in medieval times, men hunted out the prettiest girls, married them, deflowered them and then uttered the inevitable pronouncement, women's protection was assured by total cover from head to foot, to dissuade the lustful eyes of men.

'I've never heard such tosh!' I barked. 'Change the divorce laws.' I called to the waiter for a beer and, to my utter astonishment and that of our taciturn, now open-mouthed chauffeur, Muhammad, my corseted guide, turned to the waiter and said, 'Make that two.'

But at least he had engaged in the discussion. Emboldened now, I drew from the hat of sticky subjects Assad and his deceased brother, Basil. Both men choked. I feared they had swallowed kebab sticks. They shot fearful glances towards neighbouring tables as though apologising for the words of this traitor, worrying the *mukhabarat* might be at hand. I had broken the golden rule.

The next morning, I was back in the souk searching for Khan al-Sabun, 'the Khan of Soap'. *Savon, sabun*, I was surprised by the similarity between the French and Arabic words for soap. As in Lebanon, the French had been charged with responsibility for this territory when, after World War I, the Treaty of Versailles had divided up the Ottoman Empire. The courtyard of the soap inn, when I eventually tracked it down, was packed with curly-haired, dark-skinned boys with grins as wide and pink as slices of watermelon. They were standing alongside hillocks and boxes of olive-oil soaps in every conceivable colour, perfume and design. The bright-eyed hucksters, most of whom were only ten or eleven, boasted that the Prophet Muhammad had claimed seventy diseases could be cured by olive-oil, but when I asked what these might be, the boys grinned and rolled their eyes. 'You take soap, missus, strawbirry, laurel, mixture flavour.'

Aleppo was where olive soap had first been fabricated, first created, they alleged. The stallholders in Lebanese Tripoli had claimed the same. Nablus in Palestine, now a destroyed city in the West Bank, might also beg the honour as theirs. What would they say back home in Marseille?

I had read of, but had found no address for, an olive-oil soap factory here within the walls of this khan, or close to the outskirts of it. A factory where the boys wore wooden boards strapped to their feet to allow them to skate across the treacherously oily floors.

'Is that here?' I asked the young sellers.

A scrubbed-faced boy thrust a bar at me that resembled a kiwi fruit and shook his head 'Here, perfumed soaps fraught with Orient. You free take and then buy, missus?'

Beyond the courtyard, where I was now standing, smouldering vats of olive-oil liquid were possibly brewing, stirred by old men with rowing-boat oars, while elsewhere in the factory the congealing soap was poured out across a wooden floor and then cut into soap slabs the length of rulers by boys driving bladed sleighs. I longed to see all that.

'Is that here?' I asked again, staring about me at several substantial bolted doors.

'Give soap you, if photograph take and newspaper in print,' was the only response I received.

Eventually, I gave up and came away carrying a dozen and more bars that ranged from shades of raspberry to lime green.

Syria boasts 85 million olive trees, is the fourth-largest producer in the world and there had been much talk in the recent press about Italian investment in its production.

'It's a growth industry. Doing better than tourism,' said the rather elegant proprietor of my hotel over breakfast.

Was I aware that clay records, the first official documentation regarding olive farming, had been found at Ebla, south of Aleppo?

'Any idea where they are now?'

'I couldn't say. Damascus, perhaps. They date back five thousand years.'

A thousand years younger than Bechealeh, then. While we were talking, an American guest came storming into the dining room, demanding to be transferred to another hotel immediately.

'But why?' begged the bemused owner.

'The Arabs are forever calling their prayers,' she barked. 'I cannot sleep. It's getting on my nerves. Ring the Hilton!' There was no Hilton, but he dutifully found her another residence even though she had booked with him for five nights.

'Why do they come?' he moaned, after she had marched upstairs to pack her bags. 'I am a Christian, but this is a Muslim country and we are in the old town, what does she expect? There's nothing to see now at Ebla, but once upon a time, this entire region was involved in olive farming right up as far as Antioch. Innumerable old presses were found hereabouts. The olive tree was worshipped as divine because it never died; new growth shot up alongside expiring trunks. You'll see when you travel towards the coast, the limestone highlands are ideal for olives.'

After twelve days in Syria, as we motored out beyond the old city of Aleppo, my final destinations drew close – the sloping hills, the jebels, silvered by the north Syrian groves – before our descent to the coast, to the Mediterranean.

A pearly hue marked the countryside, which before had been baked leather by the sun. I was taken aback by the vegetation here. I had not expected it to be quite so fertile or to be so evocatively Mediterranean.

Olive trees covered entire mountainsides, dusky beige mountains shot with red earth. I felt perfectly at home. A one-eyed boy at a roadside curvature in the hill was selling pottery. I requested a stop to investigate and the Muhammads seized the opportunity to linger a while with the potter beneath the shade of an olive tree, drinking tea.

Olive trees everywhere, silver against iron-red earth; tractors, market towns; tobacco fields; trucks of watermelons. As we climbed higher into the mountains before descending to the coast, there were wind-blown olive trees bent like women working the fields. I spotted a stand of four, dead. It was shocking. I had never seen a dead olive tree before. Mountain shadows across mountains. Inland Mediterranean terrain, undulating and glorious. In villages, men were sleeping across rows of chairs in the leafy shade out of the midday sun. Deep green ravines. Olives everywhere against salt-white soil. Passing over the northern extreme of the Orontes Valley, gazing upon its exceedingly lush plains, I knew that, in spite of Syria's dictatorship, its politics and the isolation I felt here as a woman, the earth was another story and I loved this strange and beautiful land with its jebels, wadis and deserts.

As in the chalky Lebanese hills behind Tripoli, I was on my way to the home of an olive farmer, Abdullah. En route, down a winding country lane in the middle of agricultural nowhere with nothing but olive trees to left and right, we passed a mill, rather a spacious hangar, with, quite literally, a miniature mountain of dried paste, *bereen*, out in its yards. I was invited inside to tour it. It was a curiously lonely place set in the middle of trees. No farmers dropped by. Its sole purpose was to extract the remaining drops of oil out of the all-but-dried paste. The final pressing, the transformation to renowned Aleppo soap. One worker sat atop the mountain of *bereen* with a shovel at his side, sleeping.

Unlike Mr Dibdib, the Christian farmer in Lebanon, here it was a Muslim household that awaited me. I was in a knee-length skirt, T-shirt, wind-blown hair, sandals and was the only female at the gathering. Abdullah, my Syrian farmer, in his late sixties, appeared to be a sprightly fifty years. I was ushered on to a capacious first-floor stone-tiled terrace, shaded by vines. Cicadas sawed through the thick heat. Traditional Arab hospitality awaited me. Fresh green oil, home-cured olives laid out on a table. Abdullah was running his estate with his son-in-law and two other young male members of the family. I was not presented to the women. The wives and children remained behind closed doors, shut within an interior kitchen or living room. When I turned to find them, I saw seven pairs of dark, inquisitive eyes peering at me from between the slats of the shutters. The foreign woman travelling alone. I longed to beckon them out, to learn their names, to enjoy their shy smiles, but it was impossible and I left without being introduced to them. I was a little anxious, at first, about how these country farmers might respond to a woman directing the interview. They were too polite or shy to pose questions of their own. Only the patron enquired after our olive farm. He wanted to know where it was located, but when I told him, he appeared none the wiser.

Sweet black coffee was served by anonymous, braceleted arms, cups passed out from behind the door where the fair sex were ensconced. One of the younger men fetched and carried between door and table. From the shaded balcony, we looked out across an estate of coppery-earthed hills. In the foreground, a stand of cypress and, beyond, Abdullah's holding of 5,000 trees. In the olden times here in northern Syria, one of the bonuses of farming olives was that it allowed for the plantation of other crops beneath the trees. Grapes, for example. Beasts, too, could graze the groves. In earlier times, itinerant merchants travelled between the isolated villages, bought up excess stock and delivered it to the coast by mules or camels. Later, wagons were loaded with the oil, negotiating these steep mountain defiles on journeys that had taken days, weeks, to reach the waiting ships at Ugarit or Latakia. I learned from this farmer that insecticides and chemicals were never used here. So this is an organic farm, I confirmed. Such a notion puzzled these men. It was not a decision. Spraying was unnecessary. There were no flies or fungi to damage the crops.

I was mightily impressed. 'Do you know why this might be?'

'An unpolluted atmosphere,' suggested Abdullah.

His land was measured in *donoms*, units of 1,000 square metres. He wanted to know the quantity my husband owned. I smiled at the notion that the farm belonged exclusively to Michel.

'A little less than thirty,' I replied.

He nodded. Abdullah owned 460 *donoms* and produced four tons of oil a year. This he sold for approximately £433 a month. In Syria, this was an exceedingly comfortable income. My host was a very wealthy man. He told us that during the previous year, Italians had visited him requesting to buy oil directly from his farm. Their price was insufficient. He was awaiting a better offer. He smiled. He was keen to know the cost per litre of oil in France and was taken aback when I told him.

'Good to know, before I speak to those Italians again.'

When I asked him about his thoughts on the origins of the olive tree, he recounted a sura from the Koran in which Allah swore on the fig and the olive. This, he explained, has given both trees divine status in the eyes of Islam.

'And before Islam?' I asked.

He shrugged. In this land, so abundantly rich in ancient history, its people rarely looked further back than the birth of Islam. For these Muslims, history began with Prophet Muhammad.

'Where do you think the first olives were cultivated, Abdullah?'

'Why, here, of course.'

I smiled.

He offered me a taste of the oil. It was exceptionally fine with a clean, peppery taste, not dissimilar to our own.

'Come back, please, to Syria and bring your oil,' he requested.

In the courtyard, before our departure, our host climbed a triangular wooden ladder – a typical Mediterranean farming implement – and cut fresh grapes as a gift for our journey, while two grazing donkeys watched on. He washed them with a garden hose and handed them to me. I thanked him for his generosity and strode towards the car. Suddenly, from behind me, a commotion, an outbreak of riotous shrieking and screaming, followed by peals of high-pitched laughter. I spun round to catch the women and children rushing out on to the upper balcony, where I had been sitting with the men. They were shouting, calling to me in Arabic. And then one lovely, fresh-faced woman shouted, 'Bye bye!'

I raised my right hand to my left breast, bowed my head and called out, 'Ma'a salaama.'

How they cheered! It appeased me a little to know that I had made this minor contact, witnessed this unannounced female breakout.

'Great to see you,' I called in English. They did not understand, but it encouraged them. Their smiles were broad and warm. They jumped and waved their arms above their scarved heads, whooping like a gaggle of exuberant boarding-school girls. I shot a glance at the silver-haired patron, trying to ascertain his reaction. His expression was steely, inscrutable, but his eyes reflected no disapprobation. He wished me a safe journey. The men shook hands with my two men, bowed to me, and disappeared inside the house, while we sped off laden with fruit and information, descending towards the coast and Turkey.

Turkey

I arrived in Istanbul in a rather exhausted state. Originally, my plan had been to travel by bus up the Syrian coast to Antioch and from there to coach-hop west to the Aegean coast, where I was intent upon a ship for Greece or even as far afield as Malta. However, a fax received from Michel at my hotel in Latakia on the Syrian Mediterranean suggested he share some of this Turkish leg with me, and so I happily flipped my itinerary around. Instead of bidding farewell to my two-man team in Ugarit, I returned with them to Damascus and, from there, took a dawn flight to Istanbul. My revised, hastily cobbled-together plan was to move south from the capital, follow the Aegean coastline and then, after a visit to Ephesus, meet Michel at the airport in Izmir. From there, the pair of us would hug the Mediterranean as far as the Roman port of Antalya, turn north, travel inland to the Neolithic town site at Çatal Hüyük, then journey some distance along the ancient trade route that had once led to Babylon. Michel was booked to fly back to Paris from Kayseri in central Anatolia, from where I would aim for Greece. That was, loosely speaking, my circuitously designed new route. My first afternoon in Istanbul was sunny, but I was travel-weary, not in the mood to traipse the old town, where most of the sights and historic buildings were located, so I strolled the western bank of the Bosphorus Strait, pearly in the light, to an embarkation point where I boarded a boat, a maritime introduction to the capital that had once been Constantinople and, later, pulse of the Ottoman Empire. A young man seated at the landing stage, wicked grin, sprucely dressed, responded in faltering English to my ferry-schedule enquiries before quizzing me.

'Am I handsome? You are a woman. I am on my way to meet my girl. Am I good-looking?'

'Yes.' I smiled. 'You are very handsome.'

He bowed shyly and swaggered off, breasting the throng of Muslim families tucking into jacket potatoes served in pages of newspaper. Ours was a local vessel, a tired old crock, packed with smiling Turks on an outing that cost the equivalent of 40p. Once aboard, we chugged forth from Europe, hugging the 'mackerel-rich' western shore of Istanbul, skirting its many bays, to its most northerly suspension bridge, which, if we had continued, would have fetched us upon the Black Sea. Instead, the old ship yowled like a lonesome dog, and we tacked to the right, crossing the slender canal, and descended in a southerly direction, hemming the lovely coast of Asia. I was looking out for *yalis*, the seaside mansion houses once occupied by the Ottomans. There were one or two, renovated now, but predominantly what I saw, gazing out from the waterside, were exquisitely furnished apartments. Sailing by a mosque, I spied groups of men perched at the quay, feet dangling, fishing. The vegetation was not the world of olives. It was not Mediterranean at all, but a darker-leafed verdancy, save for the Judases on the distant hills.

Our crew served us steaming glasses of black tea while everyone chatted like old friends and a couple threw bits of lunch to the greedy gulls. A student told me she lived 'in Asia', while her friend had a flat 'in Europe'. Both inhabited the same metropolis. Istanbul is the only city in the world that straddles two continents. A Eurasian capital of confused identities, of many histories, living between the West and the faded glories of a vanquished Eastern empire, zipped together by a waterway. I had known this, but the physical experience hit home when I heard these girls and then felt the sun's rays on my arms. I turned my head towards its warmth hanging over Europe, and then I turned again to Asia. The sun rises over Asia – 'Anatolia' is an ancient Greek word meaning 'east' or 'Land of the Rising Sun' – but sets in Europe.

The following day, I awoke to torrential rain. After a breakfast of honeycomb chunks drowned in creamy yoghurt, I crossed the Galata Bridge and puddle-hopped through the narrow, decaying alleys of the old city, bristling with monuments of glorious struggles, rickety edifices, cacophonous activity and toothless, cotton-haired men. The wind was a demon force, whipping in and about the hilly curves as I ducked through flooding streets to the Grand Bazaar, a chaotic Aladdin's cave of trinkets, gold merchants, silver-sellers and vendors of intricately woven carpets, most answering to the name of Sinbad. It was an onslaught of hawker-talk that greeted me and I swiftly slid off for a glass of sweet tea at one of its interior cafés to escape the sellers and bury myself in my reacquaintance with Graham Greene's *Stamboul Train*. Drying out, warming up, I observed the bargain-hunting tourists plodding about snugly in their blue or red Pac-a-Macs, until I could stand the noise of the sharp yet amusing vendors no more. 'Hey, lady! No, wait! Lady! One minute of your time. Life is short. Spend your money!' 'Pretty lady, let me help you spend your money.'

Heading for the Spice Market, I found myself lost within tortuous lanes where no tourist trod, in a clothing district where wedding dresses and chunky bras were the retail. All around me in the squelchy, bustling *ruelles* were women in chador or ankle-length coats in variations of beige or stone. Unlike Syria, the women here wore coloured scarfs on their head. A *dupatta*, it hid their hair but left their faces exposed and eased the severity. No one attempted to sell to me aside from one poor fellow crouched on an upturned box touting cottonbuds. This was a domestic district, not related to tourism. It was animated, bawling. Some hawkers yelled so vehemently their faces grew brick red.

The rain recommenced, battering and slapping at the fragile stalls. Within an instant, I was sloshing through rivulets of water, skipping to avoid muddied hollows outside the cubicle shops, picking my way through the crowds, to the Misir Çarşisi, known to the Turks not as Spice, but as Egyptian Market. I had passed through wedding dresses to baubles, glittering knick-knacks. Still the rain flooded and guttered. Losing direction, blinded by rain-sheets, I shouted, '*Baharat?*' Dripping traders pointed me onwards. All around, stall-holders were engaged in a communal effort to haul wares in out of the flash floods. Yelling men with trays of rattling glasses bolted for cover; the orange-seller wheeling his fruits splashed by, a whiskered merchant shoved packets of dried fruits into saddlebags slung across his sad, sodden mule. I knew I was drawing close when a hundred aromas wafted my way, damp-intensified.

Plunging beneath cover, I penetrated the arabesque alleys of the *pazar*, passing beggars furled, snake-like, on the ground in layers of raggedy clothes. The ubiquitous gold-pedlars had set up shop here, too, trespassing the turf, edging out the herb merchants, but it was the dazzling cornucopia of teas, tisanes, rose waters, caviar, dried fruits marshalled in tightly packed squares on stallfronts that greeted me. Slabs of honeycomb the dimensions of laptops and jars of golden-yellow mountain honey taunted my taste buds. 'Dried mulberries,' shouted a barefoot boy. Another offered bitter oranges, a third, walnuts or fresh pistachios. Nimble-footed lads delivered tulip-shaped beakers of hot black tea on copper trays to shoppers dawdling over peppers, spices, fruits. I was moving through an Arabian paradise stacked high with hessian sacks of linden tea, sea sponges, powdered henna, blended spices and, of course, olives and oil. Before the declaration of Turkish independence, in 1923, after its Ottoman Empire had finally hit the dust, Istanbul had been an active and prosperous outlet for both Greek and Turkish olive oil, as well as a major store and transit house for its exportation. I was hoping to track down a few of the mills that had been operating back then, or the olive-soap factories once owned by Greeks, but I had no luck. I had been furnished with no addresses and every vendor I approached shook a bemused head.

I snaked my way around the solicitous traders, learning uses for rosaries of red sumac, so appreciated by the Romans. I recognised these berries from the home of Emile and Elizabeth in Beit-Shabeb. I wandered through narrow alleys crammed with teeming life, until, when the *muezzin* commenced for the umpteenth time and I heard the rain drumming its relentless rhythm against the roof, I took refuge in a turquoise-blue tiled restaurant with domes, hand-painted ceilings and glass chandeliers. A celebrated eatery, I learned, where Atatürk had lunched when in town, it overlooked the frayed glories of Galata Bridge, the Golden Horn and the river. I ordered grilled sea bass, a glass of Turkish wine, salad swimming deliciously in local olive oil and settled back to gaze at the weather blasting along the waterfront.

The proprietor had been a Greek, born and reared in Asia Minor, who had opened his first 'cook shop' in 1901 in the old fish market. Within no time he was rubbing shoulders with politicians, intellectuals, artists and journalists who crammed into his tiny kitchen to dine, but then came 1923, and he had been obliged to leave Turkey. After victory in the Turkish War of Independence, the Treaty of Lausanne declared a peaceful exchange of ethnic minorities. All Greeks born and raised here – Greeks had been living on this strip of Aegean coast for over two thousand years – and all Turks with the same status in Greece were forced to quit their homes and set up anew in the country of their flag. Millions of refugees from both sides of the Aegean departed for lands they had never set foot on before, abandoning everything. The proprietor from here had migrated to Athens.

When the sun returned, albeit short-lived, I strolled through a park where a man was cleaning his sodden white sneakers with a large leaf, streaking them green, and corncobs were being sold from tricycles converted into stalls. Down at the shore, battered-face fishermen in white cotton vests were back at work. I wandered aimlessly in all kinds of districts, hoping to chance upon one of the defunct olive factories, falling upon the misery of what I took to be a *gecekondu*, one of the many squatter settlements that have burgeoned in urban Turkey.

Scarred relics of a palimpsest of pasts were all around me cohabiting with barbers, sharp-talking hawkers, high-street malls and Starbucks cafés, but the heart of the city itself eluded me. I dawdled in bookshops, antique stores, listened to *arabesk* music out of the rain at record counters and I encountered large-hearted warmth and a friendliness that seemed at odds with the reputation of violence the Turks have been be-smirched with. Monstrous acts written in blood soil the pages of their history. The Turkey that is making every effort to become a member of the European Union has, in earlier incarnations, a chequered career; from 1895 onwards, the Ottoman government embarked upon the systematic decimation of its Armenian population. Even today stories continue to expose suppression of their Kurdish peoples. In my youth, thanks to British film-maker Alan Parker, images of the Turkish prison system as depicted in *Midnight Express* haunted the West. I walked by that prison, perched on the European shore of the Bosphorus, now converted into a five-star hotel. Due to the filthy weather – it was pelting again – I had difficulties finding a cab. I flagged shabby *dolmuses* packed to the gills, as well as official taxis, while getting thoroughly soaked. I was miserable and tired, and it was night by the time I eventually found a cabbie willing to transport me to my hotel off Taksim Square. Did he know of any olive factories used during the years of the empire? He shook his head. Swaying beneath his rear-view mirror was the *nazarlik*, the blue-eyed symbol that guards against the evil eye, the destructive powers. It was everywhere, even tiled as a mosaic into the floor of my hotel, where, after a hot bath, I fell gratefully into bed.

Louring nimbus clouds, dark and steely, threatened the morning. I could not face another drenching and with no olive history to unearth, I dedicated my day to the Topkapi Palace, where emeralds as big as the Ritz shone aplenty. By the time I reached the Pavilion of Sacred Relics, containing various body parts of the Prophet Muhammad, I was inching at a snail's pace behind queues of sightseers. The most sacred reliquary adjoined the room I was in. A notice informing visitors this was a holy shrine for Muslims requested silence. Not a whisper could be heard. I followed the crowds and peered along with them into a glass case where a wooden stick was on display, the staff of Moses; the very one, allegedly, that drew water from rock and parted the Red Sea. While I was wondering what nature of wood it had been fashioned out of, a dark-skinned man, beak-nosed, handsome, encircled by a small coterie of novices appeared. He was my height, 5 foot 5, fit, luxurious black locks, ebony-smooth skin, costumed exquisitely in pale, ankle-length vestments. Save for the hefty diamonds I noticed on his fingers, I might have cast him as a reincarnation of Moses himself. I was intrigued. One of his students stepped forward, displayed a digital camera, requesting permission to snap the holy cane. The imam, prince, preacher gave an almost imperceptible nod, then turned and exited the discreetly lit chamber. Proud, assured, understated, he cut a charismatic figure. His young brethren left off gazing into glass cases and followed instantly. One remained, a tall, fluff-faced, white-skinned member of the sect.

'Do you speak English?' I whispered.

'Yeah, I'm from London,' returned the young Muslim in a thick cockney accent, which took me by surprise.

'Who is the man you are with?'

'He's a sheik, mate. We're on a pilgrimage. 'E's been teaching us in London and is on 'is way back to Malaysia. Some of us'll go with him, but the rest of us will go home!'

'London?'

'Yeah.'

'Who are you?'

'We're of the Golden Chain, mate, the direct descendants of Muhammad, the Holy Prophet. There are companions who have formed other faith lines, but we're the real thing, mate, the Golden Chain.'

'Is the distinction akin to Sunni and Shi'ite?' I suggested.

'There are no Shi'ites here. You'll find them in Iran. Only Sunnis 'ere. No, we of the Golden Chain are the direct descendants. We're the true brethren.'

Listening to this white boy's words spoken in his very discernible London accent, surveying his pillbox hat, his apparel, recalling the bombing news upon arrival in Beirut a matter of weeks earlier, I was uncertain as to whether I was amused or made afraid by this Englishman's unswerving commitment to Islam. However, he was polite to me, a woman not draped in hijab, nodded 'cheers' and slouched off after his companions. When I exited the pavilion, the sheik and his boys had disappeared.

The motorway was peopled with farmers, land labourers, men and women journeying by mule- or tractor-driven carts. At the roadside turn-off to every small town, a sign directed newcomers to the *otogar*, the local bus station. It was Mustafa Kemal, later known as Atatürk, Father of Turkey, who switched the country to the Roman alphabet in 1928, just as it was he who outlawed the wearing of the fez. Fields of watermelons, resembling puffed-up blisters, flanked our passage. Due to the road constructions, everywhere was dusty out in the countryside, but the rains had abated and the sky was cerulean. Murat was driving at breakneck speed to make up for our lost morning.

There was so much ground I wanted to cover in the few days before Michel's arrival that I had decided to hire a car with a driver to translate for me. Murat, the young chauffeur in question, had come steaming into my hotel almost three hours late. I had hoped to reach Troy before evening, but this was looking unlikely. Gravelled stones from yet another newly laid stretch of bitumen clattered against our chassis; we might have been under attack. Fields of sunflowers hung disc-heads, as though bowed in supplication, while entire families were at work on hands and knees, gathering their seeds.

Atatürk also made Turkey a secular state, though 99 per cent of the population remain Muslim and the women's heads were never bare. Their skirts were always ankle-length, but usually floral and attractive. Their costumes enhanced their femaleness rather than negated it. Further along, tractors were at work razing the harvested crops, preparing for the next plantation. Turkey is one of only a handful of countries worldwide that are entirely agriculturally self-sufficient, a country where young men commencing their military service are required to plant a tree and where first impressions suggested the entire community was out tilling and toiling.

Descending the promontory of Gallipoli, speeding in the hope of catching the mid-afternoon ferry – if we had missed it, we would not have gained access to Troy until the following day – I barely had time to admire the Sea of Marmara. In the distance, high on a hillside, I noticed a stand or two of olive trees, while Murat said proudly, 'Gelibolu.' We had no time to stop. In any case, empty battlefields, even these fertile plains, once the scene of the bloodiest of encounters, the Battle of Gallipoli, held no fascination for me, but history was rewritten here. Here, the Turkish fight for independence was begun when Atatürk and his feisty soldiers fought to wrest this land from all takers, including Winston Churchill's forces, transforming an ailing empire into a republic, at the cost of thousands of lives.

At Eceabat, towards the foot of the peninsula, the ferry was all hands on deck. We skidded aboard and the craft set course, breasting the short span across the Dardanelles Strait between Europe and Asia. I charged up two flights of iron stairs to the upper deck to revel in images of the ancient Hellespont, inhaling the stink of diesel, fish, lavatories, briny air. This gulf has famously been the trajectory between the two continents, as well as the gateway north, to Istanbul and the Black Sea. King Xerxes of Persia scudded this passage in 481 BC intent on conquest. As did Alexander the Great a few decades later, while, many centuries after, the Ottoman armies used this route regularly during their forays into Europe and the Middle East. How many tons of olive oil had been freighted across this salty yawn? I asked myself. From my elevated position, gazing due east, I quickly spied Çanakkale bathed in the sun's afternoon light. To its rear rose a crescent of hills, while upstream, carved into a hillside, was the inscription '18 March 1915'. The date the Turks repulsed the Allied troops, giving Turkey its first opportunity for independence.

Çanakkale was my first port of call in Asia Minor, but I could not stop. I wanted to reach Troy before sundown.

Troy. The towering wooden horse that greeted my puffing arrival was an imitation, of course, an unexpectedly Disney-like introduction to the vanished city. Excavations here have unearthed levels, strata, representing nine Trojan cities constructed one on top of another. Troy VII, destroyed by fire in around 1300 BC, is believed to have been the mythical city sacked by the Greeks in revenge for the kidnapping of Helen. Immortalised in Homer's epic work the *Iliad*, its destiny was a ripping tale of love, war and military might, all for the heart or honour of the most alluring woman in literature, Helen of Troy. But no one took the tale seriously, until the 1870s, when a German amateur archaeologist, Heinrich Schliemann, used his own funds to dig here and unearthed the ancient city. Many dismissed him as a treasure-seeker because he damaged other excavations in the act and helped himself to a fair share of the spoils. But he found the place.

Alongside the wooden horse, I found a fenced garden, Pithos Garden, displaying, not surprisingly, *pithoi*, clay jars. These capacious vats with collared rims served primarily as coolers for olive oil. They also served as storage containers during maritime transportation, particularly useful for maintaining the quality of oil when the distances travelled across trade routes were considerable. I was excited to learn that these terracotta jars were already in use in the Mediterranean and Near East in the Neolithic, New Stone Age, period, somewhere around 7000 BC. In other words, a thousand years before the planting of the Bechealeh groves. Had Turkey an ancient olive history I was yet to discover?

The illustrious harbour city of Troy no longer fringed the sea. It was quite some distance inland. Its access to open water had long since silted up. Like many other classical sites, I found jumbles of stones on a hill scarred by trenches, deep holes, serpentine dust tracks, and it was almost impossible to make sense of such a confused elevation rising out of the immense plains of Troas. The glory had long since vanished and there was little evidence left to tell its story.

I could only imagine the arrival and berthing of the magnificent sailing boats, with labourers on the quayside at the ready to unload the wealth of wares. However, five thousand years ago, during its Bronze Age heyday, due to its strategic position between West and East, Europe and Asia, situated right at the water's edge, Troy was envied for its immense wealth and its high levels of craftsmanship. It was a powerful, exciting international metropolis with a vibrant cultural scene. It was the New York of its day. After the Trojan War and sacking of the city, the location was abandoned, but it was resettled later under the name of Ilion. Alexander the Great ruled over these northern provinces for a time, followed by the Romans, who chose Constantinople as their Eastern capital, thus robbing Troy for ever of its previous status and power.

It was nearing 6 p.m. I began to climb, hiking dust tracks that wound between dug trenches and stacked hessian sacks representing the outline of theatres, temples, palaces, all manner of BC urban life, to the summit of what must have been the ancient hill city, where the *meltemi* wind that blows from Egypt and southern Tunisia scorched my perspiring features. The Trojans had respected the *meltemi* for bringing with it fortune and wealth. Sailing ships pregnant with produce embarked and disembarked from a harbour destroyed long ago. Troy's maritime traffic came and went between Arabia, Egypt, Tyre (transporting the purple dye of the murex shell so prized by Roman aristocrats for their robes), from Sidon and Byblos, delivering the Lebanese cedar. Amphorae swilling with olive oil docked here, from Syria, the Levant and Palestine. And wine, possibly from the Beqaa Valley or later, around 600 BC, from Greece.

I gazed across flatlands in every direction. I felt the wind's motion drying my sticky features, heard the rotors of distant tractors at work. Beyond sight, across these far-reaching lonely steppes that once welcomed the ancient world to its glamorous quaysides, now silted and swallowed up, lapped the Aegean, where winds still mattered. I inhaled the familiar, acrid odour of wild fig trees, contorted by weather. Somewhere, though I could not spot it, snaked the Scamander river, once known as the winding Menderes and from whose name we have inherited 'meander'. I looked out upon empty wheatlands; a tableland broken up by groves of distant fruit trees; no olives as far as I could tell, nothing but dust clouds from tractors and the ghosts of the whistling Troas plains. Such was twenty-first-century Troy.

After checking into my hotel, a small haven nestling within a pine forest set back from the sea, I strolled to the beach and watched the sun set spectacularly beyond an island-studded, blue horizon with not a single Trojan warship to distract. I decided to return to Çanakkale for dinner and invited my driver to accompany me. Murat accepted reticently, regarding me with black-eyed mistrust. We parked down by the port, where brightly painted lorries laden with tomatoes for restaurants in Istanbul were queuing for the last crossing to Europe, and from there strolled along the waterfront, where I noticed that the exterior of the local police station was swarming with people. Murat, who knew every inch of the country, recounted how families came here in the evenings to sit with their loved ones employed in the force. Rather than allow their officers to wander off and drink iced tea elsewhere, the municipality had decided to transform the terrace into an ice-cream parlour. Further along, we reached a square where a troupe of Bulgarian folk dancers in national costume, working out of their bus, was entertaining a large crowd. The place was spilling over with old Turks, grinning, smoking, ogling the young dancers; dogs; children haring frenziedly to and fro; scarfed, full-bosomed matrons with whiskery, toothless laughs who reminded me of Russian babushkas. We stayed for a while, enjoying the atmosphere, before settling at a fish restaurant back along the quay. Murat had been moaning that he could not stomach the tourist food he was obliged to eat, so I suggested he choose our eatery. His profession was tourist coach driver, I learned. I was his first private client. When the waiter arrived, I requested the catch of the day, while my young companion tucked into pizza and Coca-Cola with peasant gusto. He refused wine, but insisted that he did drink and then proceeded to tell me that many of his friends were marrying 'older, foreign women' because they were angling for European or American passports. He eyed me carefully before adding, 'Even women as old as forty or forty-five.'

I smiled, repressing laughter.

'Some hang out with them for money or as a means to travel,' he emphasised.

'And what do you think about that, Murat?' I teased.

He stuffed a huge mouthful of doughy food into his mouth before pronouncing the practice 'disgusting'. I became fascinated by his bulky hands, the hands of someone who had dug and worked manually for a lifetime. His parents were farmers. They owned a smallholding inland of Fethiye. During the meal, he fiddled constantly with two mobile phones, flicking at tiny buttons with thick, split-nailed thumbs, as though desperate for a friend to make contact, to offer him distraction. He confided that he had a girlfriend who was very eager to become his bride. She was eighteen.

'Utterly lazy,' he pronounced. 'Her father spoils her by allowing her to stay home all day and watch television.'

'Are you intending to marry her?'

He shook his head. He was only twenty-two. He wanted to see the world first. 'And where do you dream of visiting?'

He shrugged. He hadn't given it any thought.

On our way back out of town, we passed a lively late-night market. It was close to midnight, but I requested a swift stop for photographs. Murat slammed on the brakes, informing me that he would wait where he was, and proceeded to operate his phones.

The market was the most sprawling I had encountered. Moths flapped everywhere, attracted by the flickering lights powered by a throbbing generator. Anything and everything was available; stalls dedicated to shoes, plastic flowers, wooden spoons, bras, copper kitchenware, bundles of garlic, sacks of fruits, olives, plastic shopping bags, snack bars. Much pandemonium ensued when the generator packed up. Many of the traders were equipped with their own miniature supply, but the others resignedly packed their wares away. In the crepuscular light, it became difficult for me to retrace my steps. I stumbled over rough ground and became lost in a maze of alleys. When I eventually found the exit, Murat was nowhere. I tracked him down, parked in a side street, on the phone.

After Çanakkale, patchy olive groves began to crop up, adding a dog-eared silvery note to the landscape. Beyond Troy, towards the main road south, rows of *oliviers* were growing in tilled cotton fields. I had never seen that before, olives in cotton fields. The trees were as arthritic as bent men carrying burdens on their backs, as though this northerly land weighed heavily upon them, but, slowly, as we whizzed southwards, the whipped-by-wind silhouettes, branches as broken and seared as the historic ruins, began to straighten up, come alive, growing in harmony with their environment.

Walnut-skinned herders in caps, scaling the hilly slopes aided by fruit-tree staffs, trailed by a stream of goats, were a regular sight, but rarely accompanied by dogs. I began to feel at home, to sniff scents, traditions of the Mediterranean; a spilling over of cultures; a marriage of East and West; tapestries of cultivations. The road system was very efficient, hardly surprising in a land that has for aeons been at the crossroads of so many trade routes. Still they were laying new roads, cutting through the countryside, creating dust everywhere. Men in hard hats sitting on hillocks of rubble punctuated the works, smoking, looking mystified.

We passed groups of women bent double, harvesting red peppers in fields. The piled vegetables rose from the earth like flames. A wooden cart with an old man and boy drawn by a limping donkey arrived to collect the bulging burlap sacks. I ran to take photos and the women waved and smiled, pausing from their labours to approach me. I asked if they objected to the camera. They shook their scarfed heads shyly and caressed the lens with their earth-worked, wrinkled fingers.

Several of them were children, not yet adolescents, dusky girls of ten or eleven. They bunched around me, bright-eyed, Tartar-eyed, curious. Their blushed skins were smooth as buffed stone. How they smelled of the earth! Emitting pungent odours of plants, of goat and of crude milk products. I was reminded of my childhood days at the farm in southern Ireland, of dairies and fresh, warm, gurgly cow's milk carted in slopping pails. In the adjoining fields, other cultivators or pickers had encased each sunflower-head in a blue plastic bag to trap the falling seeds.

And then there were olive trees. Everywhere. Had I ever seen so many olive trees? Away from the sea, climbing a mountainous road en route to Pergamum, the chalky road-sides were lined with alpine stalls selling honey, olives, olive oil as well as open wooden boxes of pistachios still snug in their red skins, fresh off the trees, just as they had been at the home of Mr Dibdib. Everywhere olive groves, no other crop in sight. Great silver deserts of them, rippling down the pale mountainsides, falling to the sea. As though they had burst right out of a sloping earth cavity, expulsions of incandescence, planted in tilled lines. There were no drystone walls here.

We got stuck behind a lorry transporting YAG – 'That means "oil",' said Murat, bemused by my excitement at the agricultural production all around us.

I spied large terracotta amphorae lying in olive fields near a higgledy-piggledy shack of a farmhouse. Clearly, they were still being used to store the oil, but why were they in the fields? I smelled freshly pressed oil, but it was impossible; the drupes on the trees were way too green; it was too early in the season. Still, as we travelled further south, the oleaginous scent pervading the air defied my reasoning, and I was not mistaken. On the outskirts of Ayvalik, we flew by a large sign designed with an olive sprig announcing: 'Tarimsal Ürünler'.

'What does that say?' I cried.

'Farmers' Association.'

'Is it a mill, a press?' I begged.

My young driver did not have a clue. I insisted we turn back. There was an armed guard at the gate, who confirmed that it was an olive factory. On my behalf, Murat requested a tour. I butted in, apologising for turning up without an appointment. The guard in his fake designer sunglasses glared through the window, appraising me. Was I mad? He barked into his short-wave radio, which crackled and splattered in response, and then relayed back the news that the manager was in Izmir and a tour was impossible. Murat fired up the engine. I touched him on his shoulder and stepped out of the car.

'I would be perfectly happy to be shown around by someone less senior.' I smiled. As I spoke, from out of the building, a brace of women in white uniforms and hats appeared. They saw me and waved vigorously. This was a response I was to find everywhere in Turkey, the joyous welcoming wave.

I waved back, and wandered off to examine a row of antique amphorae lined up against an outhouse wall, leaving the guard to convey my second request. Murat shouted triumphantly that an assistant to the manager would show us round. The guard accompanied me back to the building whose walls were adorned with the clay jars, into the head office, and introduced me to a svelte young woman with pale skin and bulging eyes who spoke only Turkish, but the guard, it transpired, spoke extremely passable English and enthusiastically took on the role of interpreter. We began our tour of what I now understood was a factory. Bulk oil, including sunflower, and quality oils were their produce as well as bottled and tinned table olives, for export and home markets. We were 150 kilometres south of Troy, inland of the resort of Ayvalik, directly across the water from the island of Lesvos. Every olive grove we had driven by since Çanakkale, with their silver tresses falling in streams towards the sea, as well as all those beyond this route that we had not yet seen, belonged to this association. I was unable to establish whether the family whose name appeared on the label owned the factory or whether this was genuinely a farmers' association and they merely managed it.

'How many trees?'

The assistant shrugged. 'Millions, but I don't know precisely.'

I met the smiling gaggle of white-clad factory women, several of whom were teenagers. They were engaged in the checking and approval of tons of olives in readiness for packaging and marketing. I stole a drupe to sample and they shrieked with schoolgirl pleasure, black-nailed fingers covering their lips. I was given a tour of the bottling and pressing areas, of the soaps on display – the entire place reeked of mashed olive fruit, an odour that, as autumn approached, I followed.

Afterwards, the manager's office, where prizes and certificates decked the walls. A pair of drawings of men in fezzes on their knees gathering and grinding olives in the old manner, executed by an artist from Izmir 'before the Alphabet Revolution, before the interdiction of the burgundy beret', hung behind the boss's desk. The turn-of-the-twentieth-century artwork was discovered at a bric-a-brac market and given as a gift, I learned, because the dedication in the outlawed Arabic lettering bore the same name as the family who headed this outfit and who had produced gourmet olive oil for three generations.

Eventually, we returned to the car, escorted by the guard and assistant manager, who shook my hand heartily and thanked me for my visit.

'No, thank *you*.'

As we set off, Murat, my broad-of-beam companion, laughed triumphantly. During our tour, the car boot had been stocked with gifts of olives and cans of virgin oil.

Before checking in at our next hotel, I requested a quick detour to the coast, to gaze upon Lesvos, the third largest of the Greek islands and seventh in the Mediterranean. It was probably first occupied by Greeks from the mainland, perhaps Thessaly, during the late Bronze Age and was also once governed from this coastline by Aeolians, Persians and the Ottoman Empire. Today, it earns its income from tourism and olive farming; 40 per cent of the island's ground was covered by an impressive 11 million olive trees. I intended to visit Lesvos later.

Between this pretty strip of Turkish coast where I was standing in the sun and the opposing island, whose mountainous outline I could just discern, was a tract of choppy blue water, but either side of that sea stretched a history of olive farming reaching back to antiquity; a tradition, a culture, possibly too ancient to be tracked down, but I was determined to try.

The following morning, we started out early, soon after sunrise, to reach Pergamum with time to appreciate the ruins at leisure. The unfolding daylight was soft, yellow as corn. Whatever hour we were moving, the countryside was animated by families working or travelling by tractor and trailer, or mule, to and from their fields. The men were at the wheels with brown-skinned, angular boys at their sides or perched on their knees while the females crouched in the trailers at the rear, clutching large woven baskets. During the evening journeys, returning home with full loads, harvest or kindling, entire families huddled up front, with the women perched precariously on the broad mudguards. Always, they waved and smiled. The women were heavy-booted, wearing *salwar*, the lovely baggy trousers frequently in floral designs, similar to the long skirts sported closer to the cities. Usually accompanied by a longish, loose shirt the *salwar* is believed to have originated with the horse-riding Turko-Iranian steppe peoples from central Asia.

Outside Bergama, which seemed unaware of the potential for tourism sitting on its doorstep and, consequently, was rather attractive, I requested of Murat to stop and pick up a young couple hitching. They turned out to be French students from Lyon and travelled with us for the rest of the day. I was rather glad of their company. Together, we discovered the sites. Pergamum was gentle, calm, lacking visitors, set inland from the sea; stark stones worn to the bone, leached to desiccation by centuries of sun, jutting heavenwards. The theatre was steep and swept up the contours of the mountainside offering unforgettable views out across the Caicus plain.

I was particularly interested by the sanctuary dedicated to Asklepios, the god of healing. Here was one of the most renowned cure centres of the ancient world. Galen, after Hippocrates the most famous physician of antiquity, was born at Pergamum and received his early training at Asklepios. I was on the lookout for the role foods and herbs played in their philosophies of medicine, looking to bolster my arguments against insecticides and the poisons in our twenty-first-century products. In the ancient world, it was held that there were hardly any illnesses that could not be cured with olive oil or using olive oil as a base.

Obsidian. I confess that I had never heard of this stone, this glass-like rock, a product of hardened volcanic lava, before I began to research this journey. I learned that I would find it in abundance in central Turkey in Cappadocia and Çatal Hüyük, but I had not expected to come across it here. What was even more surprising was that the obsidian used at this healing centre had been brought not from the volcanic areas of central Anatolia but from Lipari, a little-known volcanic island close to the Sicilian coast. This was evidence yet again of the distances travelled by the ancient Greeks. Fragments of it both raw and carved had been found here, used in the treatment of the ill, but I could not discover what function it had performed.

There were numbers of feral creatures at this classical site. Several orphan puppies, the tinctures of desert sand, were following me everywhere, licking and nipping playfully at my ankles. They were starving, of course, but I had nothing to offer them. The Frenchman, Laurent, gathered a few drupes from one of the olive trees for them. They were so hungry they tried to bite through the drupes, rolling the minuscule offerings in the sand, frustrated by their inability to chew them. Mireille, the French girl, tripped over a large tortoise on the grainy pathway and we photographed it endlessly until the hard-shelled fellow grew impatient, wriggling and scratching with miniature prehistoric limbs, before plodding off into the brittle grass. Enough is enough! A solitary white horse grazing high on a hillside above the ruins added an almost Celtic touch to the scene.

Passing through Allaga the following morning, I spied a bright-blue olive press standing upright like a tall, shiny robot in an olive grove.

'Murat, stop the car!'

I charged across the highway and began to snap photos.

Murat, flat-footed, came running after me. I felt sure that he was going to moan about why we had stopped again, but, surprisingly, he ran round the machinery looking at it from every angle, bending and peering like a policeman.

'It's for oil, undoubtedly, but oil in the ground. This is a drill,' he pronounced, staring down into its central basin.

'Murat, these are olive groves. It's an ancient olive press, but what is it doing here? Was the tradition to crush the fruit directly from the trees?' I remembered the amphorae I had noticed in the fields south of Çanakkale.

My young driver shrugged and we continued along our way. After several hundred yards, I spied a garage where four men were sitting beneath vine-bowered shade drinking tea. I hailed another stop.

'Please will you ask them about the crushing machine?' I requested of my disbelieving companion.

The four men stared as I stepped out of the car, and nodded. Above their heads, a muted television was transmitting a morning soap opera. Murat translated my questions. As a man they began to smile.

'Yes, indeed, it is an olive press. Our local community wanted to create a museum in the village, honouring the tradition of olive cultivation. The old press would have been given pride of place, but the council couldn't raise the money and so it stays in the grove. Passers-by can admire it. Those who know what it is.'

'But why is it there? Did farmers press in the groves?'

'The fruits were carried out of the fields and pressed directly after harvesting. It's there because we don't know what else to do with it.'

How I would have loved to take it to our farm.

★

Eski Foça is the modern port once known as Phocaea. In 600 BC, Greeks originally from Athens, Ionian Greeks, occupied this coastline. Phocaea was the most northern of their cities, located on the coast, north of the Gulf of Smyrna. Due to its peninsular position, it is slightly off the beaten track and not visited by busloads of tourists. I had been looking forward enormously to seeing the place, for it was the Greek sailors from here, later known as Phocaeans, who founded Massilia, modern-day Marseille. It was they who gave Provence its olive history.

Like the Phoenicians, based along the Levantine shores, the Phocaeans were excellent long-distance seafarers. They were the first Greeks to penetrate the western Mediterranean basin, founding Marseille, Antibes, Alalia in Corsica and Ampurias in northern Spain. Their trade routes extended to Egypt, southern France and north to the Black Sea. Their navigational skills offered them power and independence, until, eventually, they fell foul of King Croesus and his Lydian armies, who, in turn, were conquered by the Persians in one of the opening skirmishes of the Greco-Persian War. Preferring not to submit to Persian rule, the Phocaeans packed their women, children and possessions aboard their substantial boats and abandoned their beloved port-city, fleeing to Chios and then to Corsica. Doubtless, a few of them also ended up along our Provençal coast, where, who knows, perhaps they settled and taught the locals to farm the olives they had delivered on earlier trips.

Today, there are two towns with the name Foça: Yeni Foça, or New Foça, and the original port of Eski Foça, where the ancient Greeks dwelt. We drove first to New Foça, a modern fishing village and weekend hideaway for privileged Istanbulis. My first image as I stepped out of the car was of two wrinkled seadogs sitting spread-eagled on the quayside beneath a palm tree, slicing slender silver-blue fish into slivers while a black cat sat at their feet awaiting snippets. It was 10 a.m. I found a seat in the sun at a seaside *kahve* and ordered a cup of the local *dibek*, coffee ground in stone mortars, but I was out of luck. The waiter assured me it was still possible to find it in this region, but not at his establishment. I settled for regular coffee and then took a walk along the front, where wrinkled men and women were queuing for newspapers and bread at the bakery.

The pace of life was less than a pace and every sound resonated; the revolution of bicycle pedals ridden by retired men in hats and shorts transporting their bread and news-papers in carrier bags; the wind flapping those plastic bags; the drawing in of the fishing lines from the small groups of men and boys hoping for a catch; the gentle wash of waves against beached seaweed vulcanising in the sun; a boy's cry; the frantic mating call of the cicadas, which for an instant transported me home and reminded me how eagerly I awaited the arrival of Michel. Seduced by the quietude and lovely bay, I lingered awhile, penetrated narrow inland lanes leading off the esplanade, where the older ways of life were still evident. I paused to admire crumbling Ottoman houses, many of which were being refurbished for vacationers. I stood and allowed the sun's heat to caress my features. Although the season was moving towards autumn, the temperature was rising. I was moving south, Mediterranean-bound. A shrivelled old biddy eyed me with curiosity from her first-storey window latticed with climbing geraniums. I was photographing garlands of peppers drying in the sun. When I glanced up, she shuffled out of range of my lens. I grinned and she waved, laughing toothlessly, all gums and sucked-in cheeks. Her face was a map as eloquent as the olive I was attempting to chart. I strolled on, hearing the swish of straw sweeping marble floors, a donkey's bray, the insistent drilling of house construction. I smelled disinfectant, floor wash. Everybody smiled, everybody acknowledged.

A couple of blocks back from the waterfront, I encountered a market, not a *pazar*, but an outdoor affair in a square. Barrel-loads of dried legumes, rice, copper pots, plastic lavatory brushes, fruits, spices, freshly picked dewy mint, herbs, olives and oils, of course, as well as an array of essential oils that sent my senses reeling. Melon-hawkers sat cross-legged surrounded by hummocks of striped green-and-yellow rugby-ball fruits. Samples had been halved, ziggurat-fashion; knife still plunged into the soft flesh as an enticement to taste.

Reluctantly, I made my way back to the quay and we set off for my real destination on this peninsula, Eski Foça. The coastal drive was remarkable, virgin landscape marred only by barbed-wire enclosures, acre after acre of steep scars, rocky eminences, grazing land, dedicated to the military. On the inland flank, flocks of long-haired goats and wide-girthed olive trees were a reminder of peaceful worlds. Suddenly, I spotted a sign scrawled in black paint on the stones of a substantial ruin, offering 13 acres for sale. These were olive groves, and ancient ones at that! There was no fence. Murat pulled up on a grass bank and I ran to take photos. I did not notice the men until I was on their holding. Two of them, one seated, were in animated discussion alongside a well with water pump. A woman, further to the left, appeared from behind a jagged stone wall. She was carrying a heavy pail as well as a child at her breast and was struggling towards a second, even third, broken-down stone building constructed on the same plot. This must originally have been a hamlet that had grown up within its olive groves, but, dilapidated as it was, it seemed to be occupied. Twenty thousand euros was the asking price, so said the farmer who claimed ownership. The other, his companion, was warbling loudly. It was only eleven in the morning, but he might have been drunk, or attempting to sober up as he doused himself with water while his goats grazed beneath blue-grey olive trees. From here, there was nothing to impede a view that swept dramatically to the sea. Not another property in sight. It was perfect. I asked the farmer to scribble his phone number on the sticky palm of my hand. We could barely understand one another, but he did. I could see no obstacle to the purchase of this farmland that lacked every conceivable facility except its well. It must have been the augmenting heat, Michel's impending arrival or the fact that we were drawing closer to the south. The perfumes were familiar, ambrosial, heady; the olive trunks had girth; they were knobbly, knotted, expansive. I was as intoxicated as the singing herdsman.

Phocaea, today Eski Foça, or Old Foça, was one of the most active colonies of ancient Ionia. It gained its name from Phoça, a Mediterranean monk seal (*Monachus monachus*) that lived in flourishing pods all along this coast of Asia Minor. Once under the protection of Poseidon and Apollo, today these mammals are an endangered species with less than four hundred remaining. The locals speak of them as 'pretty seals with fearful glances' because they have been hunted almost to extinction.

I entered the old port on foot, inhaling air that was salty, brackish, of blood and fish, as one might expect from a community living off the spoils of the deep. Save for the addition of diesel, the Greeks of some two thousand six hundred years ago, in this port-city's golden age, doubtless breathed a similar mix of perfumes to those that greeted me. In Kuçuk Deniz, the smaller of Old Foça's two harbours, I visited the covered fish market. Half a dozen stalls each offered a similar choice of catch, hauled from the sea that very morning. The stallholders were also the fishermen. They were out with their *caiques*, their fishing boats, by 4 a.m., landed their nets around nine o'clock, cleaned them up and stayed until they had sold their full complement. At our fish market in Cannes, wives and daughters manned the stalls, allowing their men to sleep until their return to the sea. I asked where the women were and learned that they were tilling fields. I strolled to the open waters, following an arc round the quay, which was buzzing with open-air cafés and restaurants; moored *caiques* bobbed at the wharf-side, some for sale, others being repaired.

It was from here that their fifty-oar galleys set sail for Marseille. Their vessels possessed a passenger capacity of five hundred. And what stores did those intrepid Phocaean sailors carry? *Pithoi* brimming with oil and wine? Olive trees, almost certainly. Did they sell the trees in France, or plant them up themselves? What promise went with those unfamiliar saplings: 'The fruits of this eternal plant will provide you with light, feed you, and enhance your skin.' The Greeks were sailors rather than agriculturists. That was left to the Romans who came after them.

Were the trees from this coast? Who introduced the Phocaeans to the olive tree? They had almost certainly learned their navigational skills from the Phoenicians, so possibly traders from Byblos and Tyre. These sailors were traders, too. Ancient Foça was one of the first cities to create coinage and use it as money. Their coins bore the image of their Phoça seal.

After my brief hike, I stopped for a bite at a fish restaurant offering views of harbour life, little different from any port in Mediterranean France. Just for fun, I asked the waiter if they served bouillabaisse. He frowned and shook his head. He had never heard of it.

'How about *kakavia?*'

He grinned. It was the original and finest of all fish soups.

Even before checking into my hotel at Selçuk, I made my first visit to Ephesus. Ephesus! One of the great surviving cities of antiquity. I could not contain my impatience. It was early evening. Most of the tour groups had completed their shopping and were climbing into coaches that were hooting for all they were worth. Tubby men in cowboy hats, laden with trinkets, struggled aboard as I purchased my entrance ticket and began my tour. The evening was warm. The stones were burnished by the shifting light and seemed to drink the reflections into their old bones. Several areas such as the Terraced Houses were closed off due to renovation works, which was disappointing, but the city itself was a jewel in the crown of any journey.

A short walk along the road from Ephesus lay one of the Seven Wonders of the Ancient World, the Temple of Artemis, the fertility goddess originally known as Cybele. Soon after dawn the following morning, I arrived there. There was not a soul about, besides a handful of soldiers on duty at a neighbouring checkpoint. A dozen geese in company with a peacock flapped and honked in a shallow puddle of putrid water. Hopping to avoid other puddles as I approached the dig, I spotted, at the side of the path, a soggy newspaper displaying voluptuous girls in bikinis. I screwed it into a ball and stuffed it into my pocket to ditch in a bin. In ancient times, pilgrims journeyed from far and wide to bring gifts, pay homage and request favours of the revered goddess Artemis. Ephesus accrued fortunes from foreign pilgrims travelling to this site, while the temple itself became the richest in the entire province of Asia. It is hardly credible that in its day, well-travelled classical visitors claimed its beauty and magnificence entirely overshadowed the other six wonders of their universe.

What remained of this once-glorious, all-marble temple was precious little. So little, in fact, that no entry fee was requested and no one manned the site. Of the original 127 majestic columns, all had gone bar one, and its verticality dominated the abandoned, untidy setting. At its pinnacle, no embellishment perched. Instead, a stork's nest sat aloft, from which I spotted the bobbing heads of a couple of nosy chicks peering out through a mass of sticks and straw. Amusingly, a pointer, a suckling mother, with her puppy were roaming the ruins, circling about me with wiry energy. What with the bikini-clad pin-ups, the goddess herself and the dark-russet bitch, the place was awash with mammary symbols, but that was about all that remained of this, once upon a time, wonder.

In antiquity, when Artemis reigned supreme here, women, the mother goddess and the fecundity of nature – the magical powers of birth and regeneration – were the energies prayed to. Worshippers, pietists made sacrificial offerings to the goddesses of the earth, pleading mercy from and begging kindnesses of her. It is believed that the power of the female, her role as creator within nature, began to dwindle with the arrival of metallurgy. Once humans began to carve tools of metal, the shift of power moved from woman to man and the process of birth, regeneration and nurturing took a back seat. We remain today, I believe, in a world charged by the power of metal, the voice of the weapon.

I continued the short distance to the classical city of Ephesus. It was a little after 8 a.m. so the bus-loads were still at their breakfasts, which offered me the opportunity to get ahead of the groups and guides. Reaching the theatre, which, once upon a glorious time, had boasted stunning views across the harbour to the Aegean Sea as backdrop to the entertainment, I found a lone olive tree. It had sprung up on Harbour Street, shading the artists' entrance, where the performers, the thespians, would have waited before striding forth to the *skene* and the stage itself to entertain an audience of 24,000 spectators. *Skene* was the stage building. From it, we derived the word 'scene'. As elsewhere, the monumental harbour had silted up many lifetimes ago and Ephesus was no longer fringed by water; even so, due to its grand scale and well-presented architecture, it remained remarkable.

Michel was arriving. I awoke full of expectation at the prospect of spending time with him after so many weeks apart and I was longing for news from the farm. I had not been able to reach Quashia. Packing speedily, I checked out of the hotel to allow myself a full morning at the Ephesus museum, where marvellous statues of the multi-breasted goddess Artemis were on display. I spotted, amongst the designs on her costume, aside from lions and breasts, bees. Honey was a vital source of nutrition and healing in early Anatolian life.

I had observed that all the classical statues of females depicted pert, nippled breasts. Artemis had multiple breasts, without nipples, that sagged like hanging fruits. She wore a necklace of what appeared to be acorns or small oval-shaped tree fruits. An article I had read the day before (undoubtedly written by a man) caused me to examine her many breasts more closely. It had suggested that they were not breasts at all but testicles! I laughed aloud. The pendulous mammaries might as plausibly be olives! Priapus, a fertility god, was flashed across every postcard on sale in the tourist boutiques of Selçuk. The world had fallen into the hands of men. Why not leave us women with ancient history?

Murat collected me from the museum and because we were ahead of schedule I suggested a little detour. Twenty minutes outside Izmir, we followed a signpost that led us to the right. The road wound like any country lane and as usual we met only farming folk on tractors, passing only one café. I realised that I had not eaten, having skipped breakfast to spend more time at the museum. It was now almost 1 p.m.

'Lunch,' I said.

Murat mumbled that he had eaten and was not hungry. But I was!

'If we chance upon a rural taverna, please let us stop.' Of course, no such diner existed. Here, the tiny communities ate their prepared lunches beneath the shade of olive trees in their fields and then returned home before sunset for their evening meals. I caught sight of a lane to the right where, at each corner, began meticulously tended olive groves and I requested of my sullen young companion, who grew moody whenever we drifted off any agreed schedule, to take us there.

Its sign read, 'Havibaşi'. We were in the middle of nowhere and yet little more than a half-hour's journey from the mighty port-city of Izmir. Our approach was along an unmade track that snaked and ascended until we reached a hamlet of white-washed cube houses; a clutter of homes alongside a tiny mosque with a pointed blue minaret. Nothing else. The lovely, immaculately pruned olive groves encircled the cluster of habitations. Chickens were running in the powdery dirt, as were naked, mud-encrusted children. Two women were deep in conversation, arms folded over their Artemisian breasts, outside a house where a bank of earth, from the digging of foundations, had settled and grown weeds. Their heads were dressed with *dupattas*, and their costumes were the loose-fitting shirts with customary baggy pants, the floral *salwars*. Both were barefoot. They paid our passing car no heed at all, though how often did an unknown vehicle mount this dead-end track? I wondered how these folk survived. What might this olive community consist of? Six families, at most. Did they live an entirely self-contained existence out here amongst their lovingly tended groves that, I supposed, delivered them their incomes? I saw no satellite dishes. Did they ever venture to the city for entertainment, to catch a movie? Izmir, once ancient Smyrna, the city on their doorstep and birthplace of Homer, contestably the greatest storyteller of all time, nudged up against them and yet, it would seem, nothing of that impinged upon their lives. Perhaps they gathered together in the evenings to recount to one another their own tales, like so many communities in the past.

Eventually, I gave up on my food-hunting and we returned to the café several kilometres back in the hope of a sandwich, or, at least, a beverage while we bided time. I took a stroll round the almost non-existent and very run-down hamlet and then I sat beneath the shade of two towering plane trees whose trunks were mottled yet smooth. Murat placed himself at a separate table and fiddled with his phones. Choosing to sit elsewhere was his manner of communicating discontent. I ordered a sandwich, but the moustached owner shook his head. I settled for *chai*, and ordered another for my companion, who pretended not to hear, punching away at his toys. I began to wonder if the phones were even connected.

Round the other side of the café was a tiled yard where chairs and a couple of tables had been stacked. This was the hub of community life, then. One table was occupied by five men, all sporting moustaches and short-sleeved shirts, who were watching television, smoking, drinking tea, idling away the hot afternoon. *Keyif* is the Turkish word to describe the activity of idling time away. The men in this country had it down to a fine art.

Basil was growing all around the veranda step in plastic food containers. Wooden crates of tomatoes were piled high by the drinks and cash kiosk. Above them, attached to a tree trunk, was the yellowing face of some old weighing scales.

Suddenly, Murat rose from his seat and lumbered, thick-bodied, towards me. 'I have ordered you a sandwich. Only tomato is available.'

'Thank you.' I smiled, but he turned on his heels and returned to his phones. I was at a loss. What was he so grumpy about? Had his bride-to-be ditched him? Moments later, a doorstep of white bread ridged with sliced tomato and pressed into a cone of newspaper was served to me. I thanked the middle-aged proprietor and requested the bill. Of course, there was no bill. Instead, my host stuck his cigarette between his lips for safekeeping and raised one scarred, black-nailed finger. One Turkish lira was the sum charged for three glasses of *chai* and a sandwich, approximately 35p. I handed over the cash and nodded my appreciation. As the owner retreated, a wrinkled, cadaverous individual, plaid scarf tied round his skull as though to ease toothache, cigarette clinging to his open mouth, driving a tractor, pootled by the café, waving. All six men returned the greeting. We waved our farewells, too, and took off in the car.

What a distinct change in Murat's behaviour once Michel had cleared customs and we had begun our journey from Izmir to Mugla. The plan had been that Murat would leave us at the airport – he was to have taken the bus back to his village and we were to have stayed outside Izmir – but we had decided to spend our first night together further south by the sea. This took us in a direction closer to Murat's home. He had begged a ride. So grateful was he that he continued at the wheel. It afforded M and me an opportunity to sit in the back together and catch up on lost time.

The road south-west was nothing but olive trees. Young groves, not old, gnarled masters, ascending the stark, rocky land like mountaineers, right to the peaks where little else could survive. What a business to harvest them! Even within the recently thrown-up estates, ugly complexes or small new towns where the houses had been constructed back to back, a glance down an alley or track revealed a robust olive or two pressing its presence against the plastered walls.

'What happens to all this olive oil?' I pondered aloud. 'Rarely is Turkish oil seen on international supermarket shelves.'

'It could be sold for canning. In that case, there would be no obligation to state the oil's provenance, or its quality,' Michel suggested.

But even sardines in oil supplied to the entire world could not have accounted for the gallons being pressed. I reminded Michel that Italy is incapable of producing the quantities of olive oil it is committed to selling and buys substantial supplies from other oil-producing territories, who sign contracts binding them to the secrecy of the transaction. The oil is then sold on the open market as Italian extra-virgin olive oil. Virgin, extra-virgin or simply oil, the truth of the matter is, a fair percentage of what is sold as Italian oil is not pure Italian at all. Turkey must be selling their produce somewhere. Agriculturally, it is entirely self-sufficient, which is remarkable, but even a population of 67 million cannot consume such rivers of olives. Abdullah, the Syrian farmer, had been visited by Italians interested in purchasing his oil direct from his farm. Would that be marketed as Italian or Syrian oil, I wondered.

Murat left us at an intersection on the outskirts of Mugla. He had telephoned on ahead to a pal to collect him off a bus that, if he ran, he would catch. We offered to drive him to the bus station, the *otogar*, but he refused. We embraced and the boy wept, apologising for his manners, and skidded off along the road while we turned south to a quiet fishing village set at the mouth of the estuary of Gokova. Alas, it had been transformed into a resort where estate agents on every street corner offered 'dream homes with swimming pools' for prices quoted in sterling. Cheap property, wine and Mediterranean sunshine, Turkish-style, or, rather, British beneath a thin veneer of Turkish trappings.

As we parked the car, a phone began to ring. Not mine, not Michel's. In his haste, Murat had forgotten one of his mobiles. Michel swung the car round and we climbed back to the intersection, where we found our young friend. He came flying towards us, arms outspread, imitating a plane. I passed the phone out through the window, he grabbed it and flew off.

The quality of adventure was much enhanced by the arrival of my husband. We made do with 'British' Gokova for one night, promising ourselves to be on the road bright and early the next morning to discover unbeaten tracks. Over breakfast we took a long look at the map – such a vast land mass! – as well as at the route I had provisionally laid out, and Michel suggested we make adjustments. The distances to cover each day were too taxing. Why not go directly east and penetrate the central heart of the country? Aside from olive sleuthing at Çatal Hüyük and Michel's plane, we threw my itinerary to the wind. I was disappointed at the prospect of missing the trading ports in the south along the Mediterranean coast, but I accepted that I had expected to achieve too much. From here on, then, we were busking it.

The alpine road we chose led us in a meandering fashion towards Kale and Tavas, a region renowned for its honey. It was breathtakingly beautiful and deserted. Its surrounding mountainscape could have been the elevations that encircle our coastline in the south of France. It was quintessentially Mediterranean; limestone mountain ranges, pine lands, the perfumes and vegetation of the *maquis*. The Tethys legacy. We found beehives stacked in long rows, dozens of them, on grassy banks amongst pines and olives, and stopped to take photographs. A toothless herdsman with tortoiseshell specs appeared from an invisible track hidden by low-hanging branches. He was followed by the ting-a-ling of bells and a line of clopping goats. A black-and-white collie brought up the rear with panting enthusiasm, harrying his troupe until his gleaming eyes alighted on me. Even once his team had traversed the road and were ascending the opposite unpastured gradient, where stones and scree fell away beneath his master's heavy-booted feet, he stayed at my side, thumping his dusty tail contentedly against the dried earth, until I shooed him along, at which point he slouched off miserably.

Like miniature colonnades along our narrow route were jars of honey atop hives offering produce for sale. A pot to sweeten the unpalatable Nescafé on offer each morning at breakfast, we thought. In a middle-of-nowhere place, set back from the lane, we pulled up outside a bungalow, where the woodwork was painted the identical Matisse blue and turquoise we had chosen for our own farm. Seconds later, a plumpish woman in plastic boots came running out, encouraging us in. I stepped from the car and she embraced and kissed me, *bisous*-fashion, damp lips against my cheeks. Her skin was soft, smooth and tanned, reminding me of the women in the pepper fields. She drew me by the hand to a cluttered veranda, from which three doors led. There was a sink with cold running water, two dusty trestles stowed alongside chopped wood, a couple of chairs, an old black coat-stand hanging from which were copper pots, an assortment of hats. Honey jars both full and empty were stacked beside an unoccupied hive containing wooden-framed sheets of hex-agonal cells, within which were stored the layers of resplen-dent, gooey honey.

Beyond the terrace was an olive tree and a vine bower with pendulous bunches of grapes and, drying in the sun, necklaces of red peppers resembling sharks' teeth. Michel remained in the yard, taking photographs, leaving me to negotiate with this apple-faced countrywoman who proved a seasoned vendor. She was intent on persuading me to buy one of the honeycombed frames, which I refused. How would we trans-port it? A small jar of honey was all that was required. She turned to the jars and shook her head. Then lifted three earth-encrusted fingers. Heavy, 3 kilos. Clearly an exaggeration. I opted for the frame and she requested 20 dollars, approxi-mately £11. I was a little taken aback and decided on the jar, which, she mimed, was also 20 dollars. The price was less than I would pay in Europe but by local standards was expen-sive. Still, I pulled out the note, choosing the frame for its novelty value, and she disappeared into the house. I sneaked towards the door. Within, a paper-thin mattress covered with a coarse grey blanket lay upon a single-sized iron bedstead. Beneath it, on the bare floor, neatly piled clothes. No other furniture was evident in the primitive space. Our lady returned, smiling broadly, wrapped the honey frame in two plastic bags and laid it flat in the boot of the car. She then kissed me once more, but made no physical contact with Michel, and we were on our way.

We began to climb into landscape identical to the Alpes-Maritimes, to home. At 1,000 metres, we made another stop. The view was stupendous. Mountains folding behind mountains and not a habitation in sight. Only the sound of the wind. At this altitude, no more cicadas or olives, but a wisp of thermal heat. Fleet-of-foot goats trailing everywhere, darting up and down valleys and hillsides. Then red foxes at the roadside in broad daylight. Michel spotted them.

Kale was a concrete town set in a fertile alluvial plain. The mosque here had two minarets, sharp and pointed like rockets on a launchpad. In these upper plains, the women were harvesting a thin, upright plant with pink leaves that we did not immediately recognise. It was tobacco. This Kale was not to be confused with the coastal town of the same name metamorphosed from the Roman city of Myra, whose most famous inhabitant, once the town's bishop, was St Nicholas, more popularly known as Father Christmas.

At the Temple of Afrodisias were the ruins of a Christian church built upon her site. No visitors, bar us. I found a solitary olive tree growing there, but on the lovely plains that surrounded the temple city were thousands of olive trees. Once sacred groves? Within the adjoining museum, small clay lamps were on display. Olive oil would have been their fuel. The discovery that oil could be burned to create light must have given the tree a mystical significance for Stone Age peoples. Living in caves or windowless huts, by darkness and firelight once the sun had set, and then the discovery of a 'berry' whose juice gave light . . .

We were deep in the country now, moving towards its heart, towards a lake district not much frequented by strangers. Along our route red earth, so rich, with green shrubs growing out of it, like glorious Italian frescoes.

On the rooftops of whatever habitations we drove by, unless they were ruins, cylindrical aluminium basins had been installed, connected to solar panelling. Outside the cities, it seemed, water was heated by the sun. In a country where many other facilities were lacking or primitive, we found this impressive. But soon the face of adversity began to appear and it grew more pronounced as we penetrated the central lands. Many of the country folk we passed, trudging the long distances between village and fields, walked with stooped shoulders. Like their mules, they carried heavy loads with patience and resignation.

As daylight began to drift from the plains, we drove by fleets of heavy-booted families tramping to their homes bearing metal milk churns. It took me back to southern Ireland in the late 1950s. The deprivations. These Turkish women's voluminous clothes gave the impression of sturdiness, but it was impossible to know. We were shocked by the grinding poverty in these out-of-the-way places. Isolated villages, threadbare faces, with only the land to feed off or concentrate on. Passing through mud-housed hamlets, far from any beaten track, firelight illumined the one street. Encircling the incandescence were shadowy female figures cooking out of doors on roaring, red, sparking braziers. The folk looked frayed, old as rags, rarely waving. What we observed were regular people, hardworking, full of guts.

Imagine the arrival of oil to create light for the first time in societies as isolated as these. The power of such a discovery.

The landscape, the nature, as we drew closer to the lakes, fanned out into lush lands, arable, irrigated, markedly less underprivileged. The plains here were filled with grove after grove of lemon and lime trees. The lakes were unruffled and boundless as oceans. We stopped to take photos. Two lads in a lorry parked alongside us leaned over and offered us Coca-Cola.

We arrived into Egirdir in the dark, after 9 p.m., having travelled for many hours. Crossing a narrow isthmus to an island on the lake, it took us approximately three minutes to circumnavigate it, choose a *pension* – a little expensive, but we were too zapped to debate – dump our luggage and hurry the few steps to a vibrantly packed restaurant where only Turks were dining.

We ordered heady Turkish wine and were the only table with a bottle. Exhausted, we sat silently gazing out over the lapping water and ate freshly fished lake bass accompanied by Turkish salad and two simple *mezze* plates: aubergines with tomatoes, yoghurt with garlic and cucumber. Michel was crazy for the tomatoes here. He ate them with every dish at every meal. Afterwards, we climbed the pristinely swept flights of marble stairs at our *pension*, which reminded me of modestly priced *alberghi* in Italy I had stayed in during my early twenties, to our attic room and fell into the hard bed, waking the following morning to the glory of the lake washed by sunlight. It was impossible to conceive the beauty of this place.

Saturday. The sun was already high and I was on my haunches at the water's edge. The lake, embraced by mountains, was clear as a bell and blue as the Med. A local girl, in jeans and no headscarf – here, they did not wear veils or long dresses and we had not heard the *muezzin* for a couple of days – was hawking a trip round the lake in her motorised dinghy. She was chewing bubblegum. When I told her 'no, thanks', she shrugged, grinned and remained at my side, happily blowing bubbles. The water rippled, covering the stone steps, turning them green-gold. No clouds. Large pebbles at the water's edge, slippery and brown with algae. It was a perfect morning in the deep heart of old Turkey. There was no mosque on this lake island. Logically, the *muezzin* could have been heard from the mainland, relayed by loudspeakers across the isthmus, but it was silent. Until 1923, Egirdir had been a Greek Orthodox community.

Our breakfast at the *pension*, prepared and served by four generations of women, was a feast. (No male members of the family in sight.) Boiled eggs, olives, tomatoes – and still Michel requested another plateful – a filo pastry rolled like a cigarette and filled with cheese, *sigara böreği*. Still to the table came fresh fruit, toast and strawberry, cherry, apricot homemade jams followed by yoghurt with honey. We suddenly remembered our frame in the car!

I requested olive oil to accompany our tomatoes, but the grandmother shuffled back with a thin vegetable substitute. I was reminded that, for many, olive products are too expensive and they make do with sunflower or inferior vegetable extractions. Ludicrous when so much oil is produced here. A tour bus passed beyond the window, between us and the tranquil water, honking, ruffling the leaves and stillness. In five years' time . . .

After breakfast, I strolled in the shadows of the willow trees that lined the quayside, the paths interspersed with blossoming hollyhocks. Plane trees also flanked the street. It might have been the south of France except these were *Planus orientalis* and not our Western *Planus occidentalis*, but I could not tell the difference. Boys were washing the small islet streets with hosepipes and brushes. As they did so, their plastic shoes squelched and sucked in the puddles. Michel was down at the waterside with his movie camera.

Because we were nearing Hüyük, I thought it would be fun to stay on here for a day or two, rest and relax, but Michel argued that we should keep travelling. Çatal Hüyük was the principal reason for this leg of my route; better not to risk any delays.

We were moving eastwards along the ancient trade route between Ephesus and Babylon. Blue pointy minarets, like elongated sorcerers' hats, as we flew through the central Anatolian plateaux, where the old houses were hummocks of crumbled mud and stone and the new, garish mauves, pinks, yellows. Old men in caps, check shirts, waistcoats with wooden walking sticks and heavy boots hobbled across the sweeping fields where donkey-drawn carts delivered grandmothers to toil. The colours were a tapestry of dried yellow from the remains of the corn, striped with red-brown clods punctuated by occasional light-leafed trees, olives or willows, planted as shade for the labourers. Streams meandered through the picture. The present was the past. Empires, governments came and went, but such scenes were perennial.

We turned off on to a rutted track that, according to my map, was the direction for Hüyük. Immense stretches of flat grape orchards surrounded us. We stopped. I wanted to check the route and to photograph a towering wooden well at the fieldside. In a neighbouring vineyard, a couple stooped, gathering their harvest. They called to us. Michel crossed to say hello. They snipped a bunch of pink grapes and waved me over. A second couple, friends of the first, chugging by on a tractor, were summoned to the party. An unlikely sextet, we stood in a circle in the vineyard munching the sweet produce. The vinekeeper's wife filled a blue plastic bag for us to take on our way, refusing all payment. The bearded men wanted to know what we were doing at this out-of-the-way spot. Çatal Hüyük, I confirmed, pointing at the map. Energetic debate broke out between three of the quartet – the second woman, an exceedingly rotund female, was consuming vast quantities of grapes. Her husband, thin as a stick, in white crocheted cap, was shaking his grey head. There are two Hüyüks, they informed us, and they proceeded all at once to give directions; arms flying to all points of the compass.

'Konya, Konya,' they repeated. I nodded. The dervish city was renowned for its museum exhibiting many of the prehistoric artefacts found at Çatal Hüyük.

'M-u-s-e-u-m,' I confirmed.

Everybody nodded and fell silent, puzzling, because neither party had understood what the other was communicating. We thanked them for their kindnesses and returned to the car with much waving.

Hüyük was an insalubrious outpost stuck in the middle of vineyards. A chaotic Islamic backwater that reeked of smoke and a charred, bitter scent. Buzzards were circling overhead. I was reminded of the many vultures at the mouth of the Amazon, but this was no departure point, here were no quayside mounds of rotting discarded fish. What was their prey? As we penetrated the town, cycle bells tingled and the *muezzin* echoed forth from every quarter. These were the first prayers we had heard in days.

I had been expecting a certain cosmopolitan influence, given that an important archaeological site was somewhere in the vicinity, involving a steady influx of visitors, young workers, keen amateurs, diggers, scientists in and out on a regular basis, an eclectic mix, particularly throughout the summer months when the dig was operational. We turned around a square or two, but saw no signs. I wound down the window and hollered to two gangly, heavily bearded young men, carrying satchels: 'Do you speak English?'

'Yes, yes.' They hurried towards us.

'Çatal Hüyük, where?' My pidgin-speak.

'Hüyük Hüyük,' they confirmed, darting fingers at the

filthy street beneath their dust-filmed shoes. Clearly, we had exhausted the extent of their English and geography.

'Archaeological dig, ruins, history, Neolithic civilisation,' I tried.

They nodded furiously, but they had less notion of what I was asking than the wine farmers. Both students, eager to assist, pointed out of town, instructing us, if I read their body language accurately, to go back the way we had come and keep a straight path. We returned to the road that had delivered us to this no-man's dustbowl of a settlement and then back to a road that might have been the one we had turned off earlier. There were no signposts, no road numbers. Michel studied the map again. We were both puzzled as to why not a single indication for the site was marked.

M suggested left and I trusted his instincts. Raptors were flying low in the sky all around us, circling the cornfields that flanked this Roman-straight road, where farmers were burning off the last of the season's stubble and plumes of damson-grey smoke rose heavenwards. It explained the stench in the town. We journeyed this straight road four times up and four times down, scanning every signpost. At a loss, we stopped by a brown sign, which usually indicated an archaeological site, though this one made no reference to Çatal Hüyük. Still, we decided to follow it, winding for quite some miles until we found ourselves at an encampment, beside a stream-fed pond where a few locals were washing clothes, a family were enjoying a picnic in the shade of a willow tree and, across the water, a man was refurbishing a millhouse alongside a series of astounding prehistoric stone-carved figures.

A Czech-registered VW bus was parked at the water's edge. I enquired of the trio alongside it, unfolding a table for lunch, if they had visited or knew of Çatal Hüyük. The Czech professor lecturing at various Turkish universities, travelling with his wife and teenage daughter, shook his head.

'Where are we?'

We had fallen upon a Hittite shrine.

The daughter lent me her guidebook. I had made an utterly stupid mistake. Huyuk was an entirely different location to Çatal Hüyük, which remained a considerable journey east from where we were. It was south of Konya. That had been the distinction the vinekeepers had been trying to explain. I glanced across to Michel, who was wading through the shallow pond, taking photographs. Dark-skinned boys were splashing and swimming at its farthest extreme. Beyond, in a field, a young Muslim woman was unloading a full complement of heavy white sacks from a lorry while the men in her party watched on.

How could I have made such an error?

When Michel reached the bank, I owned up to our situation. Without a word, he went in search of our map. I grabbed the grapes and returned with offerings of fruit to the Czechs, along with their guidebook. I donated bunches to the picnicking family beneath the willow. M was chewing thoughtfully, studying our position. I was mortified and wandered off to take photos of my own.

Since prehistory, many different peoples have built civilisations on this vast land, now Turkey, or passed through en route to other continents. This soil has known a rich diversity of cultures. At the birth, 6000 BC, two thousand years before the groves of Bechealeh were planted, was Çatal Hüyük, one of the earliest known settlements anywhere, situated in central Anatolia – but not where we were right now! – close to the arterial route that crossed from Ephesus to what was Babylon, now in Iraq. Indications of primitive oil pressing had been unearthed there, which was why I was so keen to visit, to discover whether this prehistoric city had been the birth of the pressed olive.

I glanced at my watch. It was close to 4 p.m. We were at least a day's journey from my destination and there was nowhere in the vicinity to stay. I was ready to discard all plans, ready to abandon my project entirely. Frankly, I just wanted to go to the beach. As it happened, I had been asking myself whether these earliest peoples may have journeyed their produce from these central plateaux southwards to the sea. Feeling culpable, that my error had left us in the middle of nowhere, aware that we had been travelling hard, I suggested that we return for a day or two to my original itinerary and go south from here to the Mediterranean, follow the coast east and then return inland, approaching Çatal from the south. Michel agreed.

We hit the coast east of Antalya as dusk began to fall, and found ourselves in a Hades of construction sites and ugly resorts. Our trip seemed to be taking a nosedive and I blamed myself. We continued east towards Alanya, assuming that this would be less constructed than Antalya, a city with the busiest airport on the Turkish riviera. Music thumped from behind every wall and there were tourists everywhere. Was this the same country we had been travelling through together for the past week? Eventually, barely visible between five-star monoliths, we found a run-down *pension* a few steps from the sea. While unpacking the car, a very plump Russian girl, in waist-slung sarong and bikini top cutting into her flesh like string, handed Michel her digital camera and requested he take her photograph. Leaning up against a cascade of brilliant red bougainvillea, one hand on her hip and the other touching the back of her cropped and bleached hair, she posed and pouted like a fifties pin-up star. This tiny incident released a growing tension between us.

Before driving to find dinner in the old port of Alanya, I tried to telephone Quashia, but without luck. I walked down to the beach, which was filthy, to have a swim. When I returned, I learned that we had no water. We set out for the evening sticky and, in my case, coated in sea salt.

At the roadside, the perennial traders, now with paraffin lamps and moths. Here, they were selling pendulous fruits from the dust-caked banana plantations flanking the coastal highway. Alanya proved, at first sight, to be another high-rise hell until we slipped off the traffic-clogged coastal streets and followed a winding lane directing us to the castle, where, halfway to the summit, we found an attractive fish restaurant with views across the bay. Lit up, the port packed with yachts and brightly lit restaurants was, at this distance, quite pretty. The *muezzin's* cry bouncing back and forth across the ink-black water, hitting harbour walls, created a droning, mournful accompaniment to our *apéritif*. It was followed by relative silence until, from a floating discotheque, music erupted.

We argued over dinner; our only discordancy throughout our days together, seeded certainly by the afternoon's events, predominantly my inadequate research. I was also tense at having failed to contact Quashia. I was concerned for his well-being and to hear news of the farm.

After dinner, we drove up to the castle. Boys on corners at the roadside were selling bunches of blood-red roses. They shoved the bouquets through the open windows as our car spun the corkscrew curves. We were neither of us in the mood for flowers. It was Saturday night. The castle illuminations created a crepuscular, discreet hideaway for lovers. At the foot of the fortified walls, two young males were crouched on a mat, eyes locked into one another, deep in soft conversation. A bottle of raki was the sole accompaniment to their evening. Elsewhere, a group of adolescents were engaged in a private party alongside parked cars. Music blared from a vehicle's radio. Suddenly, a bottle smashed, there was an outburst of raucous laughter and a girl began to squeal hysterically. I was momentarily alarmed. Her cries were answered by drunken male howlings and yelling. Then laughter, males and females. Michel took my hand and we retreated, leaving them to their entertainment.

Still no water at the hotel. I set off for an early-morning dip. The sand was grey as concrete and pebbly. The lovely inland lakes we had left behind us were more reminiscent of the Mediterranean than this coast. We checked out of the hotel without breakfast.

Antalya and Kekova on this Mediterranean coast facing Cyprus and the Levant made excellent stations of commerce for the Greeks, Phoenicians, Cretans and Egyptians. Was it also feasible that earlier Stone Age peoples from the central plateaux, beginning at Çatal Hüyük, had arduously journeyed here with their produce to trade with foreigners from across the seas?

Kekova was formerly the Greek olive-trading port of Tristomo, the name means 'Three Mouths'. Today, it is known for its Lycian tombs, where there are fine examples of ancient olive trees shading the two-thousand-year-old sarcophagi. The Byzantine city sank into the sea after a terrible earthquake in the second century AD. We had no time to visit; it was too far back west. We settled instead on a day trip back to Antalya, to its Roman harbour, which was pleasantly green with walls clad in ivy, surprisingly sedate and untampered with, though this *yat limani* (yacht harbour) no longer resembled the photos I had seen of it from the 1950s, never mind the great Roman embarkation point it had once been. We parked the car above the port, close to a *taksi* stand where yellow taxis stood idle while their drivers played cards out of the heat beneath a carob tree.

The present-day, heavy-duty port of Antalya had been relocated to the outskirts of the city, leaving the Roman basin to perform as a yacht marina with a small mosque at its centre. I descended directly to the waterfront, past the harbour police, who requested I take their photograph, to where, on this Sunday morning, men were fishing and dark-skinned curly-haired boys were diving from natural boulders as large as chapels. The sea out to the Gulf of Antalya was satin calm. Fishermen at the rudder of their *caiques* were chugging to land with their morning's catch. Aside from a few seaview restaurants, life here was as it had been for decades, if not centuries. The harbour itself has been cut out of gargantuan reddish rocks. Most of the docked boats were wooden sailing craft employed for the transport of tourists on day cruises. Long gone was the maritime trade and traffic that fed Greece and the Middle East.

We had left behind the resorts and had regained unspoiled nature. Beyond Alanya on the road to Anamur, we found coastal ruins, delightful coves, jagged ghosts of fortresses, a fallen citadel. History was tumbling into the sea at every curve of this deserted, deliciously Mediterranean littoral. Olive trees reappeared as well as pines and rich, red earth. High on the cliffside with views that commanded the sea were the first drystone walls we had encountered. Who had built them and planted the olive groves here? The knowledge and saplings had surely been shipped across the sea from the Levant. Precious little could be constructed here due to the escarpments sweeping to the water's edge. It was dizzyingly beautiful; a mirror of what the Côte d'Azur must have been a century ago.

Anamur was curious, a sprawling little town, lacking planning. It appeared to be on a grid system with dozens of apartment blocks added later, abnormally laid out, plonked in the middle of agricultural plots. Eventually, we found a small white hotel, which was halfway down a street leading nowhere; rather attractive, with an art deco air. Our room on the first floor was small, square, clean, luminous and perfectly comfortable.

After a shower, we strolled – it was quite a distance – towards the sea, looking for the port. The women wore Western clothes, and though we had passed a mosque or two, there was little that suggested this was a Muslim state. Tourism had not reached here, yet it had a European feel about it, an evolving Turkey, not a lost city like Troy or Ephesus, but a settlement where for centuries ordinary people had lived off land and sea.

We passed an extensive training base. In fact, it operated as a summer resort for military families, which throughout the remaining months of the year was policed by 300 permanent soldiers. Anamur was two hours by boat from Turkish Cyprus.

Cyprus stands between the Turkish coastline and the Lebanese and Syrian shores. Throughout early history, its placement had been critical to the maritime powers of the day and it has been ruled by everyone from Hittites, Egyptians and Assyrians from the fertile plains of Mesopotamia to the British in the twentieth century. Turkey invaded in 1974 and today the island lives beneath the shadow of its unresolved situation; divided between Turkish and Greek rule. I intended to visit there later.

We found ourselves a fish restaurant in Iskele, the harbour

district, where we sat outside and ate extremely well, though our bill exceeded the listed prices. A query brought panto-mimic apologies. Walking back to the hotel, holding hands, the fragrance of jasmine pervaded the night air. Jasmine from the Orient. I picked several of the white, star-shaped florets to lay on the pillows in our small square room, where we made love. Harmony once more.

We checked out of our hotel at daybreak, affording us time for a visit to the ancient Phoenician city of Anamurium. It was a hillside of stones and hidden mosaics, ancient baths, theatre and odeon, sprawling beside the sea. The beach was deserted, a sweeping arc that led from cliffs broken with citadel walls back to the modern town. I walked up and down, crunching in the sand, staring out towards Cyprus and beyond to Israel, Palestine. I was trying to picture the comings and goings of those fabulous wooden vessels built of Lebanese cedar and oak as they docked at the excellent anchorages here. This would have been a strategically important trading base for the Phoenicians, and possibly earlier civilisations before them.

The descent we had already made from mistaken Huyuk and the journey we were intent upon later today both involved crossing the Taurus Mountains. If the earliest civilisations were as far inland as Çatal Hüyük, who did they trade with? How did they travel any distance? Did they reach this coast? Carrying their loads by foot? There were no donkeys yet. Might a trading chain have evolved whereby the goods were handed along, until they eventually reached the sea? Obsidian from east of Çatal Hüyük, the volcanic areas around Cappadocia, has shown up in Egypt and along the Red Sea. The site was absolutely lovely. The sun was shining and the Med was the colour of a bluebell. I regretted that I had packed away my swimming togs. There was not a soul about, not even Michel – he was scaling the hillside taking photographs – but I would not skinny-dip in a Muslim country, so I sat at the water's edge, drinking in the atmosphere, dreaming, asking questions. In earlier times, the only access to this city would have been by the sea.

We returned to town for a hearty breakfast before our long trek over the mountains. Sitting next to us in a café was a muscular, handsome Turk who seemed angry, shouting at the waitress, chain-smoking, not eating. I noticed then that he was in a wheelchair. He saw us studying our map and asked where we were headed. We learned that his great joy in life had been riding these mountains on a motorbike: the wind in his face, the scent of resin. One day, a lorry took a curve too fast. It was dangerously overloaded, as they all seemed to be, with sacks stacked far too high. He shrugged, said no more, lit another cigarette, but within minutes he was laughing and regaling everyone with football jokes. He was full-blooded, engaging.

When he learned that we were on our way to Çatal Hüyük, he shook his head. 'It is closed for the winter.'

'But I enquired in England,' I began, humiliated by the prospect of another blunder.

He instantly reassured us that a guard remained on site all year round and that as long as we arrived before 5 p.m., access would be possible. 'It will take you four hours from here.' He smiled, shaking our hands. Looking at our map, his timing seemed optimistic. But the day was young, we had hours to play with.

On the road to Ermenek, where the communities were once more traditional – weathered, striated faces, boots, flat caps, waistcoats, wooden staffs – high above an altitudinous plain, I spotted deep honey-toned rocks with cave dwellings. Who inhabited them? The species of fir pines here resembled giant cacti and reminded me of the cool-climate rainforests in northern Tasmania. Climbing higher, we came upon vast apple orchards. I jumped over a tiny fence and stole two: one red, one green. They were sweet, but not yet ripe. Further along in an alpine hamlet, a man was relaxing in the shade on the street in a barber's chair while two other chaps were crouching like monkeys in the middle of the road staring unblinkingly into the direction of oncoming traffic. Beige, stone dry, pink, honey, red were the mountains. We both agreed that this was one of the most beautiful landscapes we had ever encountered.

South of Ermenek, cave dwellings were everywhere, cut into the vertical mountain peaks. Several had been adapted, stone-fenced and appeared to be occupied. Outside one was a couple with a donkey gathering fruit from a wild tree – we could not identify it. How did the ancients ascend and descend to these primitive dwellings? Were these stopovers on the way to the coast, to where they traded goods with the Phoenicians or other, earlier seafaring peoples? Beyond Ermenek the road was closed and we were obliged to take a detour via Mut, circuitous and time-costly, but we were loath to hurry through the karstic limestone scenery, it was too beautiful. Vistas of mountains – fantastic and surreal. Rock tones that appeared as though, from the birth of time, all colour had been leached out by the sun. The landscape had a prehistoric feel to it. Olives were growing here, though, many examples of my ancient tree, and vines.

Limestone plains where the earth was almost white; the relief of intermittent green from unexpected foliage; a landscape of gorges, fissures, rocks, caverns; it was all, quite literally, astounding and we found ourselves drawn to a standstill. The ranges permeated our beings, rendering us sense-drunk.

From these altitudes sprang the upper reaches of the mighty Euphrates, flowing its 2,800-kilometre distance down to Iraq. Might the river have offered Stone Age peoples a trade route? No other cars on the road, but we lost count of the multicoloured trucks, swinging precariously on the hairpin bends, packed with squatting men or families of women and children perched high above the onion layers of white sacks. How they remained in place, how they were not thrown off and killed, we could not reason. The air was clear, clean, high-alpine scents. Above the olive groves were ranges fretted with caves and dwellings. Places of immense solitude and mystery where we both experienced the sensation that we had countermarched, had been seduced, drawn back into the distant past.

Time. It was close to 2 p.m. when we reached the turn-off for Karaman. Our only breaks had been for photography or observation. Once on the highway, we pulled in at a garage. Two policemen in sunshades were sitting together, talking, playing cards. They glanced our way, but paid us no heed. While Michel organised petrol, I hurried into the small provision store, requesting coffee, but there was none. Instead, I stocked up with biscuits and mineral water, to keep us going, and a couple of beers for later. I was unsure whether we had an opener so I requested the boy lift off the bottle caps and then place them lightly back on again. I returned to the car, storing the beers carefully. While I sat waiting for M, I noticed the shop boy approach the police. He imparted information that caused them to look my way, to scrutinise the registration plate. Back on the road, I recounted the episode to Michel.

'Booked for drunken driving in a Muslim state.' He grinned. 'Don't be silly.'

We had picked up speed, still intent on reaching Çatal Hüyük before 5 p.m., but the clock was ticking. The approach to Karaman was scenic even along the motorway. Apple farms, mountains. But we kept moving. If we failed to reach Çatak Hüyük before sunset, it would mean an overnight in Konya and then little if no time together in Cappadocia before Michel's flight. Still we were travelling too fast. Outside the city of Karaman, passing a sign welcoming us to the 'apple capital' of Turkey, we were snarled up in a traffic jam that delayed us further. Michel pulled over and, in true French fashion, began to weave his way in and out of the traffic and then we were back on the open road, flying along, bickering about the risk he had taken, when, all of a sudden, as we slowed for a traffic light, a police patrol car overtook us and stopped at the lights, where an officer was waiting. He stepped off the kerb and flagged us down, beckoning Michel to pull over.

'I knew it,' I groaned, throwing a sweater over the two untouched beers wedged between us. The officer bent low, signalled the window, which I obediently wound down, smiling sweetly. Speaking in thickly accented English, the heavy-framed man wanted to know where we were from. 'France,' replied Michel.

I was about to reach for our passports when the Turk handed me a package.

'Welcome to Karaman,' grinned the man of the law. 'The city of apples. Drive carefully now,' he added, stepping back and waving us along. I was holding a sealed pack of four apples accompanied by a leaflet detailing their local production.

On the outskirts of Çumra, the nearest town to Çatal Hüyük, there were small encampments of nomads tenanting by a stream. They reminded me of the Syrian gypsies who travelled as pickers. Livestock abounded in the dried grass around their woven tents. They were melon-gathering we

saw, where swallows flew so low they veered by the windscreen. It was half past four. We were 13 kilometres from
Çatal, but could not find our way through this milling, mud-
bricked maze. It was a curious place, almost medieval. We
asked directions. Nobody seemed to recognise the name,
Çatal. Chickens, potholes, bicycle riders, mule-drawn carts,
flat-capped men, mounds of tyres, stray yapping dogs, debris.
Someone pointed to a sign. We turned into an alley, swerving
round urchins playing in the street. Two policemen offered to
escort us to the road. We followed them out of the confusing
poverty-stricken town and on to a road with fields and trees,
full steam ahead. Then the sign, off to the right, down we
plunged, country lanes, holes in the road, flat plains in every
direction. Rurality. And Çatal Hüyük. It was five to five. I
hared to the entrance and called to the guard. A baby-faced
young man in jeans and blue shirt approached, smiling.

'Do you speak English?' I cried.

'Somewhat.'

I pointed to my watch 'This is our last opportunity
and —'

'Perfectly satisfactory,' he assured me. 'Follow this way.'

We entered the little museum at the site, which was in
reality more a digs record, but on display were two extraordinary pieces. The first was a small, black-faced, oval mirror
made out of obsidian. An eight-thousand-year-old mirror,
believed to be the first on earth. The second article, also
believed to be the first of its kind in the world, was a terracotta
spice-shaker. I found its sophistication remarkable. What it
also expressed was the level of farming and cooking sophistication these earliest of settlers must have already reached.
Their agriculture was highly organised. They reared sheep
and they hunted deer, wild cattle, boars and leopards. They
farmed the fields around the town, growing various different

wheats, barley, lentils, peas. They grew and used pistachios, cherries and almonds. They made a version of beer. Wine, too? I did not know, but the wine from Cappadocia with its black volcanic earth is judged to be the finest in Turkey. They pressed oil. But oil from what? Checking the glass cases, I saw no miniature clay lamps, nothing to suggest that they had olive oil for lighting. Cooking, then? The question was whether it was almonds they crushed or did they have olives, and, if so, were the drupes from the mountain ranges we had crossed?

Outside in the soft late-afternoon light, accompanied by the guard, we walked to the remains of the ancient towns themselves. Compared with the beauty of Ephesus, these were little more than giant craters with sacks piled everywhere to create walls and to help demonstrate the various levels of the civilisations that had inhabited the tell. The excitement lay in its primitiveness, its record as a birthplace for all that had come afterwards. I looked out across a 360-degree panorama at plains, endless fertile lands. I was standing on the dawn of civilisation, perhaps also the first faltering steps towards olive culture, though there appeared to be no olive trees in the vicinity. There was widespread evidence, however, that the people from here travelled great distances to graze their herds and collect berries and timber. There had been acorns here, too – possibly man's first food. Olives are really only one step beyond acorn and berry nutrition. To the east, barely visible, a spreading bruise in the distance, were the volcanic mountains of Cappadocia, where the coveted vitreous lava, obsidian, came from. The people from Cappadocia, a five-hour journey by car from here, traded that green-black glass with the inhabitants of this city as well as with overland traders from the East. Obsidian from this period has been found at

Jarmo near the Tigris river, west of the Zagros Mountains. For the dwellers of Çatal Hüyük, obsidian proved to be a trading jewel. Some of the very earliest merchants swapped it for goods such as stones from the Levant, flint from Syria and shells from the Red Sea. To have achieved that, they almost certainly journeyed over the mountains we had crossed. Or could it be that they sent their produce, their materials for exchange, in relays? Might they have employed mountain couriers who dwelled in the caves we had driven by, who possibly handed over the products to other couriers to transport to the sea, to Anamurium, for example, the settlement that was later to become the Phoenician site we had visited at break of day? From there, seafarers took over the job. Whether or not those sea-going peoples were from this side of the water or the Levantine, who could say?

All of this was taking place some two thousand years before the olive grove in Bechealeh was planted, but feral trees were growing in certain zones around the Mediterranean. Might the crudely pressed oil of wild fruits have been offered for trade? Were wild trees taken from Anatolia and cultivated in the Middle East?

I asked the guard if olive trees grew along these high plateaux. He shook his head. Not as far as he knew. What about ferals, were there wild olive trees anywhere hereabouts? He confessed that he did not know.

Before leaving, our kind and patient host took us to see a reconstruction of a Neolithic house, an example of how these earliest settlers lived. The oven in the living area was almost identical in style and size to the *tandirs* used by the local women in the neighbouring villages even today.

There were no lamps within the house. Unlike the small clay lamps we had seen on display at Afrodisias, we found no objects used for lighting the homes of these early peoples.

Before man understood the cycles of the sun, moon, darkness, seasons, might he have been afraid as the days drew in, as they grew shorter? The darkening of the sun? His source of light and food? Worship of the sun as power, as a god, was common and comprehensible. How terrifying must have been the notion that the sun – man's light and heat – might diminish. These Neolithic people had fire to cook by. They understood that fire died away, but what if the sun, like fire, burned out? How would they survive in the darkness of night? And then, somewhere around this Mediterranean basin, at some point not far beyond these settlers, the mashed olive – possibly a wild, inedible variety – gave oil and, with oil, man created light. The olive's oil kept darkness at bay. Is it possible that the oil from the olive was the first product from the tree to be traded?

Leaving the site, the approaching dusk had turned the sky yellowish; the endless plains were in long, moving shadows. The distant mountains were marginally clearer. The extraordinary wall paintings these Stone Age people had created must have been influenced by time spent looking at nature, at the volcanic mountains and the ebbing and flowing of light. We shook hands with our man and thanked him for his time and set off. We still had a long journey to Cappadocia ahead of us before nightfall.

As we drove through the surrounding villages, we were struck by the exceedingly basic living conditions. The dwellings were mud houses. Çatal Hüyük was first inhabited somewhere around 6500 BC. The mud houses we were driving by had barely altered from the mock-up accommodation we had just visited.

We arrived in Ürgüp in the dark and were unable to see anything of the surrounding volcanic scenery.

But what a day we had travelled. I pondered, if the ancient

peoples from Çatal Hüyük did journey to the sea for trade, how many weeks the trajectory that we had made over one extraordinary day would have taken them. This was our final evening together for a while and I was feeling my habitual pangs of loss, though thrilled by all that we had discovered. Michel's plane was not until the following evening so we rose early, breakfasted at our hotel, which had been carved out of a series of rock caves, and set off for a final tour of what promised to be a most original topography.

And it was.

I had never seen a landscape like this. It was fantastical. There were entire valleys of volcanic rock that had been sculpted by time and weather and grew up out of the grey, sandy ground like forests of soft-stoned phalluses. They were known as 'fairy chimneys', though I cannot understand why. There was no doubting what they resembled. These *peribacalari* were formed when the winds came whipping through the valleys and the rains streamed down the hillsides, wiping away the loose lava covering the consolidated volcanic ash, the tuff, leaving behind isolated pinnacles. These 'chimneys', these conical pillars of soft rock topped with sloping hats of harder rock, reached heights of up to 40 metres. The Cappadocians called them *kalelars*, which meant 'castles'.

We drove slowly, looking all about us as though we had entered a science-fiction universe. In the flat, deep-brown, almost black-ash fields, vines were growing. The region was renowned for its wine; the nitrates in the Vesuvian volcanic sand provided excellent nutrients. The proprietor of the hotel, a carpenter by trade who resembled a bandy hobbit, had told us over breakfast that the grapes were also used to make a syrup known as *pekmez*.

The sky was seamlessly blue. So pure was the colour, it all but echoed. We were saying we should walk, we had been sitting for days, when we spotted a sign to Love Valley. Michel swung right on to a sand track where the dust flew at us in whorls. We parked, got out and the heat settled upon us, creating a spooky stillness broken by the cawing of crows and a distant hum from a far-removed road. As we began to trudge up a sandy incline, puffing, I asked Michel if he had noticed the trees at the roadsides. They resembled the olive with silvery, pointed leaves and green button fruits. My breathless chatter was silenced as we entered a volcanic ash forest of giant *kalelars*. Mind-blowing, surrealistic and, for a woman, rather like Charlie walking into Willy Wonka's chocolate factory!

Michel pulled out his camera and we wandered from phallus to phallus, awed. And then the trees. 'Look!' called M.

Close up, they were shrubby and they were everywhere. Wild olives growing in the volcanic sand. There were forests of them.

We had fallen upon prehistoric olive trees in Love Valley. Michel began to photograph them. I picked a fruit. It was smaller and rounder than our *cailletiers* at home. I cut it open with my thumbnail while Michel leaned in over me. The flesh was soft but not oleaginous. Wild olives lacking oil?

When we returned to the hotel, we learned from the curious-looking owner, who had been hovering by the door waiting for us, that the trees grew wild in the sand in these parts, but they were not olives. They were a berry tree known as *aliç* whose fruits turned from green to yellow and then red by mid-October, when they were harvested for a deliciously original marmalade.

'What is the history of this tree?'

Our host could not say, but agreed that its resemblance to the olive was uncanny. I considered those earliest inhabitants from Çatal Hüyük who travelled distances to gather berries and to trade whatever – their goats, sheep or wheat, almond oil, too, perhaps – for the dark-green obsidian and possibly the fruit of the *aliç*.

I had not yet discovered the birthplace of olive cultivation, but I had possibly visited the ghosts of the first crushers of fruits or berries gathered expressly for their oil. I was moving in the right direction.

It was then the proprietor handed me the message. 'Telephone Quashia.' When I reached him, he was deeply concerned. There was a crisis at the farm. We packed our bags. Michel and I left together for Paris and from there flew to Nice.

The olive cultivators could guard their secrets a little longer.

Malta

On a warm, late-autumn morning, after an exhausting and circuitous journey from the farm, where all preparations for our olive harvest had to be cancelled because we had lost our entire crop due to olive fly, I found myself standing in the Upper Barrakka Gardens in Malta's capital city of Valletta, looking out across the island's superb, natural Grand Harbour. I had vigorously resisted all attempts by Quashia and Michel to spray insecticides on our trees and the spectacle that greeted us when we arrived home was a sea of fallen fruits, blighted and blackened by fly larvae. On this early-November day, the sun-burnished stones of the Three Cities, restored and fortified by the Knights of St John in the sixteenth century, were pleasing both to my eye and to my nerves. A gentle sea watch, one might say, that allowed my mind to wander and pick up the threads of my journey.

During prehistory, somewhere between 5 and 25 million years ago, the rocks that were to become the Maltese archipelago were forced up from the seabed by tectonic-plate collisions and continental shifts between Africa and Europe. At that stage, Malta and its two smaller outlying lands, Gozo and Comino, were attached to Sicily by a land bridge. After the last Ice Age, around 12,000 BC, as the earth's temperatures rose and all the glaciers began to melt, millions of tons of water were unleashed. Naturally, these floods, these great waves, caused sea levels, including the Mediterranean's, to surge. The result was that the land bridge in question was overwhelmed by water and submerged beneath the sea, causing Malta and its islands to be separated from the southern tip of Sicily, detached from the continental land mass now known as Europe.

Southern Europe had a damper climate in those prehistoric days and, over time, as elsewhere around the Mediterranean shores, the vegetation, shrubs, trees such as the holm oak, the carob – one of the oldest trees in the world – and flowers began to grow upon the limestone rockiness. Amongst these came the olive. Was the wild olive a native to these Maltese islands, or was it planted here by conquerors or seafaring merchants, of which there have been countless colourful fleets? The generally held belief was that Phoenicians from Tyre introduced the olive to the Maltese islands somewhere around the eighth century BC. I had no reason to question it. It was not the birth of Maltese olive farming I was unclear about, but its demise. The flourishing olive groves the islands had boasted of two thousand years ago, and historians had written about, had long since disappeared. Few olives had been farmed here for the best part of the last five centuries, but I had no idea why.

Tearing myself away from the view on that first morning, I wandered through a small paved park and paused to pick a round green fruit from a tree I did not recognise; its leaf had caught my eye because it vaguely resembled the olive. I pierced it with finger and thumb and split the fruit open. Inside were bright tangerine seeds, plump as small beans. They were not edible and their juice was not oily; it was sticky. It was a *Pittosporum tobira*, I learned later. The leaves were not as leathery, shiny or deep green as I would have expected from a pittosporum. We have a variety that grows almost wild on our farm. Down our way, it is frequently used to create sweetly scented hedges, but it bears no linkage to the olive.

I had a meeting arranged for later in the afternoon at the island's only olive mill. This afforded me a few hours and I slipped into Valletta's National Museum of Archaeology. I had not expected to be so taken with the five-thousand-year-old artworks on display. All had been discovered at Malta's Neolithic temple sites. Most of the objects were monumental slabs of crafted limestone incised with dots, circles and loops. They were quite mysterious and begged the question as to whether their markings represented a primitive language or musical notations. The obsidian mirror, the terracotta spice-shaker, the wall paintings at Çatal Hüyük had woken me up to the sophistication of such early peoples. Here, on display, were dozens of rotund fertility goddess statuettes, all breathtakingly beautiful but, alas, offering me no clues that might relate these Stone Age female-led cultures to olives or to any primitive form of oil pressing, which was what I had been hoping to discover.

Fleeing from persecution in Rhodes in 1530, the crusading Knights of St John were on the lookout for an alternative base in the Mediterranean. At this point, Spain was the power governing Malta. Leasing the islands to the knights made sense. The Spanish felt safe with Catholic Crusaders as tenants and trusted that they would protect and maintain their dependency, but the knights were reluctant to set up home here. Their first impressions of the archipelago were not positive; it was agriculturally desolate and the terrain was stark. In short, the islands could never sustain them. However, lacking alternatives, they accepted the King of Spain's offer and Malta was given over to the knights for a peppercorn rent of two Maltese peregrine falcons to be paid annually on 1 November.

What fascinated me was to discover what, between the departure of the Phoenicians who had brought olive cultivation to these islands and the arrival of the knights six centuries later, had transpired to destroy all fertility on what had earlier been hailed as a Mediterranean haven. What incident had turned Malta and its two outlying islands into bald, unproductive rocks?

Before meeting the miller, I decided to take a drive inland. Many village and town names on both Gozo and Malta were reminders of their fertile and oleiferous past. In Arabic, there are several spellings or variations on *al-zeytun* which means 'the olive': *zeytun*, *zitoon*, *zitun* are but three. Zegtun is an inland village situated on the south-east corner of the island. What I drove into was a sleepy little town caught in a shower, where I changed money at the Bank of Valletta, grabbed a quick pizza at a trattoria nestling beneath autumn-leafed vines and dawdled over the headline on a British newspaper 'Wilma Hurricane Hits Florida'. I paused, sent thoughts to several friends residing in the storm-torn state, and then continued on my way, covering the length of the main street, getting damp, in the vain hope of finding a clue to an olive past more vibrant than today's. I did not.

Two miles away was the village of Birzebbuga. *Bir* means 'well', so this habitation was once the 'Well of Olives'. I found a fishing port with unsightly gasworks and a newly constructed beach, but not one olive tree or well anywhere. Beyond the light rain, three miles from the fortified, original capital of the island, Mdina, was Haz-Zebbug, or the 'Hamlet of Olives'. Yet again, not an olive tree in sight and certainly not the groves Pliny had so admired.

Pliny the Elder, Roman historian and naturalist, AD 23–79, noted that 'The olive tree does not die but takes on new life from its trunk.' Landing at Binwerrard, on the shores of Malta, Pliny walked 'all the way inland to the capital, Mdina, beneath the shade of whispering olive trees'. Binwerrard (modern-day Burmarrad) is no longer a port, Mdina is no longer the capital, and those groves that kept the historian from getting sun-burned have long since disappeared.

My drive that afternoon revealed a bald, wave-lapped island with every building constructed out of limestone. There was little else, but it was soft on the eye, honey-toned and honey-combed, quarried from three different limestone layers: glo-bigerina, lower coralline and upper coralline. The lanes and fields, now in sunlight, were criss-crossed with mile upon mile of ancient drystone walls and irregular small enclosures constructed from the globigerina stone, known locally as *franka*. It gave the landscape an appearance of having been cable-stitched and was rather attractive even if almost denuded of trees. Prickly pears grew at the roadsides, *garrigue* plants here and there and carobs, but otherwise rocks. What had returned these green and silvered islands to stone?

Somewhere in mid-afternoon, I arrived in Wardija, an attractive inland village winding in ascending circles round its hillside, adorned with elegant houses built of vast slabs of the ineluctable *franka*, all draped in brilliantly coloured climbing bougainvillea and with pleasing views east across the island to St Paul's Bay. I strolled up a leafy cobbled driveway that led to a substantial private house, a panting black Labrador jumping around my feet, and found myself in an outbuilding in a lovely garden where an Italian pressing machine, a gleam-ing state-of-the-art centrifuge, was about its thundersome business, tamping and turning. A huddle of old-style locals, who smiled shyly at my arrival, were crowded close by the open door watching their fruits transform into oil.

'I'm looking for Nat,' I yelled.

A short, wiry, grey-haired miller stepped forward to greet me. His eyes burned with such enthusiasm they looked as though they had been stoked. Natalino Frendo had studied as a gemmologist and had made his fortune in diamonds, but his passion was olives and he was as fascinated by the tree's history and its role in the islands' patrimony as I was. His commitment to the regeneration of the olive on these islands, I was to learn, was a great deal more than a hobby. We hit it off instantly.

The annual harvests had been achieved. Pressing had commenced. One or two of the faces, broad and solid, looked on as though witnessing a miracle. Nat waved me eagerly towards them. Amongst the expectants, chatting convivially, was the 'best-bread-on-the-island' baker, a university lecturer from Valletta, and a young woman with mid-length hair and office clothes.

I expressed my surprise at such early gatherings, but Nat assured me they were already more than halfway through their season. Outside, we crossed a cobbled courtyard, where a line of men, baskets of shiny, healthy fruits at their feet, stood in the sunshine, dressed in shorts and T-shirts. Back home in France, our farmers are wrapped up warmly in winter-wear, prepared for hours of waiting in temperatures no higher than 10 degrees Celsius. Nat's mill was not underground. Still the room was coolish if a little cramped, which was why the farmers and pickers were waiting outside in the yard, standing about in groups, chatting to one another.

'Farmers travel from all over Malta,' he admitted shyly. 'A handful even take the ferry from Gozo to press their drupes with us, at Nat's mill.'

The arrangement was not dissimilar to our *moulin* at home in the hills behind Grasse: if a farmer does not have sufficient quantities of fruit to fill the machine and create a single-estate pressing – 'Very few do here because there is so little land to go around and so few olive trees' – they can leave their contribution with Nat or his assistant, Tonio, who add them to the next communal pressing, which was due to take place the following morning. Nat rises at 5 a.m. all year round, he told me. During the harvest season, he sets to work directly, cleaning up, filling the press with the mixed fruits, setting it in motion, and then strikes out for his daily hour-long constitutional.

Tonio called from across the yard. It was a message from Nat's wife, Julia, on the internal phone, reminding him of the arrival of 'the nuns' later that afternoon.

'The nuns?'

'The ladies hail from a nearby convent, whose grounds count half a dozen old trees. They took up the faith a couple of years back and without fail have delivered their drupes to us each autumn since, and every olive has been hand-picked by the "holy girls" themselves,' grinned Nat.

I was fascinated to know how he, a diamond specialist, had ended up with a press in his garden, mashing olives for the local community. Nat recounted to me the tale of his friend Giorgio, who owned a modest few trees and had wished to press the fruit.

'In 1999, when Giorgio discovered there were no mills here, he shipped his harvested olives to Sicily, but the Sicilians made his life hell. The fruits sat in customs for days, growing mouldy, gathering flies, and by the time the consignments were cleared, they were past their best and the Sicilian miller refused to allow them inside his establishment, shouting that the flies would damage every other delivery. Giorgio not only lost his harvest, but he was obliged to pay for it to be bagged up, because it could not be transported uncovered. He also forked out for its return to Malta because everywhere denied him permission to bury or simply jettison the crop. He tried to ditch it in the sea, a short distance from shore, but was nabbed by a Sicilian marine patrol, who fined him and insisted he return the consignment back where it came from, Malta.

The whole endeavour cost him a tidy sum, but he refused to be beaten. The following winter, he hired a private boat to smuggle the drupes back to Etna's island in an attempt to avoid the custom delays. Unfortunately, he got picked up again, was fined for smuggling, practically landed himself in a Sicilian jail and was still forced to transport the pungent crates back to his yard, by which time the fruits were once again too shrivelled and acidic to bother with even had there been a mill here to press them. I wasn't going to go through all that.'

It was after hearing these woeful tales that Nat ordered his own equipment and set it up in the specially constructed outhouse we had just left. His enterprise, he announced modestly but with evident pride, was already proving to be an enormous success. His machine remained the only one on the island.

Neighbouring farmers, from far and near, had begun harvesting long-forgotten trees, and a handful of them had planted one or two more. With a little financial assistance and advice from Nat, locals were ordering varieties from southern France, Italy and Spain. The word was spreading and Nat was as excited as a kid with a new toy.

'Maltese oil will soon be back on the map.' He grinned. 'But this is just the beginning,' he all but whispered.

He had greater ambitions, a grander scheme that he was itching to tell me about. We were now on a swift tour of his grounds and young groves, which in comparison even with our little farm were modest in size – it is impossible to own extensive tracts of land here, the *tomuli*, acres, are simply not available. But everywhere was well tended, except, I was puzzled to see, many of his trees still hung heavy with ripe black fruits.

'Will you be harvesting these?' I asked.

Nat's thoughts were elsewhere. His plump assistant, Tonio, in powder-blue shorts and white vest, was waving to him from the yard. Nat turned those fiery eyes back to me, but I could see he had almost forgotten why I was there.

'What? Yes, we might pick a few more if there's time. Why not meet Julia?' and with that he sprinted back across the garden and disappeared out of sight.

I strode up to the house in the afternoon sunshine, accompanied by the bounding black dog, Oliver, to introduce myself to Julia, Nat's wife. Although the phone barely stopped ringing with locals requesting appointments, the rapport between us was instantaneous. So much so that she suggested I check out of my hotel and move into their spare room, with its heavy wooden furniture, white bedspread and free-standing full-length mirror. I declined the offer, but lingered, tasting their olives and oil, assisting their daughter, Lizzie, a coltish beauty, with her French homework, and within two hours I felt as though I had become part of the family. Julia recounted tales of the days when women came to Wardija on foot to pick the olives, travelling long distances, carrying metal weights, which were for measuring the fruit loads, and, at the end of the day, they returned to their homes carrying their share of the gathered drupes in baskets on their heads.

The olive and its history were our point of contact. In our different ways, we were all digging for the ancient roots of the olive tree, searching for jigsaw pieces that fitted together and interlaced our Mediterranean identity.

Although I had declined the offer of the bed, I returned the following morning bright and early. Nat had promised to take me to visit a Roman olive grove, probably the only one still in existence anywhere on the archipelago.

It was a little after 8 a.m. when I rolled up the drive, noticing for the first time that there was a tall, scruffy emu with a curious bald head staring bug-eyed at me from behind a wooden enclosure. The yard was already packed with people and I had a strong sense that for these folk this was a social event as well as a newly discovered pleasure. I waved and they nodded courteously. As in France, several uncorked bottles of wine stood about the place. A few of the hardier farming codgers held glasses in between cracked, weathered hands. An open van pulled up and one of the handsomest young men I have ever set eyes on jumped out and began unpacking his loaded crates. Nat hurried over and introduced him to me as 'the son of . . . whose mother was married to . . . her father's farm was situated . . . once owned by . . .' I was in the midst of a tiny, tightly knit community where the mood was upbeat and welcoming. The Maltese are inherently friendly, if rather reserved.

'There are no secrets here or, rather, there are many, but everybody knows them! Let's go.' Nat tore himself away from his gang of gatherers, grabbed an ill-fitting raincoat, the cuffs of which rode high above his elbows – it was cloudier today – and we set off together to hike to a neighbouring rural village, Bidnija, across a few rock-shrubby tracts of land that sprawled around an insignificant settlement. We clambered over Phoenician tombs – 'This is evidence that the ex-Canaanite sailors were here ahead of their Carthaginian descendants!' cried Nat, kicking weeds away with his foot to show me where sailors and merchants from Tyre who never had the good fortune to return to their families and homelands were buried and whose disintegrated remains had long been forgotten beneath wild fennel and evergreen carobs. Nat and I beat a path through the sweet-smelling *garrigue* to visit a grove of twisted, asymmetrical, lopsided olive trees that had been carbon-dated at around one thousand nine hundred years old. Roman trees.

We paused on several occasions while Nat tore and ripped at the briars and weeds of the scrubland. 'Look at this! Look. Here and here!' Shrouded beneath decades of thick-skeined, thorny growth lay Roman settling tanks attached to stone channels along which the oil would have been fed after extraction. 'They are all over the island,' muttered my guide, striding onwards. I recalled a shallow stone bath we had uncovered at our farm, years back, close to the ruined vinekeeper's cottage, and how bewildered we had been by its purpose. I will have to take a closer look, I was thinking, when I return home. My thoughts fell momentarily on our empty trees until Nat's voice pulled me back to the present.

'I want your opinion,' he insisted on several occasions. 'Tell me if you think the grove could be older.' I deduced from his tone that an earlier dating was what he hoped for. 'It's a miracle they weren't uprooted or razed to the ground like all the rest on the islands.'

When we reached the stand, alone in a dip in a valley with scatterings of rubbish dumped close by their roots, it was hard to believe these sinewy, knobbled guys had slipped through the net. Had some farmer fought tooth and nail for the lives of these dozen or so two-thousand-year-old elders decorated today with small ripe fruits as dark and inviting as blackberries? Due to the girth and weathering of the trunks, my guess was that the dating Nat had received from Italy sounded pretty accurate. When I said as much, I read his disappointment. He nodded and kicked his shoe at the ground. He wanted something more, a nugget that might lead to a key, to a history more ancient than anyone had so far dreamed of. In this we were similar. Nat knew that I too was sleuthing about, hoping to hit upon an unknown fact, though precisely what or where it would lead me, who could say?

'If, in the grounds of a tumble-down monastery or a

forgotten, weed-choked garden, somewhere here, anywhere, a stand or even a single tree could be discovered that dated back two and a half thousand years, then we'd have found ourselves a Phoenician offering. Carthaginian, at least,' he said.

He and I were in agreement that cultivation of olive plantations probably began in Malta with the trading Phoenicians from Tyre, had flourished and then been expanded by the Romans and, later, the Byzantines.

'Are these the oldest trees on the islands?'

He nodded, swinging about as though the secret he craved might be standing right behind him.

'Who is the proprietor?'

The land was owned by the Church, or perhaps it was the State, Nat was unsure, but any individual had the right to harvest the trees if they so desired. I wouldn't hazard a guess as to how many generations it had been since they had been pruned, but still they survived and fruited, even if surplus dead wood was throttling their hardy crowns. It was beginning to drizzle. I snapped a few quick shots as an aide-memoire and we hastened back to the house.

Returning by another route, Nat paused to point out a stone building on a neighbouring hillside. 'You must visit that chapel,' he said. 'It's constructed on a Roman olive farm. Ask Julia.'

Back in the yard, Nat returned to the farmers and their hundreds of kilos of oleaginous fruits, while I strolled up to the kitchen to drink coffee sweetened with Julia's honey, lifted from their single hive, the taste of which had been permeated with wild thyme and carob, *harruba* in Maltese.

She served me black and green olives, both of which were extraordinarily good, and oil that had been pressed the previous afternoon into which I dunked her homemade Maltese bread. I was beginning to realise that I was in the company of a culinary goddess whose recipes for curing olives were simple but ingenious. As soon as the fruits were picked, she soaked them for five days in unsalted water to extract the bitterness. Afterwards, for black olives, she added rosemary, orange peel, wild fennel and coriander seeds before curing the entire mix in brine. For the green drupes, the additives were lemon peel and parsley followed by the same brine curing.

I had noticed as I had made my way inside and up the stairs to the first-floor kitchen that I was being peered at from many directions. Their grounds were populated with fowl, caged or strutting freely about. If one could but obliterate the thundersome din coming from the mill halfway down the garden, the air vibrated with coos, quacks and crowings.

Settled comfortably at the kitchen table with a glass of local wine in front of me, I asked Julia about the birds, a surprising collection including two pairs of magnificent golden pheasants.

She smiled and raised her lovely dark eyes. 'They are another of Nat's passions.'

'And the emu?'

The emu was Harold. His partner, Sally, had been stung in the throat by bees from Julia's hive and had dropped dead instantaneously. The following day, their sole offspring, a young female, had suffered the same fate, expiring with equal alacrity, leaving Harold a solitary widower.

'He's very lonely,' lamented Julia, ladling out spoonfuls of delicious homemade basil-and-fig compote to accompany the bread, olives and now a little goat's cheese from Gozo.

As I was leaving, with promises to return on the morrow, I went to introduce myself to poor bereaved Harold. He was a most extraordinary creature, with wide, unblinking marmalade-orange eyes, a disproportionately small head stuck on a hosepipe of a neck attached to a perfectly round, fluffy body with a turquoise pate that looked as though it had been sculpted out of enamel, or mosaic. He pumped his sinewy neck up and down, craning back and forth, imitating a periscope, in vain attempts to communicate beyond his enclosure. The poor fellow looked as though he had popped up out of a cartoon. Nat saw me communing with his bird and signalled me over. He wanted me to admire an alley of olive saplings growing in black plastic pots.

'You recognise them, don't you?'

Well, I didn't.

'I snicked a couple of dozen shoots off the Romans down in the valley, a few samples from each tree, and flew with the cuttings to an olive institute in Italy, where an expert team assisted me in propagating them.'

I gave them another look. They were fruiting. Small black olives like shiny obsidian or onyx beads and barely larger than those on the mother trees we had visited earlier.

'Quite a feat,' I mused.

'It justifies Pliny's statement that an olive tree never dies, eh? Taste a drupe,' insisted my host. I dithered. One never eats olives directly from a tree. They are sharp, inedible and must be cured.

'Please.'

Tentatively, I picked one while Nat plucked off several others and offered them to me in the palm of his hand, his eyes dancing expectantly. Confused, I bit into the drupe. To my astonishment, it was sweet, not acrid at all. It was *edible*. I ate another and found it was also sweetish. The olive is a bitter fruit. It becomes comestible once it has been marinated or pressed into golden oil, but these fruits plucked directly from a tree, albeit a tender sapling, were edible.

'This is remarkable.'

Nat was nodding excitedly. 'We, that is, Julia has also discovered that, centuries ago, a variety of white olive grew in the San Blas district over on Gozo.'

A white olive, was this madness? Was I in the company of lunatics?

Since Nat had purchased his pressing machine, farmers all around him had been awakening to the possibilities of harvesting their long-forgotten, occasional trees. 'This is worth the effort,' they were saying, and a nascent olive community was peeping through. The word was spreading, but white olives . . .

'Congratulations.' I grinned, still pondering the remaining fruits in my hand, which, due to the stickiness of my palm, were bleeding a purple dye.

The discovery that early varieties of olives might have been edible when picked directly from the tree could entirely change the story of this fruit's history. Its impact was spinning through my mind.

But before I could mention it, Nat was confiding: 'I have a vision, a grand plan. Shipping the centrifuge machine, building a mill was stage one, but it was only the beginning.' His eyes were on fire again. Someone was calling to him from the yard, but he did not seem to hear them. Two thick-waisted matrons in spotted navy-and-white frocks toddled by, carrying between them a hefty glass demijohn, wrapped in woven straw, slapping with freshly pressed oil, still cloudy with sediment. He barely noticed as they called good evening.

'And your dream is . . .?'

'To propagate and replant some of the long-lost Maltese varieties, including the white olives. I want to track down each and every ancient tree still surviving on these islands, take cuttings, and, with the knowledge and expertise I am learning in Italy, I want to plant and spread them. The

Romans, for example, you can see for yourself how splendidly they are shooting up. And imagine the advantages in kitchens if the fruit doesn't have to be cured. And then there is that white variety ... His pupils were dancing like bouncing balls. 'If we can find any still surviving. That's Julia's task. She'll source their whereabouts from her old books. I intend to return Malta and Gozo to their earlier silver, oleiferous glory. And by so doing, to assist in the reforestation of these barren, rocky lands over the decades and centuries to come. What do you think?'

What did I think? That possibly I was in the company of a visionary, but more likely a madman. White olives!

'This reminds me of that opening scene in *All Creatures Great and Small*,' observed Julia gaily, as we flew through the countryside, brushing close against vintage limestone walls in her open-top car, listening to a Reader's Digest six-CD collection, *Great Moments from Opera*. Of course, the car Julia was driving was a compact and rather elegant silver Peugeot 206 that Nat had bought her as a Christmas gift, not the bone-rattler Chris Timothy and I had rocked around the Yorkshire Dales in, in all weathers.

'Nat spoils me,' she purred. 'My family used to love that programme. We didn't own a colour television until I was twenty so we watched it huddled together at home in St Julian's Bay, in front of our dinky black-and-white set.'

I was wondering if I should mention the white olives. 'I haven't yet understood how these islands went from fertile to barren,' I admitted.

'In the written history of Malta there are many gaps,' began my driving companion, who, with her solid-framed sunglasses, tall figure and scraped-back, sleek, ponytailed black hair put me in mind of Jackie Kennedy. Even when she was out in the yard, her wellingtons sinking into damp duck feed, tossing handfuls of mushy bread and squares of homemade cakes to the flocks of honking fowl, she still sported chunky liquid-clear diamonds on her fingers.

That very morning after I arrived, Nat had shot up to the house for a five-minute coffee break in their expansive yet homely kitchen where three well-fed cats slept on the cushions of three wooden chairs, and he'd said, 'If you've got any questions, ask Julia. She'll be able to fill you in. She's terrific, aren't you, darling?'

'Oh, Nat! More coffee, Carol?'

And with that Nat was gone, scooting back to the thundering business of the mill, his mobile ringing incessantly. It was then that Julia had escorted me up to the top floor of their house, climbing as though to a secret tryst, to a room that resembled an artist's atelier, an enviably capacious wooden attic dedicated to her formidable library, writing desk and one of several 'television-lazing areas' the house possessed. A room to cuddle up together in, to spread out in, to be expansive within, to write or think in, to sit at the table by the French windows drinking a good glass of wine, or stand out on the balcony and appreciate the sea view over St Paul's Bay. I had not known that she was a writer. 'Oh, only little things,' she had cooed, waving the subject aside. 'Bits, you know, for magazines, and a couple of books. Nat will give you copies, if you like. He keeps boxes of them in the garage. I only write about Malta.'

When the Maltese speak English, there is a rhythm scoring the words that is seductive, almost soporific, and Julia spoke it as though she were being stroked, like some pleasured velvet feline.

She had pulled from her shelves leather-bound editions as

large as atlases, written in 'old Italian', others in Maltese, a photocopied piece in a Sicilian dialect, all of which she read and understood.

'Do you speak old Italian?'

Did she mean Latin? I shook my head; my modern was sufficiently rusty.

'Look, look here.' I bent to look, by which time she had closed the tome with a sigh as though it had disappointed her, slid it onto a table and smiled. 'It's hard to know where everything is. Let's go for a drive and I can show you places and we can have lunch. Do you like having lunch? I do. Then I won't have to run endless errands for Nat – he's quite obsessed, you know, but so brilliant – and I can tell you everything you want to know.'

And so here we were, hurtling about the hillsides, whizzing through glens, lapping up the late-autumn weather because Julia had expressed her desire to introduce me to the real Malta, to inland villages where the grey-haired spinsters and widows sat out by the *franka* stone walls in the sunshine, spinning wool and tales of times gone by.

'It will be a fun way to fill you in on the island's history, to answer your questions and to get to know one another. Move in, stay for as long as you please.'

I think if I had been a man I would have fallen in love with Julia. She belonged in a book.

Our first stop was St Pawl Milqi ('St Paul Welcomed'), the chapel site Nat had pointed out the previous day. It was named to commemorate the reception Paul had received when he and fellow seafarers were shipwrecked on their journey to Rome. From the hill where the chapel was situated, the salt-pan district known as the Bay of Salina was visible. To the left, now silted up, was another bay, St Paul's, featuring a statue of the apostle that pinpointed the spot where the saint's endangered ship eventually perished, spilling crew and passengers into the shallow waters.

'And when we escaped we found the island was called Melita and the natives showed us unusual kindness.'

'This stone chapel,' said Julia, leaning out, drawing the sun's warmth towards her, 'was constructed on the remains of a Roman villa, which, in turn, was built upon a Phoenician habitation. Sections of the villa have been unearthed and it was clear from what had been found that the building was part of a substantial estate where olive farming was the dominant activity. Let's go outside.'

We picked our way across precarious steps to grounds jumbled with stones, scattered with substantial grinding wheels, stone-hewn irrigation systems, underground storage caves. It was remarkable.

'See,' pointed my hostess, 'they have found several of these. *Trapetum*. Roman pressing wheels. Isn't it wonderful?'

Months later along my journey, on the isle of Lesvos, I learned that *trapetum* (a new word to me on that day) came from the Greek *trapel*, meaning 'to turn around', and that Pliny noted in one of the volumes of his *Natural History* that the first known *trapetum* was carved in Athens around 400 BC.

After the Phoenicians had been all but expunged from the planet during the course of three Punic Wars, the Romans kept up the olive estates and the extraction of oil with characteristic vigour. Wherever they conquered they expanded the 'inherited' plantations, claiming the produce for both food and light. The city of Rome was illuminated by olive oil.

'Two thousand years ago, when Rome controlled this olive farm, it was much closer to the water. The bay reached further inland, but over the ensuing centuries, due to the deforestation that eventually caused rains to wash away the island's topsoil, the bay silted up.'

Back within the chapel, leaning out through open doors atop the excavation site, we looked down upon a flattish valley, an extended dried-out gully with views marred by unsightly electricity lines, to stands of stunted carob trees and, beyond, in the semi-distance, a calm sea.

'This villa was built according to criteria laid down by Cato, who wrote that a property must sit close by a road, a navigable river or the sea. In its heyday, this estate would have pressed its oil, decanted it into jars, loaded the filled containers on carts or donkeys and transported them to the port, a distance of little more than several hundred metres. Once the waiting ships had been stowed with the amphorae, they would have set sail directly for Rome or chased the winds to the transit routes across the seas to the extremities of the empire.'

'And at that stage in the islands' history of vineyards and olive groves, the estates would have been productive and lucrative?'

'Phoenicians first, followed by Romans. Each would have reaped hefty commercial returns from the farms. Whoever was the proprietor would have been an influential and rich figure. I'm sure Nat wishes it had been him,' winked Julia. 'Recently, while building rain ducts over at Marsa, several Roman warehouses were uncovered, where oil and wine were stored before being shipped from the port to foreign destinations. Their ample size gives some idea of the extent of activity here.'

Not far behind us was a hill bearing the name Jeblazzara, the 'Hill of the Presses'. Were there other presses situated further inland? If so, how extensive had oil production become by that stage?

'Strabo, Greek geographer and historian, born in 64 BC, described Malta as a fertile and prosperous island.'

'Olive trees don't just die. Their regenerative powers are

like no other. Yet, when the Knights of St John relocated here, they encountered lands barely more arable than the original limestone rocks. So what happened between the departure of the Romans and the arrival of the knights?'

Julia replied with a smile, 'Ah, my speciality. In the written history of Malta there are many gaps even after the Romans, but what is reasonably certain is that long after the Romans had departed, their empire in ruins, the remaining resident Greeks, who probably tended the estates, were captured and sold as slaves by the Arabs, who appeared on the scene in around AD 870. Those Saracens were keen cultivators of fruit trees, particularly citrus, and it is largely thanks to them that the western Mediterranean is rich in oranges and lemons, but they were not olive farmers. Added to which, they were eager to sow cotton plantations, which were more lucrative. So they set about uprooting huge tracts of the olives and vines.'

'So, it was the Arabs who destroyed the olive groves?'

'Partially. Certainly those early stages of deforestation eventually cost the islands dearly. However, the Arab domination only endured a couple of centuries. It was during the centuries after their departure and before the knights came on the scene that our flourishing agricultural heritage began to wither through neglect.'

Still listening, I stared at the woman accompanying me. Set to one side had been the pampered beauty. Julia not only knew her subject, she was passionate about it, and lucid. We were once more walking the grounds, where a retired Englishman in shorts, brown sandals and socks with a canvas satchel over his shoulder was in heated debate with the gate-keeper – this chapel with its Roman villa farm was not open to the public. Due to their prominent position in the community, Julia and Nat had access. I was fortunate. The irate Brit was yelling that he wanted to paint a watercolour and couldn't achieve it from the far side of the fence. He was strawberry with rage and his words were not polite.

'There was no ruling power on the islands. Pirates, predominantly North African, squatted our excellent natural harbours, using them as bolt-holes and storage docks, and when the islanders attempted to drive them away, the cut-throats terrorised the enfeebled communities. So threatening did life become that those with resources fled to Sicily. The coastal areas, previously well cultivated, were deemed too dangerous to farm or inhabit. The residents uprooted to central acres, praying for protection. Trade with Sicily, Italy and Spain was all but severed because no shipping fleet felt safe with swart corsairs plying our waters. Our archipelago gained a reputation throughout the Mediterranean as treacherous. Merchant ships avoided these channels, which left the struggling inhabitants isolated and impoverished. Their lands grew neglected, olive groves and vineyards were untended, and the devastating long-term result was that the terrains lost their ability to produce. Without trees to protect the earth, to feed it with their fallen leaves and cover, the alluvial and agricultural soils lacked nourishment. Wind carried away vast quantities of dry earth, malarial fevers spread, and when the rains came, they washed away the remaining topsoil, silting up bays such as this lovely one before us. The islands were reduced to scarred barren slopes.'

'But with the arrival of the Knights of St John in the sixteenth century matters improved greatly, yes?'

'Indeed, the city of Valletta was constructed, its peninsula was fortified, and the restoration of fruit, olives and vine orchards was undertaken. The vineyards and groves were once again husbanded and oil was pressed for local consumption and for exportation.'

'So, where are those farms?'

'Tragically, financial interests took precedence yet again. In the late eighteenth century, Spain called for even greater quantities of cotton. To accommodate this growing demand, all existing estates were once more uprooted, myriad plantations destroyed. In their place cotton was sown. Zebbug, which had once boasted over eighty thousand vigorous olive trees, was depleted. The problem was compounded by the Americas. When they began shopping for cotton, the production of oil and wine ceased entirely on the Maltese islands. It was the final nail in the coffin of what had once been a buoyant olive industry. And Nat believes, if his plans come off, will be again.'

As we were pulling away from the chapel, Julia offhandedly threw in her conviction that olive cultivation on these islands did not commence with the Phoenicians. 'They brought their alphabet so written records began with them. But,' she said, 'ferals were indigenous to these islands.'

'You think wild trees were harvested?'

'Yes.' She felt they might have been a source of food and possibly inspiration for the people who constructed the temple sites, but there was no documentation to prove it.

I remembered my visit to the museum and the spellbinding temple artefacts. Those Neolithic peoples occupied these islands around the time the Bechealeh groves were being planted.

'What evidence have you for this?' I begged. By now we were walking along a deserted beach. A snack bar was serving hot drinks and pea pasties, *pastizzi*.

'I must have read it somewhere.'

'You don't remember where?'

We sat down by the water, bottoms buried deep into the sand, drinking coffee from paper mugs, watching the sea and a lone fisherman dragging his *luzzu* ashore, painted in striped bands of blue, red, green, a design of boat that has barely changed since the Phoenicians, a craft that in various reincarnations might even date back to Egypt. I recalled the fishermen in Marseille and Turkish Foça. The only difference for such men today is that their vessels are powered by diesel, not their sweat.

'No idea. I'd have to trawl through all my books.'

Julia waved and the fisherman waded up the slope of sand towards us, a lean-cheeked, middle-aged figure with mildly bloodshot eyes and hair crinkled by salt. His name was Vince. He seemed grateful to pass the time of day. I asked about the Eye of Osiris painted on his boat's hull, which I thought arrived with the Phoenicians, but I was not sure. A protection against curses, perhaps, similar to the *nazarlik* in Turkey. Vince knew nothing of its provenance, only that it kept him safe at sea. Every fishing boat in the Maltese islands displayed this symbol, this charm. Julia then wanted to know if he was carrying an olive branch aboard.

'Of course,' he cried. 'You think me stupid?'

Sailors, fishermen laid a freshly plucked olive branch close to their engines whenever they set sail, she told me, to calm the sea, keep it peaceful. 'They probably took the habit from the sprig brought to Noah,' she laughed.

Certain locals believed that a few prayers and an olive branch could lead them to an abundant catch, Vince told us. He was returning from checking on his nets, but he wasn't expecting a catch worth selling today, a few red mullet, baby tunny, a mackerel or two, sufficient for his family's needs. The day before, he'd been blessed with an excellent haul so he wasn't too concerned. Today was the turn of another for good fortune.

'The Lord looks after His own.' But life was much tougher than when he'd started forty years earlier, 'and the cost of living in Malta . . .' He sighed, not bothering to complete the sentence. His father had been a fisherman and his before him. It was in their ancestry, but there were fewer fish today. The fishermen multiplied, but not the sea creatures.

We wished him well and set off. We were way too late for lunch, but my hostess suggested a glass of wine. As we drove I noticed that the sloping hills towards the coast were studded with cube-shaped stone outposts. These were used by local trappers, explained Julia, who were intent upon the songbirds. We spotted many hunters on the hillsides and down near the coastal fringes gathering their prey.

'Bird-trapping has become a heated issue here. During Malta's negotiations to join the European Union, we were the only country granted a transitional period of change though Maltese shooting and trapping activities are contradictory to European directives. Swallows are shot for training practice, birds on reserves are targeted illegally. The perpetrators cite the French.'

'Whose hunting is strictly regulated even if there remain cases of illegal activity,' I countered.

'Carol,' interrupted Julia softly, 'they follow the example of the Italians, who shamelessly break every rule in the book. Sardinian warblers reside here. They, among other species, are threatened. Goldfinches, greenfinches, linnets, chaffinches are trapped and sold in cages. Songbirds are hunted here and songbirds spread seeds.'

We fell silent. We were sitting in a square in the inland town of Mosta, drinking glasses of local Sauvignon Blanc.

'Only two generations ago,' Julia remarked, 'local viti-culturists purchased their grapes from small-scale farmers or shipped them from Sicily and Italy, pressed them without even removing stalks and then trundled the barrels round in horse-drawn carts to sell to housewives, who waited with jugs for the filling. Today we have flourishing vineyards and tomorrow olive groves!' We toasted the moment.

Beneath towering plane trees that reminded me of home and tinged my heart with a fleeting ache of loneliness and a sense of confusion about my choices, we listened to the starlings congregating in the treetops. There must have been a thousand of them and the chatter was strident. Since the latest outbreak of avian flu, the hunters had continued to shoot but did not bother to collect the dead prey, simply left them to rot. My mind was back at home, remembering how our *oléiculteurs* detest the starlings, *les étourneaux*, because they swoop in great black flocks like locusts and strip the olive trees clean. The starlings had brought to mind the hash I had made. I had forced my organic vision upon our farm and caused the loss of an entire harvest. I mentioned it to my companion. I wondered if Julia and Nat had considered the maintenance of so many plantations soon to take root on the islands if Nat's dream became a reality.

'Will you recommend spraying the trees?' I asked her. 'It's a real dilemma for us.'

She shook her head. 'It need not be necessary.' She cited one of her obsolete books, the volume in which she had first discovered the existence of the *zebbug abjad*, white olive, where the author, a professor of natural history, had written about olive care on the islands in earlier centuries. Pruning took place in the autumn directly after harvesting, which was achieved early to avoid the risk of late fly attacks. The fields were hoed 'thrice annually', to keep down weeds and allow all possible opportunities for rain and moisture retention. I was fascinated to hear that, because when the islands were rich in olive groves these had been of many mixed varieties and the larger fruit varieties were pollinated using smaller varieties to assist the cross-pollination.

Our farm is exclusively *cailletier*, a producer of small drupes; perhaps that is why it has never needed cross-pollinating.

'But do any of your books advise on the subject of insecticides?' I pressed.

She suggested that songbirds using the groves as their billet had probably taken care of the job by feeding off the flies. After severe winters, attacks would have been slight because the hibernating pupae could not survive in the cold weather. Julia said that she was sure Nat had not thought that far ahead. She promised to look later and see what, if any, advice there was to be found on the subject. 'And when you return from Gozo, do come and stay. We can browse my old books together and you can help me sell my jams at Nat's Olive Open Day. It will all be such fun.'

I was seduced, not only by Julia but also by the possibility of discovering an olive culture here as ancient as the Lebanese trees. I had not counted on this. I changed my plans and decided to make a single day trip to Gozo and then stay with my new friends.

On the island of Gozo, I hiked to Haz-Zebbug or 'The Village of Olives'. From there, I pilgrimaged to Ghasri, which means 'Place Where Things Are Pressed'. I discovered the same legacy as the mainland: there were no olive groves aside from youngish fellows. I took a taxi to San Blas, a pretty crescent-shaped bay where the white olives were supposed to have grown. I found only citrus trees and wondered if it had been the Arabs who had planted up the original orchards here, destroying the unique white olives in their wake. After, I took an early-evening ferry back from Mgarr to the mainland, watching the local Gozitans waiting by the dock for friends, loved ones or provisions. The sea route remains the only contact Gozo has with the outside world. In that respect, unlike most other islands in the Mediterranean, it has maintained its ancient traditions.

Sailing between the islands in the rosy aftermath of sunset, watching the emerging stars, which I am incapable of reading, my thoughts were on Odysseus, departing from Calypso's Island (believed to be Gozo) intent on keeping the Pole to his left if he was ever to reach his homeland of Ithaca; the Phoenicians, navigators par excellence with their fifty-man galleys; Paul's shipwreck; indeed, all those I had so far encountered who had ploughed their way across this aquatic highway, travelling by the stars without charts or maps. Men lacking the ability to read an alphabet but who could decipher the heavens and knew the geography of shores, headlands and bays. I tried to penetrate the fears and delights of those early sea travellers, the loneliness of those sailors in the dead of night and silence of the wine-dark water, their loved ones waiting behind on distant shores, sometimes for men who never returned, the wind whipping at their loose clothing as it was at mine. I thought of the transience of all our journeys.

In the Acts of the Apostles it says of Paul's shipwreck, 'And falling into a place where two seas met, they ran the ship aground.' Paul landed on the north-eastern end of the mainland, not far from this Malta–Gozo channel, where the eastern and western Mediterranean meet, not too far from where I was landing, and not far from where, I was glad to say, friends were awaiting me.

Celebrations for the Olive Open Day were in full swing when I arrived back. This evening, the Friday, was intended as a feast for the villagers and farmers thereabouts, or for anyone who fancied a glass of wine and a slice of Julia's roasted suckling pig and it seemed that the entire island had turned up to fête the olive with my hosts in an acoustically exhausting, open-walled outhouse. To escape the thrumming crowds, I disappeared into the garden. I wandered over to say hello to

Harold, who was leaning over his fence, eager for companionship. From the emu, I sought a passage through one of the groves, appreciating the stillness, the night air, the rustling of leaves. It was welcome after the rush of conversation-making. A pack of dogs was gathering down by the open gates, possibly chums of Oliver, the black Labrador, who had been closed inside the house for the duration of the festivities. Their paws made a sound like sandpaper against the soft stone entrance. Crickets and frogs were at their nightly chatter and there was a strong smell of petrol. The narrow road was banked up in both directions with fleets of stationary cars. The generosity of this couple seemed boundless and I was thinking how unexpected had been their welcome and the inspiration of these islands, and then there was that gentle tug, all too familiar to me, the pang of leaving, of moving on. I had found a temporary family here; a situation I always searched for and had done all my life.

The following morning, the world of the yard was up and quacking. Birds were screeching, wings beating from every direction. It must have been feeding time. Julia came knocking on my door as two peahens strutted a path beyond the open window, to announce she had 'found the book'. During breakfast, the kitchen was buzzing with upbeat news, high spirits, stories and preparations for the following day, which was to be a demonstration of olive pressing. A camera crew were interviewing Nat for a magazine programme; Maria, the cleaner, had arrived with dried figs for Julia, a gift traditionally given on this day, the feast of St Martin. Picked from her own garden in August, she had left the fruits to dry in cool storage into September, then heated them for twenty minutes in the oven until they had begun to soften and spread, toffee-like. Afterwards, she had placed them in layers, adding fennel seeds, ground hazelnuts, whisky, aniseed liqueur and vermouth. They had been marinating for a month and reeked potently. Julia was drinking coffee and sewing something made out of checked cloth. She seemed to have forgotten the book and was recounting the story of Donald, a duck who had been donated to their menagerie by friends who could not keep him because he was always diving into their swimming pool and had, on one occasion, almost drowned a guest by rendering her unconscious in the water. But after Donald had arrived, they had discovered he was afraid of water. He waddled off in fear of his life whenever the hosepipe was activated. The real reason he had been discarded by his original keepers was due to his habit of diving.

'Dive-bombing into people was more accurate,' stressed daughter Lizzie.

He would wait in hiding on one of the upper balconies for Julia to leave the house and as she approached her car he swooped, full pelt, slamming himself against her. Or when she returned with shopping, the bird would descend, damaging, smashing whatever she was carrying.

'Whenever they tried to catch him, he always managed to escape, or turned on his heels and snapped at theirs. He was uncontrollable,' Julia sighed.

'What happened to him?' I asked, pouring coffee.

'I came out one morning and as usual he targeted me, but I jumped out of the way and he went slap bang into a stone wall. Nat found him later, curled up on the ground, looking snug and asleep, but he was dead.'

'Poor Donald,' sighed the lovely Lizzie.

Julia finally remembered the book and slid it casually across to me, open. I glanced at the exposed page. Nat, who was zipping in and out of the room as though attached by elastic, was waving a letter. He had secured financial backing for the propagation of 10,000 Roman saplings. *Ten thousand*!

The bank who had agreed to underwrite the project were promising to post flyers in all their branches, Nat told me gleefully, offering locals the opportunity to buy the juniors at a very reasonable price. Nat would give the new farmers guidance and support, and when the fruits eventually needed harvesting, they could take advantage of his facilities, if they wished to. The triumph for Nat was the knowledge that Malta would be reforested with its own historical olive trees.

I was only partially listening.

After promising Julia that I would sit up with her after dinner and assist with jam-jar labelling, I set off for the temples. Their beauty, placement, alignments were haunting me, so were the words in the book Julia had dug out. I needed a final root about, to penetrate something of the mystery. Understandably, all the voluptuous figurines, the fertility goddesses and the rest of the artefacts discovered within their enclosures were in Valletta at the museum I had visited on my first day, but it was not the contents of the temples that were exciting me, rather the missing sections of the structures themselves. All the temples were open to the heavens; they had no roofs. Malta possesses three temple sites. I began with the two down on the south of the island, the complexes of Hagar Qim and Mnajdra, where I was escorted by a black-faced mongrel who was eager to befriend this lone visitor and whose coat was the buff tone of the sandstone slabs. Set close to a coralline limestone bluff, with the sea sweeping and fawning at their feet and the tiny island of Filfia within view, these two temples were awesome megalithic constructions and pre-dated both Stonehenge and the Egyptian Pyramids by a thousand years. I sat with my new canine pal on a stone block, gazing out to sea, sipping mineral water, fancying I heard temple chanting, but it was doubtless just the wind gusting across the cliffs. I was contemplating their seaside position, their accessibility by water.

Then, to Skorba. The Skorba temples, towards the north of the island, pre-dated the two I had visited earlier. The setting of Skorba might have seen human habitation as early as 5200 BC, but the construction of the temples dated from around 4500–4100 BC. Approximately the same age as the birth of the groves in Bechealeh. Indeed, a touch earlier.

From their position, on a clear day, I was told I would see Sicily, a mere 70 miles north. I could not. Sicily, from where the people who designed and constructed these remarkable stone centres of worship originally hailed. It is held that the earliest settlers were farmers, agriculturalists, who crossed over on rafts or primitive boats from Sicily, bringing with them pottery, grains, seeds, foodstuffs, all that was required for the founding of a new society. The staple diet of those temple people was wheat and barley foods. They reared live-stock: sheep, goats, pigs, and they were fishermen, of course. But might they have transported with them on their seafaring timber vessels cuttings from trees, a cultivated olive? Or might they simply have brought their expertise to domesticate the feral examples they found here?

All this was long before metal. Quite possibly before the invention of the wheel. To shift, transport and position the monolithic limestone slabs used at these sites as temple walls, they would have needed to lever them with substantial cuts of wood. They might even have reached a level of devel-opment that told them round logs can roll heavy weights. Who knows, perhaps they had progressed one stage further and understood the principle that a horizontal log in between two round cuts of trunk is a moving machine. We cannot know. Whether or not they created wooden wheels, we cannot know. Because wood, unlike stone, does not preserve, which is why all these sites were open to the heavens. The solid, monumental stone doors and walls remain, the roofs have long since disintegrated, but in prehistoric times those apertures were closed over.

The book that Julia had casually mentioned and then dug out from her library was entitled *Skorba* and was penned by an eminent archaeologist, David. H. Trump. In the book there is an appendix, written by a botanist, Dr C. R. Metcalfe of the Royal Botanic Gardens, Kew. Dr Metcalfe wrote, 'Of ten samples from the early Neolithic level, six are certainly *Cerci siliquastrum* (Judas tree) and two more possibly. Some of the diagnostic microscopical characters of the remaining two are very obscure. One sample is probably *Crataegus* sp. (hawthorn), a second, more surprisingly, appears to be Ash (*Fraxinus* sp.).' He goes on to say, 'The ten samples of Copper Age material (TX, East Temple) are all olive *(Olea europaea)*. It is quite impossible to distinguish wild from cultivated material of this kind from microscopic characters.' But there was a footnote: 'The samples came from the destruction level of the temple pl XA, and must represent the timberwork of its roof. The implication is that they were well-grown olive trees, not from the wild scrub olive.'

I was knocked backwards when I read that footnote. The wood used to roof these temples was olive wood. The olive as a wild tree is shrubbier than its cultivated cousin. It is unlikely the ferals would have produced trunks sufficiently substantial to use as timbers to cover the openings. Instead of olive, those Stone Age peoples could have chosen the Judas tree, which grows a sturdy hardwood trunk. But no, they used the olive.

Wild olive trees, or cultivated? If the trees were cultivated, which seems more feasible because cultivated trees have solid trunks and would have made hardy, resistant roofs, then it implies that the cultivated tree did not arrive on the Maltese islands with the Phoenicians, around 850 BC. It suggests that the olive was being cultivated by Stone Age man here in at least 3000 BC.

While farmers were planting trees in Bechealeh, these Stone Agers were rafting themselves across from Sicily and building temples that outstrip most modern architecture in magnificence and design. It also suggests that if there were cultivators of the olive here at this period, they were farming olives not much later than Bechealeh.

At one or other of the temples, I found stone slabs into which rounded and semi-smoothed central, circular dips, like the cup setting in saucers, had been carved. Foolishly, I didn't note down at which temple, because it did not immediately occur to me that the utensil I was looking at was probably a primitive form of pestle and mortar, a quern, a crushing bowl for olives. I have since learned that no fewer than eleven querns have been found at these sites; querns that experts believe were used for pulverising olives and have been dated as Copper Age, 3000 BC.

Sicily and Italy are abundant in olive groves. Malta and its islands were equally fecund once upon a time. Is it possible that these quintessentially Med trees were growing wild everywhere on this united land mass? Is it feasible that when the Phoenicians landed here from Tyre in around the ninth century BC they had no need to carry along the olive tree to teach the locals its cultivation, because the natives were already way ahead of the game? The trees in Lebanon have been carbon-dated at six thousand years old. Seven, if one listens to the claim of the French archaeobotanist. Evidence of Neolithic man here at Skorba has been dated to 5200 BC. Simple arithmetic shows us that Maltese Neolithic man was creating a civilisation, building settlements, feeding himself seven thousand years ago, which is one thousand years before the cultivated trees in Lebanon were planted, but if we accept the French carbon-dating of Bechealeh, it would have been at precisely the same time.

While I sat in the warm November sunshine calculating dates, asking questions, two brilliantly green lizards were fighting on a Neolithic stone wall. My Mediterranean olive story was a deeper, more venerable mystery than I had ever dared to dream.

Returning back to my friends, I was greeted by Harold, peering out, pop-eyed, from beyond the cage. I was feeling upbeat after my outing and wanted to cheer up the poor fellow. He was rocking from side to side as I spoke to him and I began to imitate his movements. Slowly swaying as he did, in rhythm, keeping time, and then, as he grew excited and more exaggerated in his swaying, I mirrored that too. We must have been a bizarre sight, this half-bald bird and I, a middle-aged woman, jiving and gyrating with a tall fence between us. The more frenzied Harold became, dancing, striking the ground, slapping out a beat with his webbed feet, the more I kept pace, until he was clawing at his wooden fence, kicking and beating time, pumping his neck as though a spring had snapped and he could not keep it still and was bursting to break free of his enclosure. I was out of breath, wanted to stop but felt I had to keep dancing for Harold's sake.

Unexpectedly, Nat came up behind me, watched us for a moment, then stepped forward and whispered gently in my ear, 'You know that's Harold's mating dance, don't you?'

I froze, mortified. I had been driving the poor lonely bird insane.

That night the clocks went back. Winter. The following morning, my last few hours in Malta, a liquid, warm Sunday morning, I was to be found manning a trestle table-cum-stall selling jams, preserved tomatoes and olive paste. As the eager crowds began to amass, shouting requests at me, I struggled to keep abreast of the frenetic commerce, grappling with orders in Maltese. I glanced to my left. Alongside me, poised on a garden chair, sleek in slacks and sunglasses, my new friend was busily signing copies of her latest cookbook. Someone came charging towards me, wanting to know where I had left the jars of jellies. I shrugged. 'You must know!' they wailed before shooting off, exasperated. I had learned from Julia the previous evening – we had sat up till after two labelling her jars – that early olive farmers here had worked with the seasons and songbirds to combat tree diseases. It was not until the late nineteenth or early twentieth century that the notion of killing off olive fly with poison had occurred. Ore of arsenic was the base of several solutions. Slowly, even more than with the rampant hunting, they had begun to endanger the flocks of songbirds by poisoning them too and thus augmenting the fly infestations. I wondered then if Abdullah's farm in northern Syria was protected from blights by a proliferation of songbirds. How could I protect our smallholding and the creatures living upon it and yield fruit? Ore of arsenic is a recognised carcinogen. Pesticides constitute the largest single use of arsenic compounds. Julia had listened to my concerns and realised that it was a matter she and Nat would need to address later as Malta grew silver and bosky again.

Time to go. I placed a handful of coins given to me for two tangerine jams in the tin biscuit box Julia had supplied me with and closed its lid, smiling. I was sad to leave these passionate people, but excited at the prospect of Carthage and its navigational heroes, the Phoenicians. I was on my way to Africa.

I threw my camera over my shoulder, strolled back to the house, collected my bag, kissed Oliver on his shiny black head, waved to Harold, who looked as though I had broken what remained of his heart, and then set off for the airport, unnoticed. One last glance back showed Julia and Nat intermingling with the throng, lost in their work of regeneration, while the onlookers, clogged in doorways, bulging out of the window frames of the outhouse containing the shiny Italian olive press, watched on with fascination at a process, a way of life, possibly, surely, as ancient as Stone Age man, kickstarted into the Maltese twenty-first century thanks to the passion and vision of one man. What had I found? A gentle revolution born of the earth and the islands' history. Even a waiter in Gozo had eulogised the 48 gallons of wine he produced every year for his family's consumption. I took a bus to Valletta and another to the airport. I felt uplifted. Malta, at the heart of the Mediterranean, was beginning to beat again.

Tunisia

Tunisia and Sicily were, once upon a time, linked by a land ridge, a mountain chain that has been submerged for somewhere in the region of 44 million years. It is this underwater partition that divides the Mediterranean into its two halves, its western and its eastern basins. Situated further west and slightly south of Malta, Tunisia is at the extreme limit of the eastern basin. The distance between Valletta and Tunis is approximately 400 kilometres, a mere 216 nautical miles, yet there is no ferry, no public sea traffic, running between the two continents at these points. This was a journey I had wanted to achieve by water, but I would have been obliged to return from Malta to mainland Italy, to Genoa of all places, and make the voyage from there. Finally, I chose the swifter route; fifty minutes by air.

I departed from Valletta, regretfully leaving behind my new friends, on a fine autumn Sunday at midday. Church bells were ringing across the island while the faithful sauntered home from Mass in milky warm sunlight, preparing themselves for the weekly gathering of family and, no doubt, a *lampuki* fish pie or an invigorating rabbit stew already on the boil. On my flight were less than twenty passengers, predominantly businessmen. We landed into a French-speaking world of palm trees, *politesse* and crazily honking horns. Minarets, *muezzins* and Moorishness: Tunis on a hot, working afternoon.

How far back could this North African olive story be traced? I wondered.

I had not booked anywhere and needed lodgings so made my way to the tourist office, where an exceedingly portly Arab in a navy suit and *chéchia*, the traditional burgundy cap, bowed his head and asked how he could be of service. I explained that I was intending to continue to Carthage the following morning and would prefer a location close to the city centre. He offered to find me a place directly near the Phoenician site. I had visited Carthage twice before and had on each occasion taken a hotel in the vicinity. This time I was looking forward to an evening moseying about Tunis's famous kasbah and enjoying the buzz of the capital. I decided to stick with this decision.

The tourist officer, whose jowlish features put me in mind of a Levantine money-lender, accepted my choice without further debate and drew a thick catalogue towards him, explaining that I shouldn't bother with the five-star addresses because equal value could be had at a more respectable rate from one of the many three-star establishments. I appreciated his consideration. He nodded graciously, closing his eyelids. A cluster of moustached drivers hovered nearby hoping to pick up a fare. I shook my head, told them not to bother with me, that I intended to take the bus, but my friend from tourism advised me against this. 'The sun will soon be down. You cannot delay. You are well advised to take a taxi. They are not expensive and perfectly safe. In fact, it will be as cheap as the bus.'

He raised a podgy arm, his elbow never leaving the table, and wiggled five sausage fingers, the pinky of which was adorned with a large blue-stoned ring, and a tall driver in jeans and leather slippers stepped forward.

'I can vouch for this man,' the tourist officer assured. 'He will take you wherever you decide to go. But, first, allow me to telephone on your behalf to secure you a reservation at a good price, though you will have no difficulty finding a bed.'

I decided to busk it and requested the driver take me to the centre, to Avenue Habib Bourguiba, which was within easy walking distance of the medina, the old walled city, with its souk and unsleeping life. Riding in from the airport in a vehicle that had definitely seen better days, my driver was wheeling to and fro, crossing from one lane to the next without regard for anyone else on the motorway. He spun the wheel back and forth like a madman, but he was not alone. Virtually every other driver was tackling the task of getting to town with equal freneticism. It began to dawn on me that this battered vehicle was quite possibly uninsured and was shaving the neighbouring motors within a breadth of my life. I was in the front passenger seat – there were no safety belts – and should he swing to his right an inch further, I would be the first hit in the collision.

Whoever we drew near, my driver lifted his fist, shook it and roared at the offending opponent, railing against their appalling road sense.

'Please would you take it more steadily,' I requested, nervous of exacerbating his mood further.

'It's the same for everyone,' he explained.

'I am not in any hurry.'

'But I am! It is Ramadan. The sun is setting . . .'

Then it dawned on me. 'And folk are hurrying home to eat.'

'Nothing has passed our lips since sunrise.'

Having spent the last couple of weeks in Catholic Malta, I had completely forgotten that the Muslim world was observing the second half of their annual month of fasting, Ramadan. I cast a thought to Quashia working back at the farm. I glanced at my watch. He would be strolling down the driveway about now in his lambswool hat, eager to prepare his evening meal. When I am at the farm during this period of observance, he talks of nothing but food all day long. I smiled, missing my dear Arab friend, wondering how the recently seeded vegetables were coming along in our greenhouse. During our last conversation, I had forgotten to ask. My concerns had been about the olive loss. I had also forgotten to ask about Lola, who I had feared was pregnant, but our new vet assured me the dog was not.

'Careful, please!'

The car alongside us screeched and veered away.

Ramadan is a religious adherence I am well acquainted with, but this was my first visit to an Arab country during its conformance. My taxi dropped me right across the street from the rather characterful five-star Hotel Africa and five minutes' walk from the medina. Fortunately, not half a dozen steps from where we were parked, opposite the Africa, was a much more modest establishment. I paid the requested fare (considerably more expensive than the bus) and the driver insisted on carrying my bags inside. A swift glance up and down the famous avenue afforded me views of a puzzlingly deserted and dimly lit thoroughfare. It was as though I had arrived during a curfew. Within the lobby of the hotel, two male receptionists were seated at a table rigged up behind the desk alongside the key pegs and were tucking into a hearty dinner.

'Bon appétit,' was my greeting.

One rose from his meal and picked a key off its peg. 'Vous voulez une chambre?'

I nodded.

There remained one room available on the top floor, for the princely sum of 40 dinars.

'It is clean.' He smiled, returning immediately to his hot

food. It was precisely what I needed: simple, clean and, at £16, exceedingly inexpensive.

Fifteen minutes later, I set out to stroll the crepuscular avenue as far as the medina. As in all Middle Eastern and Arab bazaars, each souk specialised in a single trade and I was hoping to visit one of the oldest in Tunis, the thirteenth-century perfume-makers' market.

Souk el Attarine specialised in essential oils. It was situated close by the medina's Great Mosque, Jami ez-Zituna, or the 'Mosque of the Olive Tree', so called, allegedly, because its founder taught the Koran at its location beneath an olive tree. The tree-lined street was this capital's Champs-Élysées, constructed by the French during their occupation. The Greeks, Turks and British never made it here. The French were the colonisers and, second to Arabic, French is the language. Everywhere vestiges of that colonial past allowed me to feel at home. During those years, this was an elegant boulevard lined with art deco and belle époque buildings. Aside from a smattering of men seated here and there in the many cafés that stretched the length of the avenue, smoking their water pipes, drinking tea or soft drinks, it was completely deserted. Not even a fellow foreigner to break up the stillness; no one besides myself abroad. Contributing to the sombre or melancholy atmosphere was the lighting, curiously subdued, at half-mast, as though someone had forgotten to switch it on. Was it set thus because it was Ramadan, because Muslim Tunisia had gone indoors to dine, to end the day's fasting?

On a whim, I decided to slip off the main thoroughfare and wander about the back streets. Perhaps I would find more activity there. Here, if that were possible, it was even more dimly lit, but after a short traipse down streets lined with banks and tall administrative buildings with elegant white stucco façades, all heavily barred, I crossed into an untidy square and from there found myself entering a passage where a market, partially lit with paraffin lamps, was in progress.

The stallholders, all male, not a woman in sight, were sitting on crates or low stools in the evening gloom. A few were in conversation, but most were idling. As I passed through the narrow lane, rendered even less negotiable by the spilling over of boxes stacked with plastic toys, brightly coloured slippers, ladies' underwear, chunky CD systems for sale, several glared at me with stern-eyed mistrust. A couple nodded *bonsoir*, but most stared. I had never before felt intimidated in Tunisia, never felt judged or unsafe, but suddenly I did. I had dressed with consideration in a calf-length skirt and, in spite of the November warmth, was wearing a long-sleeved cardigan, but the glowers caused me discomfort and I wished Michel were with me. So uncomfortable was I that as soon as I could, I retraced my steps, hastening to the medina.

A youngish Arab, late twenties, plump with bulging eyes, appeared from nowhere at my side, attempting to engage me in conversation. '*Soyez bienvenue,*' he kept repeating.

Usually this would cause me no concern, but I had become a little jittery, uncertain. 'What do you want?' I snapped.

He wanted me to understand that nothing would be open this evening. The souk was closed. I thanked him for his concern and continued on in the direction of the old city. Moments later he was back, trailing alongside me, suggesting another market. It was an authentic artisanal street fair and this was the very last evening of a week of trading. He assured me that even if the souk was closed, this special market would be open and I would be able to purchase carpets at very good prices. It was, according to the self-appointed guide at my side, my very last opportunity to find such bargains.

I thanked him once more for his trouble, explaining that I did not wish to buy any rugs. This seemed to amaze or perplex him. A tourist who was not looking for carpets at knock-down prices – did such a creature exist? He bowed and disappeared, offering, as a parting reconciliation, mint tea at the hotel where he worked as a waiter. *'Baksheesh, madame, bien sûr.'*

The central square, Place de la Victoire, leading to Bab el Bahr, or Porte de France, the arched gateway that is the principal entrance to the medina, was almost as deserted as everywhere else. A trio of police officers were standing about smoking, a few youths were playing a ball game, their cries echoing in and around the empty arches and lanes, while an outdoor café to my right was jam-packed with men in old brown suits and various forms of head covering, smoking hubble-bubble pipes, playing dominoes, sitting at exterior tables in twos or threes, passing the time of evening. Ahead of me in rue Djamaa Ezzitouna, I spotted a couple of shirted chaps heaving crates of soft drinks up a flight of stairs and my eyes were drawn to a first-floor bay window where I saw a sign: *Restaurant*. I clambered over the crates and ascended the stairs. I was reminded of Pankali's fish diner tucked alongside the entrance to the spice market in Istanbul. My hopes were high for another such fine meal. A wooden arabesque-decorated ceiling caught my eye. Paintings recalled caravans of turbaned traders with laden camels; long-trekked desert routes. A young, slick-haired waiter stepped forward, bowing his head, wishing me *bienvenue*, welcome. An arrangement of long tables had been laid out, clearly in preparation for the arrival of a party. This surprised me. The entire Arab world was currently at its repast, eating early after so many hours of fasting. The waiter offered me a seat in an adjoining wooden room, while politely reminding me that the establishment served no alcohol. Inviting as the place looked, I declined. Solitary dining was a habit I had grown used to after so long on the road, but the prospect of eating alongside a party was not what I fancied.

I made my way back up the boulevard, looking for an alternative, until I reached the Hotel Africa, where I enquired at their reception for somewhere fairly central for dinner. 'All restaurants are closed for Ramadan,' they informed me. 'You should eat here.' It was after nine so, thinking it late, I opted for that choice.

The house security officer followed me, accompanying me in the lift without a word. Stiff-lipped, cropped head, what did he think I might be about? The dining room on the second floor was soulless, a conference space serving a buffet to a handful of foreigners: a retired French couple proving picky about their food, a party of young Japanese who giggled continuously and an exceedingly tall, black African gentleman in bright-blue and green *galabiya*. I ate my meal, head buried in my book.

Later, as I stepped from the hotel to return to my *pension*, I was astonished to find the avenue buzzing with life: horns hooting, traffic at a standstill, top-of-the-range Mercedes parked nose to tail along the kerbsides; cafés whose existence I had barely registered two hours previously had set up exterior tables and were overflowing. Waiters were flying back and forth. Families, smoking, moustached men, women in full chador with tiny children in strollers, other women in jeans, were perambulating to and fro. It was hard to believe this was the same city on the same evening.

When I rose to catch the early bus the next morning, the breakfast room where I had held out little hope of obtaining even a coffee was operating at full pelt. I was not in tune with the country's rhythm, having forgotten that all practising

Muslims were obliged to consume their only meal this side of sundown before the sun was up. In fact, those remaining were the stragglers. It was a little after five in the morning. A steaming buffet was bubbling and gurgling in cauldrons. I settled for black coffee sweetened with Tunisian honey and set off for the bus station.

By the time I arrived at Carthage, having checked into a nearby hotel, the clouds were black and the heavens had opened. I had not been lucky with Carthage. This was my third trip to the long-lost Phoenician city and, on each occasion, the sky had let rip so forcefully that I had barely completed a tour of the site. Every image I had of this place was of mud. After a trek around the adjoining museum, I returned to my hotel to read.

The North African colony of Carthage was founded by Tyrian-Phoenicians in approximately 814 BC.

Carthage is a derivative of the original Phoenician name Qart Haddasht, or the 'Next City'. It suggested expectation, new beginnings, promise.

For those supremely skilled Levantine traders, descendants of the biblical Canaanite peoples, this shift of emphasis from the Levant to a setting just south of the heart of the Mediterranean, at the mouth of the Sicilian Channel, was propitious. Tucked behind the head of a small peninsula on the south-east side, it protected them from sea winds, but gave them full view of any unwelcome fleets sailing in their direction. The chosen site also contained two natural harbours.

Carthage was not their first port in what is modern-day Tunisia, but it became their glory because it boasted, undoubtedly, one of the finest maritime locations in the entire Mediterranean. From this strategically perfect position, they more or less had the advantage over all shipping activity from east to west and from south to north. The founding of Qart Haddasht had given them the perfect sentry point for both Mediterranean basins and the perfect disembarkation stage from which to extend their trading links.

After the Assyrians captured Tyre in 720 BC, Carthage became the Phoenician capital. From their new city, they dominated commerce in the Western world. The citizens were now Carthaginians with a language of their own, Punic, which had evolved from the Phoenician tongue spoken by their forefathers in Tyre.

The French historian Fernand Braudel suggested that when the western basin of the Mediterranean was first colonised, it represented something like the New World to Aegean emigrants, with Carthage as an 'American' power. I like this analogy. The only difference perhaps is that the Carthaginians' military force was a bit of a makeshift affair. Their army, when it became an imperative, was predominantly made up of African mercenaries, many of them Libyan. Employing foreigners allowed the indefatigable Levantines to concentrate on their business, and had they been left in peace to trade, they would have troubled few. They were at odds with the Greeks over trading grounds, they sank the odd ship here and there to keep the competition out of their markets and were given to the gruesome sacrificial practice of cremating live children, but fundamentally they were not warmongers. Their strengths lay in their navigational and commercial skills, which were second to none. Wherever they travelled they created commercial bases or ports to break their voyages or winter until the winds were once more favourable. They traded with everyone, they bought tin from Spain and Cornwall in Britain, gold from the west African coast, exchanged and sold ceramics, textiles and pottery. They also counted amongst their trading partners the Etruscans,

Maltese, Sardinians, Sicilians and Cypriots. If they could not set up trading posts or warehouses where they landed, they hawked their wares directly off their boats or in open markets.

Hailing originally from the eastern Mediterranean, the olive tree and its oil were cornerstones of their way of life, and, quite naturally, they made commerce out of them. Amphorae, used for the transportation of their oils, wines and various other commodities have been found aplenty from the wrecks of their sunken ships, particularly on the route between Carthage and Marseille, and some argue that the first olive trees transported to my corner of the Med arrived with the Phoenicians in vessels that had embarked from Carthage, rather than with the Greeks from Asia Minor, the Phocaeans. It is hard to know. Certainly, Massalia is a Phoenician word. What is clear is that from the mountains of pottery shards discovered around the Mediterranean and Europe it is evident that the Phoenicians and their Carthaginian descendants shipped olive products to wherever they set sail. In that respect, we have a great deal to thank these tenacious traders for.

I awoke the following morning to a blue sky and sun. A remarkable upbeat change that cheered my spirits no end and I set off directly for the ruins.

Carthage is a breathtaking Mediterranean setting, even if the remains are less than spectacular. It takes a certain imaginative effort to mentally restore the magnificence of what was once such a legendary trading centre because the Phoenician city was completely destroyed in 146 BC by the Romans, who, once they had conquered and razed the entire place to the ground, ploughed it with salt. A vindictive gesture. D. H. Lawrence wrote that the Romans 'smashed nation after nation and crushed the free soul in people after people'. After years of fighting three Punic Wars, rising-star Rome was victorious. The Romans levelled the greatest trading empire of the ancient world and certainly crushed its free soul. Rome was determined that Carthage would never rise like a Phoenix from its ashes. But, ironically, after such ill treatment of the local soil, what Rome had won in these new colonies was the richest oil-producing spread in the Mediterranean. Even today, though it is rarely acknowledged, Tunisia produces far greater quantities of olive oil than Italy and it is, though not publicised, exceedingly fine oil and frequently discreetly purchased (at less than competitive prices) by modern Italians to feed their world-market commitments.

The Romans named their newly won colony Africa, a bastardisation of the Berber word 'Ifriqa', and they governed at first from Utica, once a Phoenician port further along the coast towards Algeria, now inland. A century or so later, Julius Caesar constructed Carthage anew, but the land was deemed cursed, good for nothing besides grazing. Still Rome eventually rebuilt and ploughed fortunes into their North African holdings, building roads, bridges, causeways, planting seemingly endless groves of olive trees the length of the coast all the way south to Djerba. Using local Berbers as labour, they pressed more oil than they had anywhere else before and they shipped it to the farthest reaches of their empire. They created a wealthy olive industry.

I found a stela close to the Carthaginian site entrance. Upon it was written a quote by one El Bekri. It read, 'Any person visiting Carthage every day of his life and doing nothing better than looking around him would every day find a new marvel that he had never seen before.' A tragic reflection. The siege of Carthage, during the third and final Punic War, lasted three years. During its eventual downfall, the city burned for seventeen days and nights before the sated flames died down. I recalled Turner's golden strokes of that hell-like conflagration. So which marvels had El Bekri been referring to? Indubitably, the landscape and surrounding countryside had plenty to please the eye, but as historical sites go, both the Phoenician and Roman remains offered poor pickings.

From literary descriptions and a model of the city I had seen, I attempted to conjure up the layouts of six-storey flat-roofed buildings that had once swept down the hillsides to the shore, the wine fields and olive presses, temples, darkened cellars and storehouses for the amphorae brimming with oil, bakeries, wheat fields. Were there teams creating perfumed oils to pour over the flesh of the rich? Where would they have stabled the famous Carthaginian elephants captured wild from the African forests? Where were housed the kitchen staff, the poor old slaves, the fleets of oarsmen to man their mighty galleys? Where had stood the Temple of Eshmun that had been the Carthaginians' final refuge and from where Hasdrubal, brother-in-law of mighty Hannibal, exited, waving an olive branch, begging for mercy – so disgusted was his wife by this act of cowardice that she threw herself with their offspring into the fires of the disintegrating city, while Hasdrubal received clemency from the Romans? How many maids poured and carried the oil for the cooking, for the kitchens? How many kitchen gardens superabounding in songbirds and mellow fruits fed this mighty metropolis? I posed this question as I stood in the sunshine and watched two mellifluous golden orioles perched on bushes in the *maquis* that had grown up through the rubbled and lichened stones, and then my attention wandered. I became fascinated by a scrawny Arab, cigarette between arthritic fingers, sweeping broken twigs off minute portions of a ground mosaic. Precious little to keep clean.

I climbed up and down and in and out of what remained of Carthage's vanquished glory, pausing to take a snap of the occasional capital or broken-nosed marble face; I attempted to mentally reconstruct form out of heavy, time-weathered stones, to trace avenues that might once have been flanked by cypresses, or squares shaded by fig trees, searched in vain for the lakes of temple olive groves as described by Gustave Flaubert, and tried to find the site of the theatre but lost my way and ended up outside a spanking-new health spa. I crossed over the tracks of Carthage-Hannibal, a dinky station decorated with blue-and-white faience that serviced commuters between Sidi Bou Said and Tunis, peered at the ancient gardens of the Antonine baths, drank tinned lemonade at a plastic table in view of the last column standing at the water's edge, took several illegal photographs of the Tunisian president's palace even though signs everywhere forbade the act, exchanged a few euro coins as a favour for a curly-haired guide who grinned that they were tips and could not be changed at the bank – coins I later discovered were fake. I then decided to take a little walking tour of twenty-first-century Carthage.

The Carthage I found was an exclusive residential neighbourhood inhabited by the president, politicians and beau monde. With palm-lined winding lanes, chic, fashionable boutiques and fabulous whitewashed cubist villas screened behind blue wrought-iron gates, it was the Beverly Hills or Super Cannes of Tunisia. Bougainvillea, in full *papier poudre* blossom, in every shade from its most common purple to a delicate, washed-out tangerine, were straddling walls, trunks of cypresses and pines, climbing like rampant weeds, creating riotous colour and privacy. Olive and banana plants towered above wrought-iron gates. Palms stood sentry. I took a leisurely stroll by the tranquil seashore, where lone figures fishing punctuated the jetties like obelisks. The peninsular location remained breathtaking, unspoilt. Its core position between the waters of the East and West still holds true, for although it is a Muslim state (after the Romans came the Vandals and then the Arabs), polygamy has been outlawed. Here, women have assertive, respected roles to play and they are entitled to dress as they please; the mores of this nation bow East to Islam and West to Christendom.

What surprised me was the army of security gathered like drowsy bluebottles at every street corner. I had never seen so many police here. Even if the majority were lolling about in vans with their booted feet on dashboards or leaning against trees, wearing black, anti-reflect sunglasses, smoking endless cigarettes, the manpower was formidable. I enquired of one what was going on and he informed me that the country was preparing for a three-day World Summit on Information, which was to be held the following week and would block every hotel between Carthage and Hammamet. President Zine El Abidine Ben Ali was assuring his international guests of the highest standards from 'this land of civilisation, culture and enlightened thinking'.

I had intended to spend several days in the vicinity but decided, before the influx, to move on. I made a swift visit to the tip of the peninsula, to the neighbouring lighthouse village of Sidi Bou Said, once so exquisite with its narrow, cobblestone, winding *ruelles* and perfectly cubed whitewashed houses with their sky-blue filigreed shutters and wrought-iron and nail-studded doors in matching blue. In earlier trips, I had loved this hilltop enclave, tracing the footsteps of Colette and Simone de Beauvoir, who used to frequent this artists' haven, where waiters wore ambrosial white jasmine tucked behind their ears like rolled cigarettes, its mosques, private whitewashed courtyards fragrant with the scents of freshly watered ferns and potted flowers. I had relished the children shrieking and running circles around me in the streets, drinking sweetened green tea with sprigs of fresh mint at the al fresco Sidi Chebaane café. Set on a rocky spur, its views down to the Bay of Tunis and across to the 'two-horned' mountain of Bou Kornein, where the distant light had a faintly blue tinge to it, were dizzying, but with each return visit I found the village had grown more meretricious, swarming with ever more hawkers and day trippers.

As soon as I could I boarded a *louage*, an exceedingly inexpensive form of transport not dissimilar to the public taxi system in Lebanon. My decision to pause at Hammamet, an overconstructed stretch of sweeping shoreline, was not to visit olive groves. This was a personal detour. A dear friend from Devon had talked of a village, dating back to the Romans, that specialised in hand-painted pottery. I wanted to pay it a visit. In order not to lose time, on what was intended to be a single-night stopover, I checked into a tourist hotel on the beach. After a walk along the sands and a delicious swim, I set off in search of the artisanal centre, which I achieved with no difficulty; it had all but been swallowed by resort spread. The wares on offer were splendidly arrayed and I bartered light-heartedly for a set of hand-painted terracotta Berber dishes. Satisfied with my newspaper-wrapped purchase cradled in the crook of my elbow, I sprinted to the bus station, hopping impatiently in between the flow of unruly traffic at a busy junction. And that was the last I remembered.

The snap of a bone cracking and the crashing of plates nanoseconds before my skull hit the tarmac were barely registered as I, momentarily, lost consciousness. Opening my eyes, a circle of Tunisians were bending over me with deeply concerned expressions. Before I could argue, I was bundled into the back of a taxi and delivered by a young couple to my hotel. They had seen my accident; I had fallen in a pothole in the road. Responsibility for me was handed over, and in spite of my embarrassed entreaties, I was carried by two porters to my room. The hotel doctor was summoned. Nothing as far as he could see was broken, but I would require a series of X-rays. My protestations were to no avail. He fed me a painkiller and promised to return in the morning. Until then I was to rest. The porters returned with a bevy of ice buckets. Nothing was too much trouble.

Alone, I lay back against the pillows, considering my plight, my route, when the phone alongside my ear burst into life. It was Michel.

'Just ringing to know that you are fine,' he said.

'Who told you?' I murmured. I judged by his confusion that no one had been in touch. How would they? I had not given any details of next of kin. I mumbled something about an accident and immediately, even within a tranquillised haze, understood that he would be on the next plane over to organise the deferment of my journey if I said more. Somehow, I managed to assure him that I was sleepy and that although I had stepped into a pothole, no damage had befallen me.

After several X-rays and check-ups, the black-haired Dr Douglas Ross of Tunisian medicine, who had driven me in his own little car from one clinic to the next, and whilst doing so had recounted tales of his life in Hamburg as a student and young intern, assured me that I had suffered shock, a sprained ankle, perhaps also a chipped bone and a small knock to my skull. Rest was all that was required and then I would be perfectly mobile, fit as a fiddle. He refused all payment. His argument was that I had arrived in Tunisia healthy and they would send me away in the same condition. I lounged by the pool for three days reading John Banville's *The Sea* and Wilfred

Thesiger's *The Marsh Arabs* (the marshlands in Iraq were drained by Saddam Hussein to deprive the inhabiting Arabs of their homeland, punishment for rebellious acts against him), and then, hobbling to the beach, sat for another three, observing, discovering.

Abu Abdullah El Bekri (1014–94), I learned, was a Spanish-Arab geographer and historian, an eleventh-century Herodotus, one might say. The difference was that El Bekri never set foot outside his native province of Córdoba. He wrote copiously on the climate, the peoples, the geographical aspects of North Africa, Europe and Arabia, but all his references were based on literature or word of mouth from travellers and merchants who had journeyed across the continents. I found quotes from this esteemed historian in which he described the marble remains at the ancient city of Carthage being so abundant that even if every man in Africa had assembled there to take his share of the booty, there would not be sufficient manpower to carry off the spoliation. He wrote that it was Africans who first plundered the city, not Europeans, and that well into the tenth century people were still stealing boat-loads of goodies. Roman Carthage, then, or partially fanciful?

Gustave Flaubert in his novel *Salammbô* described cotton plants in Phoenician Carthage ascending the trunks of cypresses. Cotton was not introduced to this part of the world until the Arabs conquered the western Mediterranean some six hundred years later. Cotton from as far afield as Persia had been brought to Greece by Alexander the Great. Egyptian cotton had in earlier centuries been farmed and spun along the banks of the Nile. Long before the Western world had discovered it, India had maintained a thriving cotton textile industry. Herodotus wrote, 'There are trees which grow wild there [in India] the fruit whereof is a wool exceeding in beauty and goodness that of sheep. The natives make their clothes of the tree-wool.' After the trade routes opened up, India shipped cotton and cotton textiles to Persia, Greece and Rome. The Greeks, Romans and Egyptians used it for their sailing ships. It must have created quite a revolution in the Mediterranean maritime world. Alexander the Great introduced cotton fabrics to Greece in the fourth century BC and as a fashion textile it quickly took off both for nobles and slaves. Given the Phoenicians' genius for trade networking, it is possible they swapped another commodity for cotton plants somewhere around the eastern basin, but as an ornamental plant, cotton would have been an unusual sight.

Were Flaubert's imaginings of the lost city as fanciful as El Bekri's?

Lying by the pearly calm of a surprisingly warm early-winter sea, surrounded by blubbery Russians for whom this hotel catered by the plane-load, foot strapped and resting on a deckchair, I concluded that the precision of such details was of passing consequence if the writers' imaginings helped recall for us lost civilisations, giving back to us for fleeting moments a sumptuous history snatched for ever from our grasp by the itchy, bloodstained fingers of war.

I had been intending to continue by *louage* all the way south, passing through the *sahel*, before crossing the Roman causeway by bus to Djerba. From there, if my visa came through, I would continue on to Libya, whose border was a mere 100 kilometres further east. Although walking was now possible without a crutch, there was still discomfort and I was concerned about taxing my ankle unnecessarily. Before leaving, I went in search of 'Dr Ross' for a final check-up and to thank him for his kindnesses. He was interested to know my purpose in his country and, having learned it, strongly suggested that I rejig my plans, rest awhile.

Almost everywhere I was discovering that the very mention of olive trees brought about Mediterranean smiles and a sincere desire to assist. This doctor was no exception.

'The olive tree is protected in Tunisia as it once was by Solon in ancient Greece. Our laws forbid the removal of even one olive tree to build a house,' he told me while checking my blood pressure.

The region in Tunisia with the greatest spread of olives was the *sahel*, the lush littoral – *sahel* is an Arabic word meaning 'shore' – where there are hundreds of thousands of olive trees. This includes Sousse and the country areas outside the sprawling industrial city of Sfax. The dominant variety, *chemali*, is similar to Nice's *cailletier*, though the *chemali* produces more fruit.

These facts I knew, but he went on to tell me that during the eighteenth and nineteenth centuries, in the sahelian south, it had become a custom for all dowries, in other words the women's wealth, to be invested in the purchase of olive trees. The demand from northern Europe at that stage for oil was enormous and created stability in those southern Tunisian economies, where women were beginning to represent a fair percentage of the ownership. It gave them independence and it became the habit for females, whenever they acquired money, to invest it in olive groves. In a male-dominated Muslim society, this gave them status. It was enlightened. No matter how their marital situations evolved, they were secure. Even before the French arrived in 1881, southern Tunisian women had a key to their security and independence: olive farming.

After thanking the doctor warmly for this nugget, I returned to Tunis by *louage* and from there took the short internal flight to Djerba. This re-route meant that, disappointingly, I was skipping the oilfields of Sidi El Kalani, but I deemed it more prudent to rest in Djerba. I had planned to disembark the south-travelling *louage* in Sfax, a place I had never visited, known internationally as Oil City, and from there take a bus inland to an area that I had learned was rich in Punic olive groves. Today, oil companies, predominantly Kupek, are drilling in these groves, which is a delicate issue. These Phoenician groves are situated a short distance from the Roman theatre of El-Jem, the largest of its kind outside Italy, and local Tunisian kids had been collecting Roman coins unearthed in the olive fields, which they sell to the oil men. I had heard that they approached the rich foreigners with the coins tied in bits of rag and haggled with them over a dinar or two. The men usually bought the entire batch and then hung on to anything worthwhile. The rest they ditched back in the fields for the kids to find all over again. More valuable was the Roman glassware: small jars, usually scent pots, which they smuggled out of the country. Punic fields, then, planted by the Phoenicians and, later, expanded and husbanded by the Romans. I had been hoping to discover olive specimens that were nudging close to three thousand years old, but, alas, that was not to be.

Djerba, *la Douce*, 'the Sweet, the Ambrosial', were the praises bestowed upon this southern island by mainland Tunisians. My first impression was of a dun-coloured, desiccated, sea-girthed flatland with white-domed habitations flanked by expiring palm trees, where the salt pans were as still as death, where tourism had not impacted. Until I learned there were four beach zones, each stringed with over-elaborate hotels, clubs and bars servicing the holidaymakers. In this way, the tourists were left to their own devices – alcohol was served in the 'zones touristiques', restaurants were open during Ramadan – while the religious sensibilities of the islanders were not affronted. Aside from these littoral fleshpots, the island was inhabited by Arab and Berber peoples and two small communities of stalwart Jews.

I found a *pension* five minutes from the sea, along a winding sand track, darkened by deep shadows. It was owned by a middle-aged Argentinian woman with strong aristocratic features and gunmetal-grey hair. Thirty-eight dinars a night, approximately £15, was the room tariff. It was as silent as a Trappist cell; white, pristine, bare; containing a single bed, chair, built-in cupboard and tiny cubicle with shower but lacking curtain or tray. It looked out upon a small grove of dried-up palms, several of which had been decapitated. Their carrot-top fronds like dead machine-gun rounds lay between marram and sand. If I stretched my torso over the ledge and twisted my body to the right, I could glimpse the choppy water, churned up and clouded by sand. An added bonus, given my recent fall: the guest house was close to one of the resort hotels where there was a thalassotherapy and medical centre. I was delighted with my find even if its austerity marginally heightened my sense of solitariness.

Everywhere was parched, the colour of old brown paper. Even the tousled palm trees were dying from the aridity, their fronds wilting like motorless wings. The Phoenician name for Djerba was Meninx, which took its roots from *me-nages*, meaning 'water shortage'. Women washed their laundry in the Mediterranean. During my inland walks, I passed wrinkled herdsmen, bent like flick knives, leaning over staffs, standing over a quartet of sheep feeding ravenously off a few blades of grass along the sandbanks. I encountered a father and small boy gathering handfuls of those tufted grasses. Was it for their beasts? I hoped so. The twisted old olives with their uncared for, lifeless crowns were growing out of camel-coloured soil. Forests of wild olives had once grown everywhere in Djerba, I had heard. Had there been a climate change? It did not seem at first viewing that forests of anything could survive here, but during prehistory this island had known the wild *olea*. Those remaining, the cultivated fellows, appeared to be centuries, not millennia old. Others I encountered were youngsters, orphans, and not faring well. All the groves were sparsely planted. This was due to the desiccation. The roots needed to spread, tap deeper, to find moisture to feed off. If the trees were planted any closer together, as ours at home were, they could not survive. The topsoil here was nothing but biscuit crumbs. I walked for miles, looking for wild trees or ancient clues, imbibing the atmosphere, passing lone figures in brown smocks and straw hats riding crocky old bicycles. The few women in the lanes were diminutive with leathered, masculine faces. They were entirely wrapped in white robes with large straw hats perched atop their covered heads, like perambulating bandages. The island reeked of mashed olive fruits, yet there was no one in the fields. The groves were deserted but not harvested; no sense of industry anywhere.

The world was hidden behind their flat-roofed, white cubed houses with Mother Mary-blue doors and shutters. White silhouettes, white cupolas of the mosques like upturned breasts against the desert. They gave off an air of freshness, air to aspirate, not this windy, clawing climate – Djerba is a part of the Sahara. In bygone, forgotten centuries, the desert was greener, less arid, perhaps that was when the forests of wild olives survived here. Many of the doors and entranceways displayed a hand, palm exposed, painted or carved. *La main de Fatma*. Fatma was the revered daughter of Muhammad. Her hand was believed to bring good fortune, protect against evil spirits. I was coming across such superstition everywhere. I learned from a Djerban doctor who examined my ankle that the fingers represented the five pillars of commitment to the Islamic faith.

The long month of Ramadan was drawing to its close. L'Aïd el Fitr, or days of feasting, were approaching. It was seeding a mood of expectancy that even I picked up on, but while the fasting endured, there continued a daily ritual of afternoon shopping for the evening meal. This brought locals into the tiny towns that lay baking in the heat and sold little aside from painted pottery for the tourists. On one or two occasions I visited the port town of Houmt Souk (which means 'marketplace'), where the men, exclusively men, were shopping, bicycling to and fro, laden with strings of fresh fish, vegetables, loaves, dressed in long, brown or blue blousons, white pillbox hats that seemed a cross between a *chéchia* and a fez or wide-brimmed straw hats, and leather slippers. Others came with wooden-wheeled carts, clopping side-saddle on donkeys, palm fronds plaited as whips, loading up before the breaking of the fast. One afternoon, I found myself stranded. I had been tracking down a caravanserai, known here as *fondouk*, lost my way, realised it was after five and that all transport had stopped. My *pension* was 13 kilometres out of town. As I had discovered in Tunis, the population burrowed itself away before sundown and the world was in a lull. I could not go to a café; they were all closed, so I wandered along the road in the stultifying heat, heading in the general direction of my monk's room. Strong winds were coming in off the water and the vegetation looked flogged. What notion of Med was this? Was this the *gregale* wind flying down from northern Greece, or the *meltemi* whistling in air channels from Turkey? Those powerful winds that Odysseus battled against.

Flamingos were wading at the water's edge, in salt pools close to the rim of the sea. Clouds of them had flown in from the Camargue and Valencia, rouging the sky. I smiled. Theirs was another Mediterranean route; a celestial crossing. I came across a solitary blue-and-white bungalow set back from the water beyond the salt pans, a short distance from the tourist zone. '*A louer*,' said its sign. I knocked, but there was no reply. I peered through a window. It was empty. I fantasised about renting it, about returning after my journeying. I was growing fond of this 1,000 square kilometres of cardboard-brown adjunct to the mainland, seduced by this sea-girdled land of the lotus-eaters, where the sun on the sand was almost primrose. Like Odysseus's men, I was losing the will to move on.

Djerba is where Homer's hero and crew, after nine days of tempestuous sailing with winds battering their curved ships, eventually put ashore. They ate a land-based meal, and before setting off, Odysseus sent two of his crew plus a third as messenger to scout inland and report back. According to Odysseus, the inhabitants the sailors encountered were 'a race of lotus-eaters that lived on vegetable foods' and 'It never entered the heads of the natives to kill my friends.' Indeed, these easygoing vegetarians gave fruits to the mariners, and after consuming the offerings, the Greeks expressed a desire to stay, never to return to their homeland. But our hero was not about to lose three of his trusty team to an atoll of hippies. He ordered the men to be boarded directly, strapped in irons and kept there until their vessel was safely scudding the open waters.

So who were these mythological love-children and what was the lotus they consumed? There is evidence to prove that there was civilisation here during the Stone Ages and that the Berbers are their descendants. Around 1500 BC, the island knew its first seafaring visitors, who either brought the olive tree with them or found it growing feral, and probably taught the natives how to cultivate it. Those pioneers might well have been early Phoenicians. From Byblos, perhaps? By the time Carthage and other sites on the mainland had been settled, Djerba had become an important crossroads for the caravans of traders trekking up through the desert as well as for the earliest mariners plying their wares along the Mediterranean rim. A convergence of merchants on an island of bohemians.

This terrain, a chunk of Sahara surrounded by salt water, probably never sustained grape or wheat cultivation. Before the Phoenicians arrived and taught the natives how to farm their forests of wild olive trees, offering them an opportunity for commerce, and before the Romans, who built the causeway, planted more trees, sent the ships in to load the produce aboard and generally knocked this easygoing pleasure-loving community into shape, what did they have? They had no amenities or crops to produce beer or wine, so what did they have?

Their lotus was the *Ziziphus lotus*, a thorny, deciduous bush with a sloe-like fruit that could be used for making a form of bread or a fermented drink. The Djerbans chewed the plant's honeyed fruits, which were mildly narcotic and, I suspect, probably a tad hallucinogenic. If so, Odysseus's sailors were tripping, high as kites, which might explain why he deemed it necessary to sling them in irons. If they had simply been stupefied, stoned, it would have been far easier to toss them in their bunks and let them sleep off the effects. Alas, the lotus-eaters' *Ziziphus lotus* has long since vanished from this island so I could not test it to discover.

I gave up on hopes of transport and cut off the track, trudging by the marshy saline waters, limping towards the

shoreline. I was wondering whether the history of the lotus-
eaters was the reason Tunisians refer to Djerba as *la Douce*,
'the Sweet One', when, galloping fast through the waves,
churning up the sand, on gleaming chestnut mares, came a
pair of young Berbers. As handsome as two Errol Flynns they
were, and roguish too.

'Why aren't you eating?' I asked, when they reined in their
horses to greet me. The sun was down. It was almost dark. The
beasts were panting, snorting, champing at the spume's edge.

'Because we're not practising,' they bragged. They were
tricked out in fetching costumes. Tight black suits with white
embroidery; heads in scarves, gypsy-fashion, like a couple of
sword-throwers or ballroom dancers.

'Rebels, then, are you? Not Muslims?'

'Muslims and rebels.' They swaggered, chuffed with the
image. They were desirous of a photo of themselves and I
obliged, but they expressed no interest in the results.

'Got a daughter?' the darker, more devilishly dashing
demanded. '*Une belle jeune gazelle*,' he grinned rakishly.

The other offered me a smoke. I shook my head. The
cigarette rolled from the packet and I noticed, even in the
gloaming light, the stitching that travelled its length like an
open zip.

'Yes, lady, it's marijuana, hashish, want some?'

'No thank you, but I'll score some sloe fruit if you have it.'

'Sorry?'

I smiled, bid them *bonne soirée* and hobbled off up the coast,
with my thickening frame, ever-swelling ankle, bare feet (I'd
taken my shoes off when I'd reached the beach) sinking into
the damp, corrugated sand. In my twenties, I would have
been rendered breathless by their lithe arrogance, their insou-
ciance. Today? I was grateful they had not requested my
granddaughter.

As usual, I was dining alone. At a neighbouring table was a Scotsman with a boyish face. He was thick-necked, tall, broad as a ship's mast. He leaned across from his table and politely suggested that as we were both 'aloone', he might join me. I made my excuses, shielding myself behind work laid out before me, but we struck up conversation just the same. He had driven in from Tripoli.

'I am going on to Libya from here,' I said, 'if my visa ever comes through.'

He offered to assist me. He could 'fix anything for me'. He was 'in oil'. Libya had closed down to celebrate Aïd. He had driven across the border to play 'a wee round or two'. I was surprised to hear there was a golf course on this island where the topsoil was as dry as crumbling bones. I had learned from a Berber working in the garden at my *pension* that they had seen no rain for three years. Occasional downpours but nothing to make a difference. Agriculture was in deep crisis. The farmers were losing heart, abandoning everything for tourism. The Scotsman settled at my side. His name was Duncan.

The eve of Aïd. I took a taxi early in the morning, leaving behind me the coughing brays of beach donkeys, to the southern coast, to Guellala, where there was a Berber museum with a traditional olive mill. After the Romans colonised Djerba, the island's pressed oil was shipped to Rome to illuminate its streets. The colonisers deemed the local product too coarse to be comestible. Nonetheless, the empire brought wealth to the casual ways of the lotus-eaters.

My driver was a Berber. It was the Romans who christened them Berber, judging those who ate animal fats instead of olive oil barbarians. When he learned that I had arrived from Malta, he told me the Maltese word for olive, *ebbu*, originated from his ancient Semitic language. Was it the Phoenicians who travelled the word to Malta? The Berbers, he said, were descendants of the earliest inhabitants of Djerba. I asked him if he knew whether those inhabitants worshipped fertility goddesses. He replied that Berber men were great lovers and gave me his card in case I felt interested in some extra-marital affection.

Set in a tranquil garden, surrounded by clay-pottery stalls and camels, the museum was a curious place of dark, silent corridors lined with wax figures encased in glass, displaying scenes of traditional Berber life; marriage ceremonies, intricately embroidered bridal outfits. The custom for a bride-to-be was to lock herself away for a month before the nuptials. Accompanied by a friend or maid, she passed her days fattening herself up and covering her skin with royal jelly and clay to render her flesh smooth and pale. A dark-skinned woman was judged less of a catch than a lighter one. I was fascinated to note that olive oil was not part of these rituals, which suggested to me that they were born of a desert-based culture. Also on display were snippets from the lives of the Jewish population of Djerba. Jews fled here after the destruction of Solomon's Temple in Jerusalem in 586 BC. The El Ghriba synagogue in the small town of Erriadh, one of the holiest Jewish sites in North Africa, is said to contain stones from Solomon's Temple, carried into exile and used in the construction of the foundations. On 11 April 2002, seven months after the World Trade Center terrorist attacks, the synagogue was targeted by a lorry laden with explosives. Twenty-one people, of whom fourteen were German tourists, were killed. Al-Qaeda claimed responsibility. I was puzzled as to why Bin Laden's monstrous gang would trouble with this windswept dot fringing sea and desert.

I followed arrows to the artisanal exhibits. Here, I found

the *huilerie*, the oil mill. It was underground as is the tradition. Beneath the sand and dust, Djerba is honeycombed with mills, *maâsera*. In 1934, there were 284 traditional oil presses in operation. These production units were all dug out of the rock and clay, invisible from above ground save for their imposing white domes and arched vaults cut with small oblong skylights, through which the harvested olives were deposited. The subterranean placement screened the heat, and the cooler temperatures, around 14 degrees Celsius, favoured the pressing, aiding the extraction of oil from paste. Our *moulin* in France is always chilly for the same reason.

I stepped down into the refurbished mill and was hit by a rancid odour. Dried olive paste and camel dung. I was rather taken aback to find myself face to face with a young camel. No waxed prototype, this was a bedraggled, forlorn creature that lived out his days rigged to a grinding stone. In olden times, camels were the brute force employed to turn the presses in Tunisia. Aside from the fact that the Arabs chose camels rather than mules or donkeys as their beasts of burden, olive crushing was an almost identical process everywhere across the Mediterranean.

The harvested and washed olives were placed on a stone bed shaped like a flat, circular feeding trough, which was elevated to somewhere around thigh height to ease the business of pouring the olives in and decanting the paste afterwards. The mill or grinding stone, known here as an *aguigua*, consisted of one or two heavy cylindrical stones harnessed to a blindfolded camel that turned round and round in circles while these hefty stones crushed the fruits beneath. Its eyes were covered to avoid dizziness. I found it hard to take, but later along my route, on the island of Lesvos, I discovered that this back-breaking process of pulverisation was performed manually by both men and women late into the twentieth century. All this was before the advent of the modern centrifuge machines.

Every so often, the camel alongside me, which was not blindfolded, probably because he was the museum's circus act, looked thoroughly bored, roused himself and loped a circuit, turning the great stone as he went. The unoiled mechanism squeaked, reminding me of the wailing call to prayer. One of the Berber guides came shuffling down the steps, eager to see what I was about, why I was spending so much time with the beast.

'The camel gets switched on Mondays.' He was eyeing my camera mistrustfully – did he think I was from the RSPCA? – and then, beaming, offered to photograph me with his mournful captive. I shook my head and the bemused Berber retreated, slapping up the stone stairs in his leather slippers, back into the sunlight.

Once the olives had been ground, the paste was placed in *scourtins*, the circular mats that resembled flattened shopping baskets. I had encountered these at the home of Mr Dibdib in Lebanon. Here, they were made from alfalfa and called *chamia*. The *scourtin* method had been in common usage right across the Med for centuries until it was outlawed by the EU. Many older farmers, even back at home in France, still claim that this method of pressing produced the finest, richest of oils. It was a fact, though, that these coconut-fibre mats could never be thoroughly cleaned. It meant if a predecessor had delivered mouldy fruit, the taste of his rancid oil was tamped into the woven material and tainted the next producer's oil.

The oil, once it had been separated from the *margine*, the vegetable water, was left to drip into locally turned terracotta jars and stored in a cool, dark space. This does not differ from almost anywhere in the Med, even today. The jars used here had pointed bases; they resembled spinning tops. Their vertical status was maintained by standing them in iron-ringed tripods. The leftover desiccated paste was not used for burning or compost here, as it is elsewhere in the Med; it was fed to the camels. The local farmers believed that it builds their strength. I hoped the poor brute alongside me was to be given a hearty meal of it before long.

Away from the Berber museum, I strode across powdered desert tracks where camels sat in the sand yawning and donkeys laden with pottery jars and ridden by men with rawhide skin in wide-brimmed hats were the traffic. Donkeys, desert, desiccation. I stopped alongside a very dried-out olive tree and picked one of its ripe drupes. Since the sweet fruits of Malta, I had been tasting varieties direct from the branches everywhere. This one was so bitter it all but took the enamel off my teeth.

I visited the nearby pottery town of Guellala, where shopping fever had been unleashed. The last day of Ramadan was children's day and new clothes were being purchased for the offspring. Plastic bags full of beans, nuts, dates, sticky cakes in eye-boggling quantities were being loaded for the evening break of fast later, on this final day of cleansing before the festivities to come. Aïd, pronounced 'Ay-eed', was like Christmas, a three-day affair. It began with prayers at the mosque for the men only, followed by a copious family meal that continued all day long. The island would shut down.

In the marketplace, I found myself in conversation with a hook-nosed Arab with a dark, stippled complexion as pock-marked as the seabed. He asked my thoughts on the museum and I asked him about the Djerban Jews, about the terrorist attack against the synagogue.

'A petrol container was driving by and exploded. It was an accident,' he said. 'Twenty-odd people killed. Most were German tourists, a couple of Italians, several Arabs, but less than a handful of Jews.'

'An accident?'

He shrugged. 'Who knows, maybe not.'

When I threw in the name of Bin Laden, my acquaintance furrowed his brow. 'I haven't heard much about him,' was his evasive end to the discussion.

The wind had calmed. I felt becalmed. I was waiting for news of my Libyan visa and attempting to find some olive gem here that might take my story backwards in time. I took a long sunset walk. Terracotta lobster pots were dotted along the beach. The locals live off the sea as much as the land. Other trades are sponge-diving – black sponges were the island's speciality – and fishing for octopus with clay jars fired in Guellala. Here, they call their coloured fishing boats *les felouques*.

The seascape was a turbulent turquoise, a prairie of shells and driftwood. The sand was furnished with dried clacky palms, several decapitated, eerie-looking fish heads, soles of rubber shoes and an iron wheel, rusted and half-submerged. I found a beached turtle. It had been dead for some time. Attached to its shell were white encrustations, possibly rock barnacles. Its eyes had been picked out and its limbs were beginning to spread shapelessly with decay as though melting. The piercing sorrow I felt for this creature washed up from its environment was illogical, not unlike my concern for the camel. It was something to do with the fragility of life, its indifference, and our cruelties and recklessness. I felt haunted by the drug-funded face of Hezbollah, training up, in waiting for the Israelis; by the Israeli air attacks on Qana. I felt this journey in search of the roots of the tree of peace was leading me into jungles.

A young Tunisian approached. He was walking until the sun had set, until he could eat, staving off appetite with exercise. He had finished work and was at a loose end. He lived in a shack abutting a wooden beach 'bar', set back from the sands on an unconstructed scrub of land. Tourists from a couple of the big hotels frequented the bar, he told me, for more reasonably priced snacks and coffees, or alcohol-free beverages. He was employed as cook but also slept there. It was a solitary existence, but it was the only work available to him.

I asked him if he was intending to spend the following days with his family, to celebrate with them.

He was not from the island. His parents and brother worked a smallholding on the continent, the mainland. They were *maraîchers*, vegetable farmers, and kept a few olive trees, but their patch was insufficient to feed the entire family so he had been packed off to find employment. I told him I was interested in olives and he suggested I look for the Olive Egg Tree in the village of Midoun.

'What is it?' I asked with surprise.

He did not know, he had never seen it, but people had spoken of it.

He earned 200 dinars a month, approximately £82. Occasionally, when he had saved a bit, he would take a *louage* back across the Roman causeway. The bus deposited him in his parents' village and cost 6.50 dinars, or double to return. 'Very expensive,' he explained.

My heart went out to him for his simplicity. He was not attempting to gain anything from me. As we parted, he invited me to drink tea at the café after the holidays.

Aïd. Finally Aïd. The Med was still choppier than I would

have expected, particularly given the temperature, 32 degrees Celsius. An Indian summer. It seemed the ideal moment to go in search of the Olive Egg Tree in Midoun.

I had expected everything to be closed down, but a scaled-down version of the tourist market was operating. A cripple was bunched on the pavement making popcorn and a number of blacks were selling spices. They grew grumpy when I did not wish to taste or buy. Most were descendants of slaves delivered to the island by the caravans and merchants from the African continent to feed the Roman slave trade. Today, they earned their living, when not selling, as musicians or stonemasons. *Jerbian* means 'trader' in Tunisian.

The narrow, winding lanes of the souk were spilling over with coloured plates, most from Guellala, the island's pottery capital. The few women about, walking with purpose, never catching my eye, were wearing the costume known as *fouta*, a flowing white robe with red stripes topped with their wide-brimmed boaters. I felt the African influence. They reminded me of the Candomblé, voodoo priestesses in Brazil. The men wore fezzes or *chéchias* covered with straw hats and the long, grey or brown tunics they called *blousons*. I failed to find the Djerban name for this garment.

When I asked after the tree, everyone shook their heads.

Then a young man in a hurry pointed me to the right. I ended up in a field where two women dressed in pink, surrounded by scruffy, untended olive trees and a few dusty goats, were deep in conversation. I called out. The older, seventy or so, waved me furiously away. She had seen the camera swinging from my neck. I signalled that I was not after photos, only seeking directions. She spoke no French and gestured to her companion, a younger, matronly woman. I explained as best I could what I was looking for, emphasising

'*Zitounet El-Adham*' in an accent that, I realised, rendered their language incomprehensible.

Eventually, the younger beckoned me to follow. The grandmother departed and I stepped after her neighbour. I was dressed in T-shirt, tracksuit bottoms and hiking boots. We arrived at her door. Teenage offspring were bidden out to greet me. They spoke French, of course. Everyone invited me in. It was Aïd. I was most welcome. We entered by an inner open courtyard. The family, excluding father, were lounging on mattresses on the floor watching Arabic television. The sole piece of furniture in the room was a low table. On it, a plate of multicoloured confectionery. It was accepted that unlike the rest of the family, I was not required to remove my shoes. Of course, I protested, but the long-winded business of untying all those laces lost my case. Avoid stepping on the carpet, they emphasised. I sat on a doubled-over mattress that sank like sponge beneath my weight. A glass of cola was delivered and I was invited to eat the plate of dainty sweets. I chose one. It was exceedingly sweet.

'Have another,' the younger, braced-teeth daughter pressed.

I refused. Everyone insisted. And another.

While I was consuming my fifth sticky delight, the father arrived. His expression as he sighted me, face full of cake, crashed awkwardly on the floor in heavy soiled boots, was priceless, but not for one second did he allow his surprise to discomfort me.

'*Soyez bienvenue, madame*,' he muttered, slipping off plastic sandals and entering.

I attempted clumsily to explain why I was gatecrashing their family festivities. Waving aside all concerns, he shook my hand and then lay down on a mattress and rested his head against the room's stone wall. He was in blue serge working clothes, reminiscent of French farmers or Chinese Mao wear. By this stage, it had been agreed that one of the sons would accompany me to the Olive Egg Tree. They assured me it was close by, but nobody was making a move and I was keen to be on my way. More patisseries were delivered and slid in front of me. I refused, but the women were adamant. One choice in particular was a festive speciality, baked only for weddings or Aïd. I had to try it. Last one, I laughed, and bit into the floury, flaky, finger-thin pastry.

'Ah, honey. Do you have bees?'

'No, it's not honey. It is concentrated sugar.'

All the while, the father was talking to me about Muhammad, assuring me that we were both descendants of Abraham but that I and all fellow Christians were successors of one son, while all Muslims were offspring of the other.

'You and I are brothers,' he smiled.

I had finished the sixth cake, not without difficulty. I felt nauseous and my mouth was dry. Speech was out of the question.

Father announced while scratching his feet that Jesus had prophesied the Prophet's coming, but it had been erased from all biblical teachings. He must have misread my inner churnings for shock because he hastily assured me that it was well over a thousand years ago and there was no point in any of us remaining angry or vengeful.

'Best let it be,' he smiled.

The room fell silent. Only dialogue from the television sounded. I needed water.

The father was looking at my hands, frowning. 'Where's your husband?' he asked eventually. Ah, my wedding ring.

'Working.' I downed the saccharined cola, which left me worse.

'Will you stay to eat with us?' chirped the mother, the

woman from the field. 'We have camel meat.'

Her eldest daughter translated, adding, 'It's a delicacy.'

'Are you holidaying without your husband?' Again the father.

'Tomorrow, when my eldest daughter gets here with her family, we'll roast a whole sheep.'

'In France you cook in wine, is that true? We use camel fat.'

'I must leave,' I rasped, struggling to lift myself gracefully up out of the sponge.

The tallest of the boys, a lanky adolescent, rose and after much handshaking and many thank yous and come agains and *insha' allahs*, we were on our way. But first, a kiosk stop for his cigarettes.

'Thanks,' he said to me.

I frowned.

'You were a good excuse to get out,' he sighed.

I expected to hear the screeches of children as we wound through the souk, passing cafés where solitary old men in white hats and tortoiseshell glasses were hunched, clasped hands resting on plastic tablecloths with flies circling. I hoped to follow the children's excited yelps until we found ourselves in front of a hearteningly ancient olive elder, which bore the appellation Zitounet El-Adham, or the Olive Egg Tree.

I asked my teenage guide about its history.

The game the children played was a form of hunt the egg. Reserved for these days of Aïd, it took place beneath not just any olive tree, but this single venerable in this country town of Midoun. From my companion I learned that each child paints an egg in bright colours – similar to the Christian tradition of egg-decorating at Easter – then brings it to the tree and secretes it somewhere about the sinewy roots for his companions to find.

'How old is the tree?' I asked.

The boy took a deep drag on his cigarette and shook his head.

We had arrived at the square. The tree was certainly a mighty fellow, growing in a central position, but there were no children. At its base a display had been set up. The roots, the trunk, its boughs were laden with pottery for tourists. It had been transformed into a stall. I stood and gazed, saddened. Then I cast about for someone who might have an idea of the tree's age and spotted a one-eyed man with wide-brimmed hat, bicycle and straw shopping basket woven from palm fronds, within which were wild herbs and grasses.

He squinted in the bright sunlight with his one good eye, appraising the twisted specimen. 'Many times hundreds,' he pronounced. A torrent of swear words followed as he accused the Tunisians of being thieves because he had never received a penny of his pension, and so it went on until I gave him a couple of dinars before learning that he was a mainland Tunisian himself.

What I had not learned from this miserable complainer or my boy guide was that the tree had not earned its nomenclature from this festive game. Beneath its pendulous silvery shade, farmers' wives had sold their chickens and eggs. This Olive Egg Tree had, for many centuries, been the island's official poultry market.

Before tourism.

The end of fasting and festivities brought people into the fields. On the outskirts of the villages, in the dusty countryside, there was activity. Women were climbing ladders, harvesting olives from twisted trees. They were singing, laughing, animated. I walked mud-walled lanes where small boys came charging after me, asking my name or where my husband was. I saw a man feeding chickens while his wife, sisters and a gaggle of girls in flowing *foutas* climbed between branches. Olives were falling to the nets beneath like hailstones. I had never seen such speedy gathering. I passed by a couple of goats and went to watch them at work. The hoary farmer with his broad smile spoke some French. The women were wearing chopped horns on the central fingers of their right hands. He called down a pretty girl. She raised her hand for me to look. The closed, pointed tip of the goat horn had been sawn off and removed so it resembled a slender cylinder, rather like a bullet shell. These horns allowed the gatherer to slide her fingers along the boughs without damaging young shoots or bruising the fruit. It was ingenious.

The farmer laughed. 'No one else in the entire Mediterranean has thought of it.'

Where did the tradition come from? He shook his head, shrugged. I asked him about wild trees. Again he shook his head.

I was stumped. Awash with fine oil and history though it was, the spirit of Tunisia's olive past, its earliest tap roots, had somehow eluded me. I had uncovered no religious or sacred significance, no ancient or surprising directions. But perhaps there was no history earlier than the Phoenicians. Wild trees, yes, but no primordial relationship with olives. In the lives of the early desert peoples living on the southern rim of this basin, these fruits probably played no part.

When I returned to my monk's cell, three messages awaited me. The first from Michel assuring that all was well at the farm but informing me of the riots in the *banlieux* outside Paris. The Scotsman, Duncan, had left his card with a note: 'Call when you reach Tripoli. Or if your visa doesn't come through, I'll help you out.' I smiled. I liked him, his wry sense of humour, but I doubted that I would call. The last was to say that my visa for Libya had been refused.

Libya

My visa allowing entry into Libya as an independent traveller had proved impossible. No agency or tour operator was willing to assist me unless I hooked up with one of their programmes. The country had recently reopened its doors to tourism, which in a low-key way was doing well. Sanctions had been lifted; in March 2004, Tony Blair had flown to meet with Colonel Gaddafi, outside Tripoli, making the first British state visit in years. But there was still no channel, save with a tourist organisation, to gain entry and I had no desire to be herded about in a bus with a group, shepherded by guides. I flew to London and tried the few contacts I knew in the British travel scene. The messages came back that to gain entry I must agree to lay out a detailed schedule, which I had not precisely planned, and travel with a group. Eager as I was to visit this ancient coastland, I was contemplating skipping Libya if this proved the only option available, yet there were sites there that had been closed off for decades. I wanted to see them, to understand their role in the growth of olive culture. I decided to call upon the offer made by the Scotsman I had met in Djerba. Duncan was neither surprised nor fazed when I got in touch. He requested copies of my documents be faxed directly, assuring me there would be no difficulty whatsoever in securing the necessary entry papers. Fax operations took a couple of days because connections were erratic, but eventually I furnished all that had been requested.

'Give me a week,' was all that was now required of me.

And, lo and behold, nine days later, I received a message saying that my papers had been cleared and a copy of the visa would be faxed forthwith. I could board a plane. Rushing about at the last minute, I could find no small token of gratitude for the burly Scotsman. Alcohol is forbidden in Libya – possession of it is an imprisonable offence – so transporting a bottle of fine whisky was out of the question. He did not strike me as a man who read books. I didn't know his musical tastes, and I did not feel sufficiently well acquainted with him to arrive with aftershave. I fired off a last-minute email asking whether he had any particular requests. His response was instant: 'A few wee rashers of bacon for breakfast.' Bacon! I was taken aback and friends who heard were horrified that I should entertain such an idea: to travel *pork* into a Muslim dictatorship. But after all that he had achieved for me, how could I refuse? He was even offering me a place to stay; without a tourist visa, booking hotels was exceedingly complicated. So, a few 'wee rashers' seemed to be the least I could do. I confirmed with my guidebook and with the airline that the importation of foodstuffs was not deemed an illegal act akin to the smuggling of alcohol. No mention was made of it so I slipped the vacuum-sealed rashers of organic pig's meat inside a new shoebag in my luggage and hoped for the best. One small niggle: the visa had not arrived. I did not have a fax machine, or, for that matter, an office in London. I had requested that it be sent to my accommodating agent, but when I telephoned, I learned that it had not come through.

Duncan assured me that it had been sent and promised to fax it again.

This went on for a couple of days, by which time I was beginning to doubt, to panic. Eventually, the single-page document arrived late on the afternoon of the day before my early-morning flight. I was at the hairdresser when my agent's assistant called to confirm she was biking it across. Hair wrapped in slivers of tinfoil, I sat staring at the flimsy page, illegible to me save for my name and passport number because it was transcribed in Arabic. I had no idea whether Duncan, from the oil industry, had applied for a working visa on my behalf or a tourist one.

I was keen to slip in without fuss. In every other country, I had declared my profession as olive farmer. I decided, in this instance, to state the baldest 'working in oil'. For the journey, or, rather, the arrival, I kitted myself out in thick leather hiking boots and cargo slacks: this actress's notion of someone ready to get dug in on the oilfields.

The plane was fairly empty. I was curious to observe what nature of passengers were travelling to this relatively obscure destination at the end of the first week of December. Dotted amongst the empty seats were faces of men (almost no women aboard) who looked travel-weary, but not from business. These young to early-middle-aged men had rough, tanned skins, an outdoorsy hue and rugged, casually dressed appearances. Oil workers, riggers, engineers.

I was seated beside a bearded thirty-something gentleman with closely cropped hair who smelled of sandalwood. A Muslim, dressed in a malt-brown three-piece suit, who introduced himself as Khalifa and, without further ado, shot me an alarming number of questions: where and with whom would I be staying? What is the profession of the man offering me board? Where does he live? Will I, a married woman – he had obviously taken note of my ring – be staying alone with him? Was the property a house or flat? When, how did I make his acquaintance? Where was my husband? My work? How many children? Endless. I began to panic, fearing that I had been seated alongside a member of Libya's secret police, that this man's brief was to investigate solitary travellers – particularly women – to assure I would cause no embarrassment to their heavily protected state. As soon as I was able, I switched the conversation to him and learned that Khalifa had worked for seventeen years in the desert, in oil. He had trained at the Oil Institute in Tripoli. Within minutes I had been furnished with his phone number, email address and offers to escort me to the olive groves belonging to his relatives a hundred or so kilometres south of the capital. A swift assurance that his children would accompany us was this Muslim's way of signalling that his invitation was honourable. I thanked him. The Libyan people are famous for their hospitality and amicability. My scepticism was probably ill-founded. When the meal was served, Khalifa asked whether the meat was halal. When the steward shook his head apologetically, my neighbour cast his breakfast aside and pulled out an apple, followed by a substantial knife to skin and quarter the fruit. How had he managed to smuggle such a weapon through security? My nagging worries reappeared and I buried myself in my book.

As the plane descended into Tripoli, I glanced out of the window. We were flying in over olive groves. Touchdown was flanked by lavender-silvery trees in every direction. My spirits lifted.

I joined one of several queues for non-Libyan passports. Within moments, a short, uniformed man – in fact, he had been waiting at the door of the plane, studying the faces of arriving passengers – stepped towards me.

'Mrs Drinkwater, Carol?'

I nodded.

'Follow me.'

Feebly, I waved the faxed Arabic document, which he dismissed, holding out his hand for my identity card. I handed it over, a European passport bearing a gilded Irish harp on its cover, and stepped obediently out of the queue. Fellow passengers were eyeing me with suspicion, or was that my imagination? Even if the authorities refused to return my passport, I was thinking, I still had my British equivalent tucked away at the bottom of my suitcase, the means to travel onwards.

I was forced to wait a very long time. Having been almost the first to exit the plane, I was about to be the last to clear immigration. Eventually, the young officer returned, signalling me back into line where my passport was stamped.

I was in Libya.

Outside, at the carousel, no luggage had appeared and it was another fifty minutes before it did so. Having recovered from my visa heebie-jeebies, I was now fretting about the bacon. They must be going through every case. Anxiously waiting, I fell into conversation with a man from the same flight. He was bemoaning the recent imprisonment of two of his colleagues. They had been caught brewing beer down in the desert at the rig. This was not unusual. The place had a secret 1,000-gallon distillation plant, but it was 'bloody rare' for anybody to 'get nicked for it'. They must have rubbed someone up the wrong way, he concluded, or not honoured an agreement. 'This is a scratch-my-back-and-I'll-scratch-yours society. The Manilla-envelope mentality, which can contain cash, air tickets, even deeds to a house . . . it depends on the extent of the favours.'

I wandered over towards the exit doors, desperate to be on my way, and spied my host waiting in the outer hall. He waved, as did I. I considered trying to warn him that I had bacon in my case and then thought better of it.

When I was finally on my way, safe within Duncan's Land Rover – the car park resembled an abandoned lot – I recounted my horror story to him and he burst out laughing. His last guest had sneaked through an entire suckling pig wrapped inside his raincoat and no one had paid the slightest bit of attention.

Oea, the original city on the site of present-day Tripoli, was founded by the Phoenicians somewhere around 500 BC, approximately three hundred years after they had set up shop in Malta and given birth to Carthage. Oea, along with the other Phoenician cities in present-day Libya, was created to facilitate their growing commercial interests right across the Mediterranean. It was a modest link in a chain of coast-based settlements that stretched the length of the North African coast, stopovers and trading posts en route to Spain, where they had lucrative metal interests, and onwards, around the horn of Portugal. What they took from here to trade were ostrich eggs and feathers, both prized in the ancient world. During that period, this coast was abounding in the birds. What they offered in return were olive trees. After the callous destruction of Carthage, the Phoenicians finally faced their crushing defeat and ceded control of the Mediterranean to the Romans. Tripolitania became a Roman protectorate. The other two cities in the *tripolis* – a Greek word meaning 'three cities' – were Sabratha and Leptis Magna. In their heyday, all were major exporters of olive oil. As at Carthage, the oil business brought enormous wealth to the Roman citizens, but Leptis Magna, which became the Roman capital of North Africa, proved to be their jackpot.

Duncan's villa was situated on the outskirts of the far side of town, close to the main road, towards Leptis. During the journey while we chatted, I was observing the roadsides, piled high with discarded plastic rubbish. Mini-mountains of the stuff. There were few pavements and those that did exist frequently disintegrated into sandbanks. Iron rods rose like floppy batons from the flat roofs of untold numbers of unfinished buildings. It was a tax dodge, I learned. Only completed properties incur charges. Years ago, Greece used to be peppered with unsightly breeze-block carcasses, for the same reason. We were somewhere on the outskirts of the city. To reach my host's villa, we had no need to go through its centre. Even so, this introduction was hardly prepossessing.

My sleeping quarters were a bunk bed made up with Harry Potter linen in one of Duncan's sons' rooms. His wife and children lived in Italy.

'What ken ee getch yer?' he called through to me as I unloaded computer and camera.

I dithered as one does in the home of a stranger. So determined had I been to include Libya along my route that it was just beginning to dawn on me what an unusual situation I had landed myself in.

'Tea?'

'Or somma ey wee bit strronga?'

I, who never drink spirits, soon found myself perched on a white sofa in a darkened room – the entire villa was locked and shuttered and I never once saw it otherwise – in front of the largest TV screen I have ever set eyes on, calming my smuggler's nerves with a hefty shot of gin and tonic, staring at Noel Edmonds overacting in an afternoon quiz show.

'I thought booze was illegal here . . .?'

As in every society where a product is outlawed, the black market rules and bootlegging was rife.

My first evening was spent at a 'do', an early Christmas party, held at a British sports club situated well out of town in an area of agriculture and ploughed fields, somewhere east of the capital. The further we travelled, the more the roads disintegrated into sand tracks until eventually we arrived at a newish construction where black manservants in uniforms stood to attention by the entrance gates. This British oasis consisted of pools, barbecues, interior and exterior bars where alcohol flowed freely. In one fashion or another, everyone was linked to the oil industry.

'And what line of business are you in, Carol?'

'Also in oil.' I could not resist it.

'Don't I know you from somewhere?'

'I don't think so.'

'Weren't you working for Shell in Uzbekistan?'

I shook my head.

'You look very familiar.'

I did the rounds, chatting to men with faces as lined as earth indented by tractor tyres, scrubbed up in clean shirts for the 'party'. Blokes who had spent their lives travelling the world 'working in oil': searching for it, servicing it, con-structing rigs, overseeing the accounts, hiring out equipment or knowledge, whatever. Short, stocky George, another Scots-man – so many were Scottish because they had trained on the North Sea rigs – this one with a crushed nose and features like a tired boxing glove, eulogised nights in the desert where grown men, 'cynical buggers', dismissive of the miracles of nature, would sit together in silence, hour upon hour, spell-bound, staring at the stars. He conjured up images of camel herders appearing from out of nowhere, looming up like phantoms out of the emptiness; men digging holes in the sand and 'shitting in them' only to find their naked buttocks blackened by flies; the multiple eyes of packs of dogs staring from out of the darkness through the tightly closed windows of trucks transformed into bedrooms after sundown; the shift-ing face of the sands after the wind turned; the ineluctability of it; its beauty and indescribable power. To my amazement, several of these hardened 'buggers' spoke to me in words of poetry.

One chap, a non-drinker among a crowd of serious boozers, knew about olive oil. 'Best oil comes from the escarpment region south of Tripoli,' he told me, but he could not remember the name of the location. Yet he'd been in the country for years.

'The Gebel Escarpment, perhaps?'

'Could be. Also there is good oil from the Green Mountain district, east of Benghazi. There are mills all over the place. Wine is cultivated here too.' He registered my surprise. 'And produced by Libyans. They consume it as well, whatever Islam states. It is described by the expats as washing-machine wine because once the grapes have been harvested, they are placed in washing machines with several pounds of sugar and wrung. The liquid from this process is the wine.'

I could not imagine what this might taste like. I was to find out later in Benghazi.

'Nowadays, there are no foreign-owned vineyards of course.'

Under the strong arm of Colonel Gaddafi, better known here as the Leader (of the revolution), only Libyans were entitled to possess property in his sovereign Arab Libya.

I glanced about me at a room that was bursting at the seams with red-faced Europeans dancing, jawing, guffawing beneath a ceiling hung with looped, coloured paper chains. I hadn't seen such decorations since I was at school. The place was awash with wine and spirits and the club members were emptying and refilling their glasses as though a drought had been forecast. Disco music was blaring out of two humungous black speakers.

'How does the booze get here?' I yelled.

Each refused to reveal his contacts.

Later, I learned that the sale of black-market alcohol was serious business. A bottle of whisky fetched £60, whereas wine reached £15. The alcohol was cargoed in at advantageous rates for the diplomats. The embassies were privileged, their importations never searched. In any case, the Libyans were happy to turn a blind eye to what went on within the expat scene so long as it remained behind closed doors and the alcohol was not sold for profit. However, it was sold, and at exorbitant prices.

The evening grew rowdier. As the Europeans got more drunk, so the music and chatter grew in volume and I stood like a wallflower watching on, or shouting questions at sozzled oil employees, but when my voice grew raspy and my throat scratched, I wandered outside into the moonlight, admiring the lush plants growing around two swimming pools and kiddie slides, while three black-as-jet Ghanaian barmen served and poured the endless waterfall of alcohol, all the while smiling graciously. This was not at all what I had been expecting. Still, it was a modern twist, another chapter in this country's long history of oil.

There are no trains in Libya. Aside from private cars, there was precious little transport whatsoever. If the government's bid for the 2010 World Cup had proved successful, they would have invested in laying down tracks. However, South Africa beat them to it, so this vast land of desert and coastal steppes remained difficult to access and hugely expensive to penetrate. My limited choice of transport was to hail a black-and-white taxi, the prices of which were extremely reasonable, or service bus, otherwise known as *siara al-arma* or *taksi*. These were capacious vehicles, 'people carriers', used as public taxis. They were recognised by a thick yellow band painted the length of their frame. Their destinations, more flexible than our notion of a bus, were written in Arabic on large cuts of card and stuck inside the windscreen. The driver waited for trade at roadsides. When the vehicle was bursting with passengers, off they went, hurtling here and there, careening to and fro. I was strongly advised against the use of them. They were hazardous, I was warned, and regularly involved in accidents, which was due to the poor standard of driving. Several had overturned in the city centre quite recently and a string of passengers had been severely injured. Yet again it was looking as though the only real option available to me was the hire of a private car with driver. I would not have attempted to drive myself. Pedestrians and drivers showed little regard for safety, suggesting most had grown up with no concept of roads.

Friday, sabbath. After breakfast, served up by Duncan's Filipino cook, I hailed a black-and-white taxi out on the street and requested Leptis Magna. The weather was louring, threatening rain. The road, the main route that followed the coast the thousand kilometres east to Benghazi, was lined with litter, predominantly plastic bags and the carcasses of rusting cars. The slender fingers of the minarets, skyward projectiles, rose up out of the squalor.

Many of the dark-eyed faces on the streets were as worn, as neglected as the buildings all around them, fretted by wind and salt. The population appeared to lack purpose. Arabs, black Africans hanging about with nothing to do, in the midst of mountains of garbage. Plastic is a by-product of petrol. Why bother to clear up or recycle when there was plenty more bubbling up on a daily basis out of the desert or from the seabed? It was less expensive to drill than clean up, it seemed.

Leptis Magna was sprawling, monumental, excessive. Constructed originally along the promontory of its natural harbour by Phoenicians in around 1000 BC, as at Carthage, precious little of that Semitic settlement remained, but, unlike Carthage, the Roman Metropolis had worn well and there was the thrill of mentally sketching its well-organised classical layout with its vast circular harbour sited at its spumy reaches. I stood in the wind, beneath December clouds and drizzle, attempting to bring to life that city of power and pomp, with its capacious vessels, docking and scudding forth, breasting the winds beyond these quays of Africa, this limestone and marble extravaganza. Olive oil was major business all along this sea coast when Tripolitania was at the height of its glory. To give an idea of the extent of production here, Caesar levied an annual fine against Leptis of 300,000 measures of olive oil as a punishment for supporting his rival, Pompey.

The Romans built olive farms and presses everywhere along the coast. At the height of its productivity, somewhere in the region of 1,500 olive mills were active in and around the capital. Olive oil must have been almost as lucrative a business for the Romans as crude oil was proving to be for the foreign investors today.

I was one of perhaps a dozen at the little-visited site and a lady at the ticket booth described it as the most crowded she had ever seen the place. Broken marble columns lay about the grounds, but less so here than at many other Mediterranean sites. Today, both the original harbour, a basin of almost twenty-five acres, and a narrow canal, Wadi Lebda, where smaller craft once berthed, had sanded over. Dusty tamarisks, bamboo grasses and stunted vegetation inhabited the marshy, whistling-in-the-wind wasteland. Still, the reach of the once-industrious port, with its extensive seaborne traffic, was evident. I traced the remains of what were sprawling dockyards, entrepôts and quays. Here the jars of oil would have been kept in storage caves. From here, too, gold was shipped and black slaves awaited exportation, taken from southern Africa, transported along the trans-Saharan routes. I could picture the teeming Metropolis as it must have been. Hungry traders from across the Mediterranean who had set a course for here, spending time in this magnificent coastal city while their boats were loaded with tall amphorae, bales of wheat, ships stowed with shuffling chained Africans. Both here and along the Tunisian coast, the Romans used slave labour to work their considerable estates, their latifundia. Their wealth built upon the sweat of others' lives, they grew rich off this land and its golden gallons, leaving the surrounding desert peoples angry and resentful.

As I returned from the beach where sections of the circular harbour had fallen away, the clouds cleared, the rain stopped and a rainbow straddled the horizon.

I ate lunch, a bowl of vegetarian soup at a very sombre restaurant alongside the ancient city and drank a tin of rather bland alcohol-free beer. Afterwards, my attendant taxi drove me back to town, to the modern port of Tripoli. Tripoli, Tarabulus in Arabic, once known as the 'white bride of the Mediterranean', due to its famous medina of square whitewashed houses, is, today, Libya's principal port. Before I alighted, my chauffeur – we muddled along with a few Italian, Arabic and English phrases – was keen to show me the walled perimeter of Colonel Mu'ammer Gaddafi's palace. Not far from the city's downtown areas and docks, it consumed an entire district. Every few yards, on the exterior side of its concrete enclosure, armed soldiers were posted. Apertures, resembling steel letter boxes, had been cut out. Through these the legions of interior guards kept vigil without intruders peering in. Like every piece of machinery or equipment that protected Gaddafi, the flaps had been bulletproofed. He counted numerous enemies but few allies, within international Islamic communities as well as the Western world. It was essential, as my Arab driver observed, 'to keep a watchful eye against a sabre in the back'.

During our circuit, one of the gates opened and I stretched to glimpse within the palace environs. I saw another wall of equal height, just as impenetrable. The estate was said to be a maze of concreted and bulletproofed structures spiralling to a central nub where stood his palace, a super-luxurious tent. He was born to Bedouin parents somewhere in the desert near Sirt, in 1942. Gossip said he preferred to live in a tent. Air traffic was forbidden in the vicinity so it was impossible to know whether this was fiction or fact. Beyond the royal compound and the hillocks of plastic rubbish, there were posters and billboards everywhere of the Leader, sometimes sporting dark sunglasses, always wearing his familiar pillbox *chéchia*, always striking one of a series of vainglorious poses.

On our way out of town we stopped for petrol. To fill the tank cost 10 dinars, approximately £4. Petrol was the cheapest commodity on the market here. Libya was producing 2 million barrels of top-quality crude oil a day. Across the semi-completed forecourt was a two-bit kiosk where a tattered, ill-starred Arab was purchasing two cigarettes. Two cigarettes! How to explain the grubby poverty on display all around me.

'Where does all the money go?' I asked myself. Two million barrels of oil a day returns a hefty income. I calculated that if the money was apportioned fairly and squarely to the Libyan people, it might be possible that every single family would be a euro millionaire. Unfortunately, the revenues rest with five colonels and their immediate families. A certain amount is shared with the bereaved families of their fellow revolutionaries – the seven deceased colonels and their kin – but little is put back into the State. Of course, Gaddafi would, no doubt, hotly disagree with my reading of his economic policies.

When I returned to Duncan's house, the bill for achieving my visa had been faxed through. It was €350 or £240. I was staggered. I was bearing witness to the discrepancies between the scratched existences eked out by the populace and those working within the oil industry, and it was difficult not to compare, or imagine, the similarities between today's conditions and those of the Roman colony.

Around the sixth century AD, desert tribes besieged Leptis Magna. They sacked the city until it was eventually abandoned, left to the winds, engulfed by desert sands. Could such a force of resentment arise here? Might the day arrive when the disregarded bodies I saw lolling about the filthy streets storm Gaddafi's palace?

The following morning, I took a trip downtown by service bus, which was indeed a cramped and rather hair-raising experience, to drop in on the souk and the medina with its famous white houses, its fortified wall and to book an onward ticket to Benghazi. As souks rate, it was less lively than many, but no one hassled me. It was easygoing. The market existed primarily for its locals and, to a smaller extent, for foreign residents. The country had not yet been impacted by tourism. I took photographs, engaged in conversations with a few traders, struggling with Arabic and rusty Italian, which, particularly amongst the older generations, remained the second language. I came across a cinema displaying several posters of *La Dolce Vita* and advertising a couple of early de Sica films. Souvenirs from, or nostalgia for, the nation's Italian period? Sellotaped to the glass door was a large black-and-white photograph of a curvacious young Anita Ekberg seducing the passers-by while outside on the streets the real women were covered from head to foot, honouring, or simply obeying, Islamic dress code. The Ottoman and later the Italian colonial periods had left distinct architectural traces everywhere, both were rather elegant. I was to see this again later, in and around Benghazi.

I strolled by the old palace. After the coup of 1969, when Gaddafi and his military comrades snatched the reins, King Idris's home was given over to the people as a library. It was the first moment I had felt any positive energy towards this system. I learned that study of *The Green Book*, Gaddafi's equivalent of Mao's *Little Red Book*, is compulsory for schoolchildren and young men doing their National Service. Quotes from it are to be found on his posters, at airports and in public arenas everywhere. After a visit to the fishmarket down at the quays, where they were selling whole young sharks as well as splendid specimens of junior swordfish and a fabulous array of other slithery Mediterranean creatures, I dropped in at a travel agency to book my ticket for Benghazi. They were closing. It was 2 p.m. I asked whether they would be open later and the assistant replied, 'Yes, but in secret.'

The citizens, shopkeepers, were obliged to be present at a fortnight-long series of meetings of the People's Congress. Many avoided attendance, because the decision-making rested with 'the Leader and his henchmen'. The young man from the agency advised me to return another day.

He warned that he was unable to reserve seats and the sole means of payment was cash. One step up from desert trading, Libya remains exclusively a cash society. This would not impact on tourists because all travel arrangements are included within the price of the tour. Going it alone, I was not shielded from the complications of a non-credit-card society.

I was keen to begin travelling. Time with the oil crowd had been fascinating for certain aspects of Libyan society, but I was itching to be on the move. The problem was hotel bookings, and flights were proving nigh on impossible to arrange. In one sense, my determined independence had tied me in knots. I took a solitary walk along the city shoreline, where the Mediterranean was thumping against the rocks, throwing up ice-blue spray. A handful of Arabs were dotted here and there, fishing, a few blacks were kicking their heels, killing infinite unemployed time along the grubby strand or lolling against the breakwall smoking, while behind me the traffic screeched, belched and sped by. I had to find a means of crossing the country.

Thanks to Duncan, a driver had been organised to take me south to an olive-growing region, to visit groves and local mills, but each evening a message came through saying he was 'tied up with Halliburton business' and would not be free until the morrow. The same message greeted my return from the city with an added explanation: one of their 'head honchos' was in town and Dick Cheney could be on his way.

Dick Cheney?

Duncan had invited two guests over for dinner, both employed in the oil industry. Pete and Alex, yet another Scot, were drilling and measuring experts. I sat with rapt attention listening to their tales of the international sites they had set up or worked on and their lives within or, rather, on the periphery of societies that were completely unprepared for the discovery of crude oil and its massive investors. Uzbekistan, Tunisia, Iran. These men had arrived into towns or villages where, at best, there may have been one tiny guest house and they had departed several years later having witnessed the construction of skyscraper hotels and office blocks and having participated in the restructuring of local values, particularly towards money.

'It's time to get out,' said Pete, 'when you sniff the contents of a bottle of mineral water before sipping it.'

I assumed this was a comment on the quality of the local drinking water, but no. Alex then went on to recount a tale of an occasion when his wife had hosted a canasta party, an all-day event for thirty ladies, one of whom was diabetic, suffered from kidney failure and weighed twenty-odd stone. While the women were inside rapt by their card game, Bill's children were outside in the beating heat playing by the pool. Thirsty, they had grabbed from the garage a bottle of mineral water, the contents of which had been replaced with 'flash'. Fortunately, the nanny caught the girls before they had sipped the liquid and hurried inside to store it in the fridge, out of harm's way, before returning her attention to the offspring in her charge. Meanwhile, inside, the obese woman was in need of refreshment and was directed to the fridge, where she could find chilled water. Needless to say, the woman opened the bottle containing the 'flash' and downed great glugs of it before she fell into convulsions on the floor. Pandemonium broke out while all fought to save the woman's life. Fortunately, she survived and retained no memory of what had triggered the incident, apologising instead for inconveniencing her hosts by 'having one of her turns'.

The trio of men present at the dining table now hooted with laughter, eyes streaming at the memory of the hapless female and all that befell her.

'What is "flash"?' I asked.

Flash was a distilled concoction of water, sugar and yeast, creating pure alcohol. If the distillation goes awry, it can cause blindness. It tasted and smelled like floor polish. Later, down the track in Benghazi, I was able to vouch for this observation.

'A white desert truck linked itself to Gaddafi's security convoy . . .'

The tales spun on. I slipped off to bed, leaving the men, still carousing, each looking one glass short of unconsciousness.

Up early the following morning, I was at my makeshift desk from where I had access to Duncan's Internet connection, eager, before setting off for Sabratha, to discover a few facts about the Texas-based giant, Halliburton, the world's largest oil- and gas-services company, which had fingers in pies worldwide, including Libya. Their presence in Iraq had caused much press coverage. During Dick Cheney's tenure as Halliburton's CEO, the company signed contracts worth more than $73 million, principally to supply oil-production equipment and spare parts to Iraq as well as the billions of tons of provisions required on a daily basis for the US troops. Today, the company holds more than 50 per cent of all American rebuilding contracts in that war-torn region.

Halliburton is a products and services provider to the petroleum industry, and during the previous evening's repast, the men had been discussing its role in Libya. Naïve on my part, but I had been surprised, given the acrimonious relationship until the recent removal of sanctions between Gaddafi and the United States, to learn that Halliburton had long been very active in Libya. When asked about Halliburton's involvement in this desert country, Dick Cheney had acknowledged they did business with this state but only through foreign subsidiaries. That response did not seem to tally with the picture that had been painted during the previous evening's meal. The table gossip, albeit drunken, had also implied that Cheney, Halliburton' s CEO between 1995 and 2000, retained ongoing involvements with the company.

'Is he coming into town?'

'Nah.'

I had just come across a quote from the *New Yorker*, stating that Cheney had earned $44 million during his CEO years at

Halliburton and was still receiving annual 'kickbacks', when Duncan appeared at the door in dressing gown, looking decidedly worse for the several bottles he had consumed the night before, but in habitually good humour. He was a 'wee bit' too hungover to go to his office so was offering to drive me to Sabratha.

It was a delightfully warm winter's day. There were many olive trees at the roadsides, but most had partially expired. Deprived trees that lacked irrigation and urgently required pruning; inglorious groves; products of neglect. Several different people had remarked that the olive oil produced in Libya was frequently rancid. If the harvests were as sluttish as the groves, I could understand why. These farms would have been expertly husbanded during the Italian occupation. The Italians landed here in 1911 and treated the people cruelly, but they did look after the narrow agricultural belt that was situated between sea and desert. However, when they were kicked out by Gaddafi's team in 1969 and the lovingly tended farms and acreages were redistributed to Libyan Arabs, no expertise was bequeathed with them.

On the road out of town, I asked my host what he knew about Halliburton and how they had negotiated long-term involvements in a country that had been ostracised by the States for years.

'The Great Man-Made River Project commenced over twenty years ago is, indirectly, theirs.'

'But how can that be? Their entire board of directors is American, predominantly Texan,' I argued.

Gaddafi's vision to pipe water from the southern deserts to inhabited zones all along the Libyan Mediterranean coast, known as the Great Man-Made River Project, has been a controversial and fantastically expensive enterprise. The contract to install these millions of dollars' worth of subterranean water channels was won by a South Korean firm, Dongah, which subcontracted out a hefty percentage of the work to Brown & Root. In 1962, Halliburton bought up the shares and took control of Brown & Root (also a Texas-born company). Gaddafi seized control of Libya in 1969. The first stage of the Man-Made River Project was inaugurated in 1991. The USA only ended trade sanctions against Libya in September 2004. Trade sanctions that had been imposed in 1986 by Reagan during his presidency. It would appear that Gaddafi has by default, or not, been in bed with the Americans since the outset and Halliburton was and remains one of the largest players in the resource fields of Libya.

I was beginning to understand why the only way in here was with a guided tour. Towering eucalyptus trees flanked the roadsides. I spotted grey herons flying low, skimming the multiple mounds of plastic trash. At a T-junction, four Africans were sitting in a semicircle beneath an unpruned olive tree, a couple of aluminium cooking pots lay at their feet. They had slung cotton sarongs across the leafless branches, presumably to create shade, protect against the wind-blown sands, and appeared to have set up a dusty temporary camp. One of them was glueing the sole of his shoe back with a tiny tube of adhesive. Three were in slacks, bomber jackets, sneakers and baseball caps, Western wear, albeit shabby, while the fourth, a wizened old geezer, wore tired green slippers, a white blanket, a *jarde*, wrapped around him in the style of desert Bedouins and a small skullcap, a *capuse*. A dejected group of rag-pickers beneath an ailing olive tree.

We pulled over. I requested a photo. All nodded, bar one.

'I want money,' he snapped, holding out his wrinkled palm that resembled chocolate-coated papyrus. He spotted my rather elegant silver pen attached to my shirt and tried to snatch it.

I shook my head and held up the camera. 'May I?'

He shrugged and I took a couple of snaps. His companions were amiable, but he pouted, eyes elsewhere, letting me know that he was 'pissed off'. Back on our way, I recounted the exchange to Duncan. He swung the truck round, returning us to where the Africans were sheltered and the guy was still looking sore.

'Give them these.'

I ran, arm outstretched, proffering a couple of plastic Biros with Duncan's company details printed on them. The homeless young African whooped with childlike delight. I felt utterly ashamed of myself.

Sabratha's location was exceptional. This once-upon-a-time Phoenician port still sat on the fringes of the sea, dominating a ravishing stretch of coastline dotted with Mediterranean pines. Used only as an occasional stopover for the Phoenicians, somewhere around the first century BC when their light had been extinguished, Sabratha became a Roman city.

On that late morning, its fabulous three-storey theatre, all pillars, balconies, apertures, rust-hued sandstone, a crowning landmark, was set against a relief of cobalt and emerald; clean Mediterranean topography at its most glorious. We wandered, individually, not a soul but us, waves lapping. Duncan called to me. Tearing myself away from the theatre, I reached the approach to a ruler-straight Roman street marked 'Oil Press Street'.

Yes!

In the warm winter sunlight, I trod the length of the paved walkway. At its extreme, Oil Press Street spilled upon the shoreline and would have been ideally located for the stowing of oil into vessels. I came across a massive stone basin lying on its side. It was the lower section of a crushing machine.

The Greeks named such a stone *katopetra*, or 'downstone'. I did not know the Roman name.

The oil-filled terracotta jars, the amphorae, would have been stored in the ships' darkened holds before transportation. I gazed to sea, squinting, conjuring up those days of laden vessels ploughing through benign waves on journeys to Rome or the outer reaches of its empire, when I noticed two black container ships outlined against the cloudless horizon, anchored far beyond the coast, and I traced an invisible line with my finger back to shore. They were awaiting berths in the scruffy port town of Zawia. Sitting high on the water, the empty tankers would soon be loaded with thousands of gallons of crude oil, Libya's twenty-first-century 'liquid gold'.

I found an archaeological organisation that was ready to assist my journey east towards the border. As soon as I had visited the Tripolitan olive groves, I planned to get going.

It was a relief, then, when Abdusalem, the driver, finally became available. Our destination was south to Guaran, towards the desert, a well-established olive-growing region. On the outskirts of Tripoli, we passed queues of Egyptians and Africans squatting at roadsides. They hung around busy intersections every morning, hoping to be picked up for a day's employment. They were impoverished, thin as straws, bony-kneed, with tobacco-blemished teeth.

Clear of the city, the landscape transformed. It grew flat, rose-tinted, sandy and boundless. The terrain was hinting at its desert nature, promising what lay a mere 200 miles south of where we were. Ahead of us, looming up out of the soft sand, was a massive, sweeping escarpment, pink as a flamingo. There lay Guaran. While I stared out of the window relishing the infinite space, I listened to Abdusalem, amused by the manner in which he chattered. How he bragged and swaggered, how he attempted to impress with his talk of money and cars. He was employed exclusively by companies servicing the oil industry. Although against the rules of his faith, he drank alcohol with those guys and he was a man just like them. Beyond the windows, infinitude was marred by a staggering number of pylons, mile upon mile in every direction. Libya supplies Tunisia, Egypt and sub-Saharan Africa with electricity. It also pipes gas to Sicily, which, in turn, transports it to France. Twenty per cent of all French oil is from here. This vast land mass of desert and coastline is fabulously rich in natural resources, yet lethargy, penury, social disorganisation were everywhere to behold.

We passed through several army checkpoints. Unlike in Lebanon's Beqaa Valley, they weren't concerned with me, but Abdusalem was obliged to show his national service papers. Prison awaited those who had avoided the army, he explained.

The earth grew redder, as rich as the terra-rossa pottery on sale from makeshift stalls at every turn along the winding ascent. The slopes were fringed, fretted and chiselled with narrow, winding wadis. Once we had climbed the snaking road to the higher levels of the ranges, the olive groves returned. Here, they were healthy and tended. Many mills lined the streets of small, undistinguished towns peppy with rural activities. Stacks of hay were being loaded on to trucks at the roadsides, and ironmongery appeared to be an active business, too. An inviting mill façade caught Abdusalem's attention and he screeched to a halt. He had been recounting to me how an uncle of his had bought a smallholding of 2 hectares for 2000 dinars, approximately £830, from the State in the early 1970s, after the Italians had been shoved out. I asked if anyone had taught his relative how to husband his legacy. Abdusalem shrugged. He had no idea.

The owner of the mill was Ramadan, named after the

month of fasting. He was a bullish young fellow with a bushy beard, dressed in navy overalls; a gift from his brother who was working in the 'other oil industry'. Olive oil sells here for 2 dinars a litre, close to 70p. It costs more than petrol, but is a far less lucrative business. With Abdusalem translating, I expressed my desire to see the machines in operation.

Ramadan welcomed me warmly, though his staff seemed confused by my presence. In spite of the time I had been in the country and the poverty I had witnessed, I was still taken aback by the depressing conditions. The miller's passion for his trade was uplifting, though the dingy, dirty establishment reeked of so many unpalatable odours. Splotches of machine lubricants stained the floor, and I was shocked to see that a few stray olives on the ground were swept up into the next assignment of fruits to be pressed, along with dust, leaves and general detritus. The drupes would be washed, but even so. This mill's method of pressing was an old-fashioned version of modern, which was to say metal, machinery made in Italy, but decades out of date. Given the unwholesomeness of the conditions, when Ramadan offered me oil to taste, I declined, pretending that it was too early in the day, but I was beginning to understand the claims that oil from these parts was rancid. We said our farewells and I left with the distinct impression that I had been visiting a garage rather than an olive mill. There had been no farmers present, no sense of that joy that accompanied the ever-thrilling moment when the first drops of liquid began to drip through.

And then I realised. It hung everywhere about me, that low cloud of joylessness. The weight of oppression.

Driving deeper into the ranges, beyond the elevated one-street towns with their pick-up trucks and stacks of wooden boxes, where black-as-night Africans herding sheep, swathed in white scarves, exposed little aside from glowing eyes and

piano-key teeth, I began to spot groups of women in countryside groves, gathering fruits. Frequently, petrified almond
trees shared the fields. Lack of irrigation. Farmers were standing on oil drums to prune their trees. Were they too poor to
own ladders? Women, too, pruned as they gathered.

I requested of Abdusalem to pull over so that I could meet
them, but the women scampered for cover when they saw
me, burying their giggling faces behind raised hands or leafy
branches. Fortunately, their timidity was outweighed by curiosity and inherent friendliness. Patience, and they crept out,
peeping from behind silvery foliage, smiling, congregating,
until the instant Abdusalem penetrated the groves to translate
for me. Then they shrieked playfully, wrapping coloured
scarves over their faces, hiding all but one eye, refusing to
engage in verbal intercourse with a male. Interestingly, his
city brashness and money-confidence, all that he had emu-
lated from the oil men, fell away. Here he was an Arab kid,
returned to local traditions.

'Don't photograph them without permission,' he pleaded.
'I have no intention of doing so.' I laughed, having already
shuttered the camera. Even when the women refused the
gaze of my lens, slipping gracefully beyond sight, they always
left with an invitation to photograph their trees or sup mint
tea with them. Success came with several whiskery grandmothers who had but a trio of molars between them. I found
gaggles of them in brightly striped robes, buried deep within
the orchards, collecting drupes or, more frequently, slumped
on the crumbly earth, cracked and stained bare feet, legs
akimbo, substantial frames leaning against gnarled trunks,
gorging. They expressed no concerns about exposing their
faces or their wrinkled femininity before male company and
they gladly posed for my shots, clawing drupes off sprigs with
henna-painted fingers or laughing raucously alongside their

sons and young male relatives. Abdusalem, at my side, was nervous, jittery, throwing glances over his shoulder. Fearing the arrival of a jealous husband with a shotgun, he fled on several occasions, abandoning me to negotiate the brittle earth of the groves, explaining my purpose as best as I could. One old biddy, hair hennaed a brilliant orange with a navy tattoo from her lower lip to the base of her chin that gave the impression she had sprouted an Oriental beard, dragged me by the arm, pinching me, insisting that I return with her to her home. We had no time so, tears in her eyes, she unburdened her heart beneath the shade of her olives. Her son was in England; she was worried sick.

'We must all be friends and forget war,' she cried. 'I fear for him in London, a land of bombs and warmongers.'

I tried to calm her. 'My family carry the same fears for me during my days in Libya.'

She was incredulous. 'Fearful of Libya, but why?'

On my last evening, nocturnal rains and thrilling lightning ripped the trees apart, bringing down clumps of vegetation, causing the streets to become even more cluttered with detritus. I was happy to be on my way, but taken aback to learn that Duncan had cancelled the sketchy itinerary I had painstakingly put together and had arranged for a 'friend of a friend' to meet me off my flight in Benghazi.

'Why?' I cried.

'You'll be safer with our crowd.'

Flying in from the west over the lagoons of Benghazi, I spied flamingos from the Camargue wading about in the salt pans, while the refreshing simplicity of the white cubed houses led me to believe I was entering Arabia.

The Green Mountain of Cyrenaica, the capital of which was Benghazi, was first colonised by Greeks from the volcanic island of Thera, modern-day Santorini, and later, fleeing from the Spartans, boatloads of refugees from the city of Messini on the Peloponnese during the area's city-state wars. The original city was christened Euesperides. This entire coastal green belt must have been paradise for them, a great granary. Whether they brought the olive tree with them or they found it here, I had yet to discover, but what they certainly sailed into was a vast fertile garden of mountainous land where anything and everything could be cultivated. Unlike the native Bedouins, who were never agriculturists, being herders and nomads, the Greeks by this stage, the sixth century BC, were well-practised farmers.

Later, the Romans took control, though they were never as present here in the east as they were in their lucrative western Tripolitania. Once the Turks had been ousted after the fall of the Ottoman Empire in 1917, the area had been colonised by the Italians, who made themselves profoundly hated during their half-century rule, but left architectural and agricultural legacies Libya could be proud of.

I had been excited about this stop along my route. I had hopes that it might prove to be a highlight of my journey. My late father had spent time in Benghazi during his days as a young entertainment officer in the RAF during World War II and he had frequently eulogised its Italianate beauty when I was a child. The city was later gutted during that same war so I knew that the place I was about to visit would not bear relation to the one he had known in his youth. Still, it was fabled to be the site of the ancient Garden of Hesperides, which had been a lush paradise planted with pomegranates, mulberries, myrtles, laurels, creepers, olive, pear and almond trees. Even if that Eden had long since vanished, this eastern side of Libya was lovelier and more verdant than its western counterpart. It promised plenty, though I was concerned that all my well-laid plans, sketchy though they had been, had been cancelled. I had been looking forward to seeing the country through my solitary traveller's eyes and not through the protected, comfortable lens of the petroleum industry.

I stepped from the plane into a country-town airport where no one awaited me. I hung about, looked outside. Not a soul, and I had nowhere to go. In Libya, you cannot just walk into a hotel and request a room. I experienced a moment of panic and then, as I was asking myself what I could do, a harassed, bespectacled figure came hurrying towards me, jangling car keys in his right hand.

'Might yous be Carrl?' he called in a broad Dublin accent.

I nodded.

'I've only just heard about you,' was his apology. He lifted my case off the ground and, turning towards his parked car, called over his shoulder, 'I'm Seamus, by the way.'

Seamus O'Brien, director of operations for an Irish construction unit. He slung my luggage and camera into the boot of a seriously tatty Japanese saloon and in we climbed. En route to what he described as a 'camp', we drove by a cement works that was belching dense columns of smoke from its numerous chimney stacks and Seamus asked what it was I required. I was taken aback, having assumed that Duncan had informed him. I explained quickly that I was in need of a bed for a couple of nights. I had booked a hotel, but . . .

'And then what?'

I wanted to discover the Green Mountain area, travelling as far as Susa and, if time permitted, east of it.

'How?'

'Local transport.'

'Alone?'

'Yes.'

'No fecking way.' He concentrated on the road, frowning.

Feeling awkward, I remarked on the pollution.

'The whole fecking dirty place is shite,' was Seamus's response.

I stared out of the window. It was like passing through a sandstorm. Everywhere was veneered with a membrane of cement dust. Given that there were homesteads in the adjoining fields, I was appalled that such pollution would be allowed. It was well over thirty years since the factory had been serviced, was Seamus's response.

'I'm going to have to find a spare man from the crew to go with yers.'

'Thank you, but I really would rather—' I was casual yet firm, unwilling to lay responsibility at this man's door.

'And let me be held accoontable for what heppens to you in this fecking place! No, ye'er my responsibility now! Ask Steph, she'll tell you all about the filthy devils.'

We had arrived at the 'camp', which consisted of a series of tin dwellings, reminiscent of Nissen huts, in a small plot of land, where the vegetation looked as though it had been talcum-powdered, at the edge of a busy intersection. It was impossible to have imagined the desultoriness of the place. My hut contained three areas, separated by plywood sheets, used as staff sleeping quarters. It was temporary accommodation for technicians passing through en route to oilfields or back into civilisation. There was also a living space, a blokes' communal room, containing a large television and DVD player and a pile of well-thumbed Clancy paperbacks lying on a table. The antiquated fridge was empty save for half a packet of digestive biscuits. After the privileged existences led by the Tripolitan 'oilies', this utter disrepair quite bemused me. Seamus had gone off, promising to sort out my situation. He closed the door with a sigh, shaking his head. His parting words were, 'Oh, make sure you lock yourself in, in case I'm too fecking drunk to remind yers later.' I sank into a chair. A sense of despair flooded through me. It was one of those what-the-hell-am-I-doing-here moments. First thing tomorrow, I'll get on the road to Susa, I was telling myself as I wandered through to 'my quarters'. The bedsheets had been slept in by whoever had been here last. Dead fag ends littered an ashtray on a bedside cupboard. I peeped gingerly into the bathroom and wanted to vomit. By the water outlet stood a yellow bucket. From within it a length of red piping fed into the tobacco-stained sink. The bath did not deserve the title. I could not imagine how I would set foot in it. It was so utterly grotty that I tried to cheer myself up by taking photographs. This'll make them laugh back home, I kidded myself, but the fact was, I was facing one of the only moments throughout the entire journey when I wanted to cry, to throw in the towel.

The door opened and a man peeped in. He nodded a shy hello and retreated instantly. He was followed, moments later, by a knock that delivered a young female of Amazonian proportions, swaying in a marginally sloshed fashion, 6 feet 2, in an outfit one size too small revealing cleavage and soft fleshy breasts. Originally from the Wirral, Stephanie had been employed to teach English at an international primary school.

'Seamus'sss trying to find shomeone,' she announced.

'Please, I'll take the bus into Benghazi and find a hotel.'

'There aren't no booses and in any case you'll probably get raped. You have to stay. Come next door and have a drink.'

I followed this giant staggering woman along a narrow wooden walkway into a neighbouring hut. What else was there to do? I had no transport, my mobile had no signal, I was not even sure precisely where I was. What I knew was that if Duncan, who had by now taken a plane back to his family in Italy for Christmas, had been standing in front of me, I would have wrung his neck.

I entered a cosier, cleaner, marginally more spacious version of the set-up I was to doss in. Stephanie offered me a drink. '7-Up and flash?'

I declined, but she insisted. At least I was now able to verify that it smelled and tasted of floor polish. Stephanie had seated herself at a dining table across the room and was engaged in the business of cutting out and painting teeny Christmas cards. Seamus flitted in and out through the door, trying to figure out what to do with me. I was mortified.

'Who are you?' quizzed the chirpily sozzled woman.

While we waited I learned that she hated everything about Libya except the sausages. 'Sausages?'

'They're camel meat.' She spilled out lurid stories of sexual misconducts perpetrated by the locals against foreign workers. Slavic nurses had been the recent victims. After yet another two generous shots of flash and 7-Up, she confided that she was having a 'thing' with Seamus, but that I was to say nothing because his wife back in Dublin would be 'none too pleased'. By then it was clear to me that she and Seamus were cohabiting in what had originally been his digs, which explained the unlikely domestication of the room.

An hour and several tipples of flash later, a handsome late-thirty-something Arab knocked at the door. This was Jamel. He was to be my driver for the upcoming days on my journey east and had been instructed by Seamus to take me on an evening tour of Benghazi. It was close to 10 p.m. I had already been protesting, insisting, that I really would prefer to take a bus and make my own way back later with a local taxi, but Seamus would not hear of it. He strongly advised me against going anywhere alone. Stephanie, who was absolutely plastered by this stage, sprawled out on the sofa admiring her silver Christmas cards, supported him wholeheartedly, citing, as best she could speak, yet more reported incidents of rape.

These negative warnings were beginning to irritate me. However, when Jamel and I reached downtown, I started to understand what had fed the concerns, even if grossly exaggerated.

The seaport town of Benghazi was reminiscent of a faded masterpiece, scuffed and bedraggled, a picture of somewhere that had once been exquisite, and not for the first time on these Middle Eastern legs of my journey, I longed for the company of my father, to walk this esplanade with me. I wanted to listen to him spirit up images, tales and memories of his service here. I remembered a collection of fezzes that he had bought in the souks and kept in the garage. They seemed so exotic to me then, the brimless cone-shaped burgundy headgear with its shiny black tassel. But, alas, that was never more to be and I had little choice but to imagine the elegance and past reincarnations of this second city of Libya.

Jamel was to escort me whether I cared for it or not and so we began our tour that evening along the seafront. My companion was a local man, born and raised in Benghazi, but, unusually, had travelled a fair amount, spoke decent English and, though I could not verify it, even better Polish. He had lived with a dentist's assistant in Prague and then with a nurse for six years in Warsaw. Both of whom he had met here and both of whom, when the relationships had split up, had returned to Benghazi. He was married now, had settled with a Libyan Muslim woman, who had borne him two children. He had returned to the fold.

'I practise my faith, but sometimes I stray. I explained to my wife that occasionally I drink homemade wine – it's low-grade stuff here, not like the Bulgarian wines – and sometimes I frequent parties thrown by Westerners. She would be happier if I were a good Muslim, but she does not believe that I am a bad man. I am weak.'

We debated Jamel's perception of life amicably. Weakness or an independent choice? I suggested that perhaps he might be following a path of his own, his definition of Islam, but he would not hear of such an interpretation. He judged my words blasphemous. He was a weak man who had strayed from the path. Full stop. I said no more. Whatever our differences of opinion, I felt at ease in his company and content to have finally arrived over on this eastern coast.

As we walked, I noticed the decades of neglect. Small boys with the hollowed-out faces of old men were kicking balls about in the filthy, echoing streets. There was not an open café in sight, certainly not a bar. All along the wide and partially paved promenade, reclaimed land, I saw lovely old Italian buildings, still inhabited, all but crumbling into the sea, and for the hundredth time since I had arrived in this confusing yet evocative land, I asked myself where was the phenomenal income generated by the oil industry being syphoned; 1.4 million barrels of crude oil a day selling at approximately sixty cents a barrel. How much was fed back into the local economy? The Man-Made River Project had lost an estimated $25 billion. Where was the rest? Was it all sitting in anonymous Swiss bank accounts?

Sand, beige and gritty, like granulated sugar, was blowing everywhere, carpeting the already dirty streets. Plastic bags were sailing through the night air like schools of flying jellyfish. The young Arab men on the streets – there were no women, of course – had angry eyes and many were as obese as young Westerners, products of the fast-food culture. A brooding frustration darkened their faces. Disenfranchised youths, tattered souls. They slouched on plastic chairs or at the kerbsides beneath decomposing arcades playing cards or staring as we passed by, puzzled by a female out this late. The parked cars were wrecks and every now and then one screeched to a halt, a quartet of young men piled out and mooched along the waterfront where the moon was high, illuminating a wafer-slice of gently rocking water.

I asked Jamel what entertainments, amusements existed for the young here. Were there clubs, youth centres, community activities? The answer was nothing.

'So what do they do?'

My companion shrugged. 'Hash and booze have brought shame to the Islamic community here,' he confessed. 'There have been a couple of cases of . . . European women targeted. Day trippers to the Green Mountain.' There was a significant Slavic population working and living here. Bulgarians, Poles, Czechs employed as nurses and doctors.

I broached the question turning in circles in my mind. 'What is happening to the petroleum revenues?'

Jamel fell silent and I feared that I had overstepped the mark.

'It is what we are asking ourselves,' he admitted eventually. 'Why are we, the people of Libya, not benefiting from this propitious time of wealth and commerce?'

Driving back out of town, we passed by an area heavily constructed with blocks of flats. This was Olivit. Before the coup d'état in 1969, it had been fields of olive groves, but the Leader had instructed that housing be built for his people and the olive groves had been razed. When farmers protested, they were told, 'We don't need agriculture, we have oil.' Sad though I was to hear about the loss of the trees, I was heartened to hear that homes had been created, but it had been a long time ago.

Before I attempted sleep in my tin shack, Seamus dropped in, followed a few minutes later by Stephanie, who was so sloshed she was bouncing off the walls. In her hand, she waved a thumb-sized card. 'I made thisss for you,' she slurred. 'Happy Christmasss.'

I requested clean sheets, which she generously provided, and I settled to reading. I had not eaten since breakfast in Tripoli and fell upon the McVities in the fridge, scrunching two along with a sugared cup of black Nescafé. Such was my first evening meal in the romantic land of Benghazi.

The night was bitter. I was cold, shivering, craved to be on the road. I woke with dust between my teeth and up my nostrils. Cement fallout. Graham Greene in *Ways* of *Escape*, talking of his time in Africa while writing *A Burnt-out Case*, expressed his desire to be at the Ritz in Paris cupping a gin and tonic. I hankered not for the gin and tonic or even the glamour of grand hotels, but for the Champs-Élysées, for the hustle and bustle of the Western metropolis, for fragrant wintery perfumes such as pine needles on a Christmas tree, for log fires burning in the hearth, fresh coffee brewing and other familiar comforts. I strip-washed in cold water at the sink and prayed that wherever the following night found me, it would be an improvement on this. My breakfast was a repeat of the previous evening's supper: two biscuits, one black coffee. Munching the digestives, I imagined our newly constructed greenhouse back at the farm and I pined for the salads, fresh vegetables and fruits Quashia, Michel and I had planted together the last time I was home.

Oil men, otherwise known as 'oilies', refer to roads that have been tarmacked as 'black tops'. 'Fours hours of black top and then three of sand' is an example of how they described journeys that took them south into the desert. Along the road from Benghazi, we travelled stretches of black top inter-mingled with mile after jolting mile of dusty potholed tracks.

There were plenty of examples of olive trees as well as another narrow-leafed silvery tree that put me in mind of the *aliç*, the tree Michel and I had mistaken for feral *olea* in Turkey. How I longed for Michel.

For much of the early part of the journey, it was flat, stony scrubland. We chose to hug the coastal plains, where I spotted several heavy vessels that had been wrecked and beached by the strong Mediterranean winds. I wondered about ancient shipwrecks submerged here.

Our first stop was Tolmeta. Resembling the last place on earth after all final wars had been fought and lost, it was a ravaged bomb site of a windswept coastal settlement with chickens, gloomy Bedouins, rusting boat hulks, shelled buildings with interestingly decorated doors – one could no longer think of it as a town – in the middle of absolutely nowhere. The occasional stranger, such as myself, showed up because it was the entry to what once upon a time had been Ptolemais. In Tripoli, I had been warned that I would find the mentality in these eastern parts different. The people are Bedouins, was the explanation. The faces of the men were darker both in skin tone and expression. They seemed moodier, morose. They stared, frowned rather than interacted, and the further east we drove from the Green Mountain capital, the more apparent this seemed to become. Here in Tolmeta, I could not raise a nod.

Beyond the scrappy town, I found a pastoral idyll of flowers and fields where sprawling jumbles of ruins, including theatres, a Byzantine church and splendid Roman aqueducts, employed for crop irrigation in the hillsides surrounding this once-fertile city, were dotted over several undulating acres. I found no stones used in olive crushing. Still, once upon a time, this city, named after Ptolemy, inhabited by Greeks, Romans and, later, Arabs must have been thriving. Certainly its situation, sandwiched as it was between the rolling blue waves, sands and a backdrop of verdant escarpment, would have made it a highly desirable agricultural zone. Today, there was not a soul on the land save for a scarved, silver-bearded Berber in a grey-blue tunic and leather slippers, strolling with his goats and sheep. He shouted repeatedly at me, 'Italia? Italia?' and looked sufficiently advanced in years to remember the Italian occupation. Had I a day to idle, it would have been fascinating to roam these gently curving fields and gaze out upon the sea and try to interact with these mysterious desert people.

West of Tolmeta, along a bumpy road that could have taken us the 300 kilometres to Egypt, before the commencement of our ascent into the Jebel Akhdar, the Green Mountain itself, we found olives as tall as spreading oaks. Fine examples growing in deep-red earth amongst abandoned vineyards and antique terraces. Perfect olive terrain. The Greeks must have been astonished when they first approached this coast with its generous spread of natural bays. The moment when land came in sight, after days of sea travel, their boats drawing close to a solid green phalanx of forest. Once disembarked and on terra firma, they would have found wooded slopes, crystal waterways running fast from the mountain's summit and fecund soil. Given that this region was such a natural paradise, I had been wondering why the Phoenicians never created a trading or shipping base for themselves here, and the only answer I came up with was that it was too close to Tyre, to home.

The scenery as we descended into the gully of Wadi Kuf and then the ascent beyond was very dramatic. Jamel had been keen for me to see it. We avoided the suspension bridge and chose the ancient, more serpentine route where there were dozens of capacious red-rock caves, all of which had been occupied by the Libyan resistance fighters who took up arms in the 1920s against the Italians. This gorge and its cliffs hold a special place in the hearts of Libyans because the spirit of the rebellion was born here. Their leader was one Umar al-Mukhtar, who was eventually captured and hanged by the Italians but lives on here as a local hero.

I took a walk and discovered wild olive trees growing up the banks and in the stone-dry gulleys. These were the first wild forests of any significance I had encountered anywhere along my journey. The Djerban farmer, whose women were harvesting with goats' horns, told me it was almost impossible to tell the difference between a genuinely feral olive and one that had been sown wild from cultivated stock. Both have a shrubbier, stumpier look than a domesticated tree and sometimes their florets blossom with a greener tinge than the standard white. I had no way of knowing if these forests around me had always been here, whether when the Greeks arrived in 500 BC they found ferals along this coast, whether these came from stock imported by them or even by the more recent Italian occupation. One bird carrying a cultivated olive in his beak could have sown the first wild tree. If grown from stones, olives return to their feral state, unremembering of the millennia of cultivation; of picking, pressing, pruning. To propagate cultivated trees, they need to be grown from cuttings, as Nat had done with the Romans in Malta, or from suckers shooting up around the overground root base.

I picked a drupe and tasted it. It was almost sweet, not as ambrosial as Nat's saplings, but for Stone Age man, whose choices had been less sophisticated and whose sole access to sweetness was honey, such 'berries' could well have been palatable direct from the branch. Michel and I had seen in central Turkey that prehistoric man was a splendid husbander of fruit trees. If certain varieties of olives were edible from the boughs, might Neolithic man have gathered them as berries, and then discovered oil?

Back along the route, there were dozens of pretty but disintegrating country farmhouses built during the Italian occupation, sitting in the centre of neglected olive or fruit fields. A few had recently been reoccupied, squatted by Bedouin families. Bedouin men and boys were driving their flocks at the roadsides or over the stony ascending scrub. Their heads and faces were wrapped in scarves, all except for piercing Arabian eyes.

Occasionally, unexpectedly in this rural landscape, we passed a mosque. Religion seemed irrelevant here. Nature, indubitably, was the supreme goddess. Richly fertile, this was some of the loveliest countryside I had encountered anywhere along my journey. Barely a construction in sight save for the lighthouses dotted along the rocky littoral, and the air was sweet, scented with Mediterranean herbs and alpine plants.

By the time we reached the ancient Greek capital of Cyrene, dusk was approaching, so we drove directly to Susa, where Jamel promised a decent hotel. Given my previous night's experience, I was looking forward to that more than the sites.

Our descent led us from the ancient hillside of Cyrene, where banks of Italian cypresses were growing inside the lonely, forgotten city, to the town that, two and a half thousand years ago, had been Cyrene's harbour of Apollonia and is today the coastal settlement of Susa, past dozens of rock tombs, Greek or Roman, cut into the cliffs, strategically sited to look out across the plains to the sea, but they had long since been looted and appeared to house nothing but goats.

It was so beautiful, this steep, sweeping panorama, opening out on to fertile plains, tapestried with cultivation, with rust-red and madder-brown earth, fringed by turquoise sea, colours melting one into another, that in those moments I believed I could have stayed for ever. I requested Jamel stop the car so that I could walk awhile. Even on this winter's afternoon, there was a light breeze and aromatic scents. The Greeks knew a thing or two to choose this setting. In summer, when the heat was at its fiercest, how perfect it must have been to enjoy the breezes at such an elevation, while watching their ships berth and disembark in the distance, loaded with olive oil, wine, wheat and sylphium.

My hotel room overlooked both the Greek harbour city of Apollonia, built as the trading port for Cyrene, and the sea, and, as if to complete the scene, there was a full moon rising above the winter-green Mediterranean. Evening would fall soon, but, impatient, I set off to make a brief tour of the site. At the entrance booth, a young ticket collector, though I needed no ticket, asked after the whereabouts of my 'friend'. I was confused. Ah, Jamel.

'He's sleeping,' I replied, and he waved me in.

I hurried to the rocky track above the shore, where waves lashed against red rocks and spread like falling pearls. Rising out of the water to the horizon was my second Libyan rainbow. I was thrilled to discover numerous ancient storage vats chiselled out of the rocks, right at the water's edge. Countless generations of maritime activity, of spinning current and spume had eroded and left them with barnacled lava-like surfaces. It would have been from here, from this very spot, the port's quays and dazzling dockyard, that the vats and amphorae, stained with the sweat of men, were hauled and loaded, brimming with produce for export. I stood face to the wind, inhaling the power of crashing waves, conjuring images of two thousand years ago, picturing young Greek or Roman stevedores and navvies shouting and shunting.

Suddenly, incongruously, I heard the *muezzin* start up. The tinny call to prayers, as though from a scratched vinyl, was hailing the faithful from the loudspeaker of a pretty green-and-white mosque in the narrow lane directly behind the ruins. Another layer of history.

A plastic water bottle was rolling in the wind, bouncing to and fro, hitting the stony ground like the repeated clopping of goats' hoofs. It was a little spooky in this setting, this falling light. Further along, I found a seaside theatre – a classical end-of-pier playhouse! – with a wind-arched palm growing like some bent old thespian centre stage. It was a dramatic, blustery location for a play. So taken was I, above all by the atmosphere and haunting dusk setting, that I did not immediately register the man.

I had thought I was alone in the ancient harbour city, and the stranger was keeping a discreet distance, slipping with the shadows from one monument to the next. It was not the booth boy but another, an older, stockier figure with a beard, in a leather jacket, stalking the red-earthed and honey-toned buildings, following me. I was puzzled, alarmed, but not afraid. He was a police officer or some secret-service employee, I felt sure, but why was he shadowing me? He could not have supposed that I would not eventually notice him, given that we were the sole visitors. I continued my path, remaining alert to his whereabouts, until it grew too dark and I considered it more prudent to return to the hotel. By the time I had reached the ticket booth, where the collector was waiting, the stalker was at my side.

'I am police,' was his introduction.

'I thought you might be,' was my response.

'You have a very good camera. I was making sure it was not stolen.'

Such an unlikely explanation, graciously spoken. I stood a

moment, bemused, and then, pulling myself together, thanked him with equal grace.

I had failed to obtain a mobile-phone signal since our departure from Benghazi and I was eager to let Michel know that I was safe. I was surprised to learn from reception that this end-of-the-earth, windswept billet boasted an Internet café. After an early breakfast the following morning, I went in search of it. Instead of crossing the road directly in front of the hotel and continuing on, I turned left and ventured off alongside the ruins, past the mosque from where I had heard the *muezzin*, moving in a direction that took me away from what little activity this town possessed.

A quintet of waving children on a balcony screeched gleefully when I snapped a shot. Further along, two youths, one hopelessly handsome, faces branded by the sun, heads and ears wrapped in strips of scarves, like scrappy bandages, to protect against the sharp desert winds, were shifting mounds of earth and rubble from the roadside. Their smiles were wide and warm as they hailed me to take their pictures, too. After the surliness of earlier stops, I was delighted to make contact and showed them the digital results and we attempted conversation in sign language but did not get far. Across the street, a man holding the hand of a little girl exited his house. I asked directions for the Internet café. A ludicrous question in this unkempt corner of the earth where the ancient ruins were the dominant images. He shook his head and disappeared. I continued along my way to where all habitation melted into fields. I was bending, photographing plants and noticing that there was hearteningly less rubbish here than elsewhere. On the whole, the east was not as filthy and was better tended than the western coast, and the hedgerows and roadsides were not so cluttered with plastic bags and rusting tins.

A blue pick-up truck swung from out of a desert nowhere, and pulled up beside me. A man, one of two in the cab, stepped out. He offered me a lift, which I refused, explaining politely that I preferred to walk and could find my own way. The second stepped out. They waited expectantly. A menacing hiatus. I thanked them for their trouble and had turned back towards town when the first called after me, in English, 'I am police.' They did not look like officers of the law. But what did that mean here? My instinct warned they were untrustworthy. I thanked them again, a firmer tone, and turned away, leaving them to drive off. They continued to town, I hung about in the lane.

Having dallied in the sunshine, enjoying the ruins and sea vista from a different perspective, I decided that there was nothing further along this path so I doubled back, intending to enquire again at the hotel for the Internet café. My progression was halted by the arrival of Jamel in our car. His face was black as thunder.

'Get in,' he snarled. The police had rung his room, disturbing him while he was barefoot at prayer, insisting that he shod himself and get out immediately to find me because I was out and unescorted. They had quizzed him about me: who was I travelling with, where had I flown in to, what was the purpose of my trip to Libya?

'They have been tracking you since Tolmeta and I am not to let you out of my sight,' he informed me. He was very angry.

I sighed. 'Have I landed you in trouble?'

'Of course not, but you are not safe.'

I sighed again. 'That's preposterous.'

He reminded me that the day before, at Tolmeta, when we were leaving the ruins, a man had hurried over, requesting that we fill out a paper. I had understood that the local municipality was carrying out a survey, a tourist's impression of the site, but because we had been pressed for time, I had left the form empty. Jamel was now explaining that it had been my passport details they had required. Since then, from every police control along our route, they had radioed on ahead to inform the next control the direction I was approaching.

'I find this incredible,' I murmured.

'Tourists are forbidden to travel unaccompanied, and you have aggravated matters by being a woman. Why are you here, and where is your husband?'

'Jamel, you have lived in the West. You know that it is perfectly acceptable for a woman to travel alone. It does not mean I have indecent ulterior motives.'

'But you are not a tourist, are you?'

Suddenly, I understood that I could not afford to be so careless. I did not want to create the wrong impression. Suddenly, I feared for all my material.

'I am looking at olive trees and the way of life in the Mediterranean. I am not a journalist, politician or spy,' I joked.

'I am not letting you out of my sight.'

And he was good for his word. From there on, Jamel took on the role of bodyguard, whose duty it was to keep a beady eye on me and to deliver me safely back to Benghazi. He remained perfectly polite, but he grew sullen and mistrustful of me as though I had tricked him in some way. He accompanied me everywhere. If I disappeared to read, he would call on the internal phone every half an hour to find out what I was doing, or he knocked at my door. What are you doing? What are your plans? What shall I order for your supper?

Every meal, from breakfast onwards, was consumed in the cavernous, echoing dining room at our largely empty hotel, the only choice in town. He collected me from my room and escorted me down in the lift, ordered my food. The only other guests were two small groups of Swedes and Dutch, all men. If I had wanted to give Jamel the slip, which I longed to do, it would have been quite impossible.

Later, in the evenings, after dismally dull dinners, when the desert wind blew north and froze us in the streets, Jamel drove me to the Internet café – a matter of 500 yards – and waited outside in the car, to bundle me back unharmed, untouched, to the hotel.

I felt a prisoner, but I was still enchanted by the location. 'Is this necessary?' I begged, or possibly snapped.

Somewhere along that half-a-kilometre trajectory between the windy, palm-swept, red, beaten rocks and the bank of computers – it did not warrant the name café – we lost touch with the Mediterranean, even if all that remained of Mediterranean life was a distant echo of some forgotten past. Even that haunting on the wind fizzled out as we inched up streets where male stares were uncompromising and life looked miserable.

Jamel intimated at an 'unfortunate incident' that had occurred here involving a foreign woman, which explained why the police were trailing me and why I was to be constrained. They wished to protect me. But I was not convinced. I judged this to be a repressive, paranoid regime that worried about foreign opinion and was revulsed by interaction. The irony was that the few locals I did manage to come in contact with were relatively easy to engage with. The Internet café, such as it was, was always jam-packed with young men queuing for computers. Hair as black as unstarred nights, frequently bearded, with soulful eyes, unfathomable as the desert. Smoking, waiting, smoking, standing in line. Young Bedouins wanting a go on a machine. They seemed to have been swallowed up by directionlessness, wading within any one of several cultures. There was nothing to occupy them in the evenings. Stand in line here or – what? The only action on the streets was the scrub rolling in from the desert. The *ghibli* wind kicking empty tin cans about, and due to the ruling of Islam that kept all unmarried females shut up, the young men, hungry for female companionship, occupied themselves how?

'There had been an incident, involving a foreign woman . . .'

What secret sites were these guys surfing? What were they accessing on the Net? So intensely did they stare into those screens. Yet whenever I experienced difficulties, messages in Arabic that I did not comprehend and, droll though it was, confusions born of working with a machine that, even in English, wrote from the right side of the screen to the left, any number of these Bedouins – boys that should have been men – would rise from their seats to offer assistance. I felt no danger here, no threat. I felt profoundly sorry for them.

Like a pair of pensioners, Jamel and I set off on our days, dipping in and out of deserted bays, exploring the coast, which must have been ravishing when all the Italian farmhouses were in good repair, when the homes, lanes, fields were less neglected and sad. I was looking for remains, stones, ruins of ancient olive mills. Given the number of wild trees, there must have been considerable production activity when the Greeks were resident, though the Romans used this side of Africa less than their fabulously remunerative west-coast cities.

We found no mills, but made discoveries that even Jamel, who came camping to this region regularly with his family, had never known. Pursuing donkey tracks that led us through a buried three-house hamlet, we came upon a lonely Byzantine church set on a blustery bluff, a location so idyllic that exaltation of God was precisely the sentiment that fell from both our lips. We found ourselves in the midst of a village nestling behind hedgerows set back from open fields and the sea where wedding preparations were afoot. Here, I learned of *lagbi*, a juice extracted from the date palm, claimed by Arabs to be exceedingly good for the health if consumed fresh, but if left in the fridge for two days, it became alcoholic and was deemed haram, forbidden by Islam. Bleeding off this sap from the palm tree, stealing its heart, according to Jamel, risked mortality for the trees.

The women were squatting outside in an untidy yard, preparing a syrup, boiling the dates on an open fire. The concoction had been simmering for several hours, explained a brown-eyed stranger who had invited us to the wedding preparations.

While this was happening, four lads attached palm fronds and hanging lights to the wall of a house across the street, which was where the groom resided; a marriage between neighbours. One of the women poured a few drops of her boiled liquid on to the sandy ground, where it settled in tiny balls. This signalled the syrup was ready. I was offered a mouthful on a piece of soft bread. Aside from being hot, it tasted, unsurprisingly, exceedingly sweet, but had a slightly bitter, burned flavour like molasses. They were intending it as an ingredient for a wedding cake.

Walking back to the car, Jamel remarked that these recipes had originated in Iraq, which had always been proud of its 30 million date palms. He went on to say that in 2003 Iraq lost its entire crop due to American weapons using depleted uranium. Farmers had not pollinated their palms, fearing toxic pollution.

'I heard about it,' I replied softly.

He asked me, with a tangible note of accusation in his voice, whether I knew that the percentage of babies born in

Iraq without eyes and with cancers such as leukaemia had escalated since the use of depleted-uranium weapons.

I had read of it, but I made no comment.

It had become a profound sadness for me that the divide in Libya, between local and foreigner, meant that there was nowhere for me to ask, to find out, to discover except by chance. Few possibilities existed to engage or to learn, to immerse myself in local life or the history I sought, and this one opportunity I had been given – Jamel – had been poisoned by state interference. In Jamel's eyes, I had become a symbol of the corrupt West.

We followed roads that wound up behind Apollonia, gazing back at the patchworks of dark-red earth and green square fields, knitted together by old stone walls and traced through with tracks to grazing grounds, searching for Roman aqueducts, plunging into wadis, chasing water conduits or natural springs, falling upon sarcophagi buried beneath overgrowth. We wandered about the fabulous site of Cyrene together and when we found millstones or made small, incidental discoveries, his gloomy mood lifted and he treated me as a partner in adventure rather than a transgressor of Islam. If he tired of the stones, trees and irrigation systems, he perched on the seats of Roman theatres or leaned against fountains or marble columns, watching me happily traipsing about the graceful ruins, discovering antiquity. But we never regained the early confidence that had been natural and comfortable in Benghazi.

Cyrene, today a UNESCO World Heritage site, was magnificent. Red earth lay in hummocks where archaeological works had once been in progress. A trio of cows were grazing the deserted sports arena. Fresh water from the Fountain of Apollo ran right through the ancient city, giving it a life and music of its own, even today. Dozens of slabs of stone olive presses, wheels, settling tanks, lay about the hillside, while wild olive trees were pushing up through the long-vacated city streets.

The Greeks who landed here, and those who followed after them, Egyptians, Romans, claiming even larger tracts of the local land, were so far removed from the local inhabitants both in time and culture. The Libyans were desert peoples, herders, nomads. They lived in skin tents, while the Greeks had already built a classical empire, had navigated and put down roots across the Mediterranean Sea. They appreciated philosophy, music, art, politics. In short, they had little in common with the Bedouins they discovered abiding here except a desire to stake this same glorious stretch of coast. The natives resisted the influx of strangers, but it was to no avail. This coast was fertile and it possessed natural treasures that offered the Greeks great wealth. Sylphium was one of those treasures. A plant that resembled wild fennel, it grew exclusively in these green belts of eastern Libya, and because it was available nowhere in the world but here, it was worth a fortune and was much sought after for medicinal purposes. The Greeks, later the Romans, harvested and shipped it until its extinction.

Olive oil was another treasure. If there were feral trees in existence before the arrival of the Greeks, I doubt they had been touched. The Greeks probably brought the olive tree to this eastern coast, certainly knowledge of its cultivation, while the Phoenicians planted up the western shores.

Meanwhile, the local population continued as nomadic desert peoples and the glories and riches were enjoyed by foreigners who settled; the privileged few. It was impossible not to liken the situation to present-day Libya.

Libya, magnificent Libya. This had been the only stop on my route where I had felt saddened by the results olive farming had achieved, but perhaps I was looking at history and its place in our present through new eyes.

Time to break camp. We returned to Benghazi. Greece, Israel, Alexandria were beckoning; still, I left with a confused heart.

Greece

A Phoenician named Cecrops founded a settlement on an impressive rock inland of the sweeping coast of Attica. The gods of Olympus proclaimed that this fabulously sited city should be named after the deity who could produce the most valuable legacy for mortals. Athene, goddess of wisdom, planted an olive tree, symbol of peace and prosperity, on the Acropolis, while salty old Poseidon struck the rock with his trident and up sprang a horse, symbolising his strength and fortitude. The gods chose Athene's gift, saying that mankind would be better served by an olive tree than by Poseidon's war weapons. Make peace not war, was their vote. Thus Athene gave her name to what was to become one of the most illustrious cities of all time. She was proclaimed patron goddess of this state and, in the words of Hollywood, a legend was born.

I landed in Athens on a Friday evening close to midnight, exhausted after a two-hour delay. Too late for a bus, I took a taxi. The ride into town with a twenty-something Greek on a mobile phone, funk playing loudly on the radio, demonstrated to me how the city had moved on a millennium since my last sojourn a decade earlier. Athens was a destination I had visited regularly in my early twenties. Greece's entry into Europe and its hosting of the Olympic Games in 2004 had offered the opportunity to face-lift its neglected capital.

The hotel I had chosen, situated towards the apex of the

Lykavittos Hill, booked by Internet, offered a reasonable winter rate of €55 (£38) per night and promised magnificent views.

From my room, leaning my body over the railings of a strip of balcony, I could just about glimpse the floodlit Acropolis. Was that it? But the following morning, I made my way to breakfast on the sixth floor and found myself staring into the face of the noble summit. The view from where I was sitting, in the hazy, warm January light, took me as far as Piraeus, the country's principal port and, for several million tourists in summer, a springboard to the islands. The harbour used to be half a dozen miles south of the city, but today they are one and the same. So much has this capital eaten its way into the countryside on its march to expansion.

I collected from the buffet a dish of yoghurt and honey, Kalamata olives and feta cheese and sat gazing out upon the cluster of buildings and, crowning it, its classical *pièce de résistance*. A thousand memories returned of young Carol, hungry for life, tanned as polished cherry wood. There had been a summer – can it have been the summer of 1972? – when I had fleetingly fallen in love in Piraeus. The object of my passion had been an Egyptian-Frenchman, dark, lean, mysterious. We had been living as neighbours on two elegant wooden schooners. I, with a French crew I had met up with at Epidavros, down along the Peloponnesian coast, with whom I had hitched a ride back to the capital rather than take the bus, and he as captain of an elegant Egyptian vessel that was never occupied. We had indulged in our brief romance, played out between the two sailing yachts, limbs entangled within cramped, creaking teak cabins. The waves beyond licked lasciviously at the boats' hulls. Our passionate liaison had lasted until he tired of me, alas, a mere few weeks later. It was sweet to cast my mind back to a moment I had completely forgotten. I wondered where he might be now.

In those earlier years, I had come to know Athens quite well, but I had never visited the summit of the verdant Lykavittos Hill. I decided it would be my first port of call. Lykavittos means 'Hill of Wolves' for, once upon a time, wild dogs prowled its wooded slopes. Most of the pines had long since been felled and replaced by a fashionable district that sweeps to the city's centre. There is a funicular for the faint of heart, but it was January, pleasant weather, and the winding hike to its apex was well worth the exercise. The views, of course, in every direction were panoramic. It was a clear day – I could see as far as the islands of Salamis and Aegina – and it demonstrated why this location had been chosen by those early Phoenician mariners who were always on the lookout for the ideal landing base. The basin of Attica stretched inland across a flat plain to the feet of a protective, encircling trio of mountains, Parnitha, Imittos and Egaleo. A perfect position for a harbour and good flat land for construction and cultivation.

The whitewashed houses, so characteristic of Athens's urban sprawl, were bathed in sunlight, while the amphitheatre of mountains were coated in snow. Alongside me, a fluff of blossoms, not almond, ornamental cherry perhaps, were blooming. Variations on a theme of white. To the east, where one of the mountains had been gouged open for its limestone – a quarry ziggurat, gradations like monumental steps, was covered in ice, a spectacular frozen waterfall, the gods' playground. In contrast to the white, the black. The old crows, the iconic Greek widows, clad from head to foot in weeds of mourning, hard at work housekeeping the interior of the impeccably whitewashed chapel of Agios Giorgios, St George. They clucked and cackled together like a gaggle of farmyard fowl. Outside on the porch were two wooden chairs with rush seating, so reminiscent of the Greece I had fallen in love with three decades earlier. In between the bell tower and chapel was an olive tree. In Greece, olive trees are frequently planted by churches; it is a laudation of rebirth, of life everlasting.

It was the season of oranges, of tangerines, perfect weather to sink into the city, weave through thick tufts of traffic and rise the hilly streets again at the Acropolis, where I had hoped to begin with the Odeon of Herodes Atticus, but it was closed for winter. I was then refused entry to the summit because I was carrying a rucksack. The quartet of ticket collectors obliged me to deposit it in a shack way down the hill where there was an irate queue attending an Englishwoman bickering about bags and cameras. I almost walked away. I had seen the temples on many occasions, but I stuck it out and, once there, was glad I had not lost patience. From the heights of Parthenon Hill, I went directly to look down upon the Herodes Atticus theatre.

On that first travel outing of mine, aged twenty-two, I attended many performances here during short hops into the capital, the first of which had been the opera *Carmina Burana*. It was during the Greek Junta, when the colonels ruled the country. On that occasion, Georgios Papadopoulos, the president who was born of poor rural stock in a village called Elaiohori, Olive Ville, was due to attend, and, as with royalty, nothing began until he had been seated. I was overawed by the display of military might and by such charismatic Athenian society, bejewelled and extravagant. I was a budding actress, a keen observer, entranced by a real-life drama I did not comprehend, played out against a sunset, starlit, visually magnificent setting. The politics meant nothing to me, until a few days later, when I stopped to buy a cold drink at a street kiosk and fell into conversation with the vendor. The bearded fellow selling me juice was also an actor. He was not street trading because he was out of work but because his outspoken criticism of the colonels had left him blacklisted. It was the first time I had given a thought to the imperatives of freedom of speech. Papadopoulos was later overthrown by his own military.

I crossed the Acropolis summit to the Erechtheion, where a young olive tree was growing, flanking the small temple. Here was where Athene had planted her legendary tree and where religious worship to the goddess took place. This latest one must have been stage-set by the municipality to please the Olympic crowds.

A pasty-faced, wiltingly thin woman with mousy hair scrunched high on her head, held in place by a bone, addressed me. She was French, working in television, but her real passion was alternative medicine. She walked up here every week, she revealed, because in ancient Athens, the Acropolis had been the religious centre of the city and she felt it imbued her with positive energy. The idea that I was in some way involved in olive oil sent her into paroxysms of delight and she tagged along beside me as I began my descent, hanging about while I collected my bag. I was on the point of bidding her *au revoir* when she asked me whether I knew the sequel to the Athene-olive legend, the story rarely told.

I did not.

In honour of their patron goddess, the sixth century BC Athenians founded a festival, the Panathenaea. As with the Olympics (which it might have been set up to rival), it was to be held every fourth summer. A religious affair, it involved a fair amount of blood-spilling and animal sacrifices offered to the goddess. (This gave my narrator the shivers because she was a vegetarian.) There were also poetry recitals and sports events. Its athletic games were highly competitive and the winner of each event was awarded a Panathenaic amphora, a substantial jar filled with olive oil pressed from fruits harvested from the sacred groves surrounding Athens.

So essential was the quality of the victory oil that from the fourth century BC onwards, the city ruler was given responsibility for the oil's production. The prize for each event varied according to the status of the game. For example, the victor of horse racing scooped the top prize, 140 jars of sacred oil. A typical storage jar contained 36 kilos of oil, which meant that certain victorious athletes stood to win up to 5 tons of olive oil from one event.

'Is this accurate?' I asked. I considered the production at our modest farm, approximately 400 kilos of oil a year.

'That is the point,' emphasised Cécile, whose name I had now learned.

The quantities were so excessive that the athletes did not know what to do with their prizes and so a black market was created to channel this sacred liquid to foreign traders. There was good money to be made in the traffic of victory oil and many of the successful athletes were set up for life. I was fascinated to discover where those sacred victory jars ended up.

It was time to sail my wine-dark sea, although, in this season, the water was more reminiscent of a ruffled pigeon's breast. I had been hunting for sailings to Haifa or Alexandria but was having no luck. All maritime exchanges between Israel and Egypt had been cancelled five or six years earlier, I learned. Before travelling to Kalamata at the western extreme of the Peloponnese and on to Crete, I decided, first to sail north to the island of Lesvos, the island I had gazed upon from the shoreline of Turkey, across the blue Aegean, on a sunny afternoon several months earlier. Lesvos had somewhere in the region of 11 million olive trees and a long history of farming; it warranted a trip. I had also heard that there had been a time during Turkish occupation when the farmers of Lesvos hid their olives from the Turks and used the money from the sale of the oil to fund a resistance. I was keen to learn more about it. It began to rain and rain hard. From Athens, the ferry to Lesvos was ten hours. The night before my departure, I enquired at reception as to whether this change in the weather would affect sailings. The lean-boned Athenian assured me that the ferry would sail, but when I arrived at the port of Piraeus – so changed from the stage setting of my callow romance – the departure had been cancelled. A force-ten gale was whipping the Mediterranean. All vessels were embayed.

A flight was leaving at half past two. I hailed a taxi and requested the airport, calling ahead to make a reservation, which the airline agreed to hold until midday. It was now eleven thirty. My taxi driver was handsome; a friendly, bearded Greek originally from the northern part of the mainland. He was easygoing and chatted as he drove. Fifteen minutes later, not 20 yards past the toll, his taxi ground to a halt. Lorries were hooting, cars were swerving to avoid us, but try as he might he could not fire the engine back into life. I had no wish to abandon him, but it was evident that we were as grounded as the ferries. Someone from the toll booth called a rescue truck. My driver stepped from the cab and began waving his arms in a dangerous attempt to flag me another ride, which he managed. I paid him the full fare, knowing the rescue truck would probably cost him a day's pay, wished him the best of luck and climbed in alongside a Dutchman who was perfectly happy to share his transport.

My arrival in Lesvos was greeted with the force-ten gale that had halted all shipping in Athens. It was a bumpy landing. Inland, dark mountains hemmed the rattling runway. The sea, directly alongside us, was choppy with whitecaps racing in from Turkey. I was relieved not to have seen all that before we touched down.

The transport to Mytilene was sparse. I ended up sharing a taxi with a pair of Orthodox priests with black brillo-pad beards, black stove-pipe hats, walrus waists, mobile phones, chewing gum. Halfway to my *pension*, the cab pulled up on a corner while yet another of their brethren toddled across the street and was crammed into the car. No one spoke. The short journey in the howling wind was solemn and I could not see past their beards to gaze out of the window at the shoreline. In some remote past, Lesvos was connected to the coast of Asia Minor, the coast I could not see.

The east, southern and central areas of Lesvos were rich with olive groves and forests of *Pinus brutia* (sometimes, but not in Greece, called the Turkish pine), oak, fir, plane and chestnut. The west was bald and rocky. I was excited at the prospect of discovering it all.

As we approached the harbour of Mytilene, the wind was jigging along the seafront, forcing all in its wake earthwards. The small hotel I had booked by phone was not on the front but down a lane so narrow the taxi could not penetrate. So I was obliged to walk with my luggage. As I stepped out of the car, the cold wind slapped my features. I set off, bidding good day and *efharisto* to the ecclesiastical trio, but not a man glanced my way. The track was just that, potted and puddled.

The hotel did not accept any credit card I was travelling with. Would I settle my account in cash? Although the sums involved were minimal, on a journey of this length I had insufficient local currency to cover any expenses more substantial than bus rides or snacks. Weary, I decided to stay one night and defer the decision till the morning. I dropped bags, coat, computer, wallet, all possessions, in my room and hastened back outside to one of the six Internet cafés I had spotted in the lane. The wind all but whipped the door off its hinges as I entered. Inside, mirrored bar and thumping techno music were more in keeping with a nightclub than a Greek-island café. I sent mails and hurried back.

Later, I went in search of food and an investigatory walk round the harbour. The winds were whipping the waves across the straits. Dozens of travel agencies, all advertising boat trips to Turkey. I had been hoping to make a day trip to Ayvalik, back across to where I had stood in September, but no boats were running.

The bad weather? No, bird flu. 'It has struck Asia Minor and is killing infants at the rate of knots,' a salesgirl informed me. I was surprised to learn this, but then I had seen no news, read no papers.

High-tech lounge bars and hip cafés with white sofas, deafening music, serving cocktails, screening snappily edited video clips, were everywhere along the front. Mytilene was a university town, but even so I had not expected the island to be quite so *branché*, switched on. There were no signs of traditional Greece anywhere until I reached the farthest extreme of the harbour where half a dozen *caiques* were moored, slapping back and forth against the stone quay. Here, I found two bars packed with old crooked Greeks in woollen hats, nattering, drinking ouzo, watching terrestrial TV. No snappy video clips for these wrinkle-faced walruses. Either of these smoggy establishments would have been where I could dig up a few olive stories, but there was not a woman in sight and I, aside from basic words, could not converse in Greek. With a sigh, I swung away from the harbour front in the direction of the library. I knew it would be closed, but locating it would save me time in the morning.

Dusk had fallen. I was frozen and went in search of dinner.

Up and down the warren of curving lanes I searched, beneath stylish, but neglected buildings. Many fine examples, I saw, of solid bourgeois houses, a faded opulence, and my guess was they were legacies of the four-hundred-year Ottoman rule of the island.

Set back from the esplanade, authentic life was more evident. Even at this late hour, I sighted young women on balconies, worked to the bone, clothes-pegged fingers hanging out washing. Eventually, I followed my ears and the deafening strains of bouzouki, Greek blues music, and found a simple place where a young couple were furiously engaged in spring-cleaning. Assuming they were closed, I asked if they could direct me to a taverna. 'Here,' the man replied, whisking buckets out of sight. I was grateful for refuge from the cold, though the interior reeked of bleach and was glaringly lit. I ordered my food. It arrived within moments, all dishes served together.

Snow had fallen and carpeted Athens causing chaos in the capital, the television in reception announced as I descended for breakfast. The same weather was expected in Lesvos. Yiannis, of Yiannis and Georgios, the two young brothers who owned the establishment, told me that his wife was a teacher and the schools had been closed. The children travelled from far-flung villages and the buses could not negotiate the icy altitudes. He warned against hiring a car and informed me the airport would shut down. Unless I flew out immediately, I would be stranded. These arctic lows had only been recorded once before on this island. If I chose to stay, Yiannis had tracked down a friend with a furniture shop who would accept my credit card. I asked my host if he could put me in touch with an elderly olive farmer or two. Shrivelled belsires, grandfathers, with memories, stories from the crumbling days of the Turkish occupation. He looked at me strangely, promised to try and I agreed to stay on.

The snow arrived, settled. It was so dense there was nowhere for me to go. I took the opportunity to work in my snug room, scribbling notes from my little black books, facts photocopied for me by Julia in Malta, or picking through the history of this island from a book lent to me by Georgios. By afternoon, I emerged from the hotel, sleepy, in need of sustenance. I had found an unassuming little restaurant that must have been a converted boathouse just across the lane. It was too modern to be described as a taverna, but a family business nevertheless – mother cooking, daughter serving. Simon and Garfunkel tunes crooned in Greek. I sat by the window looking out at the swirling snow beyond the panes. Inside, the furniture was wooden, painted bright red. Candles were burning on the tables even though it was only afternoon. I felt as though I had landed in Sweden. Geography all jumbled up. But I liked it. I had nested.

On the second afternoon, I ordered a small pitcher of red wine. It arrived chilled and demi-sweet, and I opened up my computer. I was the sole customer, settled in a corner like a forgotten sack, until the door flew open and a howling wind rushed in like the hoary fingers of frost, followed by two young girls. Chattering, laughing, long hair starred with melting snowflakes, they ordered hot chocolate. Greek music now, reminiscent of the Italian *chanteur* Paolo Conte. I was comfortable, warm, happy, observing the winter world of the harbour. Alone with my olive dreams, I was content to take refuge, to hunker down, as long as the snow beyond the windows fell in creeping sheets.

The snow continued.

Striding portside, at the treacherous water's edge, I was on the hunt for a bookstore owned by an old-timer, Petros. The mountains all around the city had turned white. Neither Georgios nor his elder brother, Yiannis, had tracked down any octogenarians who could furnish me with the past I was looking for and I was growing concerned that I might not achieve anything here, that I might be losing the thread, losing purpose. Then Yiannis suggested Petros.

The snow was scratching at my face. Everywhere around me I heard the weather drumming against flimsy shop canopies. The lamps outside the techno lounges were swinging back and forth, circling and bucking as though ready to hurl themselves into the sea. I had heard that winter in Lesvos was an inhuman business, but there was something melancholy and beautiful about it, like a damaged print in shades of grey and white, with its dark and louring sea slapping at a windswept harbourside, neither Turkish nor Greek. But I could not remember when I had last felt this cold.

The shop, tucked back along an alley off the semicircular esplanade, sold stationery, not books. I pushed at the warped door, which set a bell ting-a-linging, and found myself within a dark grotto barely larger than a kiosk. It had probably last seen paint more than half a century earlier. Tight against a solid, free-standing paraffin heater in the centre of the store stood a very elderly, faded gentleman with a full head of grey hair as stiff and upright as quills. He was wearing a scarf and grey overcoat. Alongside him were two marginally younger females, both smoking. One was darning thick, beige stockings. The place reeked of a forgotten way of life: chalk, ink, rubber, paraffin, mothballs. Shelves stacked untidily with notebooks, blocks of paper, blotting and carbon sheets, old maps, crayons, typewriter ribbons, heaven knows what else, all partially covered by a display of large black-and-white photographs Sellotaped to the wooden planks.

'*Yassas. Kalimera,*' I said. The trio nodded.

I attempted to explain my mission, but they spoke no English or French and my Greek was woefully inadequate. I soldiered on with sign language. They stared at me, not in an unkindly way, but with expressions that told me it was too cold to be fussed and my business was unclear. Eventually, one of the women shuffled to the door, crossing to a boutique selling lingerie. We waited, nodding awkwardly. Moments later, she shuffled back accompanied by a heavily made-up girl wrapped in a fur muff.

'*Yassas*, I'm Sally.' She grinned.

Now, old Petros was only too happy to recount his tales, but my hearsay that olives were used subversively to fund a resistance against the Turks was inaccurate.

He shook his head. 'Never heard that one,' he muttered.

Olive oil had been hidden from the Germans during World War II, but never from the Turks. The women, like a double act, nodded in agreement. A small crowd was gathering. Elderly or middle-aged folk in heavy navy coats, earmuffs, high zipped boots, who had come to purchase Biros, one envelope, or had been told by another in the lingerie shop, perhaps, that important island matters were being discussed. Everyone had an opinion, an interpolation. Petros was in his element. Bloody words against the Turks hissed from every dusty crevice. Stories were narrated, too fantastical or racist to repeat. Entire Greek families slaughtered in their sleep, drowned at sea. But a tale of Greek resistance against their oppressors and olive oil? No. Heads shook despondently, more cigarettes were lit. As folk began to disperse, out into the bitter, howling morning, Petros hobbled out of sight, beyond a lank curtain at the rear of his warren and returned clutching a brown cloth with the vigilance of one carrying a reliquary. He laid it on a pile of grey exercise books. The women stepped closer as though a rite was about to be performed, while the spiky-haired storyteller unfurled the cloth and revealed a packet of folded sepia documents, like parchments. These he opened up proudly and handed them, one by one, to me. Yellowed with age, folded so long they were disintegrating at the seams. All but one were ink-written in Arabic, each with a stamp at the foot of its page. Petros smiled, nodded, knowing he had won my attention.

Arabic, he confirmed. I agreed. Turkish had been written in Arabic script until Atatürk had enforced the Alphabet Revolution in 1928, switching his new republic to Roman characters, nudging it closer to the West.

'So, these documents pre-date nineteen . . .?'

I glanced towards Petros and he nodded again. 'Nineteen twenty-eight.'

His grandparents came from Turkey. These were land deeds of the olive groves they had owned and farmed somewhere north of Izmir, groves they were obliged to abandon when they departed as refugees for the mother country after the Treaty of Lausanne stipulated the exchange of Greek and Turkish refugees; all Turks born and raised on Greek territories and all Greeks on Turkish land were legally obliged to uproot and reinstate themselves in the land of their flag. Only one of Petros's documents was in Greek and even with the help of Sally I could not ascertain what this one represented: land purchased on the island of Lesvos? It seemed not.

Before the ruling Turks, pashas of the Ottoman Empire, were driven from Lesvos in 1912, the canny ones sold their properties to the wealthiest of the island's Greeks and left with cash in their pockets. The land that had not been sold was divided into cadastred plots, noted on slips of paper and placed in jars. The arriving Greek refugees from Turkey were invited to extract one of the squares of paper from the kitty and whatever allotment they had drawn was theirs to own and farm. If they had olive groves, they had potential wealth.

'And what of your family, who had been olive farmers?' I asked him.

He shrugged, shaking his head modestly from side to side. 'We were fortunate,' he admitted.

I cast my eyes about the walls. Way above, almost beyond my range of vision, hung a curious picture of small boys lying on mattresses, skinny and sick. It put me in mind of Belsen. I pointed to it. 'What is the story behind that?' I enquired.

Petros lifted his hand as though to silence me and shook his head sadly. 'The hunger. Not fortunate.' Immediately, he directed my attention elsewhere, to another faded sepia image hanging from the shelves. A small boy with a rather handsome, tall, slender woman in long frock, pinafore and headscarf, feeding chickens in a backyard. 'Petros,' he explained. The woman was his grandmother and the photograph had been taken in Turkey before they had made that short journey across the strait, leaving everything behind them, never to return.

After examining the photo, I turned to Petros. He was weeping. His tears seemed to have welled up from a deep part of him; not a new pain but one that had been contained for many a decade.

'We came from the north. We walked across the border with a pig on my father's shoulders, a few chickens. My mother, folded in a blanket to keep out the damp, was pregnant with my small sister, who lived only a few days,' said one of the women standing by the heater. Her hands were trembling as she lit another cigarette.

I had intruded sufficiently into their history. Shaking hands, expressing my gratitude for their time, I promised to visit again before leaving the island. The two smoking women nodded. I had no idea who they were or what relation they were to Petros. I set off for the library.

The sea had grown sullen, grey as a liquefied whale.

Lying in bed, I heard the wind at work in the unmade lane beyond the window, whistling and clattering like a drunk falling out of a bar, slapping itself against the electricity lines and the rusted metal doorways that led from here to the sea. I turned on my narrow mattress, stretching and flexing my toes, thankful that the room was warm, that I could keep my socks for my boots and did not need to wear them in bed.

The following morning, a lady from the local library rang me at half past eight, just after my breakfast, to tell me that she had found a book in English that could be useful for my studies, if I cared to drop by later.

'We are open all day till half past one in the noon,' she assured me.

When I arrived, the librarian, perched at her desk behind her computer, seemed thrilled with her discovery. A picture book of the island.

Beyond the window by the table where I was sitting was a fig tree. Its leafless branches clawed and tapped at the panes eerily, as though the island's past was scratching to be let in, to have its say.

Many of the photographs had dates, place names in French. 'Why?' I whispered to my librarian friend. From the eighteenth century, France made a trade agreement with the Ottoman Empire. They purchased its olive oil for the soap factories of Marseille, which in turn supplied the textile mills of Europe with soap for the manufactured cloth.

I thanked the librarian for her trouble and she insisted on writing me her name and phone number, in case she could help me further. Cleopatra, she was. This pretty, tubby lady, full cheeks like a hamster, eyes large, willing, doll-like. She regretted that she could not take me to meet her father-in-law. He was a hundred years old with a 'young wife of eighty-six to tend him', but although he was in perfect health, he had no memory now; he would not remember that he was six when the Turks finally departed from the island in 1912, the year Lesvos was returned to its Greek inhabitants after 350 years of Turkish occupation. She confirmed Petros's opinion. The resistance here was during World War II, when the island-ers assisted the Allies, particularly British soldiers, to escape, stowing them on ships bound for Asia Minor, from where they made their way to their troops in the Middle East.

Before I left, Cleopatra gave me the name of the cousin of a colleague, a professor she felt I might like to meet. She told me then that during a major earthquake in the mid-nineteenth century (the Aegean isles are susceptible to earthquakes), much of Lesvos was damaged and the Turkish chiefs doled out the reparation works to the native Greeks. The pashas were lazy and the olive farms were in a sorry state. The Greeks nurtured the plantations and possibly hived away more than their entitlement. Perhaps that had been the seed of the story I had been seeking, she suggested. Many Lesvian families became very wealthy shipping their produce abroad. Her hundred-year-old father-in-law had owned a soap factory in Constantinople, but after 1923, he no longer had access to it, and lost all his assets there. Other farmers did business in the Black Sea or Alexandria and used their fortunes to found shipping dynasties. All from their local olive oil. The irony was that it had been the Ottomans who had forced the islanders to dig up all the vineyards – as Muslims, they had no need of wine – and cultivate extra olive groves. Before the Turks, the Venetians, who had many colonies in Greece, mainly the

Ionian Islands, south-east Peloponnese and Crete, kept a very tight rein on oil cultivation, making certain that all of its produce was shipped back to Venice. The Ottomans had profited from this policy, extending it, allowing it to flourish, feeding the coffers of Constantinople. The good news was that it had promoted and intensified the olive industry in Greece and even today olives remain the principal source of income on Lesvos. The olive tree is its foremost natural resource, its wealth. Of course, tourism was fast changing that balance.

I asked Cleopatra if there was a secret to her relative's longevity, hoping she might mention the local oil or a diet of Greek goat's yoghurt with aromatic honey every morning for breakfast.

'He never got nervous,' smiled Cleopatra, the enchanting librarian.

Battling my way back to the hotel, buried beneath two scarves and three sweaters, I strode by a few examples of the ornate mansion properties. They had been constructed not by the Ottomans, I had learned from Cleopatra, but by local Greek merchants, funded from the enormous profits they had gleaned from the export of their olive oil.

I paused to admire the view across to Asia Minor where the mountains were decked in white. I recalled my journey with Murat and the family-run factory we had visited almost directly across the strait from where I was now standing. I wondered how this cold weather had affected their harvests, those trees that had been heavy with fruit when we had passed through in September.

I noticed the force of the waves on the water, directly beneath me. Until now, there had been little movement within the harbour. All the crashing and swelling, the tossing and turning, had taken place beyond its walls, but levels were rising, rolling towards the quay.

That very morning, I had found a booklet of island folklore: the Aegean 'bares its teeth' in winter, and when white horses scuff the sea and race towards the shore, mothers lift their babies towards the water and cry, 'Look! Here come the spring lambs. They are swimming to us for Easter, arriving from the east.'

I prayed the waves would not be swimming this way until Easter!

Later, a meeting in a café with Professor Skampanas, Cleopatra's contact, whose specialist topic was Ottoman history. With him I drank hot, velvety chocolate and from him I learned that local taxes were paid to the Turks in oxen, that many Greeks volunteered to fight with the Russians against the Ottoman Empire in the eighteenth century because they wanted the opportunity to avenge themselves against their oppressors, that over on the west of the island the petrified forest was made up of prehistoric sequoia trees and, more importantly for me, the Church had substantial interests in the olive groves of Lesvos. One in particular, the Monastery of Limona, possessed fine examples of old presses. Sadly, none of this could I visit, due to the freak weather.

The professor recounted how the women, in their traditional costumes, had picked olives by hand from the nets, while the men beat the trees with sticks and they sang traditional songs together. When they arrived at the mills for the pressings, they had another canon of songs, tunes of celebration. The tradition of olive harvesting and pressing had been a joyous season on this island. Unhappily, the local Greeks no longer cared to harvest the fruits themselves. They employed Albanians for the labour-intensive work. These labourers lived here on a year-round basis, working on construction sites outside the olive season, but they were not popular. In some instances, the arrangement was similar to the one we had with René, our neighbour at the farm. The gatherer kept the oil from all that he had harvested, returning but a minimal percentage to the farmer. The island was keen to find alternative methods of combatting olive fly, he also told me. Even the Church had its own label of organic oil for sale.

Had he any idea how they maintained organic standards? He shook his head.

Had he any idea when he thought olive cultivation commenced here? Again the professor shook his head. 'After the Peloponnesian and the Cretan cultivators,' he replied, 'though there were cave settlements here at Thermi on the coast from around 4300 BC and there was archaeological evidence to prove they were trading commercially with regions in the east and other Aegean islands as well as mainland Greece.' A quick calculation reminded me that while those masterly Lebanese trees from Bechealeh were being planted, here man was still living in caves, albeit seafaring cave dwellers. Did they have wild olives?

The bars, the cafés were packed from morning to night. I ventured into them now to read and guzzle hot chocolate instead of breakfast at the hotel. They were crammed with students at every hour, playing backgammon, *tavli*, or Scrabble, rolling cigarettes, chatting happily in spite of the loud music. I calculated that I must be twice the age of most who frequented them. It was curious to observe this indoor Greek way of life. After one such excursion, I returned to the hotel via the lanes and found waiting for me in reception a Professor Katris, colleague of Skampanas, seated on the beige, plastic sofa, in patterned wool sweater, denim jacket and jeans. He sported a full bushy beard and longish dark hair that hung like a fringe from a bald pate. His left eye was permanently closed as though locked in calculation. He looked as though someone had pressed on the top of his head with a heavy weight and squashed him. Between both hands he dandled a folder within which was his book. His labour of love. It had taken him seven years to accomplish, €7,000, or £4,825, to publish, reimbursed to him by the island's treasury, though I did not understand which particular department, and included 220 photographs. I feared he might be there to request help in achieving publication abroad. I misjudged him.

The book was unique in that it represented a history of the island as told through the mills and ancient crushing stones used to pulp olives. He knew every centimetre of his terrain, he and his two children, who always accompanied him for this work, achieved at weekends. He had scoured the entire island in his search for olive-related stones. During his travels, he had learned why a village was perched this way on a mountain and not another, beneath or above a bluff. He had commissioned his pupils to enquire, to seek, to return with news of ancient mill sites. Farmers had threatened him with the police or, worse, at loaded gunpoint, with hunting rifles, because they feared that the archaeologists would follow in his wake and their land would be closed off and rendered useless to them. Many had hidden rare examples of stones so that he would not find and record them, but he had managed to unearth them, frequently digging them out himself, and in one instance removing the cement casing that was used by a certain local farmer to disguise and bury a classical settling tray.

Of course, his subject, his passion, his obsession, was not everyone's cup of tea, he admitted. 'My wife is threatening to leave me.'

But I was more than happy to while away a couple of hours

in his company and grew enthused by his vision. On this island, olive trees had been cultivated wherever there was as much as a handful of soil, and, where it was lacking, the peasants carried it up the mountainsides in wicker baskets. They built terraces of drystone walls out of the rocks – the same principle as we have back home on our farm – to contain the floods of falling water, to irrigate their newly planted saplings, and these walls they called *podomes*. It was an ancient word, the professor informed me. When the snows disappeared, if I still had time, he would show me how these stones criss-crossed every inch of the eastern half of the island. He slid across the table a photograph of a grey-haired grandmother, who was leaning forward from a small wooden milking stool, hand-crushing olive drupes with what looked to be a preposterously heavy cylindrical stone attached to a handle of iron. 'That was taken in 1980,' he said. Handpressing in the twentieth century, it was hard to credit. Such traditions had existed here for millennia. He drew me exquisite diagrams to demonstrate how the various stone forms operated, he taught me the original Greek word for each piece; he talked until he was worn out and then he paused, took a deep breath and said, 'So many times I have questioned why I do this. I don't even own a camera. I was obliged to borrow my cousin's, but if I don't record this history, who will?'

'But the stones, the mills won't go away, will they?'

'They are drilling, demolishing them,' he sighed. 'They simply don't understand that this is our heritage; it is the history of mankind's evolution.'

I smiled.

He had written to every museum and archaeological establishment in the eastern Mediterranean, requesting photographs, diagrams, pamphlets, explanations. Most of the

responses he received were in English, which he spoke fal-
teringly, but he had read every word of the material painstakingly with dictionaries.

Professor Katris, who, I learned, taught physics and
chemistry at a secondary school in a humble outlying
village, possessed no car, no camera and no computer of
his own. On his salary, such items were luxuries. He had a
dishevelled appearance, yet his fingernails were immaculately manicured and I had the feeling that, like his artwork,
the inner man was impeccable, precise in thought and
detail.

'The pressing culture,' he smiled as he shook my hand,
heartily delighted that I had shown such an interest, 'is integral
to the island. These are dying, forgotten traditions, ways of
life. I have to record them before it is too late.'

Afterwards, I lunched at a tavern whose hessian-clothed
ceiling and frail walls quivered and rocked with every gust of
wind whistling down the alley. When I returned, Yiannis and
Georgios assured me that the forecast was for clearer weather.
Tuesday, they had claimed, the aiport would reopen. Now,
they were promising Thursday. I had been marooned on the
island for seven days. I had olive farmers awaiting me in
Cyprus, but this delay meant that I no longer had time to visit
them. And here, I had still not ventured beyond Mytilene due
to the treacherous roads.

The sun had come out. I awoke to an island that had opened
up like a flower sucking at the sweetness of life. I heard
laughter beyond the window and the kick-start of scooters in
the lane. Tan mongrels were sleeping all along the quay. The
exterior tables of the bars were littered with solitary figures
in woollen hats and anoraks, tobacco-stained fingers like
rusted old fish-hooks, smoking, drinking coffee, drinking in

the sunlight. Looking out from my second-storey room, across the water, I saw that the snow was slipping away. The mountains were patchworked green, peat brown and white. The roads must be clearing. The airport would be open even if the sea links were not. All being well, I would take the following day's dawn flight to Athens.

News came in a text from M in Paris. Hamas had proven the victors in the Palestinian elections. I crossed the street to one of the Internet cafés to see for myself, and, indeed, it was confirmed. 'The World is Shocked,' stated one of the headlines. I felt rather heartened by the results. With a legal voice, the terrorist acts might end. I was looking forward to my approaching visit to Israel all the more keenly now.

Before leaving the island, I decided to take a bus to Loutra, a village in the hills overlooking the Gulf of Yera, renowned for its vast forests of olive trees. Here, there was an olive factory owned by an octogenarian farmer who had agreed to meet with me in the afternoon. Within twenty minutes of winding ascent, the route was surrounded by densely popu-lated groves of silvery sturdies, many with stupendously girthed trunks as pock-marked as slabs of old Swiss cheese. In the crook of many branches were pockets of snow. The views over the water to Molpos Geras were breathtaking. I exhaled deeply. It was such a pleasure, a release, to be back out in the countryside, to be within proximity of my botanical soulmate.

A handful of Albanians, also travelling on the bus, alighted at the same stop. I climbed the cobbled lanes of Loutra. Although this was no distance at all from Mytilene, it was already a world away and closer to the traditional Greece I remembered. There were scrawny feral cats at every turn, purring beneath cars, skitting across the lanes, tearing at the piled-high plastic sacks of garbage. The air was cold and silent.

The patter of melting snow hitting the cobblestones sounded softly in the gardens all around me. There was a sharp, spicy scent of newly picked vegetables. I noticed it more keenly each time I walked by a store with its produce displayed out front, gathered from the garden or greenhouses that very morning. A fine choice, given the season, with leeks and aubergines and tomatoes as fat and round and misshapen as the *anikto* crows.

I strode out from the village in every direction, first through deserted groves where bowed boughs had been cracked by the inclement weather, back along the route to town, through the village to pause and gaze at the view down over the gulf. The trees tumbled in swathes all the way to the shoreline, where they skirted it, fronds moving in the wind, bending over the sea, like Narcissus drinking in his own reflection or a leaning woman washing her hair.

It was growing bitterly cold again as I strutted briskly back into the village for my four o'clock appointment with Georgios Kiniklis, who was eighty-four years old and looked a spruce sixty-five with his splendid grey moustache, flat grey cap and navy overalls, Bic pen in his top pocket. He bowed as I entered, smiling his welcome. '*Yassas, yassas,*' he muttered.

In the yard, a trio of rather handsome if somewhat dusty, dark-haired Albanians were shovelling into wheelbarrows from a mound of dried olive paste; the residue after the very last pressing, after every final drop of oil had been squeezed from the crushed fruit. Beyond extra-virgin, beyond soap oil. This desiccated by-product provided excellent fuel for heating water at the mills or for heating the mills themselves. Nothing from an olive went to waste. At every stage of its cycle, there was a use for it. This mill with its tall, narrow, brick chimney stack reminded me of nineteenth-century industrial plants in Britain, a Dickensian factory. From the outside, it resembled no olive mill I had ever visited, and, indeed, here they spoke of factories, not mills. I had noticed that in Turkey, too. The first factory was built in the port of Mytilene in 1853, Georgios told me as he showed me around. All the earliest machinery had been of cast iron and supplied, both here and in Turkey, from England.

Georgios was born in Lesvos. His parents were on the last refugee boat to depart Ayvalik. They travelled over with his father's brother, who had been a soldier in Turkey. His mother was heavily pregnant. It was a difficult crossing, although the journey was short, transporting their possessions, leaving their home. Two months later, Georgios was born. He had never visited Asia Minor, never felt the desire to discover his family's history. His uncle, the soldier, founded this olive factory and after he died he willed it to Georgios, who had spent his childhood on the olive farm they acquired after they arrived here – they had 1,700 trees on 90 hectares of land, or 900 *stremmata* in the local measuring system. A mere 250 farmers used his mill.

I was taken aback by this figure. It didn't sound a sufficient client base on which to build a business. But there were three factories in this village alone.

He pressed from late November through to early July, an exceedingly long season. Several varieties were crushed for oil. Unusually, 80 per cent of the fruits from the Kalamata were used for oil, whereas in the Peloponnese, this variety is predominantly for table olives. Kalamata olives are famous worldwide. All those big, black Greek olives sold in supermarkets were of the Kalamata variety, he said proudly. The other varieties he pressed were a Turkish olive from Ayvalik known as Adramitianes, Koloves and another called Ladoelies, which was also the word here for 'olive oil' and is very similar to the ancient Mycenaean words *elaia*, meaning 'olive tree', and *elaion*, meaning 'olive oil'. 'So, our tradition goes back, at least, as far the Mycenaeans.' He smiled.

I asked Georgios if he had ever heard of a resistance created by olive farmers against the Ottoman rule here, funded by resources from their olive oil. He wrinkled his face and thought hard.

'In 1822,' he said, 'locals from Mytilene destroyed a large Turkish vessel. They were part of an organisation known as Filiki Atairia, a resistance group, but they weren't olive farmers. In response to this act,' he continued, 'the Turks slaughtered many Greeks on the island.'

'But no resistance organisation underwritten by olive farmers?'

He shook his head.

Then he confided that when he was twenty, his finest hour, judging by his expression, he joined the resistance in his village. They were working with the British against the occupants, the Germans. His family hid British soldiers in the cellar of his home. His watery eyes crinkled into a smile. 'We found them boats to escape,' he admitted. The island was occupied between 1941 and September 1944, and during eighteen months of that time, the islanders went hungry. There was nothing to eat. Only the fish they brought up from the sea and the olive oil that was not snatched from them. Rats, dogs, turtles, donkeys, they ate all these meats when times grew desperate. Seventy from his village had died of starvation. They hid their oil from the Germans, who tried to take it. Out of every 100 litres pressed, they were allowed to keep 10. The Germans installed a soldier in every mill to keep an eye on the accounting. The villagers secreted extra litres and cured drupes in the homes of those who had no land because the soldiers did not search those properties.

I found myself growing silently uncomfortable. Michel has

German family, and although he has been in France since his teenage years and was not even born during the last war, anti-German stories disturb me. And then I reminded myself that these are no different from all war stories, with their incidents of man's cruelty to man and his destruction of the environment. The gods were wise to choose Athene's gift over Poseidon's.

I remembered Petros and understood that the photograph hanging high almost out of sight on his shelves was almost certainly a part of this story. His son, perhaps?

To change the subject, I asked Georgios about the Albanians. There were twelve employed by him. Only the trio I saw outside worked here. The others laboured in his fields. Young Greeks were not interested in farming or the land. They wanted the cities, they wanted Europe. He intended to pass the farm and the mill, the factory, on to another member of his family, when his time was up. 'But I won't be retiring for a while yet,' he grinned As a parting question, I asked what kept him so young, so fit. He had never smoked, he ate plenty of fish, consumed olive oil every day and loved the tending of his trees. A sacred trade, he winked.

Back in Athens, rubbish was piled at the roadsides like trenched walls, the encircling mountains were white with snow and the twenty-minute journey into the centre of town, bumper to bumper with growling traffic, took over two hours. Evidently, the recent Siberian weather had laid the city low and I could not imagine what effect it was going to have on my immediate plans. I was still attempting to find boats for my crossings to Crete, Israel, Alexandria.

Up and out of bed early the next day to climb the Lykavittos Hill again before breakfast, before my departure on the bus to Sparta. The surrounding mountains were still clad in snow and the sun was rising from behind the most easterly. It had not yet burned off the mist that was hanging over the distant seafront. I paused for breath and imagined what it must have been like when this Attica basin was nothing but nature and hectares of sacred olive groves. In ancient Greece, when Athens ruled the Mediterranean world, the orange trees that decorate the city today would not have been here: they were introduced to the West later by the Arabs. But olives, carob, Mediterranean evergreen oaks would have been. As I climbed, I inhaled the scents of rosemary, lavender and so many familiar perfumes enhanced by the early-morning dew. The vegetation here was no different from home. Twin Mediterranean territories. If the tale of Cecrops, the Phoenician founder of Athens, was fact, then was it possible that Levantine peoples – before the Phoenicians as we think of them today – transported the olive tree here? The original Canaanites perhaps? Who gave the olive to Crete? Or were the trees growing wild everywhere all around the Mediterranean basin and each Neolithic or Bronze Age culture discovered its cultivation for themselves, perhaps with the aid of botanical expertise brought to them by seafaring traders?

As I ascended to the summit, the pealing of Sunday-morning church bells was heard not only in Athens, but all across the Attica basin. It was wondrous, a rousing melody on the wind, and as I trod the last few paces to the top, the Agios Giorgios Chapel bell began to sound, deep and sonorous, startling me. The old crows were silent this morning. Heads bowed for the service in progress. I crept inside and lit five candles. Incense clouded the tiny space. There were few attendants. One or two elderly matrons I had passed, climbing the hill to the chapel service aided by the willing arms of their sons. Quite a trek up the mount to God.

★

The bus station was in a dingy neighbourhood where much industrial garbage lay strewn. A far cry from the face of 'new' Athens. But the bus left on time and was reasonably empty, so I could settle comfortably to reading a history of the Peloponnese peninsula. It was a lovely, sunny Sunday afternoon.

We were swiftly out of the city and into the mountainous areas, all construction left behind. Now it was olives and orange groves, or olives and stunted vines that resembled nothing so much as fire kindling, but I had been told that this peninsula produced the finest wine in Greece. After the offerings from Lesvos, I looked forward to sampling it.

The bus swung on, climbing into the afternoon, twisting to ever more vertiginous heights where the limestone had been carved and nobbled for epochs by the descent of rushing water from snow melts and winter torrents. Here, the olive roots were rugged in snow. How did they survive? Who scaled these altitudinous slopes to husband the groves? The trees marched to the highest peaks. No holding them back, the endless silver forests as far as the eye could see, hanging by twisted roots to the chutes, boring into the rocks, filling out the clefts, clinging for vigorous life. Finally, our escalade rose above them to surrounding ranges, awesome and infinite. Fissures whittled with unruly shrubs. The scenery was magnificent. Occasional shacks, higgledy-piggledy, lopsided, like damp cardboard boxes, but no sturdy habitation. Crossing from one mountain to another, we traversed high plains, plateaux patched with out-of-season vineyards, scrunched as old birds' feet, buried beneath snow, unbelieving of future fruit. Here, a few homes, scratched-living poor, run-down, reminiscent of a long-gone Greece. Pre-twenty-first century.

The land was so still, so quiet. A silence that frequently accompanies snowfall. A whispering complicity.

Gazing beyond the window, it was hard to imagine that for so many centuries pre-Christ, this peninsula was a war zone, city-state against city-state, whose downfalls had eventually been brought about by their greed for power and land.

Throughout this bus journey, I had not seen anyone harvesting the olive trees and there were no nets laid out on the snowy, stony ground. On the island of Lesvos, the harvest season commenced in late November and continued through till July. I remembered that the Kalamata olive cannot be gathered before it is entirely black and that it ripens early, in late November. So, if these trees were Kalamata, which was the dominant variety on this peninsula, the farmers had long since completed their harvests.

Our approach to Tripoli – the third Tripoli I had encountered on this olive quest – took us through lovely, fertile plateaux that reminded me of central Turkey. Sun-splashed days shared with M. He would enjoy this, too. It must be glorious here in spring with the ground carpeted in flowers. Tripoli itself was an industrial settlement slapped into the middle of rugged nature, and on this Sunday afternoon as the coach passed through, there was not a soul about.

I arrived in Sparta, found a hotel with a tiny, dark room but acceptable, deposited my luggage and set off to locate the olive museum. I needed to be there sharp for opening the following morning if I was to see their displays and catch the last of the two seaward buses, departing at 2.30 p.m. to Kalamata on the coast.

Sparta was a very undistinguished town, particularly given its history, difficult to imagine the strides of mythological gods, soldiers, warriors, generals across the fertile plains. They who razed cities to the ground created maritime mayhem and held many of their neighbouring city-states to ransom. My walk through its centre produced a couple of Internet cafés, several bars where bored young men were hanging about smoking, a surprising number of fast-food joints, lingerie or air-conditioning shops and a pizzeria. I found the museum without difficulty, along a street flanked with white or ice-pink apartment blocks. Although I was two hours from the coast, they put me in mind of seaside condominiums built to resemble the prows of ships. Cannes offers an upmarket version of same.

Beyond them lay the olive museum, quite literally on the edge of town. There was nothing after but building works (an extension to the museum, I discovered later) and then forested land against a backdrop of mountains. I confirmed the opening hours and then spotted a pebbled track beyond the building works. I decided to take a walk. The air was high-altitude clean. I passed a few olive trees in pitiable condition – unusual here – and then found myself at the muddy edges of a riverbank where a woman with her back to me was waiting while a three-legged dog on a lead did his business. Impeded or not, the yappy brute made for me, snarling. The woman turned and beamed a smile that would have melted any heart. She had that tanned, fresh mountain skin we came across everywhere in Turkey. I nodded and retreated back the way I had come.

I was toying with my options: read in my room, rent a DVD to watch on my laptop, walk the dull town. I thought of Michel arriving in Paris about now from attendance at a documentary-film festival in Biarritz. With a sigh, I headed into a bar, where four youngsters, two boys, two girls, were lolling over the counter, ordered hot chocolate and pulled out a book. The quartet stared at me as though I were from another planet. Perhaps to them, I was. So, this is Sparta, I thought.

Around the sixth century BC, Sparta was the most powerful

city-state within the entire Peloponnesian region. However, its kings, its rulers, its democracies desired more. They were jealous of others' trade routes, they were unwilling to work with and alongside their neighbouring states, they fought over colonies, most importantly Sicily and olive-clad Corcyra, later rechristened Corfu by the Venetians. Sparta challenged Athens, warred with them on several occasions, and was, overall, the victor. They also led wars against the Persians, who were hell-bent on conquering Greece, but when it suited them, these central Peloponnesians switched allegiances and fought with the Persians against their fellow Greeks, the Atticans.

Here lay one of the seeds of their downfall, for, while these southern states were jockeying for power, struggling within their own communities to find a means of government, or warding off the epic invasions mounted by the power-hungry Persians, another force was gaining muscle, the Macedonians in the north of Greece. Until then, no one had taken those hill peoples seriously. In fact, the southerners had written them off as barbarians. Lacking civilisation and breeding, speakers of 'bar-bar' tongues, not the Greek language. But from out of those hills rode Philip II, the father of Alexander the Great, and soon after him, Alexander himself, twenty years old, full of intelligence, philosophy and military skills, who had been educated by none other than Aristotle himself. Within no time, the charismatic Alex had trounced the southern city-states, including mighty Sparta, before moving on to greater and more distant victories. But perhaps even without the arrival of conquering Alexander, followed by his early death of a fever in Babylon, Mesopotamia, in 323 BC at the tender age of thirty-three, the glory that had been Greece was already on the wane. Centuries of internal and external warring as well as a devastating plague in Athens, which had probably been transported by trading ships from Phoenicia, had bled the Greeks of resources. But, most importantly, they had not been paying attention to what was going on just across the water to the west: Rome. Western Mediterranean territories consolidated, including the heartless destruction of Carthage, Rome was now pointing its acquisitive fingers eastwards. By this stage, the Greeks were a worn-down nation, lacking cohesion, and easy prey for the Romans, who were victorious wherever they despatched their armies. After defeating the Macedonians in the north, destroying the lovely city of Corinth, gateway to the Peloponnese, Rome took control of this peninsula. They spared the Spartans their cruelties because this city fought with them against Antony and Cleopatra, but, nonetheless, the great Greek civilisation was at an end.

Standing outside the bar in the fading evening light on a late-January evening, encircled by purpling mountains, snow, orange groves and olives, I could do no more than imagine the power of those humans who once strode these plains.

Twenty-first-century Sparta was a town you passed through on your way to the western beaches or as a detour en route to Mount Olympus, once the playground of the gods and birthplace of the Olympic Games.

This modern town may have seemed as dull as ditchwater, but the surrounding countryside was quite beautiful, an agricultural paradise, and I roamed lanes out beyond the residential area without fear. Everywhere there was a greeting, even if there was little prospect of a delicious dinner. If the hot chocolate was anything to go by, I held out no hope. In the centre of town, I found a large open square – *plateia* – with an elegant building that looked as though it might once have been the town hall. I approached, hoping for a restaurant with its white parasols and teak tables decking the terrace, but it was yet another café. So, dinner at the hotel.

The sun was shining on to a town all but transformed by its light. On the way to the museum the shops were open, several of which were agricultural stores selling the latest Italian stainless-steel containers for the newly pressed oil and the small, curved, serrated-edge blades used for pruning the olive trees. Outside the pizzeria, stacked olive logs with their creamy inner flesh awaited the oven fires. The white mountains beyond the town were sharp at the edges, outlined by the clear light of day and a heavenly cerulean sky. Beneath the snow levels, where the distant slopes had been quarried, the soil bled deep red. In contrast, rising up out of the earth were the silver and dark-green silhouettes of olives and cypress spires. A striking palette.

Passing by a fish shop, I noticed a quartet of old crows sitting together in a line, hands clasped, gossiping, jawing. Whiskered upper lips and beady eyes staring at the iced counters displaying today's fresh catch, they looked for all the world like a row of ravenous black cats.

The museum, all stone, steel, clean modernity and visitor-friendly, was housed in the city's erstwhile electricity building. From here, in the 1920s, four brothers, whose photo was on proud display, made their fortunes supplying this isolated city with electricity. Curious to think of the great Sparta as marooned, lacking facilities. It did feel, though, like a place that had been cut from a map and slapped down in the middle of nowhere. The beating heart of the community must have been beyond the town, out in the groves and agricultural zones, and I was sorry not to have had time to discover it. In the sunshine, though, this stopover had grown attractive, the nature surrounding it splendidly dramatic and the museum excellently informative. Exiting the refurbished electricity plant, I paused a moment to reflect upon the fact that until the quartet of brothers delivered electricity to Sparta, or to any farming community throughout Greece, the agricultural populations, right into the twentieth century, had lit their homes with olive oil. So, this building seemed a fitting home for the museum. Heartening news I had discovered within: the olive culture in Crete pre-dated the Greek mainland by possibly a thousand years. Beyond Kalamata, my next port of call would be Crete.

The Spartans of today proved themselves to be a warm-hearted bunch, willing to lend me a hand and ease the confusions of a lone traveller without the language or alphabet. At the bus station, destination Artemesia, where I changed buses for Kalamata, everyone attempted to point me to the correct bus, while the drivers were yelling and calling out locations as though they were stallholders in an Arab bazaar.

Twisting and swinging, ascending again the hairpin mountain passes, flying by castles, churches and villages lost within the snow-clad altitudes, and while the sun was shining, these high groves were busy with farmers harvesting and pruning.

In the pretty alpine village of Artemesia nestling near the crown of the mountain, I waited in the crisp afternoon for the bus to Kalamata. Two black-clad widows were sitting outside on white stone steps stripping spinach leaves off stalks, screeching in high-pitched voices as they worked. Here, the street lamps, so recently installed, still sported the prices crayoned in white on their glass panes. Men in black berets with wooden staffs limped from the solitary café after an ouzo or two. Here, the silence was complete until a car, a youth at the wheel, came careening round the hillside, skidding out of control. I noticed in Sparta that young men at the bus station were storing boxes with pink tickets into the luggage holds.

The buses were working as a delivery service. The peninsular Federal Express. A pile of ticketed cartons sat at the roadside waiting for the bus to Kalamata, just like me.

I breathed the scent of burning olive wood. There was plenty of it in this pruning season. A truck chugged by and the young man and woman seated in the open rear alongside the sacks of gathered fruits, the sacks of their labours, smiled shyly, lowering tired eyes. Their faces, rouged by wind and arduous work, were chapped and perished. Silence again. Birdsong. Wood smoke and then the clip-clop of a donkey and a squeaky old motor. On the pine tree in the square with fountain, where we were waiting, the cones were minuscule yet fecund with yellow pollen. Olive groves descended like waterfalls into the sleepy hollows beyond this elevated village. The farmers pruned hard here, lopping close to the central trunk. Rising from out of the valleys were upstanding plumes of smoke fed by field workers burning the leaves and twigs they were not carrying home for their fires.

We were on the move once more: five passengers in a creaky old bus. In between the mountains and lower hills were gorges, wadis, with fast-flowing water echoing as it fell. Shacks with stones holding the corrugated roofs in place, to keep the winds from whipping away the covers (Quashia had done the same with our water basin at the farm), wooden ladders leaning against branches in the groves, a few single-storey houses on stilts built in the lower terraced olive groves: these were the signs of life, of industry. Little has changed here in millennia; the traditions of the landscape. There was history in every clod. And there were caves along this route. The scenery reminded me of Turkey and Libya: rugged, cavernous, spectacular.

My first sighting of the distant port city of Kalamata. Looking down upon it from on high, in the hazy, weak sunlight, I spotted three tankers out on the water. In ancient times, they would have been sailing vessels transporting oil from here to distant colonies, loaded with tall terracotta jars of oil for sale at various stops around the Mediterranean basin. The Greeks and Phoenicians plied similar routes, desired the same territories for expansion, and this was cause for war between them.

When did Kalamata acquire its name? Were the olives named after the settlement, or the city after its renowned olive variety?

The fields abutting our spiralling descent offered only olives, all pruned in a manner I had not come across before, cut to encourage the crown's growth while the outer branches, those that at home fall loosely earthwards like swirling skirts, were lopped off entirely. It gave these trees a punk-like, shocked appearance. Each parcel of land displayed a sign with handwritten lettering. Denoting ownership, a licence to produce or a farm's registration? On the outskirts of the town, several gypsy encampments, ebon-haired men sleeping on mattresses in the rear of their vans.

Kalamata was yet another sprawl of concrete disappointment. I had hoped for more. I took a long evening stroll down at the port in search of a livelier, more evocative quarter, but was out of luck. Quayside, I discovered that the ferries to Crete only ran during the summer months. Had it not been late in the afternoon, I might have been tempted to take a bus straight back to Athens.

After I had checked into a hotel, I sat in a bar down at the quays and considered my options. The young waitress, when I asked her how the town had acquired the name Kalamata, told me that it meant 'Good Eye' and was a fairly recent appellation. The story was that a statue of Mary in one of the local churches was found to work miracles and an Ottoman pasha living locally was so taken with the cures that he himself converted from Islam to Christianity. Kala Mata. I knew that *kala* translated as 'good'. I had not known *mata* meant 'eye'. Even so, I was not convinced by this local legend and determined to dig deeper.

The following morning, back at the central station to peruse the outward-bound timetable, I got chatting to a Greek bus driver who spoke some English. I recounted the waitress's tale. His response was, 'Poppycock.' There was an older meaning, a different twist to the translation, born from the local dialect, he told me. Kalamata, in his opinion, meant 'Good Welcome'. It set me thinking.

I was now bound for the hills, the sole passenger on a bus wending its way to the village of Mauromati. I was in luck. This driver spoke excellent English. The name Mauromati meant 'Black Eye', he told me, and took its title from a water source in the heart of the village. The spring that coursed the hillside, down through and beyond ancient stones, had once irrigated the mighty city of Messini.

'Why would the village have been named "Black Eye"?' I asked him.

He lit a cigarette and shook his head. 'No idea.'

The local olives, the renowned Kalamata variety, were large and oval and resembled deep-brown sloe-eyes. If picked for eating rather than to press for oil, they needed to be harvested ripe, black. Was it too far-fetched to suppose that the 'eye' in both appellations was inspired by this very distinctive olive drupe?

Looking back across the centuries the ancient city-state farms produced little if anything else. Olives were the wealth of the peninsula and would have been transported from the port that today is Kalamata. The olive industry gave Messini its wealth and was no doubt one of the reasons the avaricious

Spartans hungered to get their farming tools into this coastal corner of the mainland.

Rich-producing olive groves in every direction and an excellent seaside position: undoubtedly, the Spartans envied the Messinians.

My arrival into the tranquil village of Mauromati was greeted by my first sighting of an almond tree in blossom. In the Mediterranean, these paintbrush dabs of pale pink, puffs of new life, herald spring; it was a joyous welcome. There was not a soul about. The bus deposited me close by the font of the famous spring, which was impressive. Once upon a time, it would have been the hub, the meeting point, for the women with their laundry, where their village gossip would have been exchanged, mulled over, debated. The small houses and bungalows, a few had been renovated, were witness to the olive culture that was everywhere to be seen: sacks ready for pressing stacked upright on terraces, olive leaves scattered at the kerbsides, that pungent, unmistakable aroma emanating from a distant mill.

In the sweep of a high plane at the foot of this cliff-top village lay the remains of the ancient city. Silence reigned over the silver-forested countryside save for the burble of descending spring water. This landscape had barely altered in three thousand years. I decided to walk on through the village and climb down directly to the site. There was a slight nip in the air and the movement would keep me warm. On the way down the hill, I passed a middle-aged fellow carrying a bag of freshly cut greens.

'*Kalimera*,' he nodded with a smile.

Down at the site, I came across a couple of gardeners in old jackets and balaclavas hoeing between the stones. I was the sole visitor yet they paid my arrival not a moment's attention. Penetrating a little further into what was an immaculately preserved city, I realised that the dozens of olive trees that had grown up within the ancient settlement were being farmed. I spotted a car among the ruins and then a quintet of men, villagers, harvesting in ancient Messini.

A little higher up the hillside, a stone-cutting machine began to whirr. Two masons were dissecting slabs of marble to shore up the capitals. I had rarely sensed such a profound union between man, his environment and his history. In the distance, half a dozen bearded archaeologists were chipping at stones or cleaning up antique slabs. The industry was con-centrated but easygoing. One or two nodded, but most con-tinued with their tasks, tasks as old as the site itself. Messini was not the most spectacular ancient city I had visited, but it was immaculate, lovingly maintained, and what was more, it was not set apart from the local community. It had been integrated into it. Messini and Mauromati seemed, to me, to be one and the same place, inhabited, evolving, over eras.

It felt uplifting to be here, to clamber around the seating at the ancient hippodrome, to sit in the sun and telephone home from my mobile, thus sending ancient Greece to France, to hear how our tiny puppies were faring (Lola, our Alsatian, had given birth to ten puppies in early January) and to quietly imbibe the glorious mountainscape of silvery groves and well-honed hills sliding to the Mediterranean.

From here, produce was shipped to Alexandria and to the colonies of Magna Graecia in southern Italy and Sicily. (I learned in Athens of villages south of Bari, in the region of Kalvaria, down on the heel of Italy, as well as others in Sicily, founded by Athens in the heyday of Magna Graecia, where even today the inhabitants speak ancient Greek. They are known as Grecani. One village is Kalimera ('Good Morning'). The children from those villages are regularly invited to

Athens on school trips, offering them an opportunity to stay in touch with their classical roots.)

It was clear why for three hundred years Sparta held this region in servitude. It would have been an excellent sea access for a city that controlled the midland plains. Eventually, with armies from Thebes, the Messinians freed themselves of Spartan oppression and built their city anew, constructing a defence wall from where they could keep a watchful eye on their acquisitive neighbours, for they were warier, more afeared of the Spartans than of any foreigner approaching by water. I could see the wall from where I was standing. Much of it remains intact. I wondered if they thought of those grasping Spartans as black-eyed people or neighbours who coveted their black-eyed fruits.

I wandered over to the harvesters, who were a little surprised by my arrival. Three of them, I saw now, were Albanians, employed by an older farmer who smiled and greeted me. The Albanians stared at me a little mistrustfully or uncertainly. They were gathering up their nets and loading up the truck with sacks, bulging with oleaginous fruits, and a small machine used for sifting leaves from gathered crop. I watched for a while, offered to help, which made them giggle, and then wended my way, bidding them a good day.

I heard the regular thwack and sweep of a gardener's brush, running water from the spring, myriad songbirds, the tock-tock of a hammer and chisel against marble and the lonely hiccup-honking of a faraway donkey. This was the Greece I remembered and I was heartened to rediscover it.

In 399 BC, expelled yet again from their homeland by their perennial enemy, the defeated Messinians fled by boat to Euesperides in Cyrenaica, modern Benghazi, where they took refuge and started afresh. Their homeland defeat was irrevocable.

Might those boat-loads of Messinian refugees have taken olive cuttings to that fertile Green Mountain of Libya? Were the wild trees I had walked amongst before Christmas seeded from stones once born of saplings from here?

The bus back to Kalamata was not due for another two hours, so, after a brief visit to the museum, I strolled back through the village, where pockets of *Iris cretensis Janka* were in blossom at the roadsides, and I chanced upon a family house operating as a café. Inside, in a capacious room, a father sat lunching with two children at a marble-topped table by the door, while his lean, drawn but pretty wife in a dark-grey dress, black cardigan, pinafore, with red, swollen hands was washing stacks of cutlery in a stone sink and wiping down the surfaces of a simple wooden bar. I asked about food, agreeing to take whatever was available, and was served beer and a plate of chips. The other customers were a trio of men at one table whose lunch had long been terminated. They sat together smoking, downing the last of a carafe of rosé. They were dressed in baseball caps and woodland camouflage fatigues. One of the three had his foot in plaster. He looked on intently, legs outstretched, while the older fellow next to him was reading aloud the contents of what appeared to be a gripping official letter. Agricultural or municipal business, it seemed. I wondered what the literacy rate was here.

The wait for the bus was interminable. I passed time admiring the marigolds and sweetly scented narcissi in blossom along the banks as well as, astoundingly, bluebells. Dogs came out to play, bark, worry and then disappear again. A man in an orange saloon pulled up, yelling from his window. In his boot were stacked packs of bed sheets for sale, but I saw no takers. A little while later, a man and a boy in a red pick-up with a loudspeaker drove in, calling their wares, bags of potatoes. A pick-up truck laden with olive sacks passed from one direction, while, from the other, another beat its path carrying substantial churns of oil. The farmer I had encountered earlier at the site passed by, transporting his Albanian crew, waving to me like an old friend.

When the bus eventually arrived, over an hour late, it was no real surprise to discover that it was the same driver as earlier. We set off, just the two of us, rolling and swinging round the bends and curves. Beyond the window, I saw men hard at work trimming olive trees and a woman herder in a peaked woollen cap, pantaloons, boots and a billowing skirt, in company with half a dozen sheep.

There was a bonded sense of community here in this village of no more than sixty houses. I noticed it in the café with folk popping in and out, asking questions of, giving information to, the bedraggled wife after her husband had returned with the youngsters to his groves. Her hair hung in stray wisps and she wiped them off her sweat-beaded face with her wet wrist, sleeves rolled past her elbows, calling to this person across the way and engaging in this chore or the next, feeding one farmer after another as they arrived from the fields or the mill. All living out the life of a tight-knit community. Each resident maintained his or her section of the hillside, at the same rhythm, marching to the seasons, in time with nature. All pulling their weight for the landscape, whatever petty squabbles or disagreements may or may not ripple through. They ate and drank in the café run by the pretty, toiling wife of their fellow farmer. They burned the wood from the olive cut in this season, getting warm from the work and from its produce, and in this season when there were no tourists, no visitors, and the world outside had turned its thoughts elsewhere, they took care of their hillside with its ancient site and its black-eyed history. I felt privileged to have spent a few hours as an observer in their midst in this season of oranges and olives and goats at the roadside. The day had transported me back decades, centuries, millennia, which was part of the purpose of the journey, riffling through the roots of time, of nature, of olive secrets. Here, I had felt close to its origins, to its timelessness. The tree of eternity.

An old crow hailed the bus and ascended, yelling to the driver, who made no response aside from a nod, not even bothering to accept her ha'penny fare. She plonked herself down opposite me and began to pummel my shoulder, needling me and yelling toothlessly. I shrugged, explaining that I did not understand, so she yelled all the harder, spittle flying from between hirsute lips.

We arrived – only the driver and I again now – back into the urban banality of Kalamata as though having emerged from another universe, another time frame. He, who had lived many years in Canada, which was why he spoke such good English, asked me where I was staying and when I told him, he delivered me in the bus directly to the front door of the hotel.

'Carry the memory of the good eye!' he called out as I waved my thanks.

Crete

After a long bus journey back to Athens, I boarded the overnight ferry for Crete from the port of Piraeus at a little after half past seven in the evening and went directly to my cabin to deposit luggage. The next I knew, I was being woken by the hum of a vacuum cleaner. It was a quarter to nine the following morning. The liner had berthed at Chania an hour and a half earlier and I was the last passenger aboard.

In the old Venetian port of Chania, now lined with cafés, *kafenions* and *ouzerias*, I found myself digs facing the waterfront, looking north towards the Sea of Creta, for the princely sum of €40 a night. The ascent up winding wooden stairs was dark and steep and the washing facilities were basic, but I was perfectly content to be settled into one of those lovely old Italianate buildings. Peering from my first-floor window, I heard pigeons cooing on the crumbling balcony and the exuberant cries of children clambering over a cannon, riding it like a fairground beast, at the Naval Museum steps from my *pension* down on the quay.

What had won my heart was that there appeared to be no hotel proprietor, no one in charge. I had been walking by, vaguely considering somewhere to stay, when the owner of the neighbouring café had called out, offering me coffee. He'd said, 'If you're looking for a room, go next door, pick whichever you fancy, first floor. The key will be in the lock.' I had chosen the one with the view. A handwritten notice in reception on a wooden table, where a bowl with apples and another with sweets had been placed, said, 'Plees, wen to chick-out, leef euros uder doore. *Bon voyage.*' I thought, this is the place for me.

The café owner struck me as a true Cretan, solid as an ox. In face and stature he might have been sired by a bull, with wrinkled features chipped out of stone. Back down in the street, I confirmed my decision and a man, looking hungover, sitting in the sun, called, 'Good choice.'

I offered my name, passport or credit card and, tea towel slung over shoulder, the café owner shrugged. 'Why? Stay as long as you like. Pay when you leave. It's simple.'

I was exceedingly happy to have returned to this marvel amongst islands, the fifth largest in the Mediterranean basin and an early Eden. During the days of the ancient cradle of Western civilisation, its position, set between Europe, Asia and Africa, had proved ideal. It was a land of mysteries, Crete.

My plan was to travel up into the mountain range directly behind this harbour, the White Mountains, cross to the southern shore washed by the Libyan Sea and move east, hugging the coastline, to the ancient city of Festos. From there, I planned to retraverse the island to the capital of Iráklion in the north, turn west along the coast until I refound Chania and my outward-bound ship. This trajectory covered only a patch of this elongated island, but it was really all I needed. The eastern tip and its surrounding shores both north and south had become overrun with tourism. The western quarters, though far less constructed and exceedingly beautiful, held no secrets, as far as I knew, to olive history. So, this waistband of the island was my circuit, my hunting ground. Before landing, I had foreseen achieving these trips by buses, but it was February, out of season, and there was little if any public transport heading where I was going. I decided to hire a car. There were dozens of agencies offering deals that were 'give-away prices', €39, or £27, for five days. I settled for a slightly dearer option but one that offered a recovery service. I was off into the mountains, after all. Directly across the street, hunting for a map, buried behind scaffolding, I discovered a bookshop, an Aladdin's cave, where I pottered about and purchased more books than I could reasonably carry as well as a map of Kriti recommended by the owner's son. It was a delightfully fusty old place. From its exterior, it resembled many other crumbling, unrenovated façades that greeted you at every turn here, but it was a true find. Pelekani's bookshop, reminiscent of Petros's stationery store in Mytilene, but without the photographic display, with plenty of options for the non-Greek-reading philistine such as myself. I returned later in the day to swap one of my choices. 'Will that be a problem?'

The old man replied that it would be.

'Oh.'

'It would be a problem if you don't have the book you want to read,' he explained.

It was a family-run affair. 'Established a million years ago,' smiled the daughter.

'Since nineteen thirty-two,' chipped in her father. 'We are the oldest *biblia* on the island, possibly in Greece.'

I was thrilled to have found them. Had I not been in search of a map, I might well have walked by.

I took a late-afternoon stroll around the harbour to the old Venetian lighthouse, which was also bedecked with scaffolding, undergoing renovations. From across the water, looking back across the bay, behind the harbour town, to the White Mountains, peaked in orange-tinged snow from the fading sun, I stood awed by the image and plays of light, a palette that would have caused Cézanne to gasp with delight. It was where I was headed.

I ate dinner in a little fish restaurant along the front, where the bouzouki player invited himself to my table and ordered us wine. His story was a sad one. His wife had died of cancer and I sensed his loneliness.

'Will you allow me to buy you dinner tomorrow evening?'
I thanked him, but explained that I was leaving.

'But you have only just arrived! Where are you going?'

'Into the mountains to see olive trees and then to Festos.'

'I have olive trees. Everyone here has olive trees. We'll sell beach apartments to the bloody Germans, but we never sell our olive trees.'

'Why is that?'

'They are our history, our livelihood, our relationship to the earth. My farm is thirty kilometres from Chania. Meet me there at midday tomorrow and I will show you olive trees!'

I thanked him, but refused.

'Why not? Is your husband jealous?' he bellowed. He was a large man, pouring with sweat and emotions, and with long, grey curly hair that reminded me of a Grecian statue.

'Why can't you promise that when you return to Chania you will dine with me?' he demanded. Watching him play, he held his bouzouki lightly, resting it on his thighs, strumming it with thick fingers and then, quite suddenly, dancing across the strings with dexterity, and when he thought I was watching him, he put even more 'soul' into it. Still, I refused to be bamboozled into a date I did not care to keep.

It was Sunday morning in the Venetian port of Chania. The portside world was drinking coffee, reading newspapers, smoking, too, of course. Some were sailing, sallying forth from the harbour out into the breezy sea, which, reflected in the hazy light, was corrugated and the colour of an oyster shell. A handful were at the water's edge, fishing, in silent communion with their Mediterranean.

I left sufficient euros under the door of my room, which I was sorry to leave, picked up the hire car and set off into the White Mountains, or, in Cretan, Lefka Ori. I was quickly immersed in olives and the harvesting of them. Entire families were engaged in the process. All along the roadsides there were trucks, pick-ups, vans, four-wheel drives, which was about all that had changed in this gathering ritual that had been played out on this island for close to five thousand years.

Entering a small town, the fruit-wood-staffed old men were accompanying their black-robed partners to tavernas for lunch. The crows themselves had been to church, while their husbands had sat in bars, talking, smoking, playing dominoes, backgammon. Passing through a village where an entire community was gathered outside the church. Man, woman and boy in black. A funeral, then.

As I climbed, I found the world of fields and groves at work, oblivious to the holy day. The agricultural yards were open for all manner of tools, sacks of earth, hay. The olive crowds were about their finger-splitting tasks like every other day. The nets they set at the roots of the trees here were black, not white or green like our own. They hung the slopes like widows' weeds.

The vegetation was similar to the south of France. The Greek name for the *garrigue*, the aromatic scrub growing out of the chalky soil and limestone, was *phrigiana*, whereas the *maquis*, the low, dense scrubland made up of rosemary, rock roses, laurel, thyme, myrtle amongst many others, was also *maquis*. I spotted a dead badger along my path. Roadkill, no doubt. I stopped to clear it from the route of passing traffic, dragging it to the rocky cliff edge, dragging it because it was stiff as a board. There were goats everywhere. Most were domesticated herds, but I came across a few wild fellows with great curled horns; the *kri-kri*, standing proudly on boulders as though posing. I was obliged to pull up frequently while the goats frolicked in the road or chewed the spiky roadside scrub. One jumped on to the bonnet of a red truck and began to chomp his way through the rubber of the windscreen wipers. Pity the farmer, off gathering his olives, thrilled by the destruction when he returned.

The sweep of valleys and lower plains as I climbed higher was lovely, softly silvered by my tree, though the clouds above blowing from the east grew louring, threatening. Higher, the olives were bent like whipped, tortured beasts. Moments further, I encountered a handsome bearded shepherd herding his shaggy-coated sheep round the precipitous narrow curves. He had no dogs with him, but rounded up his troupe with yells and the crack of his stick against the bitumen. He smiled but looked puzzled by my solitary passage in this season, in these arduous inclines.

There were griffon vultures on the road tearing at the carcass of some inanimate creature, possibly a red squirrel. Lone sheep browsed these upper roads, crossing at their leisure, oblivious to this stranger, or I encountered them in herds, accompanied by a few goats, bells clunking. The sound was reminiscent of home, of the *picorns* worn by our local stock.

These elevations offered a pastoral idyll. Pure nature. Of course, the work involved in survival, in earning a crust, was not paradisical. I passed dozens of the widows in black, always alone, immense sacks bulging with gathered greens on their bent backs, trudging slowly up the steep inclines, solitary souls, with only canes for company. I saw them sitting outside their homes on the steps, nipping off the stalks of the spinach or dandelion leaves. They never looked up.

Donkeys were still employed here, clopping home with the day's load of olive logs, sawn that very afternoon. One old codger with flat cap, black waistcoat, sturdy boots led his mule by a rope. They were transporting four loaded hessian sacks of olives to the mill. Sacks still delivered the drupes. In France, we would be turned away from our mill with sacks. Forbidden by the European Union, for reasons of hygiene. I wondered that Greece ignored the ruling. In Lesvos at the factory of old Georgios, the Albanians had been unloading them, too.

Even though it was Sunday, the mills were operating and the mountain air smelled richly of herbs, dung and crushed paste. I pulled the car off the road and set out to walk, moving briskly. There were valleys, gorges, summits all about me and then an extraordinary happening: an eagle soared by, dipping low, flying alongside me, almost within arm's reach. I felt its power, the indomitability of Crete, saw its wings steer in the air, the tip of its broad body before it flexed, wheeled and disappeared swiftly, leaving me astonished.

Eventually, plunging into the breathtaking view, I descended to the south coast, into a windy, remote village nestling at the water's edge, surrounded by mountains that enclosed its perfectly deserted beach. The place was a ghost town, boarded up save for one café, where I encountered three men and a woman drinking out of large red mugs with 'Nescafé' written on them, huddled round an antique stove burning olive cuts, of course.

I smiled. '*Yassas*. May I come in?'

The quartet nodded, watching me.

'Might I have a little refreshment?'

The woman, wispy, youngish with hunched shoulders and died chestnut hair, served me a glass of beer. To my surprise, she spoke English, but her accent was not Greek. Two of the men also spoke English. The woman was originally from Yugoslavia but lived here with her husband and son, who was born in this village of twenty adults and ten children. In summer, due to the influx of foreign visitors, the population exploded to over a thousand. But for six months of the year, they were an isolated community who farmed olives and lived off the profits they had gained in the hectic months.

'Where are you headed?' asked one of the men, who, it transpired, was the café owner.

'Along the coast, east to Festos,' I replied.

They began to chortle.

'Not from here. This is the end of the line. The only road out is back the way you've come. Or a boat across the sea to Africa, but there are no boats.'

'No way through, to east or west or south,' confirmed another, a bulbous-nosed gent with a florid complexion, who resembled the early twentieth-century film actor W. C. Fields.

I pulled out my map and took a slug of beer. The proprietor, handsome, lean, rose and stood over me.

'Is it inaccurate?' Had I made yet another map blunder?

'No, you read it wrong. Look.' He seemed to be telling his neighbours, not me, and they chuckled again, but not in an unfriendly or malicious fashion. The fourth of their party was rocking back and forth on his wooden chair, humming to himself, not quite of this world.

The proprietor, who was hurrying to return to his groves, proposed an alternative circuit, which involved climbing back up to the mountain's peak and proceeding east from there, following a snaking path that would take me through the Omalos Plateau, just north of the Samarian Gorge, which had been closed due to damage caused by recent snowdrifts. Over €100,000 was required for repairs, to remove fallen trees and boulders before the tourists flew in. They were muttering, shaking heads at the contemplation of it. The boss departed and we fell into silence, save for the simpleton's drawling. I sipped my beer, considering whether or not to request a room for the night. It was close to 4 p.m. Driving about in the mountains after dark was not an appealing option, while a night in this seaside village, a blustery stroll along the beach, suddenly seemed attractive. To strike up conversation again, I asked W. C. Fields if he also owned olive groves.

He replied, 'I hate olives. I want nothing to do with them. The second my mother died and I inherited the estate, I gave my sister the house and sold off every tree, every terrace, the whole lot and I skipped off to discover the world. I was captain on a sloop working for a Greek shipping magnate. I discovered the sea is good for fish but not for man. So I saved my money, bought property and now I rent out rooms – and they've all got refrigerators, mind. I work like a dog all summer pleasing the tourists, and in the winter, I do nothing. Six months of relaxation and leisure; it's a great life. I earn a fortune.'

'He's the village capitalist,' chimed in the Yugoslavian woman.

'Rubbish! The poor farmers' lives are beggarly.'

'You are happy to take the pocket money!' she interrupted again, hooting and bouncing on her wooden chair.

'Pocket money?' I asked.

'When April comes and the gathering season is over, the farmers give us pocket money. That's what we call it, "our pocket money". Whatever is left on the trees, hasn't been harvested, we can have. Those of us without trees. It's a custom here.'

'But if you hate olives . . .?'

'Oh, I feed greedily on olive oil and olives. Couldn't live without them. Staff of life, but I hate farming them.'

'Why?'

342

'When I was a boy, before we had those nylon nets to lay at the feet of the trees, my mother used to make me go into the fields and pick up every drupe from the ground by hand. These are the White Mountains. Have you any idea how taxing that was? When the wind blew . . . long hours on my hands and knees. I'm Paulos, by the way.'

'He's looking for a new wife.' The Yugoslavian slapped her hands together with glee.

Moving directly on from this remark, I asked Paulos if the housewives in the olive communities hereabouts were known to make soap. I had read of this Greek tradition at the museum in Sparta. He nodded that it was still a common practice in the region. His own mother had been an expert.

'She used the sediment from the unfiltered pressed oil as well as oil that had been used for cooking, to which she added water, salt, this and that. The whole mix was boiled at a fierce temperature and left to solidify. As a prayer for its success, she, all housewives, picked two sprigs from a young olive and placed them in the shape of a cross over the mixture and left it "to marble". The soap was ready when it rubbed off her hands like fish scales.'

The conversation turned to the tranquillity of winter, how jealously they protected these months. That very evening, their entire community of thirty, adults and children, would eat together at the café and the talk would be of the day's harvests. I rose and paid for my beer, gathering up my bag and map. They shared their homeland all summer long with tourist invasion. I was sorry to leave and would have dearly enjoyed the conversations over dinner, but I decided against intrusion.

'Come back in spring,' Paulos commanded as I wished them a good afternoon. 'I'll rent you a room with a refrigerator.' And I nodded that I would. Perhaps not this spring, but another.

They requested just one parting favour: 'Don't tell anyone the name of this village. We enjoy our winters as they are.'

And so I promised.

There was snow everywhere except on the higher screes, which were grey as gravel. From olive groves, I had ascended into a hoary terrain with tall, needly pines rising like obelisks and spires out of virgin snow. This was an altogether different landscape, grittier, menacing in its inflexibility. As I swung the car round the alpine bends, my thoughts were with the folk in the village. Departing, I had felt isolated, the outsider moving onwards along a journey that gave me purpose but kept me apart. Beyond the windows was winter, stark and unremitting, and I was alone in it. I envied those villagers for their unity, their hearth, their tight-knittedness. Olive farming offered me a sense of community. I had no family in the immediate sense, a caring husband but married to his work, and I asked myself, driving through these awesome snowy crags, whether life, my life, was not simply a reach for human contact.

Passing through the Omalos Plateau, the hamlets of modest shacks and bungalows were all boarded up. No one could survive here in these conditions. They must have been summer residences, then. Mile after mile and I did not encounter a soul. The snow was melting fast and running in rivulets across the hilly, winding roads. Where the ice remained frozen in great boulders at the road's edges, begrimed by muddied earth, it resembled sleeping lambkins.

Night was falling and I was in the middle of nowhere. My stomach was growling and I was resigning myself to a night in the car without sustenance when I came upon a sloping village, just a few houses either side of a street, but one had a sign painted in red: 'Rooms Rent'. I pulled over and knocked. It was an age before the curly-haired woman answered, lilac cardigan pulled tight. I had already turned back towards the car. Without a word, she signalled to a bedroom at the end of a hallway. It was freezing and clearly had not been slept in since the previous summer, but I accepted and handed her the requested €15.

'Heating?' I begged.

She disappeared. When I returned from the car with my bag, she was plugging a blow heater into the wall. Outside, snow was beginning to fall and the wind was yowling. I asked if there might be somewhere to eat and she pointed me further down into the village. I was somewhere east of the gorge, which might explain the serendipity of this stopover. In summer, this nowhere habitation was probably teeming with tourists, which could be the only explanation for the restaurant. It was a true Cretan dinner of baked mountain lamb and dark-red wine I was served.

I narrated my encounter with the eagle to the young waiter, Christos, who spoke extremely passable English and said it was not an uncommon experience. He told me how, when he was a boy of six or seven, his father had trapped an eagle and kept it in a cage, which was illegal even then. The local taverna owner offered him the equivalent of €300 to take the bird, to kill it, stuff it and hang it on the wall in his diner. In spite of the sum, Christos's father refused. One morning, about a month after the eagle had been captured, Christos went into breakfast and found his father holding its limp carcass. It had committed suicide.

At first I assumed Christos's English had faltered, but no. 'The bird had killed itself.'

I placed my cutlery upon the table, shocked.

'With his talons he had ripped out his own throat. He was too proud to be caged,' explained Christos, fingers scratching at his neck to demonstrate.

'Or was he going crazy enclosed in such a confined space?' I countered.

'The bird's eyes burned with that same fire I had seen so often in my grandfather's. We Cretans could never accept domination, even during the last war.'

'What did your father say about the eagle?' I asked.

Christos smiled. 'He regretted not selling the creature when he had been given the opportunity. What could he say? He saw how disturbed I was by the incident.'

The island had an awareness now about its flora and fauna. The hunting of songbirds had ceased altogether in Crete. I mentioned the case of Malta.

'It will come,' he smiled. 'There was resistance here, too, but now they understand their value.'

Without any prompting from me, he touched upon another subject. The White Mountain mafia. The feuds here, I had heard, were as bloodthirsty and revenge-driven as Corsica. Whole families had been virtually wiped out by neighbouring enemies who had taken justice into their own hands and killed whoever deserved annihilation, according to their private laws.

'But now there are too many police,' Christos sighed. 'And people snitch on neighbours, betraying their own kind. This will end in a bad fashion.' Even from the lips of this gentle and rather sensitive waiter, it had the ring of a chilling threat.

Crossing the eastern extremities of the White Mountains, late the following morning, the wind blew harshly at the periphery of the snowy ranges. It was a lonely route with none to nod to. Callused scree terrain. No olives. Sheep and goats. Outside these earlier months, once the temperatures soared and the days grew rainless, grazing was a critical issue. Those rights here caused the very family feuds Christos had spoken of. I spotted not occasional fleeting glimpses of *kri-kri*, but small flocks of the since-time-began Cretan goats. Some, close to the roadsides, had risen on to hind legs to devour the scrub, waltzing on two feet like dancers. Or stately with curved horns, high on the crags, watching. They struck me as mythological creatures.

The sky grew black and it began to rain. I was once more on a southerly course towards the sea, further to the east, making my way to Festos, the site of one of the two principal Minoan palaces that ruled Crete four thousand years ago.

There are two astounding stories that accompany archae-ological discoveries on this island and both concern the eminent doctor of the digs, Sir Arthur Evans. The ancient cities of Troy on the coast of Turkey and Mycenae on the Peloponnese were both discovered by the German adventurer Heinrich Schliemann, in the late nineteenth century. Defying all scientific opinion, he uncovered both these mythological cities, which, until then, had been regarded as no more than make-believe, invented locations from ancient Greek lit-erature. But he proved the world wrong. They had existed. Once he had finished with them, he turned his eye to Crete. The fabulous tale of Theseus and the Cretan Minotaur, the half-man, half-bull creature, progeny of the illicit sexual liaison between Pasiphae, wife of the King of Minos, and a beautiful white bull was yet another fabulous, fantastical tale from the mind of Homer. Or so the world believed, but Schliemann argued otherwise. This fabled land of the Minoans was, as far as the German archaeologist was concerned, the home of a very ancient civilisation and he was fairly certain he knew where to start digging to uncover their secrets, their ravishing history. Unfortunately, tragically for Schliemann, he failed to strike an arrangement with the Cretan farmer who owned the land where, he believed, the northern site lay buried and, in spite of interminable negotiations, the German died without ever revealing this island's treasures.

A little while later, in 1890, the eminent British archaeologist Sir Arthur Evans had better fortune with the farming community and was able to put his shovel precisely where his deceased German colleague had failed. The resulting finds proved to be one of the greatest revelations of modern archaeology. Immersed within the layers of Cretan hillside was a palace of such wealth and, from what one could see, great elegance and beauty, Knossos on the northern side of the island, close to the present capital of Iráklion, where I was going later.

The palace site has since revealed many of the secrets, traditions, ways of life of an entirely independent civilisation, the Minoans. Bulls and olives, both potent images for the Cretans, were depicted in many of their frescoes. The very people, in fact, that Homer had romanced in his epic tales 2,800 years ago.

While Evans was digging away in the north, another team of scientists were at work on the south side of the island close to the sea that faces directly towards Libya, and what they discovered there was Festos.

Festos, the southern Minoan palace site offered myriad details of the day-to-day lives of these extraordinary communities. From all that has been uncovered at these two sites as well as at various other less spectacular locations on the island, it has become clear that somewhere around 3500 BC there existed on this island a people, known to us as the Minoans, whose lives were, it seemed, close to idyllic. They lived off the land and lived very well. Crete was and remains remarkably fertile. They fished, they produced wine, they were great makers of music, lovers of dance, and their artwork, their craftsmanship was remarkable. They were more than ordinary seafarers who travelled distantly, taking their wares to all parts of the eastern Mediterranean; they were the masters of the sea during that period. Only the Phoenicians, who followed some time later, matched them in navigational skills.

Amongst so many other talents, it has also been held that the Minoans were the earliest civilisation to cultivate olives. Certainly, olive farming was fundamental to their day-to-day lives and diet.

It was a mere short hop, across the way from here, to where five hundred years earlier, unidentified farmers had been cultivating groves in Bechealeh.

Needing to stretch my legs, I parked, stood atop a range at a height of approximately one thousand four hundred metres, ate a boiled egg in the rain and wind, tried to call home and listened to water coursing into the valleys. I heard small birds, saw martins, I think, at such an altitude, but not a human footprint. It was both exhilarating and daunting to be so isolated. Michel had been attempting to telephone, but the calls would not connect. And I, in turn, could not get a line out.

Passing through a canyon I could not find on my map; face to face with the sheer enormity of the mountain; a river running fast and echoing around the enclosed space. It was stupendous. The mountain was my shadow and when I finally descended to it, the sea became my mirror.

The rain was falling at such a tremendous rate when I eventually reached Festos that a visit to the archaeological site would have been a miserable experience, sloshing about in the mud, soaked to the skin, so I swung the car, direction Matala. I knew that the southern fishing village, once so hip, had become touristy and ghastly, but, today, there would be no such crowds. I had not organised anywhere to stay and as it was only a few kilometres along the coast, I decided to look there. Extraordinarily, as I pulled into the car park right behind the bay, the rain stopped and the sun came out. I got out and trudged across the damp sand to the water's edge. To the right, the winged limestone cliff that jutted into the sea, dramatically enclosing that side of the bay. Within it, the curious collection of caves hewn by man as ancient burial sites, Greek or possibly Roman. These caves had become famous in the 1960s when, it was claimed, singers such as Joni Mitchell and Cat Stevens lived in them.

Twenty-first-century Matala, out of season, was streaming with mud and banks of damp leaves. Everywhere was closed. The sand was sodden charcoal. Another ghost town, but this one I knew.

That summer of 1972, after Marseille and Athens, Matala had been my final destination. The formation of the bay had not changed. The small fishing homes perched all along the left cliff were as I remembered them. The place was scruffier, but it had retained its seventies, hippy look with its wooden shacks and rickety painted restaurants, but they seemed sad and forgotten now. The beach was littered with driftwood, drink cans and perished rubber shoes. The sea, I remembered now how steeply it had shelved. How dangerous it had been with the African winds and currents that were frequent along this coast. I pictured me walking in the direction I was now facing, wearing shorts, handmade Greek leather thonged sandals with plaited straps that wrapped round my ankles and lower calves, a striped pink-and-white shirt. There had been eight of us living over on that nudist beach, a hike across a tortuously steep cliff from here, Red Beach. All strangers, at first, but it had proved to be a carefree summer. We had set up our own Olympic Games, playing out our opening ceremony on 26 August of that year. Each evening round campfires, braised meats, local wines, guitars, one of our party, Gideon, a German Jew from Munich, who was our leader, I suppose, set out the rules and organised the rota of sports for the following day. It was a piece of fun, nonsense. Until 5 September. On that day, the massacres in Munich began. Two Israelis were killed in the morning by eight Arab commandos, and nine hostages taken. The remaining nine were murdered that same evening in a shoot-out with the German police. It was several days before the news reached Matala, or before it reached us. As long as I live I will remain haunted by Gideon, standing behind a boulder, naked, as we had been all summer, crying, blubbing like a big, flabby baby.

I went over to him, tried to touch him, but he shrugged me violently off him. 'Fucking wars,' he had said in English. 'Fucking animals.' The following morning when I awoke and climbed from my sleeping bag, he had packed up and gone. Summer was shockingly over. Within a day or two, we all packed up and left.

I swung round now and saw a man in a red sweater and goatee beard waving to me. He was running a fish restaurant and it was open. I climbed up creaking wooden steps and entered. Four men, at two tables, were lunching, even though it was close to 5 p.m. One of them, a youth, was tucking into a huge plate of chips and sausages. He was obese and the fourth obese Cretan I had seen since leaving Chania.

Only on this island was such a fact remarkable.

After World War II nutritionists visited here to ascertain what physical deprivations and long-term damage had been endured during the years of occupation, but to their astonishment they found that the Cretans were in excellent physical condition. After research, it was concluded that the diet the islanders had been living on for the past three to four millennia was the healthiest in the world. The life expectancy here was well into the eighties, with many members of the community reaching over a hundred. Today, the Mediterranean diet is fêted the world over. Its basis is olive oil, fish, fresh vegetables and salads. The tragedy is that since tourism came to Crete, the islanders have changed their eating habits. To please the foreigners traipsing in and out every summer, they started to serve French fries, sweet, fizzy drinks, fast foods and over the last two decades the life expectancy of the average Cretan has dropped by 30 per cent. Obesity has become a national problem for the first time in their history.

'Want lunch?' asked the owner. I shook my head, thanked him and left.

I hiked the cliff in spitting rain to Red Beach, but got lost before the apex, stones slipping, loose beneath my feet. I scrambled to find a path. It was growing dark. Wind was buffeting the heights, knocking me off balance. I just wanted to ascend to the summit, to gaze upon that bay once more, but I couldn't reach it.

Try as I might, I lost footing. The wind was really picking up. I paused, drew breath. Dusk was falling. I turned back, trekking to the base without even having glimpsed the sands. I was trembling from head to foot, but, somehow, it seemed fitting that I could not return there, could not change that summer or that girl of so long ago. I walked back to the fish café and asked about rooms, sat and drank a mineral water, thinking of the past, while Antonios, the man with the goatee beard, arranged a bed, though it was not in Matala. I was glad it wasn't. The memory of Gideon had shaken me. I had not intended to return here.

In an inland village not far from the sea, or from Festos, my *dhomatio*, rented room, was one of eight in a Greek apartment block knocked up quickly to make a swift killing out of the tourist trade. But it was a place to sleep and it was set off the road in an olive grove, albeit a neglected one. The room had not been used or opened up in months. Zabia, the young widowed landlady, tidied it hastily, gave me sheets and towels and then hurried off, explaining that her *oma* had died that morning. Her grandmother's funeral was to be the following day. There was much to prepare. Zabia's grandmother, a hundred years old, had woken in fine fettle, drunk a glass of milk and keeled over five minutes later. A true Cretan.

'But it is all good, this life,' Zabia assured me as she accepted the €25 for the room, which was as cold as a refrigerator. The blankets smelled ghastly and there was nowhere in the vicinity to eat. I strolled across to a *bakeria*, bought crisps and tinned beer and prayed that the night would pass swiftly. I must have fallen asleep at some point because I was woken by lightning illuminating the room, an almighty crack of thunder and the fall of yet more rain. In the morning, I climbed out of bed to a world completely sodden by the ongoing downpour.

'The rain is good for the trees,' said Zabia, waving me hello when I drove to her home to return the keys. Her eyes were mildly swollen. 'These rainy Mediterranean Februarys are precious to the farmers for the growth, but not so splendid to bury one's *oma*.'

She invited me in for coffee. Shivering, I accepted gratefully. I learned that she had been married at sixteen to a man of twenty-nine, and had born him four children before he was killed, falling from a tree with a chainsaw at the tender age of forty. She had raised the children alone with her 'Rooms Rent' business. Her sole support had been her *oma*.

The island had suffered without rains for almost three years and her olive crops had diminished to less than a quarter of what they had been before. She could not have raised and educated her youngsters on oil funds, not without her tourism interests and *oma*. We drank another coffee. I felt absolutely wretched after little sleep. I perused the family album. It had only four photos in it. One of each child. I wished Zabia the best for the funeral and wended my way to Festos. The lanes led me through acres of lovely olive groves, which were quite deserted due to the weather but well tended and clearly not abandoned.

En route, I saw a sign for Kommos. I turned off the road and followed the arrows, winding all the way to the beach. In that summer of 1972, I never visited the remains of the Minoan harbour town of Kommos, the principal port for Festos, and a busy one it would have been. Today, there was little to see. The stones and trenches, resembling the foundations of a large house, had been fenced in. The rain had opened up hundreds of wild anemones, pink, red, white, small and delicate, growing everywhere in the olive groves behind the sand-dune grasses.

The beach was epic with waves crashing against the deserted, forgotten shoreline. In spite of the rain, I decided that a windswept walk might alleviate the stiffness in my muscles and the hangover I was suffering due to sleep deprivation and a bed that had been cold and damp.

As I strode forth, I paused to look towards Africa, lying unseen beyond a sheet of grey mist. My position was approximately two hundred and eighty miles north of Libya and three hundred east of Egypt. Odysseus had claimed that from here to the mouth of the Nile was a five-day sail with a favourable wind.

The Minoans, as far as we have discovered, founded two principal cities. Knossos was in the north and Festos here in the south. The southern inhabitants would have had plenty of dealings and interaction with North Africa. More so than with Greece, to whom they were not politically connected in those far-off days, and it lay a fair sail north from here, around the east or westerly tips of the island. The Levantine city of Byblos was an active trade centre during the existence of the Minoan civilisation, estimated to have been 3500 BC. Bechealeh perched in the hills behind Byblos. Did the Minoans barter for or purchase Lebanese cedar logs from the traders of Byblos to build their boats? At the height of the Minoan civilisation, the Bechealeh olives would have been in the region of five hundred years old. Were the successors of those olive planters travelling by donkey to the coast with jars of oil, sacks of fruit for sale? Might Minoan seafarers, docked at the shipyards to buy their wood or order new boats, have seen stripling olive trees for sale? Tasted its fruits, its golden juice, taken a few trees back home? Or might the Cretans have taken the mystical tree to the Levant? Cretan oil storage jars have been found in Troy.

From Byblos, there were interior trade routes via the Homs Pass to the Syrian hinterland, to the olive groves and markets of Aleppo and from there to Mesopotamia and Anatolia.

Festos in the pouring rain. I was completely sodden, but thrilled by the discovery of so many ancient stones used as primitive pressing equipment. This palace and Knossos, both known as palace states, controlled most of the very extensive olive groves on the island of Crete. The earliest written testimony about olive farming comes from Crete, from these palaces, written on clay tablets. Preceding alphabet forms as we know them, therefore preceding the Phoenician alphabet, using what was known as Linear A and B, a simplified system of writing, the Minoan people wrote of the production and circulation of their olive oil. It would appear that they were transporting aromatic oils, which would have been herbs and scented plants steeped in olive oil. The first creators of perfume? According to the tablets, it was a very profitable and successful business for the economies of Festos and Knossos. They traded these perfumed oils in many of the busy eastern Mediterranean markets, and it has been suggested that the Minoans even ventured as far as Malta and the Sicilian islands. If the Maltese and Sicilians were already crushing their own olive oil – and I put it that they were – what would the Minoans have bartered with them? Their pottery and perfumed oils, and in return they might have carried home obsidian, which is as common on the volcanic islands around Sicily as it was in the centre of Anatolia. I recalled the exquisite polished mirror carved from obsidian Michel and I had seen at Çatal Hüyük.

The Minoan tablets also recounted details of olive oil offered to their deities, who were female. This was a mother-goddess culture. Fertility and nature. As was the civilisation at Çatal Hüyük. Before metal and man took the reins.

From Crete, the spread of olive cultivation went to the Peloponnese and further north to such locations as Lesvos. But is it possible that oil production landed here from the Middle East, from farmers near Aleppo in the Levant or in and around Bechealeh? Yes, I think so. Might the Minoans, some five thousand five hundred years ago, have learned olive husbandry from the Bechealeh farmers, or their neighbours, their ancestors, and then travelled with the knowledge, the fruits of that knowledge, to other areas within the eastern Mediterranean basin? Exoticising the oils by adding aromatic plants? I think it is very possible.

Whether these extraordinary people took the olive and its culture from the Levant or whether they cultivated their own wild trees, it would seem that they took, at least, the name of Europa. Europa, from Tyre, kidnapped by 'Greeks', searched for by her brother Cadmus. Within the mythological cannon of Minoan stories, Europa was the mother of Minos, who became king of, and gave his name to, the Minoans.

By the time I left Festos, the site was a swamp. I squelched to the car and swung a course north to the capital, Iráklion, crossing the central band of the island, through the hilly vineyards of Crete, intending a stop on the way at the Palace of Knossos, but, due to the bad weather, the archaeological site of the ancient palace had already closed. I drove directly to Iráklion, one of my least favourite cities in Europe, in search of a hotel. By the time I arrived and found somewhere, overlooking the Venetian fort, I was soaked to the fibre of my being and exhausted. My mind was swimming with the mundane minutiae of journeying. No boats or flights from here to Israel. I was obliged to sail back to Athens. I had run out of clean clothes: socks, underwear, sweaters. The Greek winter had caught me by surprise. My stocks of hair conditioner and skin moisturiser were at zero, and my curly locks required my hairdresser. Into this bleak inventory came a call from Michel, finally managing to contact me and bolstering my mood with the unexpected news that he had bought a ticket and intended to meet me in Tel Aviv.

I was on my way in the rain to the Museum of Iráklion, and very excited by the prospect of it. The second mind-blowing twentieth-century discovery connected to this island and this remarkable ancient Minoan civilisation is almost a detective story. It all started sometime around 1926, when a small Cretan boy was taking lunch to his father who was at work in his vineyard. He caught sight of something glistening in the earth and when he bent to look he found a golden ring. As in so many small rural communities, advice was sought from the local priest, who was shown and given the ring, and kept it. News or rumours of the ring's discovery began to spread.

The archaeologist Sir Arthur Evans, having completed his work at Knossos, believing that there was a site close by that he had failed so far to locate, decided to give his search one last try. Whilst at work on the new project, Evans heard the gossip of the ring and sought to know its whereabouts. As good fortune would have it, the priest went with the ring to the Archaeological Museum of Iráklion. Impressions and photographs were taken both by the curators in Crete and by Evans, who had no doubt whatsoever about its authenticity. Evans located the priest and expressed his fervent wish that the precious object be acquired and displayed as a national heritage. The outcome of whatever negotiations may or may not have taken place was that the ring was declared lost, stolen, spirited away. The priest claimed that his wife had buried it and could no longer remember its whereabouts.

Evans, despairing, wrote about the subject in the *London Illustrated News*, heralding the importance of such a find. There was much scepticism about this elusive golden treasure, about all Evans claimed it represented and as to whether it had ever really existed. Evans died and the ring was eventually forgotten, until 2001 when a descendant of the 'owner' of the ring came forward with it and offered it to the island's museum in Iráklion. Its authenticity has been proven, and the precious piece of jewellery, dated at around 1450 BC (late Minoan), was displayed for the very first time at the Museum of Iràklion in the summer of 2003.

When I heard this Agatha Christie-like tale of intrigue and lost treasures, I was determined to see the object in question, but I had not expected it to impact upon my journey in search of olive secrets in quite the manner it did.

The ring was remarkable not only for its stunning craftsmanship, its beauty, its well-preserved condition, particularly given its age, but most of all for what the design on it represented. According to the notes that accompanied it, its engraving confirmed the core, the heart of Minoan religious ideology.

The ring's incised picture clearly shows that those extraordinary people, inhabiting this island as far back as five and a half thousand years ago – a Neolithic people lived on the same site previously – were worshippers of trees. The design has several images. In the first, a goddess is descending, floating to earth. In the second, she is seated observing two figures, a male and female, who are in the foreground of the image and who are joyously in communion with two sacred trees. In the lower image, the last, the goddess is in a boat, punting, journeying on water. In effect, the pictured tale recounted on this long-sought-for ring is that of the Minoans' own relationship with land and water. The goddess symbolises and fertilises nature and she has power over the sea, or protects the sea. It was how the Minoans perceived themselves and their relationship to the physical world around them.

What excited me about this find, this revelation, which I had not known of when I went to see the ring, was the power of the tree in the psyche of those sophisticated prehistoric peoples. In the palace frescoes, the olive tree was consistently drawn as the tree that brings happiness and fruitfulness. And light, of course. One image in particular offered a group of priestesses dancing in the sacred palace olive groves while an audience of men and women watched on with delight. It was the olive tree, no other, that was always present in their symbolism. In a society where nature and women were the power, the creative and regenerative force, the olive tree was sacred.

What eventually happened to this extraordinary civilisation on what appears to have been a Garden of Eden island is anybody's guess. Their disappearance is one of the greatest mysteries of ancient history.

Some scientists speculate that the Mycenaeans from the Peloponnese, who were supposedly jealous of these almost mythical people, might have overrun them, but no signs of any such devastating war have yet been found.

Others believe that the Minoans were destroyed in the greatest of all volcanic eruptions, the most spectacular cataclysm in all history, even more dramatic than Vesuvius's destruction of Pompeii in AD 79.

Some sixteen hundred years earlier, the ancient island of Thera, modern-day Santorini, began to experience movement and eruptions from a volcano that had been inactive for aeons. This gave the inhabitants warnings but nothing prepared the archipelago for what was to come when, somewhere around 1450 BC (the date of the ring!), the island literally exploded and was all but wiped off the face of the earth. It created a cloud of burning ash that spread far and wide as well as a colossal tidal wave or waves, a tsunami of such force and strength as the populated world had never seen. (This confirmed catastrophe might have been the inspiration for the story of the flood in the Old Testament. At the end of which, the dove returned to Noah with a sprig of olive, proof that the waters had sunk sufficiently low for the bird to pluck off a branch, and, for the religious, a declaration from God on high that he was no longer angry with his people, that the world was returning to calm, God was making peace with his people. This explains why an olive branch is perceived as a symbol of peace.)

Whatever the cause, the disappearance of the charismatic and powerful Minoan civilisation in neighbouring Crete – 120 miles south of Thera / Santorini – pretty much coincided with the after-effects of this geological misfortune, and there is no doubt that the waves and volcanic fallout destroyed much of the Cretan landscape. The waves rushing at the island were believed to have been over sixty feet high.

Darkness would have lingered over this part of the world for some time. The ash was carried on the winds as far as Egypt and even up along the coast to Syria. It took on biblical proportions. There are some who, in spite of Plato's claim, even today believe that Crete and its Minoan idyll was the legendary island of Atlantis and that this extraordinary natural disaster was its 'sinking'. (I rather like the idea that Atlantis might have been an olive-worshipping society.)

The Cretan survivors, such as they might have been, fled to the very western corners of their island, which seemed to have been less badly hit, or, when they could escape, to the Peloponnese. What certainly happened is that shortly after this monumental tragedy, the Mycenaeans, who had long been angling to get their hands on Crete, took possession of the island and built their own civilisation here.

When I arrived back at my starting point, Chania was flooded. The waves were rising high up above the stone quay like bucking winged horses, slapping their angry wings. Passage round the harbour was impossible unless I wished to be swept away. All ferries had been cancelled. I risked being marooned for the second time in a month. I smiled. I had read in Lesvos that all the sea-bordered lands in Greece, Crete too, light olive oil in the lamp of St Nicholas, protector of sailors. Fishermen, in the olden days, when the sea grew wild, would pour a few drops of olive oil into the waves to calm it. Sometimes using blessed oil that was rubbed on to children at their baptismals. Peace in the sea. Surely, somewhere, this and the sprig brought by the dove to Noah's Ark must be related? I recalled the fishermen in Malta, who never set sail without their olive branch in place near the engine.

I was meeting Michel in Israel in a few days and was determined that on this occasion, dearly as I loved this island, I would find a way off it. Running to move my hired car from where it was parked by the ancient Venetian city wall, I was slapped by spuming, licking waves and soaked yet again. The water had risen above quay level. Pick-up trucks were speeding to and fro along the harbour front, spray bucking high either side of their passage, to gather up parked scooters, work tools, whatever had been left out, delivering all belongings to safety before the angry swell consumed everything in its wake.

I found myself lost in the labyrinthine maze of the Venetian port, water streaming down the cobbled lanes. About me, shutters were tightly fastened. The harsh storm locked out, while the city revealed its winter face, its darker aspects. The angry Med. The local residents were unpanicked, knowing that it would pass and that the destruction would be whatever it was, while for the farmers inland, who had been victims of drought and the lack of winter rains for too many seasons, this was possibly cause to praise the heavens. Not unlike the priestesses in the frescoes at Knossos, they would be dancing in their groves.

But I was a traveller in these parts, not one of the land, not an olive farmer here, and I was at the mercy of the Mediterranean's unpredictable weather for the second time in a month. I bought a plane ticket for Athens, got myself to the airport and grabbed a seat on the first flight. As my plane took off, buffeted by winds, I closed my eyes and visualised that golden Minoan ring. I had found a civilisation that valued highly the yield of nature. A people who found joy and artistry in the world about them. Nothing in their artwork was an expression of aggression. Here was an island where the tree of peace, the tree of light had been celebrated.

After Athens, I was headed for Israel, a young state with a four-thousand-year-old history that has yet to find its peace.

Israel

I passed thirty glorious hours in Athenian comfort. Having checked myself into one of the swishest hotels in Syntagma Square, I indulged in scented soakings in a marble-floored bathroom, overpriced meals, strolls around the neighbourhood before reading on the bed in the quiet of my room with its balcony overlooking the cold but sunny central square. I felt that I deserved the hedonism after my Cretan deprivations. In any case, I was leaving on a flight for Tel Aviv, which departed at the godforsaken hour of 1.20 a.m and was due to arrive around four. I had been warned that clearing customs and immigration in Tel Aviv could be arduous, so I argued that this little parenthesis of luxury was worth every euro, and it certainly gave me the opportunity to catch up on sleep.

It saddened me to leave the classical world of Greece and the inspiration of the Minoans, particularly as I was beginning to get to grips with the alphabet and rudiments of language and I was moving to a land I had never set foot on before, into the world of Hebrew, a tongue I spoke not a syllable of. The word 'Hebrew' meant the 'Crossing One' and had been used to describe Bedouins, nomads. Amongst their points of settlement, Egypt was where the Israelites first embraced the idea of monotheism.

Aboard the flight, I sat opposite two Jews, Haredim (the ultra-Orthodox Jewish movement that originated in Eastern Europe during the eighteenth century) who, even as passengers were shuffling down the aisle, were already engrossed in the pages of their Bibles, their Torahs. A few moments after I had settled, two Arabs appeared. One of the arriving pair had been allocated the middle seat in between the two Orthodox men, while his companion had the identical central seat in the row behind. The Arab quickly sized up the situation and stood deliberating, causing a queue to bank up behind him, while the Jew on the aisle buried his face deeper into his prayers. A look of consternation crossed the chunky Arab's face. He hovered, unwilling to confront the young Jew. He would have preferred not to take up his allocated position, but what was blatantly clear was that his potential neighbour had no intention of affording him the choice. The situation was resolved when a woman directly behind rose and offered her seat to the Arab, which meant that he and his companion could travel together, and the Jews were left in peace. The scenario only took a matter of minutes to play out and few besides myself and the compassionate woman now seated further back had noticed it. However, it was a reminder to me that the land I was about to enter was being torn apart by racial and religious strife.

I was met from the flight by a young gentleman whose task it was to guide me swiftly through immigration. I had not arranged this blessing, nor did I know it was going to happen. In fact, so immersed was I in trying to figure out whether the slabbed stones used to build this luxurious new airport were genuine limestone or fake that I almost missed the card bearing my name, but I was extremely grateful for the assistance. In my luggage was extensive material pertaining to the Arab countries I had visited along my way. My young escort led me directly to the exit marked 'Crew', where a ferocious female immigration officer offered me the choice of receiving or refusing an Israeli stamp in my passport. I chose against it, and was immediately quizzed as to why I did not want it.

'You gave me the option. If it is a problem . . .' I responded as calmly as I could.

'Do you visit Arab countries?' was the steely young woman's accusatory demand.

I was exhausted. It was close to five in the morning and I had images of my undeclared Irish passport, locked in my suitcase, with its tapestry of Arab visas annotating all recent entries and exits.

'Do you?' she pressed. 'We need to know the reason you have requested not to have your passport stamped.'

'Yes, I do,' I answered with sanguine voice, but pumping heart, breathing deeply.

She gazed at me with narrowing eyes, weighing me up, and then tamped hard on to a sheet of paper. 'Welcome to Israel,' she bid. 'We needed to know.'

When I awoke later, it was close to midday and the world of Tel Aviv was closing down for Shabbat, the Jewish sabbath, due to begin later in the afternoon. I hurried to the bank, but it was already closed. I had sufficient shekels for coffee and that was all that seemed to matter on this sunny Friday lunchtime. I sat in the street in a leather armchair outside a kooky and slightly sixties café and devoured the largest *pain au chocolat* I had ever been served while the world around me went about its daily life. The disrepair even in this area so close to the beach and one street back from the US Embassy took me by surprise. The marble magnificence of the airport had promised a city of substance. A horse-drawn cart passed by, transporting two chaps, their complexions burned dark by the sun, and a motley selection of disused, rusted ironware. I had not seen tinkers or rag-and-bone men since my childhood in Ireland and had certainly not expected to find them here in what I had thought was going to be a twenty-first-century city, the economic heart of Israel. I glanced up and down the avenue, noticing shells of buildings, sooted or bombed out, in amongst the high-rises and apartment blocks Washed linen hung from open windows and several of the buildings were grimed with dirt or smoke. Many of the passers-by looked downtrodden, impoverished.

What did I hope to find here? I did not yet know why, but Israel, Palestine, felt like the completion of the journey. I wanted to connect, across a war zone, with those ancient Bechealeh olive trees. To complete a circle. I had no idea how. I was hoping the country would show me, would take me where I needed to be.

I struck up a conversation with the slender, well-toned waitress who had served my breakfast. A pretty, extrovert girl who had recently completed her military service and, like any newly qualified student, was full of the experience. She had trained with the army engineering corps and spent the majority of her two years, from eighteen to twenty, studying motor devices and explosives. Once qualified, her duties had involved teaching pilots the skills she herself had been trained in: detonation and dismantlement. She had spent a fair share of her time in 'occupied territories', learning weaponry, learning to shoot, and had frequently been given the order to pass on her expertise within a forty-eight-hour time frame to the soldiers in her charge before they were despatched on missions. She was never furnished with facts about those missions. Today, she said, only seventy-five per cent of young women served in the Israeli military. 'You can see the difference between those who have and those who have not. The discipline the army provides is vital. Today's figures are a poor show,' she sighed. 'We need to be trained up. Made ready.' Her expression softened when she confided that she had met her boyfriend in the army. He had been a medical student and was now her doctor.

I was biding time. There were people I was expecting to meet, but so far no one had returned my calls, responded to emails, and, on a personal level, Michel was flying in. We had been apart for too many weeks and his three-day visit was intended to close the gap. Aside from that, he was concerned that this leg of my journey could be dangerous and wanted to offer support.

The sun was shining. I decided to hike along the beach to Old Jaffa. The waves were slapping hard against the sand and gaggles of teenage boys were stepping into wetsuits, wading into the water with surfboards. It put me in mind of Sydney, not the tideless Mediterranean, except, here, the air was permeated with a sharp, acrid odour. At first, I thought it must be some saline, seaboard plant that I could not identify, but as I drew closer to the old city, I recognised the stench of feral cats.

I approached the Ottoman port from the north plage, hugging a strand that led me round by hangars and warehouses, one or two of which had been transformed into fish restaurants while the rest hung in decay. Further along, I came upon a boat graveyard where imposing hulks lay beached and rusting in the mud. Several bore names such as *Berenice*, painted in Roman letters, and I wondered where they had washed up from and what their stories were. Arab families were playing at the waterside or fishing. The women wore headscarves and long dresses but lacked facial veils. Mark Twain's first impression, stepping off at the port of Jaffa, was of a desolate country where the soil was rich but given over to weeds. A century on, I sensed that desolation.

I climbed up into the old town, winding in and out of

alleyways, my footsteps echoing beneath silent, stone-arched occupancies, spruced up and transformed into Israeli artists' galleries. I looked about for a café, somewhere to grab a bite, but everywhere was closed. It was Shabbat.

On my walk back along the beach, the sun was setting. A stream of brilliant orange bled against the gloomy city walls of Jaffa, burning off its desolation. I found a waterside fish café, which was open, even on this holy day, and, more surprising, its speciality was shellfish. Two women in jeans and leather jackets were on the wooden boardwalk, wrapped around one another, silhouettes lit against the sinking sun, kissing passionately and openly.

'Welcome to Tel Aviv,' smiled a stunning young waitress, an out-of-work actress, 'Israel's Sin City.'

I fell into conversation with a rather trendy, handsome couple seated at a table to my right, Adam and Beth, both first-generation Israelis, and charming. We were discussing how the present stalemate had arisen between Palestinian Arabs and Israel and how the olive tree was being used in this country. Not an uncomplicated subject!

'Although Jewish immigrants have been arriving on this shore for over a century, the State of Israel only came into being in 1948. We're a young country. Prior to 1917, the composition of land now referred to as the Palestinian Territories (West Bank and Gaza) and Israel belonged to the Ottomans. The appellation Palestine was first coined by the Romans —'

'Hadrian retitled Judaea, calling it Syria Palaestina.' An interruption from husband Adam.

'Sure, but it was the British who rechristened it Palestine when they took control after the Ottomans, and it was the League of Nations who mandated the divide of that Palestine into two states, one for its resident "Palestinian" Arabs and the other for the displaced, persecuted Jewish peoples.'

Adam was from German-Polish parents, while Beth's 'folks were Lithuanian'. I was noticing that most Israelis spoke English with a pronounced American accent.

'So the State of Israel was founded. But the Palestinians still await their lands, why?' I asked, sipping white wine from a vineyard in the Galilee region.

'Unfortunately, the Arabs hotly objected to the creation of a Jewish state within their territories. They took up arms —'

'But they lost the war. The outcome was that though Israel was founded, the territories that should have been allocated to the Palestinian Arabs were shared between Israel and Jordan. This left over three-quarters of a million Palestinians as refugees.'

I suddenly recalled my taxi driver from the camp in southern Lebanon. No distance, really, from where I was sitting. Only a war away.

'Eventually, after international intervention, it was agreed that Israel would evacuate the West Bank, which comprises the vintage territories of Judaea and Samaria, as well as the Mediterranean coastal strip of Gaza. The Palestinians grew hopeful that some of their homelands, at least, were to be returned to them.'

'But tragically, this compromise never came about either.'

'A series of Palestinian terrorist attacks caused the deaths of innocent Jews.'

'From our side, Orthodox Jews, now known as "settlers", convinced that Judaea and Samaria are their God-given right and that our Messiah will only come when we Israelis are in possession of every inch of this land, screwed it all up.'

'Our extremists began to illegally "settle",' explained Adam, 'in the disputed territories of West Bank and Gaza. They are building towns, "settlements", on Arab farmlands.

They go about it by kicking Palestinians out of their homes and by chopping down their centuries-old olive groves, claiming the land to be theirs.

'Even though Ariel Sharon, before he fell sick, ordered the settlers out of Gaza we remain caught up in a spiral of hatred. Negotiations have been halted and the situation grows steadily more acrimonious. Revenge, misunderstanding and violence perpetrated by extremists on both sides have caused a stalemate where dialogue is proving impossible.'

I listened with a heavy heart, but I was not here to judge. I was here to track the olive tree and nowhere on this journey of mine had I felt more concerned for its future, its place as a cornerstone of the Mediterranean culture, than I did here.

'You know, if you're interested in olive trees, you should check out Tu Bishvat. It's this weekend,' was Beth's parting thought. 'Enjoy!'

Tu Bishvat. For two thousand years Jewish ghettos all over the world kept faith, through prayer and rituals, with the promised homeland of their forefathers, the Israelites from Judaea. When the first flush of Zionist pioneers arrived on this eastern Mediterranean shore and began to build communities – many were atheists or non-practising Jews, their dream was a secular one – they made an astonishing discovery. The calendar that had been fanatically adhered to in the black-clad ghettos of such icy northern lands as Lithuania and Russia fell perfectly into place. The dates made sense here, fitting like a glove with the Mediterranean agricultural cycle. What meaning had there been in celebrating the New Year in September in Russia, while others all around them were working from another clock? But here, the olives are ripe, their harvest is beckoning and the summer fruits and vines have been gathered and stored for the comparatively mild winter that lies ahead. One vital cycle of the farming year had been completed and another, the olive harvest, was about to unfold. This came as a revelation to these new settlers: their Jewish holidays married with the earth, with this earth. Passover falls at the end of the wheat-sowing season. The seven weeks after planting were a time of waiting, of uncertainty, not yet knowing if the crops had taken, or whether they would produce a healthy harvest. No harvest, in past times, meant famine. The Jewish law that denied the cutting of hair during these weeks was now understood. It was interpreted as a warning not to arrogantly anticipate the fact that there will be something to cut: the wheat. To people who had been exiled for two thousand years, who had been buried in austere ghettos in far reaches of the world, who had lost touch with the soil, the rhythms and calendar of agriculture, of the earth, all this came as a revelation – Israel, this strip of Mediterranean territory was their paradise – and the Zionist leaders, adherents or not, welcomed it with open arms.

Unfortunately, today, in twenty-first-century Israel, fewer Israelis toil the earth, the *moshavirn*, Jewish agricultural communities are sparser, so this bond between land, man and the seasons is disappearing fast, losing context once again.

Tu Bishvat, which falls in February, had been one of those forgotten dates. Originally, long before the Old Testament expulsion of Jews from Israel, Tu Bishvat was the date when the age of a tree was registered for tithing purposes. Broadly speaking, in Jewish law, fruits were forbidden to be picked and utilised by the farmer during the first four years of a tree's growth, so its declared age became crucial and Tu Bishvat evolved as a period of tree planting and registering. In the modern Israeli calendar, Tu Bishvat is a time to eat dried fruits and plant trees in celebration of the beginning of nature's new year, rather like a spring festival. The tree that has come to symbolise this date, the tree that heralds for Mediterraneans the arrival of spring, is the almond. It is the first tree in the Mediterranean to flower and is in full and glorious tender-cheeked pink blossom in mid-February. And, as luck would have it, I was in Israel to witness it.

Michel had arrived and I was exceedingly pleased to enjoy the comfort and wisdom of his company. I missed home, my own corner of Mediterranean earth, and these early days in Israel had been disquieting. What I was seeing and hearing was unsettling, and the face of the military was everywhere. A documentary film-maker I chatted to in a café remarked, 'The dream of those pioneer Zionists has turned sour. Respect for the land has been replaced by consuming hatred.'

I had been planning to visit the West Bank, to penetrate territories that today are war zones, where the planting or uprooting of trees, most particularly olives, had taken on grave political significance. I had people to meet, but I was still awaiting responses to my calls, so I decided that it would offer a welcome alternative if M and I could participate in Tu Bishvat, to experience what had been described as a joyous and uplifting aspect of modern Israeli Judaism. If there were people out planting trees and celebrating the beginning of spring, I was keen to be included.

Sataf is a forested, mountainous region close to Jerusalem, in the heart of biblical Judaea, where, according to the English edition of the *Jerusalem Post*, almond trees grow in profusion. Michel and I hired a car and set off from Tel Aviv, intent on country roads in preference to motorways. At that stage, I had not fully comprehended the impact of where we were headed. When we neared the midland of the country, we found the signposts confusing and we became lost. It was not clear to us why. Michel is an excellent map-reader with a keen sense of direction, even if I am not, but as soon as we slipped off the highways, we were confronted by barred routes or we found ourselves on the outskirts of newly constructed townships. In fact, they were 'settlements' with barbed-wire fences and gates, and for added security, each of these settlements was manned with several armed guards and roadblocks. I found this faceless world of armoury profoundly disturbing. Where were we? Why was nothing signposted? Israel was beginning to freak me. Even so, neither of us immediately understood that we had penetrated Israeli-annexed tracts of the West Bank. These guarded townships had, until recently, been Palestinian farmlands, now snatched by Israeli extremists and built upon.

And then, before we knew it, we were on the outskirts of Jerusalem. Although we had not intended to visit the city, the road we had travelled had led us directly into Mea Shearim, a quarter that was inhabited exclusively by Haredim. Later, we learned that roads were being constructed across what had been Palestinian farmlands, directly into the Israeli quarters of cities. From settlement towns, the inhabitants could drive to work in the city on routes laid down exclusively for them.

Mea Shearim was like returning to a past century, another civilisation. It appeared far more extreme than any Jewish ghetto I had visited in other international cities. The men wore black frock coats, knickerbockers, black stockings. A few sported slightly more modern suits, but always black. Shoulder-length, ringletted sidelocks, pointed beards, black hats and skullcaps. The women, also in black, wore their hair swept and coiled beneath snoods. The mood of the place was sober, solemn, intense, purposeful.

Eventually, after twisting and turning, up and down, losing

our way around this ancient of ancient living capitals, we reached the wall of Jerusalem's old city, where we parked. Entering through Herod's Gate, I was assailed by the colours of the fruits, the clothing, the light; a bustling Arab souk. We pressed a path through the crowded narrow streets. Tracing the cobblestone lanes, passing here a doleful-faced Arab vendor pushing his freshly baked hoops of sesame bread on a wooden cart in and out of the milling shoppers, and there a seated vegetable farmer, lacking her teeth but rich in bouquets of spinach, sage and parsley. Along Via Dolorosa, we trod the steps of Christ struggling with his burden, passing by several Stations of the Cross. The streets were enlivened by the chatter and discussions of Irish-Catholic priests, Greek Orthodox fathers, Armenians and an entire community of Arabs. Only an absence of Jewish Israelis, but as suddenly as I remarked it, an army truck entered through one of the walled gates and sped towards us. Two scruffy Arab boys, of five or six, on hands and knees, playing marbles together on the ground, using the markings of a drain cover as a games board for their glass toys, leaped to their feet and pressed themselves tight against the heavy stone walls of the old city. I, too, was forced off my path as the truck skimmed dangerously by, forcing me up against a parked van. Inside the truck sat five Israeli soldiers sporting dark glasses, rifles at the ready. Their speed was a provocation, a threat to the inhabitants of this old city, but the Arabs continued with their business and took no notice. I suspected it was a regular event.

We drank Turkish coffee in a small cafeteria and then took off again for the hills, passing out of the troubled biblical capital down into a valley forested with pine trees. As we left the divided and occupied urban territory behind, I sighed deeply, though neither of us, at that stage, had really taken on board what we had been witnessing.

In the village of Ein Kerem, we stopped again to ask the way. This was where Christ's mother, Mary, came to visit Elizabeth, where she learned the news that her cousin, barren until that time, was now expectant. The child of her womb was John the Baptist.

Ein Kerem had a trendy, easy air about it with boutiques selling embroidered materials and clothing. We spotted several coffee shops and a pretty, vine-covered restaurant and terraces sweeping down the hillside. I considered Mary's journey from Nazareth. It would have been quite an arduous undertaking for such a young woman alone and on foot.

The Sataf region was blissfully arboreal. Several Israelis who had given us directions described it as a magical spot where underwater springs irrigated the land. We parked and climbed up towards the forested levels. On a carved stela, we read that the vegetation on these hills had been destroyed by fires, but, during the last decade, they had been replanted, thanks to generous contributions sent from overseas; Zionist donors, predominantly French and German, according to the commemorative milestones placed every few steps along our upland trek. Two, larger than the rest, Michel translated for me from inscriptions carved in Hebrew and German, were the exception. They represented 20,000 trees donated from the region of Weitzlar in the former West Germany as an offering of peace and reconciliation to the Jews of this earth.

Climbing the man-made tracks, we ascended above the designated reserve to hills that were still in their natural state. From here, we looked down into the valleys, where a patch-work of young olive groves had been planted. But nowhere did we encounter observants of Tu Bishvat. Not a planter in sight. It was no matter. The historic trees were equally a cause for celebration.

At this altitude, we were on land that had been farmed for

more centuries than we could count. The proof was the stone terraces long since fallen into rubbled piles, water tanks that had been dug out a thousand years, if not more, ago, as well as mounds of tumbled buildings, the jagged remains of stone cottages not dissimilar to the ruin on our land. Here, we found vintage almond groves with hundreds of trees in blossom. I was intrigued by an irrigation system we discovered and remembered that one of the young men who had given us directions had mentioned the subterranean sources that provided spring water for the farmlands lower down the mountainside.

'I believe these channels and underground tanks could be part of a system that was created during the Roman period of occupation here, if not earlier,' I said to Michel. 'They are known as *qanats*. The fellahin, peasant farmers, dug them out. They existed here and in parts of what is now Jordan, Syria and Lebanon. Along the Levantine sweep, in fact.' I lifted my arm and waved in a general direction towards what I guessed might be the Israeli–Syrian–Lebanese borders. 'The technology is antiquarian, pre-dating aqueducts, underground courses. They channelled water from natural subterranean springs to lower ground levels where populations had been driven back from the sea and were forced to find means of survival.'

I stood and looked about us. The terracing up where we were standing looked as though it was as old as the history of man. There were many almonds with occasional olive trees. Back then, there might well have been forests of cultivated olive trees. The almonds would have been planted later, when the farmers had found a means of irrigation. The olives could have survived on little. There would have been goats and sheep grazing up here, too. I could make out the remnants of plenty of stone cotes. Shepherds' abodes, no doubt. Judging by the remaining stones everywhere, it looked as though there had been a tiny hamlet or, at minimum, a house or two, right where we were. On the outskirts of Jerusalem, we were deep within the traces of rural farming communities that had almost certainly commenced, at least, two thousand years before Christ.

'Which way to Lebanon?' I asked of Michel. He thought for a moment, calculating, lifted his arm and pointed. In kilometres, if not politics, we were no distance from those mighty trees of Bechealeh. If the roads had not been blocked, if these countries had not been at war, we could have driven from where we were at that moment to where I had commenced this journey eight months previously in the space of five or six hours. I was nudging towards the roots of my search, the heartlands at the birth of the modern Mediterranean. I was closer, I felt it, than anywhere I had visited since I had left the Levant. I was fairly certain that if history, politics had followed different courses, I might have been standing alongside another grove of six-thousand-year-old trees.

In the light of our non-tree-planting Tu Bishvat outing, I picked six olives, *ziyat* in Hebrew, from an *olivier* in Tel Aviv and slipped them into an envelope, which I placed in my pocket.

I had expressed a desire to visit the disputed area of the Golan Heights. It had been Syrian land until 1967, when it had been occupied by the Israelis after their unexpected victory against the surrounding Arab states in the Six Day War. Our route was to take us north and east, up to the Sea of Galilee, passing through land flanked by Jordan to the east, and upwards to the tip of the country, smacking against the borders of Lebanon, Syria and Israel. An unholy trinity.

Along the route, I spotted a crippled Arab boy dragging

himself up a steep, hilly olive grove. No terraces here. We
drove by a prison where the detainees, all Arabs, were filing
out into a yard to exercise. IDF (Israeli Defence Force) soldiers
patrolled with rifles. Up around Mount Tabor, the rolling hills
were green and fertile. Plenty of olive groves set against rich,
dark soil. The Lower Galilee area abounded in blossoming
fruit trees, olives, almonds. A basin of fertility where the fields
were dotted with spires of wild red tulips.

When we reached the Sea of Galilee, there were thickly
planted banana and olive plantations growing frenziedly right
to the lakeside. We stopped for lunch in Tiberias (honouring
the Roman emperor Tiberius), ate *mezze* at the water's edge
while watching the gulls diving for pitta bread tossed by
diners. The sea, actually a lake, was still and pellucid. We
observed the antics of the only boat on the water, a small
fishing vessel that appeared to be upturning while its quartet
of fishermen seemed unable to resolve the instability. Later,
though, after lunch as we strolled the shore of this rather
touristy town, we passed the same four men selling their
wares: plastic buckets piled high with small, flapping, silvery-
scaled fish. Somehow they had managed to bring in their
catch. Curious to think of Christ here with his fishing apostles.
Judging by the weathered faces of the crew, they might have
been the very same fishers of men. As we said farewell to this
over-constructed resort, we drove by the city walls, originally
built by Bedouins and built upon later by Crusaders.

We saw a signpost to the Mount of Beatitudes, where the
earth was dark as chocolate. It began to rain. Another sign,
to the village of Kurassi, where Christ exorcised evil spirits
from a sufferer. The spirits fled the man but took up residence
in a herd of pigs, who threw themselves in the Galilee lake
and drowned. All around us were signposts tempting us on
journeys back into the New Testament. Passing through

Capernaum and then Tabcha, where the miracle of the loaves and fishes allegedly took place. I had recently come across that same parable, or similar, in an Egyptian text written during the fifth century BC. Arab horsemen, Middle Eastern cowboys, were herding cattle in the fields. After Zefat, we turned east on to a narrower, less frequented route and soon found ourselves up on the heights. The region was exquisitely beautiful, reaching deep into valleys in every direction. A bus flew by. It had been reconstructed out of the cab of a lorry and the carcass of a coach, spares salvaged from the ruins of bombed war materials, soldered together. The windy, wet weather created a moody atmosphere. We were climbing vertiginously high. Yet again our map was not always accurate and more than once we found ourselves driving in circles, ending back at the same crossroads or T-junction. Eventually, our ascent led us on to a rocky plateau, a high-altitude plain. The Golan Heights. There were military barracks and fenced-off zones everywhere. The landscape had grown craggy, almost Scottish, and the dark, louring weather played its part.

Eucalypts and old grey stones. Bleak yet fertile. Was it the British who imported the eucalypts? Occasional, tiny herds of cows – who tended them? – and small vine fields. In the days when Syria possessed this territory, there would have been no vineyards, but centuries before Christ, Palestine was renowned for its wines. Today, Golan Heights wineries are lauded in Israel; the Rothschild estates were involved in the establishment of viticulture in these parts. What we were passing through now were unfarmed acreages, wasted land, productive until four decades ago. Dotted everywhere were remnants of abandoned stone houses, bombed out, ripped down. Syrian, Druze, Bedouin farmers and herders had inhabited them. I saw many traces of antique terracing. Stones everywhere, ancestral tomb sites, witnesses of antiquity. We were penetrating ancient history. These heights were first inhabited five thousand years or more ago. The Aramaeans, those who spoke the language of Christ, arrived during the second millennium BC.

Once in a while, a lonely almond tree in full blossom, a note of cheeriness. We kept moving forward, towards the northern frontier, driving slowly, passing not a soul. To left and right, barricaded zones, abandoned army camps, chains of bunkers and the husks of stone homes; the ghosts of dead or fled lives. I suddenly feared the land might be mined. 'Not on the road, silly,' said Michel.

Somewhere, not far from where we were, lay the Valley of Tears, where some of the bloodiest battles of the Six Day War were fought. I was looking at the map, peering out through the rain, trying to locate our precise position when, silently, as though we were being curtained in, or out, *Brigadoon*-fashion, a fog descended, swirling about us on tiptoe. Like a lethal gas, it enveloped us. We reasoned later that it must have been clouds we had driven into. Whatever the explanation, our vision was now impeded. We were caged in, and the atmosphere had grown markedly eerie. We commented, both of us, almost simultaneously, that it was as though we were entering a zone known as End of the World. Moving forwards on our way to Nowhere. And then a large, round sign of warning painted with an X informed us that the route ahead was barred. The end of the line. Michel stopped the car and we pressed our faces against the glass, peering into fog, rain and clouds. The path, though narrow, was straight and continued on as far as we could see into the distance.

'What do you want to do?' Michel asked me.

There were no turn-offs in any direction. The choice was return or continue. 'Keep going,' I replied without hesitation.

I glanced at my watch. It was close to four o'clock. I knew that on the lower plains and at the coast of Tel Aviv the sun set at around five thirty. Night was not far behind us. 'But if you feel uncomfortable about that, we can turn back.'

Michel deliberated, then slid the car into gear and forwards we rolled. From here on, carcasses of beige Centurion tanks dotted the jagged, tusked land, every one trained towards Syria. I wasn't entirely convinced that they were abandoned, but Michel assured me they were. Eventually, after several slow-going miles, we arrived at a notice that read, 'Military Only Beyond This Point'. We were at the farthest extreme of Israel. Lebanon lay to the north and north-west. Syria probably about half a kilometre to the east. Directly in front of us, a matter of a hundred yards, rose a tall, radar-equipped lookout tower. To the right, a huddle of bombed-out abodes; to the left, a tiny lane at the beginning of which was a rusted upturned Centurion tank hanging from a pylon by its tail like a monstrous-sized dead grasshopper. Had the force of an explosion catapulted it up there?

I stepped out of the car. All around me the herbs smelled sweet and rich from the rain. Wild fennel was growing at the roadside. The land promising goodness was unexpected. Overhead, a flock of birds passed silently beneath a low-hanging black cloud barely higher than a slate roof. Silently. I closed my eyes for a second. Was there any sound at all in this desolate war zone? Yes, the rain. I could hear its soft descent. I dug into my coat pocket, into the open-flapped envelope and scrabbled for the six olive drupes. I had no idea whether anyone at the observation tower could see me, was watching us, had been tracking our trespass, our illicit arrival, so I fumbled to achieve this quickly, hoping military eyes would not mistake my gestures for the projection of hand grenades. I took the first olive and slung it towards Marji'yun, Lebanon, the second towards Syria, the third backwards to Jordan, another flew towards the Palestinian territories, and then I spun on my heels and threw the final two, swinging my arm forcefully like a windmill, back in the direction we had travelled: the Golan Heights, today Israel. Aware now of the altitude we had reached, it was unlikely that, even in my wildest dreams, the fruits would take root, but no matter. I was no distance to speak of from those six-thousand-year-old, mysterious, mythical, magical trees that were still fruiting, still bearing witness to history playing out its sad and bloody games. Here, reaching out from beyond where I was standing, forming a radius, a far-reaching sacred circumference, lay Jordan, southern Syria, Lebanon, Israel, West Bank, Gaza, Palestine, Judaea, Samaria, call them what you will. The Middle East. Landscapes that were once full of terraces, cisterns, silos, wine and olive presses and today were ripped to shreds by anger, dissension and strife. I believe this is where the story began. The history of the domesticated olive. Almost certainly. Perhaps in other corners of the Med's heart, the cultivation was almost simultaneous, almost, but this, as far as I was concerned, was journey's end. Almost every culture I had visited had taken the olive and made something of it, out of it, celebrated it. The tree of eternity. The tree of light. The tree of peace.

I had come full circle and would have closed the gap to Bechealeh had not the snipers, the blocks, the wars forbidden me. I lifted my face upwards into the rain, breathed the fresh, chilly air and then stepped back into the car.

'Finished praying?' joshed Michel. 'Because if you have, I think we should get out of here.'

Dusk was upon us. The fog or low clouds were dense. The rain was heavy. We were moving at a snail's pace. Then, suddenly, looming from out of nowhere, a silhouette appeared. Eyes glaring. A large dog. A Labrador or long-haired retriever, cream-coated, at the roadside, it shot out in front of the car from right to left, pausing a nanosecond directly in front of the engine. Its eyes trained upon us. Michel slammed on the brakes. The creature loped off. Where had he come from? Who did he belong to? Had we not been two to witness this extraordinary apparition, I would have reasoned he'd been a phantom; a spirit lost in the war stalking the craggy edges of Purgatory.

Nazareth (pronounced 'Nar-Zar-reet' by the local people) appeared closed when we drove in. Our supper was in a restaurant that had, until a couple of years earlier, been a private residence, situated alongside Mary's Well and a few doors from a fabulous Arab spice shop where we purchased fresh pistachios, almonds and a greedy portion of saffron, all for the princely equivalent of £3.50. The name Tishreen was chosen by its Arab owner because it was the month the restaurant opened. Tishreen, translated, was 'October', 'autumm' or 'harvest-time' in Arabic. How glad we were to have found this elegant yet unprepossessing establishment, decorated with straw on its walls. A symbol of harvest, of course, but it had possibly not occurred to the young Arab proprietor that the straw walls created in the mind of every hungry Christian a memory of those first weary travellers who had set out from Nazareth by donkey, trekking across what is today the West Bank territories, and found a welcome, a place to rest and feed beyond Jerusalem in Bethlehem. We were undoubtedly less needy than Joseph and Mary, but still we had travelled far, through spooky zones, were ravenously hungry and ready to be seduced by new flavours and tastes. At Tishreen, both our hearts and stomachs found satisfaction and we agreed that this was the best dinner we had fallen upon anywhere within Israel or Palestinian territory.

'And you know what?' smiled Michel, as we raised our glasses to toast the last evening of his too brief stay in this troubled land. 'It's St Valentine's Day.'

Two days later, I was up before daybreak to catch an early train to Jerusalem. It was packed with young Israeli soldiers, puffing on cigarettes and awkwardly negotiating their rifles. Some wore a badge on their sleeve that I thought was of an olive tree. Peace! Many of the girls suffered from bad complexions. The army diet, or adolescence. I was feeling profoundly unsettled. The treatment Michel had received at the airport had disturbed and angered me: he had been obliged to unpack and repack his case three times. Every item was scanned again and again. So long had all this taken that by the time he reached the check-in counter he had been informed that the flight was closed. It was with great difficulty that he managed to secure a seat. Now, taking seed within me, was a foreboding that I could not shake off. Our Valentine's dinner of two evenings previously already seemed a long way behind me, as did my life at home in France.

After the city of Bet Shemesh, meaning 'Home of the Sun' in Hebrew, the unveiling curtain of untouched nature was simply spectacular. I must have been somewhere close to Sataf, but I had no sense of geography in this confused country. Rolling hills, verdant countryside, almonds in blossom, passing through deep gorges where I spotted forests of green oaks, cypresses and long, silvery sweeps of feral olives growing close to fast-running streams. All piped water sources were encased within barbed-wire fencing. Water was a political weapon in this land. A source of power, of course.

Richly coloured small wild cyclamen at their feet, the olive trees were shrubbier than their domesticated kin. The terrain opened out into flat, fertile land where cultivated plantations were growing. Here, there were hosepipes snaking the rows of trees and, sometimes, stone terraces. Passing by the first village since Bet Shemesh, there were flat-roofed houses, built into a structured hillside. Once again I spotted the fences and barbed wire, 'razor wire', and the armed lookout towers. The train was approaching Jerusalem; I was growing nervous.

I had a rendezvous later that afternoon in Bethlehem with the sister of a Palestinian whose name had been given to me by a film-producer friend of Michel's. I knew almost nothing else about them. When I phoned his home, I learned that he had left for Jordan that very afternoon to renew his passport. 'But I can talk to you,' his sister, Amla, assured me. 'Come to Bet Lehem' – Bethlehem is spoken and written as 'Bet Lehem' and the 'h' is guttural like a Spanish 'j' – 'and I will meet you at the checkpoint.' She had not elaborated.

'I better ring again from Jerusalem,' I added quickly, feeling uncertain about so little information.

'If you want, but I will be at the checkpoint at three p.m. I cannot come sooner. I am a physiotherapist in the Caritas Hospital in Bet Lehem. I look forward.' And the receiver had been replaced.

That conversation had taken place two days earlier, and now here I was in Jerusalem, a stone's throw in modern travelling terms from Bethlehem, but a world away in every other sense. How would I reach the checkpoint? Was there just the one? Would a Jewish-Israeli taxi driver agree to take me? Were there buses, shuttles of any kind, organised perhaps to transport returning Palestinians carrying special exit passes back to their city beyond the wall?

I had no idea what to expect.

With several hours to kill, I made my way from Jerusalem station to the Mount of Olives. Eight of the trees growing vigorously in the Garden of Gethsemane were reputed to be over two-thousand years old. They resembled prehistoric creatures in flight. Gethsemane, or *Gat Shemanin*, meant 'olive-oil press' in Hebrew.

In comparison with my patriarchs in Bechealeh, or the long-undiscovered history of the domestication of the olive, this tiny grove here at Gethsemane was relatively young. As young, give or take, as Christianity; these trees stood silent witness to Christ's all-night vigil, his long hours of fear and spiritual torment, before his arrest and consequent crucifixion. Time spent alone, while his three apostle companions slumbered, even though he had begged them to remain awake, to pray with him.

I strolled the fenced perimeter photographing, observing, attempting to picture the scene back then. The olive trees were growing alongside other, far younger specimens, in a garden that was more reminiscent of landscaped Cap d'Antibes than a working olive grove. They were thick, gnarled, twisted, one or two of them had sections of their trunks bolstered by stone crutches, a few daffodils were in blossom at their feet and they were well pruned and of lusty demeanour.

This was a spot to which Christ came regularly. He and his companions used it as a meeting place. If our Christian Easter is an accurate anniversary, he was crucified in the spring. In those final weeks before his death, this olive-pressing area would have been active. The air would have been permeated with that pungent aroma of crushed and pressed fruits. There might have been small hillocks somewhere near the press – where was it situated? – of the dried, used paste (*jift* in Arabic, *jefet* in Hebrew), the residue after the fruits had been crushed.

In those days, it might have been laid around the trees' roots as compost or, a Middle Eastern habit, the waste, the dried olive cake, was given to the beasts as animal feed. In Libya, camels are still fed olive paste. The pruned foliage from what would have been recently harvested trees would have been fed to the herds of goats and sheep that doubtlessly were grazing these hills of Jerusalem. In Jordan, dried olive paste is used to make charcoal. Who knows, perhaps during that tortured night of the soul, Christ was able to keep himself warm burning olive waste, building a campfire or feeding cuttings into a primitive brazier, used in the day by land labourers? With an altitude of over seven hundred metres, Jerusalem's winter or early spring nights would have meant Christ had to endure long cold hours of darkness. These gnarled old masters that kept him company that night would have been juniors then. An olive press in those days would have been of the Roman style or something akin to those I had seen photos of in Professor Katris's book on Lesvos.

In between the pruned branches of the trees, I beheld the golden domes of the ornate church, situated higher up the hillside, dedicated to Mary Magdalene. The perfume in the tiny flask Mary carried to anoint Christ's feet was oil of myrrh, similar to frankincense in that it was extracted from pine resin. It was also possible that the perfume bottle she carried contained olive oil aromatised with myrrh.

In the distance, I heard the *muezzin* start up. The Muslim prayers, *salat*, ringing from every Arab quarter, echoing round the Mount of Olives, were one of the quotidian reminders that these lands are shared by three monotheisms. Another was the basilica, abutting the garden; an exquisite modern vision belonging to Franciscan fathers, designed by the architect Barluzzi. I crept inside, entering through impressive doors fashioned with cast-iron branches of olive trees. Olive motifs adorned many of the church's mosaics. A mass was in progress. The priest, in bright-red robes, was black-skinned. Close by the altar, where the rite was in progress, stood the rock that, says tradition, Christ sat upon during his solitary night. Even in here, olive boughs watched over him.

Descending from the Mount of Olives, strolling towards the valley beneath, I stopped to visit Mary's Tomb. An amusing moment occurred when a dishevelled and grizzled Arab, sitting hunched on the steps outside, carving wooden babe-in-mangers to sell to tourists, rose, shuffled over and shook my hand. His fingernails were like iron files.

'My name is Joseph and I am from Bet Lehem,' he announced, requesting a shekel or two.

It is possible that his name was Yusef and that he had originally hailed from Bethlehem – he might well have also been a Christian – but even if he had once lived there, he no longer did because he would not be allowed through the Israeli checkpoint (where I was soon headed!) to pass into Jerusalem, but the poor fellow looked like he needed a meal and his introduction had raised a smile so I gave him the price of it.

At the base of the Mount of Olives, Kidron Valley, I found olive groves, Christian graves and monumental tombs, as well as what seemed from a distance to be stones that resembled the remains of antiquated presses – the area was fenced off. I could not get closer, but might this have been where the press was situated that gave the garden above its name?

In antiquity, this area had been the eastern boundary of Jerusalem city. Here, declared the prophets of Israel, Judgement Day would take place. As a consequence of that prophecy, several sprawling burial sites have grown up. For those keen to be first in the queue!

On my way back to the walled city from Kidron Valley, it

began to rain. A few taxis pulled up, inviting me on 'free' trips around the sites and Christian churches. I preferred to walk. When the rain grew as sharp as needles, eventually turning to hail and then snow, I fled for shelter beneath a roadside olive where two Frenchmen had already taken cover, shoving my camera beneath the flap of my leather coat.

'May I share your olive tree?' I cried.

I waited alone there after the men had continued on their way. I was at the foot of the city wall, in sight of a collection of tombs and time-worn caves and remnants of an earlier wall – Canaanite, I believe – upon which this city of Jerusalem had been constructed. Across the street were the offices of UNSCO, the United Nations Special Coordinator, working to support peace in the Middle East. I climbed the steep hill alongside the outer fortifications, repeatedly checking my watch. I had three hours to kill until my rendezvous in Bethlehem.

Over a glass of wine, I perused the *Jerusalem Post*. An article and a photograph with caption caught my attention. Both on the celebration of Tu Bishvat. Front-page news reported the gathering of Jewish families in rolling hills close to Gaza. These Israelis had come together to plant olive trees a short distance from a territory that until six months earlier had been their 'settled' homeland. The evacuation of Jewish settlers from Gaza had proved a very contentious issue. Ex-Prime Minister Sharon had intended it as a first-stage gesture towards a peaceful compromise with Palestine, but for the Israeli right-wing 'settlers', it was perceived as betrayal. These extremists and ultra-Orthodox Jews believe that all Palestine is historically and divinely their heritage. For such people, there could be no compromise, no sharing of territories with the Arabs. When the crowd reached 2,000, convening near the Gaza checkpoint of Kissufim, they planted trees. 'It is our way,' they said, 'of maintaining a bond, a connection to land that is ours, the land of Israel.'

Elsewhere in the newspaper, and elsewhere geographically, in the village of Salem in the West Bank, 300 Israelis, many belonging to movements such as Plant for Peace, had met with Palestinian farmers living in the neighbourhood. Together they had planted olive trees transported by horses to the field where they were to be placed in the earth. It was a gesture of reconciliation, a protest against the recent acts of vandalism, the destruction of Arab olive groves, suffered at the hands of Israeli Defence Force soldiers or settlers.

I was fortunate with the taxi driver I hailed. He was a Palestinian Arab living in Jerusalem, but he knew where I was headed. During the journey in the pouring rain with windscreen wipers barely able to keep the flooding at bay, I asked him about his life and how it had changed.

'It is bitter,' he told me. 'The "Defence Wall" that snakes around the city has been all but completed. It is shutting the majority of Palestinians out of their capital or locking the rest of us into it. Life, for those of us still living in Jerusalem, existing within depopulated communities, has become very expensive. We are charged high taxes if we remain here. We are struggling to survive,' he admitted. 'And new Jewish "settlements" are springing up everywhere on land confiscated from us. These settlements ring the city. Their wall, their "security fence", imprisons us. Our neighbourhoods have been transformed into ghettos. Gone are the thriving communities we knew before. We are being pushed out,' he sighed. 'If Israel has its way, we will be expelled altogether. They want Jerusalem for themselves.'

I asked him which passport he carried. 'Palestinian,' was his answer, but it got him nowhere, not even to other parts of

Palestine. 'I am issued with an annually renewable ID card, which can be revoked at any minute, but as long as I have it, it gives me the right to remain in my city. Still, I am cut off from the rest of our country. I have a sister living in Bet Lehem and I have not seen her in four years. She has no permit, no means of exit from Bet Lehem and it is difficult for me to visit her.'

The ride in the beating rain cost me approximately £3. I offered extra, but my driver did not accept it. 'It was good to talk,' he said. 'Be safe,' were his parting words.

I stepped out of the car into a lashing storm with wind whipping at my scarves. I pulled my rucksack back over my shoulders and stood looking up at the checkpoint. It was imposing, to say the least. Naïve, undoubtedly, but I had visualised something more benign. I made my way up a winding path, past a sign instructing all comers to have their ID papers at the ready, and reached the first sentry box. The soldier, a boy, asked me in Hebrew for my papers. I was anxious. I had told no one where I was going because I had felt uncertain about imparting this information on my mobile or from my hotel-room phone in Tel Aviv. I reached into my bag and drew out my British passport. He waved me on and I breathed deeply, thinking that was the end of it, but I was mistaken. I had entered a capacious concrete shed with metal turnstiles every few yards. It appeared deserted until I glanced upwards. A soldier on a ramp above my head had a rifle trained on me. He waved me along with the tip of his gun. I pushed myself through a couple more turnstiles and a security X-ray system, passing by a towering poster pasted to a wall which read, 'Israeli Tourism. Go in Peace.' I now found myself outside in a large, stony yard, lacking any greenery or plant life whatsoever. I looked about expecting to see the woman I was due to meet, but there was no one. I soon realised that this was not yet Bethlehem. It was no-man's-land. The rain was streaming so hard and fast that my hair was glued like ribbons to my face. I could barely see through the rivulets running down my face. I had covered myself, over my scarves and long leather coat, in a red plastic Pac-a-Mac, but it was being whipped away in the wind. I and every article of my clothing and bag were saturated. I hurried back the way I had come and called out, 'Hello? May I wait inside?' I was given the choice by the sniper overhead: 'Move on or return to Israel.' I chose to continue. Sprinting across the yard, I reached the checkpoint for cars entering Israel. To the right of me was a watchtower. It seemed as though night was falling in grey strips. Again there was nowhere to take refuge from the rain, no one to meet me. And then I noticed it. How could I have missed it? A matter of feet across the muddied pathway, beyond the checkpoint: the wall. Eight metres high. I had read of it frequently, but standing face to face with it was another experience altogether. A sodden concrete mass of threat. To the left, about twenty yards into Bethlehem, a handful of taxis were parked. Their chauffeurs had no rights to exit from here, to ply their trade. Their sole hope of a fare was an arriving passenger such as myself, but I had no idea where I was going and there was still no sign of the woman, Amla, I was to meet. I hoped this was not a wild-goose chase. I knew nothing about her, except that she was the sister of a contact. It was a very slender thread. Suddenly from above, a searchlight was trained upon me and a male voice was yelling in Hebrew. His gun was aimed directly at me. From out of the car check-in booth appeared a soldier.

'What are you doing here?' he yelled in Americanised English when I explained that I didn't speak Hebrew.

'I am waiting for someone from Bet Lehem.'

'Move on! You can't wait here.'

Orders were cried from on high again and the light would have been blinding had it not been for the screen of rain.

'Move along,' he shouted in my face.

I was wetter and more bedraggled than a river rat. I crossed the waterlogged path and pressed myself up against the juggernaut of a wall in the hope of some protection, but again I was chivvied away. I decided to walk to the taxis. Perhaps I could negotiate a temporary seat of refuge in the rear of a cab for a few shekels, but as I took the first steps, a drenched, hunched figure wrapped in navy coat and hood plodded towards me, waving. I hurried in her direction and we embraced awkwardly, like dripping logs bumping against one another on a downstream course.

'Thank you for coming. We better hurry.' Amla led me to a waiting taxi already containing three Arabs plus the driver. The closed air was heavy with cigarette smoke and blasts of dry heat, but I was grateful for it. After what appeared to be a trajectory of little more than a kilometre, during which time I desperately tried to peer out, to see something of Bethlehem, without success – this was the birthplace of Christ; 'Away in a Manger' was singing in my head – Amla and I descended. She handed the driver a couple of shekels and signalled me to follow her. Up we went, climbing dozens of stone steps, weaving our way in and out of tortuous lanes, steep alleys, battling against the wind and horizontal sheets of rain, until we reached a door that admitted on to an open, rectangular courtyard with a central well, buckets, flowers, drowning pot plants, two bicycles lying on their sides; signs of communal habitation. Crossing the courtyard, she led me into her home, calling to her mother, Malida, who greeted me with a kiss while Amla apologised for the fact that her mother spoke no English or Hebrew. I was guided to a mattress-cum-sofa alongside a small paraffin heater. As I took off my coat and scarves they left huge puddles on the floor. Arabic coffee was served while sweets and biscuits were laid out on plates in front of me. Malida began peeling apples and oranges and slicing them into a dish, which was then offered to me. All the while Amla talked, pouring out facts and incidents in erratic order and broken English. She was a tired-looking unmarried woman of thirty-something with worried eyes and a rush of energy, and I listened, shivering, teeth chattering, while she recounted how, in numerous West Bank locations, the Israeli settlers had force-entered privately owned Palestinian farmlands with digging machines and weapons. Theirs, she was anxious to assure me, was not an isolated case.

'And your story?'

Men had arrived at midnight with bulldozers to their estate, 100 acres of olive and wine fields set on a hilltop 15 kilometres south of Bethlehem, declaring that they intended to take control of the land there and then, to commence construction of a road. These Israeli settlers had surrounded the family's living quarters, still a simple cave, with Jeeps and machine guns, shooting into the air, claiming the land was Israeli state territory and they were entitled to it.

Trained dogs attacked Malida, Amla's mother. Her elder brother Daoud was badly hurt by the extremists while trying to defend his property. Using her mobile, Amla had telephoned for assistance to a Danish pastor living not far from the site. He came at once, begging the settlers, who by then were hacking down the olive trees, to be reasonable and lawful, but to no avail. That night the family lost 350 mature trees from their groves.

'Is the cultivation of olive trees fundamental to the Palestinian way of life?' I asked her.

'It is our source of livelihood. Without our olive trees, we are impotent. You know, the date the Israelis celebrate as Independence Day is known as "Nabka" by Palestinians. It means "catastrophe".'

Since that traumatic nocturnal incursion, the family had never left their land unprotected. Always one member slept in the cave. On the positive side, they have been offered support for their battle from many unexpected sources. A rabbi, with a group of young Israeli students, donated and planted 250 olive saplings as an offering of recompense, rectification. When I expressed surprise, Amla reminded me that there are several organisations such as Rabbis for Peace who are working to find solutions to the strife in the Holy Land. Fifty monks turned up from Tel Aviv and said mass in the cave. Volunteers from Switzerland, Germany, Italy and Britain flew in to assist with the planting of young groves and maintenance of the estate. Donations towards the ceaseless and expensive court cases they have been involved in, in fruitless attempts to prove their legal ownership, have flooded in from everywhere.

'My grandfather bought the land in 1924,' Amla explained, while her mother, still peeling fruits though I had not yet touched any, nodded.

'We have all the registration and purchase documents. Daher's Vineyard, we called the property. My grandfather's name was Daher. He lived in the cave on the land where my father was raised and where we, as a family, enjoyed many days of my childhood. Daher's vision was that one day this magnificent site where you can watch the sun set beyond the Mediterranean might become a place where people from all nations could come together, spend time in discussion, drinking our wines, sharing our different cultures.'

I smiled, remembering my own, not dissimilar dream for Appassionata.

'Curiously,' continued Amla, 'this is precisely what is happening. Daoud, who is so sorry not to meet you, heads the organisation we have founded for that very purpose, the Tent of Nations. So, as long as we have success in the Supreme Court and the Israeli legal system doesn't find loopholes that can justify the confiscation of our property, Daher's dream will be fulfilled.'

At some point during all these explanations, the door opened and a stocky, handsome man entered, kissed Malida on the forehead and sat down. This was Chris, the youngest son. He offered to accompany me to the land, but dusk was falling, the weather was getting worse and I had to be on a late-evening train back to Tel Aviv. They begged me to return again later in the spring. 'Bring your husband.' With that, it was time to be on my way. Chris insisted on driving me to the checkpoint in his decaying Mercedes. It was not dissimilar to Michel's old bus, except this one could barely move and its windscreen wipers were out of action. Amla ran to find a thicker overcoat, while Malida hugged me. She seemed genuinely upset by my departure and handed me, as a 'gift from the Holy Land', a manger with the newborn Christ hand-carved from olive wood. I smiled, recalling innocent, childhood images of baby Jesus, and the Arab Yusef, who had attempted to sell me his wares outside Mary's Tomb.

Amla accompanied me the last few steps beyond the taxi station towards the checkpoint and then turned. 'This is as far as I can go. When you are back home, out there' – she was pointing beyond the monolithic, wet wall – 'please remember us and our plight.' She bear-hugged me, then walked resolutely away without looking back.

I ran those last 20 metres, splashing through the deep puddles, anger rising, noticing rain swirling beneath the bright lights and large graffiti artwork on the inner circumference of the wall. The concrete cage. One image depicted a lion tearing its startled prey to shreds while a fountain of blood spurted from its ripped throat.

I was obliged to show my passport, twice, and still found myself locked in an enclosed area between metal turnstiles while the charade of earlier – armed soldier overhead, orders barked at me through a loudspeaker in Hebrew – was played out again. I attempted to remain cool. Still no exit was available to me. I waited and waited until eventually I called out, 'I don't speak Hebrew. I am a European citizen and I want to leave. Please unlock these gates.'

After endless moments, I heard the disembodied click of a turnstile lock and I pushed my way through it, stepping towards Israel, when a voice called, 'Stop! Lady!'

'Yes?'

'Passport!'

I rummaged in my bag, trembling, losing my make-up and the olive ring made for me by Marie in Byblos. All fell to the floor and I lacked the emotional strength to bend and retrieve them. I laid the passport on the counter. The kid gave it a cursory glance and nodded me on my way.

Outside, in Israel, it was night, the weather was lousy, and there were no buses or taxis. A group of soldiers had encircled a bunch of Arabs, who were turning out their pockets. I had no means of transport. I spied a white van and ran to the window. I had twenty-five minutes to get back to Jerusalem and catch my train.

'Are you a taxi?' I yelled.

A swarthy fellow leaned over and rolled down the window and I repeated my question.

'I could be a special taxi,' he leered.

I stomped off, and at that moment, a small saloon car pulled up and out piled a young couple. As they ran towards the checkpoint, I hurtled in the splashing rain and banged furiously on the window.

'Are you going to Jerusalem?'

A handsome young chap, no more than twenty-five, opened the door. 'Get in,' he said, which I did.

'Thanks.'

Further down the track, we passed groups of soldiers frisking arriving Palestinians who looked as though they didn't have two shekels to rub together. There were dozens of them. My chauffeur remarked that he hadn't seen so many soldiers here before. He was German, a voluntary worker in medicine. Blond, Aryan and well presented. It seemed an unlikely place to find him. Six months he had spent already and had another six to go. This place is tragic, was his analysis, and bloody awful.

'For a people who have been through what the Jews have, many of them, the extremists, fundamentalists, at least, certainly know how to dole out suffering.'

I looked out of the window at the passing night, and sighed. This land was remarkably potent, evocative, yet I had rarely been anywhere that engendered such a hash of emotions within me. 'It's heartbreaking.' My remark was softly spoken, barely audible.

'Yes,' he returned, 'exhausting.'

In the rolling hills between the Mediterranean Sea and the Jordan Valley desert, Arab villagers, both Muslims and Christians, have dwelled alongside one another in communities where lives have long been interwoven. They have tramped through their olive groves to visit brothers, cousins, lovers, in-laws and friends. They have herded their goats, used the tracks as paths and lived out their rural existences on and through this land. This way of life has continued for as long as man has farmed the earth.

In the recent past, in retaliation for shocking acts of violence perpetrated by Palestinian suicide bombers, the Israelis have, as a 'security measure', sent in diggers to many West Bank villages and have torn up the land, ripping from the soil olive trees that have been growing on these hillsides for centuries, possibly longer. In place of these groves, they have constructed barbed-wire fences and concrete walls, severing villages from neighbouring communities or, in certain cases, cutting directly through the heart of homes, driving families apart, blocking access to wadis and precious water sources, denying local populations all possibility of exiting their hamlets to farm their lands or earn their livelihoods. These 'security fences', claim the Israeli extremists, are a means of protecting Israel against Palestinian suicide bombers.

A silent, mournful expanse of wasteland best described the sprawling patch where we were to plant the sapling olives.

I had arrived at the Central Tel Aviv train station ahead of the appointed hour but found without difficulty members from the party of peace activists, all of whom were Israeli Jews ready to give up their day to plant a tree under marginally risky circumstances. The gentleman who had invited me was an eighty-two-year-old journalist who had emigrated to Israel when he was ten. He had been a member of the Israeli parliament, the Knesset, until he had decided to give up mainstream politics to independently promote peace in the Middle East. He knew the whole story of this deeply troubled land and had witnessed most of its recent history through his own compassionate blue eyes. His name was Uri. He had a shock of pure-white hair and a healthy beard to match. He was sprightly, handsome, fit as a fiddle and formidably knowledgeable. I had been trying for almost two weeks to meet with him but saw instantly that this was not going to be the opportunity to engage him in conversation. A documentary film-maker, Jacob, living in Finland, was following his every move, and as the founding energy behind much of what this peace group was about, he was sought after at every second.

I introduced myself and found a seat on their bus. Fortunately, my travelling neighbour, Samuel, round as a doughnut, balding with a few remaining untidy wisps of hair, was a full-time activist and well able to fill me in on the history and events that were the background story to the village of Qaffin, where our bus was bound. Born in Israel of Zionist pioneers and kibbutzniks, he spoke English with a thick mittel-European accent, stuttered painfully and related to me the entire plot of *The Spy Who Came in From the Cold*, which, he admitted, was his favourite novel. I smiled, wondering whether his chosen calling had not been influenced by his passion for thrillers.

Our discussions were interrupted by a sandy-haired, blue-eyed gentleman who took up a microphone alongside the driver to make a lengthy announcement in Hebrew. Moans and reactions of anger were the response.

'What did he say?' I asked Samuel.

'The army have reneged on our agreement. We had negotiated for the villagers of Qaffin to be allowed to join us for the tree planting, but a message has just come through to say that they will not be given permits to leave their village. The situation is being renegotiated as we approach.'

The countryside beyond the window was lush and well planted. There were palms, bananas, waving fields of young wheat, olive trees, grove upon grove of citrus fruits. I remarked on this and was reminded that this coastal plain was the agricultural heartland of Israel. The irony was that this land was never Israel, not even during the biblical period.

This was Canaanite territory. The Israeli forefathers rarely descended from their hills to these flatter, coastal lands; they were in terror of the chariot-riding Canaanites. I recalled Sour, ancient Tyre. It was so many months ago since I had walked that seafront, looking left towards this region. I had never dreamed my journey would bring me to this.

These lush plains were irrigated with water piped from the Sea of Galilee; piping that had not been routed to the West Bank, which is why the Palestinian areas were drier, desiccated, and why they were suffering debilitating water shortages. The aridity became apparent as we – we were a convoy now that two other buses and several cars had joined the party – drew closer to the West Bank boundary. The properties, too, became less ornate. There was a more obvious air of struggle about the surroundings. Shy scarved women hanging out laundry on flat Arab roofs stared in at our passing faces with puzzlement. Here, I saw the shells of many abandoned properties, while gardens everywhere were jungled with olive trees. As we pulled into the village of Bak'a al-Garbiya there was a minor traffic jam. This hen-scratched street was not used to providing parking for coaches. The chickens whose habitual feeding ground this was were running about excitedly in the puddles and mud. Someone pointed out to me a single old border stone, explaining that it marked the pre-1967 Green Line. Ahead of us, beyond a patch of land piled high with mounds of rubble and broken bottles, was the 'security fence'. Beyond that, out of sight, lay the Palestinian village of Qaffin. These acres, its inhabitants' farming lands, were inaccessible to them without a permit to pass through the security fence. In between, slicing right through what until four years ago had been mature olive groves, lay a newly dug road bordered on either side by a high barbed-wire fence. Its grim kilometres of razor wire had been mounted with electronic 'early-warning devices', while about fifty yards along the road, once sloping hillside, was a military roadblock. I looked about me and saw that our numbers had grown to several hundred, including children and a collection of dogs. Quite a few were carrying banners that showed the two flags of Israel and Palestine in union and displayed the slogan 'Two States – One Future'.

We made our way in straggly file to the rubbish dump, where uneven holes had been dug out of the rich, white and dark clay soil in between the hillocks of junk. The chickens came, too, and there were others pecking around the roots of the few olive trees that remained here. An Arab woman was washing dishes in a plastic bowl on the ground in her yard. A small boy with dark skin and big, brown eyes was playing at her feet. Beyond the dump area, a large yellow JCB was at work. This was the creator of the holes. People stood about in the sun, appraising the site, wandering to and fro, taking in the desolation. If the Israeli army forbade the Palestinians access to the land today, there would be no trees to plant. This peace organisation, each individual member, had donated the money for the trees to the Palestinian farmers several days earlier and it had been the farmers who had arranged the purchasing of the saplings. Now we had to wait.

It was a hiatus. People sat on the large flat rocks that were part of this Mediterranean soil and began to unpack sandwiches. Uri and the film-maker, Jacob, were walking towards a gate in the fence and I went with them. Here, Uri fixed his banner of the two flags united while he and other practised activists examined the padlock and thick chain, which it didn't need an expert to see had rusted solid and had very evidently not been opened in the four years since this section of the wall had been erected.

'It's a farce, placed here for the Supreme Court,' was Uri's verdict. 'If anyone contests the fact that the Palestinians are imprisoned within their villages, locked out from the land that is theirs to farm, the army can show this gate and say, "Nonsense, they have access to and fro whenever they need it. It is only locked today for 'security reasons'."'

Suddenly, at the checkpoint 100 metres distant, a Hummer appeared on the elevated horizon. The army had arrived. I felt a cold wave wash through me. What if matters grew violent? This was intended to be a peaceful demonstration, but who could tell what might trigger aggression? I watched the armoured vehicle intently as it reversed, swung and parked itself at a right angle, closing off access, creating a roadblock.

An Israeli Arab living in Nazareth, a coordinator, came to announce the news that negotiations with the IDF had reached a conclusion and ten Palestinian farmers were to be allowed out of their village to plant with us, but they had to be back on the other side of the fence by two o'clock or they would permanently lose all rights to an exit permit. I glanced at my watch. It was almost midday. Two hours of freedom, they were being granted. Moments later, travelling from the opposite direction to the checkpoint, from the distant village of Qaffin, came a white open-back truck. In its cab were four Arabs and in the rear dozens of olive saplings and three more farmers. They stopped at the locked gate where we were still positioned and shook hands with us through the gaps between the vertical bars. Attractive men with jet-black hair, lean frames and outdoor dispositions. They climbed into the truck while we made our way back to Bak'a al-Garbiya, passing the JCB, which was lower down in the grassier parts of the field now, beyond the detritus, still digging holes. By the time I arrived back at the village, most of the activists and planters had already helped themselves to a sapling or two from the rear of the truck and were making their way back to the site. I smiled with joy as I passed lines of Israeli Jews of all ages, children too, cradling small olive trees in their arms like babies. The sun was reaching its zenith and the day was growing hot. I stared into the distance, eastwards, to undulating Samarian hills. The view was soothing. Peaceful, rural. A glance in that direction and who would guess that this was a war zone, that this productive soil was the root of so much acrimony? An Arab handed me a sapling. It was surprisingly heavy, its earthed roots packed tight within black plastic wrapping. I looked up at him. 'Thank you,' I said in Arabic.

He nodded, his eyes still trained on mine. He had a strong nose, slightly hooked. A profile that I think of as particularly Semitic. Ruggedly handsome.

Back at the site, the Israelis were busy digging and the mood was upbeat, like that of a summer party, yet there was a strong sense of purpose underlying our presence here. People were laughing and calling to one another. All around I could hear scraping and beating sounds. The planters had found any old implement, bits of stick, rusted strips of wire, plastic chair legs, to use as tools. The hole I found to plant in was a scruffy mess. I would have to go further to the bottom of the field now if I wanted better, for the others had all been taken, but I was happy to think of this little tree of mine struggling for all it was worth to hold its own here.

I silently welcomed the stripling to this soil and placed it in the hole. 'May you live to be six thousand,' I grinned. I saw amongst the piled earth alongside it a child's tiny shoe and a broken plastic turquoise chair.

The Palestinians were moving between us now with farm implements resting on their shoulders. I spotted the handsome farmer in the beige zipped cardigan and jeans. He caught my eye, smiled and moved to other planters. Several

Israelis and Palestinians came to help me secure my tree, for the spot I had chosen was not very negotiable. Nearby, a stunner of a Palestinian flirted with two pretty Israeli girls and all three giggled as they worked.

When the planting was over, we all descended to a flatter, greener tract of the land, where Arab coffee with cardamom was being offered to us from the back of an open van, which also contained cartons of bottled water and tubs of food. Arab hospitality. It would be an insult to send us away without having fed us even though time was running out and they would have to be back across the fence within the hour. We were invited to sit on the ground. Speeches began. Words were spoken by one farmer in excellent English. He told us that the village of Qaffin had possessed 10,000 *dunums* of land, approximately equal in acreage, and that now they owned only 4,000. The rest had been confiscated for 'security fences'. The community had owned 100,000 olive trees and in the territories of this village alone 40,000 had been razed or burned. There were more fences to come, they had been warned. Eighty-five per cent of their community was now without a means of income. They could not leave the village to farm the few trees left to them, they could not leave the village to find work elsewhere. Their means of survival was sacks of flour brought to them by the Red Cross. 'Our source of existence has been taken from us, but we do not want to fight. We want peace. We want to talk to the Israeli government and find a peaceful solution to this problem.'

A chubby-faced Israeli, Doran, in loose shirt and sandals, leader of a local kibbutz situated a short distance from Qaffin on the Israeli side of the fence, spoke next. He told us that he and his people maintained the groves for the farmers, weeding, pruning, harvesting, doing all they could to keep the fields clean. If the weeds were not uprooted, then, during the desiccation of summer, fires started and the trees were destroyed, particularly given that no Palestinian fire brigade would be given permission to exit the villages and extinguish the conflagrations. 'This land rightfully belongs to these farmers,' he said, 'and we are housekeeping it for them, our neighbours, our Arab friends.'

There were other speakers, both Arabs and Israelis. No one shouted, no one raised their voice, no one heckled or butted in. We sat on stones in the increasing heat and listened. I noticed that growing in the patchy grass around us were exquisite scarlet-red wild anemones.

'There are threats of more walls to come.'

'They are intending to annex all our Palestinian lands.'

'They are taking away our source of life, denying us our heritage.'

I glanced about me to the distant hills. It was hard to imagine that in late antiquity Palestinian wines and olive oil from here were lauded and shipped everywhere around the Mediterranean, transported as far as Britain.

'We are trying to convey a message of peace. A peace that supports two states for two peoples.'

A slender young Israeli woman with a mass of black frizzy hair that, because the sun was behind her, looked like a rubber-tyred halo, working for an equal rights for women organisation, said, 'Please stand with us to see the wall removed. Let's uproot the wall! We are Israelis with a vision of a different Israel. We do not want to close ourselves off, to live as though in a ghetto, surrounded by a monstrous wall.'

'What remains of life is short. We must plant the seeds of peace. Our olives are a symbol of peace,' spoke one of the farmers. He and the Israeli woman were friends. I watched them hugging, tears in their eyes. They had not seen one another for four years. He had not once been granted an exit permit from his village during these years.

While the speeches were in progress, a message came through to the Israeli Arab from Nazareth, from an army official within the IDF. The coordinator told us that what had just been phoned through was the threat, 'Tomorrow, we'll move in and take those saplings out.'

'They uproot and we replant and we'll replant again,' was the response voiced amongst the crowd gathered there on the outskirts of Qaffin.

The Nazarene coordinator assured everyone that he would not allow it to happen and that, with the assistance of inhabitants from the kibbutz, the land would be tidied and cleaned within a fortnight; all rubble removed in order that the sapling grove could begin to flourish.

A young man beside me, fluent in both Arabic and Hebrew, was translating in my ear. Several of the Palestinians were speaking to their Israeli allies in Hebrew, which surprised me. 'They would have learned the language in former times while working in Israel or more recently – not these farmers, but others elsewhere – could have picked it up whilst serving sentences for political crimes in Israeli prisons,' explained my neighbour on the grass.

I recalled the detention centre M and I had passed on our way to Galilee and the Golan Heights.

During all these words, these high-voltage sentiments, two army Hummers patrolled us from the road just beyond the fence, not 50 yards distant. I was a bit afraid. Even so, the image of their presence caused me to smile when I remembered the chariot-riding Canaanites of many epochs back who had caused such terror in the hearts of the Israelites.

And then there was lunch, served from the rear of the van on paper plates. The freshly baked pitta bread was our cutlery and with it we enjoyed houmous, tzatziki, fresh tomatoes and crunchy cucumbers. They were so delicious and reminded me of the Lebanese ones I had eaten with my dear friend Maryam, all those months back, an entire journey ago. The food we were guzzling had been grown and prepared by the women of Qaffin, none of whom were present. In the hot late-February sun, amongst these strangers talking two languages, neither of which I understood or spoke, I felt that I was profoundly privileged. I felt grateful to be in the company of these Jewish Israelis who cared, who were ashamed of this 'Apartheid Wall', this blatant cover-up for the annexation of land that did not belong to Israel, who were sufficiently concerned and compassionate to stand up against their own people, Israeli hardliners, and I prayed that there were groups just like them working within Palestinian circles who would show the same courage in the face of their extremists, their Islamic-jihad fundamentalists who refused to even acknowledge Israel's right to existence, who were, as we were planting olive trees, training kids to blow themselves up taking innocent people with them.

My mind returned to the giants of Bechealeh and I twisted my bottom on the grass and looked up the hill to my own little effort, slightly crooked close by the plastic chair and shoe. I had begun my journey, my search, with, as far as I knew, the oldest living olive specimens on earth and I was completing it with the tiniest, the most fragile of juniors, and I prayed, as I sat there with these welcoming strangers and peace-seekers in the sun, that these sapling trees would know the joy of harvests for thousands of years to come and that the hands who delivered their fruits from tree to press would be from every nation, creed and race and that it would be with peace and love they came together to harvest, with the joy of the Minoans, not driven by war, avarice or hate.

It was time for the farmers to return to their village beyond the barbed-wire fence. Jacob the film-maker, was intending to accompany them as far as their checkpoint and I asked if I could join them. No one seemed to object, so while they gathered their materials and farming tools together, I ran up to the rubbish site to take one last look at my tree. For someone who claims to be an olive farmer, I had certainly not shone in the exercise of planting. My poor little fellow was stuck in the thick clay at quite an angle. I trod my hiking boot down hard, pressing on the other side, near where the graft was, hoping to realign it. An accented voice behind me said, in English, 'It'll grow up straight and strong, don't worry.' I turned and the Palestinian I found so attractive was standing behind me, smiling. 'Where are you from?' he asked me.

I laughed. 'France. Originally, Ireland and England, but I live in France.'

His comrades were calling him. He held out a hand. 'Thank you for coming to support us. It means a great deal to us.'

'I am coming with you,' I replied.

He looked surprised and turned to wave to his fellow villagers, who had climbed aboard the back of the truck – it still contained about twenty saplings – and then he hurried up the hill. 'I must go.'

Jacob, was travelling in a clapped-out red Peugeot belonging to the kibbutz leader Doran. I followed the others, hauled myself up into the back of the truck and travelled with the farmers. We had a journey of about 5 kilometres. It was a tough trundle as the van rolled in and out of potholes, up the hill, down and round. The saplings and loose earth slid about the floor. I was holding on to a railing for dear life. We passed through a village, perhaps a section of Bak'a al-Garbiya, and I saw that here the wall had been installed with tall concrete blocks, similar to Bethlehem, and I learned that where the 'security fence' passes through a populated area rather than agriculture, although it is far more expensive to construct, it is built with concrete. This stretch cut right through the centre of a living community. I saw it with my own eyes. Tiny houses and yards on one side and the same on the other and there was no means of communication whatsoever between one group and the other.

'What is your name?' asked the handsome farmer.

I noticed that the sun had flecked the tips of his short, dark-brown hair chestnut. I told him and asked his, but I never heard his reply. The lorry rumbled in and out of a hole and we had reached the checkpoint. Everyone descended. The army, half a dozen teenagers, boys and girls, with rifles, sur-rounded us. The farmers were ordered to walk the last stretch to the sentry box. I shook hands with each of them and wished them luck.

'Come and see our village,' my new-found friend said to me. He turned and walked down the hill. I followed at a distance taking photographs. Jacob was filming down at the block, bearing witness. Each Arab was ordered to approach alone. The others were instructed to wait back, and when each man had received a clearance on his permit, his shirt had been lifted and he had been body-searched and given the all-clear, he was told to make his way back through the barbed-wired semi-open gate that led to a lane that presumably led to Qaffin, their village out of sight. Then the next man was signalled forward. The indignity of what I was witnessing outraged me, but this day, this assembled planting, this meeting of strangers, was an expression of peace and so I turned my gaze towards the hills of Samaria and concentrated on the beauty of the nature beyond. The tree of peace, planted for peace. A small flock of birds – swallows, I think, but my eyes were blurred with tears I was determined would not fall – was rising and diving overhead, outlined against the clear blue sky. When my friend passed by, he paused and we smiled at one another.

'Goodbye,' he said and strolled slowly on through the gate to join his companions, all of whom were waiting in a group until the last man was through and the gate was once more padlocked.

At which point, I swung on my heels and walked slowly back up the sandy tract of hill.

On the bus back to Tel Aviv, I telephoned Michel, as I had promised, to let him know that I was safe and that our mission had been accomplished.

'One day,' I said to him, 'I hope that you and I will visit Qaffin and harvest "my" adopted tree with the man I met and his wife and family.' I had wanted to suggest to the assembled crowd that we book a date to reconvene at that rubbish dump, nurtured to fully fledged olive grove on the outskirts of Qaffin, to harvest the fruits of those trees in peace and freedom as a group of allies from many cultures. If we fix that date, we have a goal towards peace, I was thinking, but I had not found the courage to speak out. The day had not been about my ideas so I had kept quiet, but in the silence of my heart, I promised that I would return to Qaffin.

A few days later, the Israeli driver who took me to the airport told me that he was entering politics.

'There is no other way forward,' was his explanation. 'I am not a radical; I have joined the Labour Party.'

'How do you see the future between Israel and Palestine?' I asked. The question was like a detonator and he began to shout and rant. It was half past two in the morning and I wished I had not brought up the subject.

'I care nothing for the Palestinians. I don't give a damn how miserable their lives are. I would prefer to see them wiped out. All I want is that my wife and children can go to the mall without I worry about them. Also, I want our army to go into Iran and bomb them out of existence, which is what they want to do to us.'

'You don't think there might be a more peaceful solution to the problems?'

'It states in our Bible that if a man wants to kill you, then get up early and kill him first.'

This was my final exchange in Israel. After everything, it was such a pity. I stepped from the taxi, wishing my driver and his family safe passage. I had decided against mentioning that it also states within biblical Jewish teaching that one should never cut down an olive tree, not even the trees of one's enemy.

All across the earth, there remain trickles, delicate traces of tribes and societies who lived, had been living, would still be living, in fashions that were in tune with nature. Singing their songs to the spirits of the rocks, the trees, the heavens above and the beasts. Offering their sacrifices to their myriad deities.

But we, with our monotheisms and intolerances, have leached the spirits out of the universe. With our advancements and our greeds, we have put paid to their ways. We have stolen, confiscated lands, allocated them patches, cut down their forests and forced them to live another way. To make the earth a better place?

We can destroy, I was thinking as the Israeli immigration officer grilled me about why my husband was no longer accompanying me, quizzed me about what had I been doing in the country alone and why was there no stamp in my passport, but until the last man passes from this earth, there will be someone to sow another seed, to plant one more tree and Nature will nurture it. Nature is regenerative. Individual elements may die but the act of regeneration, of renewal, is written into the intrinsics that go deep beneath the surface of our earth's crust. It is one of its mysteries. And a blessing for our everyday accursed blindnesses.

Back at the Farm

It is Easter. I am lazing out in the garden fragrant with the perfume of jasmine climbing every terrace wall. A perfume of the Orient. Ah, the Orient. I have been back from my travels for four weeks. I returned to Paris, to Michel, and together we drove south. I was rather too shaken to make the journey alone. At home, we found a pack of ten lively puppies awaiting us, not forgetting our two adult Alsatians and a very good-natured Algerian, who was more than delighted by our return. Quashia had, with his usual tender-heartedness and generosity, cared for the hounds during our absences. I found good homes for eight and we have kept two, a girl, Cleopatra, named after the delightful librarian in Lesvos, and a boy, Homer, the father of all storytelling.

The days have been hot and delicious since my return. I have spent many of them sitting in the shade, deep in thought, attempting to get to grips with all that I have seen and experienced. It has not been easy. Our olive trees are showing the buds that will soon break into lacy-fingered flowers. The talk is already of the upcoming harvest, of how this will be the best yet. It is true that the new groves have shot up and are promising us generous yields. There is also debate about last year's crop failure, of how the spraying cannot be avoided, and we are at odds. Quashia is determined that I do not cause us to lose this year's growth. Michel sees both sides, and I remain adamantly against the use of insecticides.

We have owls nesting in one of the taller pine trees. They

hoot close to our bedroom at night. There are more songbirds than I can keep track of. Has the lack of spraying made a difference? Michel shakes his head. Results do not happen overnight, and in any case, we do not live in isolation.

'But we have to begin somewhere,' is my rejoinder. 'It is ourselves as well as the earth we are polluting, poisoning.'

The oranges are coming into blossom and I see Michel down in our tiny grove gathering the last of the fruits. He calls me to join him. At the foot of each tree, a ring of extravagantly violet irises is in blossom. 'Take a look,' he says.

After we bought the farm, the irises surprised us, growing wild, fringing the perimeters of many of the ancient drystone walls. They multiply fast. Every few years we dig into the edge soil, pull up some of their rhizomes and break them into segments, which is rather like cracking old bones apart. Once they have been divided, we plant the tubers everywhere: encircling the feet of these citrus trees, skirting our fences, beneath hardy old oaks, and when spring comes and the skies are cobalt, their deep-violet flower is a striking addition to the garden.

'The structure of the iris head is a wondrous example of the ingenuity of nature. Pick a blossom and take a good look,' Michel says to me. 'See how the lower petals hang and see how, upon them, a furry yellow-and-white stripe, like a miniature ski run, has been designed. When a bee, the plant's pollinator, lands on this brightly coloured pad, it is led directly into the mouth of the flower, deep into its throat, where the nectar awaits. That fur on the landing pad acts as a grip for the bee, keeps it from sliding off before its foraging labours have been achieved. And, as if that were not sufficiently resourceful, upon entering, the bee is obliged to pass beneath a lip, which is part of the plant's female sex organ, and as the bee wriggles through, pollen grains collected on its body stick to the lip and germinate the iris. Isn't that remarkable?'

Yes, remarkable.

The olive tree has been around since before our Stone Age forefathers. It has borne witness to the courageous journeys of seafaring Phoenicians, mysterious and artistic Minoans, Judaean kings and prophets who interpreted the bounty of its harvests as an expression of God's love or anger towards them, the Greeks with their hunger for power and learning, the empire-building Romans, Etruscans, Arabs, Crusaders, Ottomans, to name but a few who have fought for control of this Mediterranean basin, its inland seas and territories. And always, one way or another, the olive has been involved in their stories. But perhaps, since returning from all my journeying, its provenance, the whereabouts of its first pressing, are no longer the vital questions. What have we lost or gained in the trans-Mediterranean crossings, in the cross-pollinations of six thousand years since those mighty beasts of Bechealeh were first planted, is this what I am asking myself? What might those early peoples have known that we have lost sight of? A childlike sense of discovery, of joy, respect for the minute details of life?

I had intended to visit Alexandria, I had been looking forward to it, but after Israel I did not. I was emotionally drained. I felt the need to come home. Perhaps I will begin my next journey there, who knows?

I learned along my way that the oil from the olive is the most ancient source of light, and that in Alexandria, pre-Christ, and quite probably in other areas of Egypt and the Mediterranean too, as dusk fell and folk had filled their little clay lamps with olive oil ready for lighting, there followed the ritual of *lychnokajia*, or the moment of 'lamp-lighting'. Performed by every household simultaneously, this 'lighting up' was reported to be spectacular, a magical moment, perceived as a celebration of light. Celebration. Is that what we are fast losing? The appreciation of simple yet ingenious miracles? The value of life itself?

While Palestine and the Middle East are being torn apart by intolerance and hatred, a tiny yet mighty miracle is taking root in that territory. When the Romans conquered ancient Judaea, thick forests of date palms grew there. Nothing was thought to remain of those forests until thirty years ago, when, at an archaeological site near Masada, date seeds were excavated and carbon-dated at two thousand years old. Three of those seeds were planted on Tu Bishvat a year ago and they have taken. Two-thousand-year-old date palms, trees that Christ may or may not have walked beneath, a variety of palm that was lost to mankind, regenerated.

Our appreciation of such simple yet ingenious miracles. The blessings bestowed upon us of light and darkness, of day and night, of sun, heat, rain, of the seasons, of the earth's ability to provide for all our needs. The ability to be born anew.

Index

Abdullah (olive farmer in Syria), 92, 93, 94–5, 131–2, 195

Abdusalem (driver in Libya), 260–1, 262, 263, 264

Abraham, 233

Acropolis, Athens, 289, 292–3

Acts of the Apostles, 72, 187

Adam (acquaintance in Israel), 369, 370–1

Adramitianes olives, 314

Aegean, 97, 109, 127, 306–7

Aeolians, 116

Afrodisias, Temple of, Kale, 135

Agios Giorgios Chapel, Athens, 291, 317

Aïd el Fitr, L', 220, 224, 228, 230, 232, 234

al: *for names beginning with prefix al- see under following element of name*

Alalia, 120

Alanya, 143–5

Albanians, 307, 312, 313, 316, 330

Aleppo, 74, 86–91, 355, 356

Alex (oil worker in Libya), 254, 255

Alexander the Great, 41, 106, 108, 214, 215, 321

Alexandria, 288, 294, 305, 316, 329, 417

Algeria, 77

All Creatures Great and Small, 175

Allaga, 118–19

Allies, 305

Americas, the, 182

Amla (acquaintance in Bethlehem), 386, 393, 394–7

Ampurias, 120

Anamur, 147–8

Anamurium, 148, 155

Ananias, 72

Anatolia, 29, 50, 64, 79, 97, 99, 139, 142, 155, 355

Antalya, 97, 143, 145–6

Anti-Lebanon mountain range, 62

Antibes, 8, 120

Antioch, 91, 97

Antony, Mark, 72, 322

Apollonia, 277, 278–9, 286

Arabia, 109

Arabs, 6, 68, 180, 186, 214, 274,
317, 365, 368, 369, 370, 375,
379, 390, 398, 399, 417 see also
Palestinians
Aramaeans, 381
Aramaic, 75
Aristotle, 321
Armenians, 103
Artemis, 125, 126, 127
    Temple of, near Ephesus,
    125–6
Artemisia, 324–5
Asklepios, 117
al-Assad, President Bashar, 67,
68, 69, 89
al-Assad, Basil, 67, 69, 89
al-Assad, Hafez, 67, 85
al-Assad family, 66, 67, 72
Assyrians, 35, 41, 147, 206
Atatürk (Mustafa Kemal), 101,
105, 106, 302
Athene, 289, 293
Athens, 178, 289–94, 295, 298,
312, 316–17, 321, 329, 334, 357,
362, 363, 364
Atlantic, 41
Atlantis, 361
Attica, 289, 291, 316–17
Atticans, 321
Aubenas, Florence, 7, 66
Ayvalik, 113–14, 115, 297,
314
Aziz (driver in Lebanon),
45–6

Baalbek, 65
Bab el Bahr (Porte de France),
Tunis, 203
Babylon, 97, 139, 142, 321
Babylonians, 35
Baghdad, 7
Bak'a al-Garbiya, 402, 404,
410
Bardaouni river, 64
Barluzzi (architect), 388
Baron Hotel, Aleppo, 87–8
Bay of Salina, 177
Bay of Tunis, 212
Beauvoir, Simone de, 211
Bechealeh, 24–30, 36, 50, 58, 64,
65, 74, 108, 155, 182, 191, 193,
194, 308, 349, 355, 356, 367,
378, 383, 387, 409, 417
Bedouins, 78, 83, 274, 277,
283–4, 287
Beirut, 1, 14, 15, 19, 28, 30–6, 49,
53, 55
Beit-Shabeb, 14, 15, 24
Bell, Gertrude, 77
Ben Ali, Zine El Abidine,
President of Tunisia, 211
Benghazi, 246, 252, 253, 255,
264, 265, 268, 269, 270–2,
273, 282, 288, 330
Beqaa Valley, 17, 19, 55, 56, 61–5,
109
Berbers, 221, 224, 225
Bet Lehem see Bethlehem
Bet Shemesh, 385

Beth (acquaintance in Israel), 369–70, 371

Bethlehem (Bet Lehem), 76, 384, 386, 389, 392, 393, 394–7

Bidnija, 169–71

Bin Laden, Osama, 225, 229

Binwerrard (Burmarrad), 163

Birzebbuga, 163

Black Sea, 106, 120, 305

Blair, Tony, 2, 238

Bosphorus Strait, 97

Bou Kornein, 212

Braudel, Fernand, 206

Britain, 2–3, 44, 206 see also British, the

British, the, 147, 305, 315, 369 see also Britain

Bronze Age, 108, 116, 317

Brown & Root, 258

Burmarrad (Binwerrard), 163

Bush, George W., 2

Byblos, 28, 35, 49–55, 109, 124, 222, 355

Byzantines, 171

Cadiz (Gades), 40

Cadmus, 40, 356

Caesar, Julius, 208, 249

Café d'Orient, Beirut, 33

Caicus plain, 117

Calypso's Island, 187

Canaanites, 33, 39, 402

Canada, 53, 55

Çanakkale, 107, 109–12

Capernaum, 380

Cappadocia, 50, 118, 148, 152, 154, 156

Carmel (Lebanese boy), 47, 48, 49

Carthage, 40, 41, 42, 43, 86, 195, 198, 205–11, 214, 321

Carthage-Hannibal station, 210

Çatal Hüyük, 29, 97, 118, 132, 138–9, 140, 141, 142, 143, 145, 148, 149, 151–2, 153–6, 157, 159, 356

Catalonians, 10

Cato, 179

Cecrops, 289, 317

Chafeek (chef in Beirut), 32

Chania, 334–8, 361–2

Château de la Mer, Saida (Sidon), 37

Cheney, Dick, 254, 256–7

China, 79

Chios, 120

Chris (acquaintance in Bethlehem), 397

Christ, 45, 47, 48, 76, 379, 387, 388, 389, 394, 397

Christians, 18–19, 21, 34, 35, 38, 43, 44, 48, 75, 233

Christie, Agatha, 87–8

Christos (waiter in Crete), 345–6

Churchill, Winston, 106

Citizens' Theatre, Glasgow, 8
Cleopatra, 72, 77, 322
Cleopatra (librarian in
    Lesvos), 304–5, 306
Colette, 211
Comino, 160
Constantinople, 108, 305
Copper Age, 192, 193
Corcyra, 321
Corinth, 322
Cornwall, 206
Corsica, 120
Côte d'Azur, 1
Crete, 29, 294, 305, 316, 317, 324, 326
    travels in, 334–63
Croesus, King, 120
Çumra, 152
Cyprus, 22, 86, 147, 311
Cyrenaica, 264, 330
Cyrene, 277, 278, 286–7

Daher's Vineyard, 396
Damascus, 49, 64, 68–75, 97
Dardanelles Strait, 106–7
David, King, 40
Deir al-Zor, 79, 81
Dibdib family, 57–60, 227
Djerba, 208, 215, 217–37
Dongah, 258
Doran (acquaintance in
    Israel), 406–7, 410
Druze, 19, 37–8
Duncan (acquaintance in

Tunisia and Libya), 224,
    236–7, 238–9, 240, 242–3, 244,
    254, 257, 259, 264, 266, 268

Ebla, 74, 91
Eceabat, 106
Egaleo, 291
Egirdir, 137–8
Egypt, 37, 50, 64, 65, 79, 86, 109,
    120, 148, 214, 261, 294, 361,
    364, 417 see also Egyptians
Egyptians, 35, 79, 147, 215, 287
    see also Egypt
Ein Kerem, 376
El Bekri, Abu Abdullah, 208,
    209, 214
El Ghriba synagogue, Erriadh,
    225
El-Jem Roman theatre, 217
Elaiohori, 292
Elizabeth (acquaintance in
    Lebanon), 16, 17, 18, 20, 21,
    22, 24, 30, 35
Elizabeth (mother of John the
    Baptist), 376
Emile (acquaintance in
    Lebanon), 16–17, 18, 19, 20,
    21, 22, 23, 24, 30, 35
England, 79
Ephesus, 97, 125, 126–7, 139, 142
Epidavros, 290
Erechtheion, Athens, 293
Ermenek, 149, 150
Erriadh, 225

Eski Foça (Old Foça), 120, 122, 123–5
Euesperides, 265, 330
Euphrates river, 67, 81, 82, 151
Euphrates Valley, 81
Europa, 40, 356–7
European Union (EU), 58, 102, 184, 227, 340
Evans, Sir Arthur, 347, 348, 358

Fareed (professor/driver in Lebanon), 56, 57, 59, 61, 62, 63, 64, 65, 66, 67–8, 80
Fatma, 219–20
Fertile Crescent, 61, 81, 82
Festos, 335, 337, 341, 347, 348, 349, 354, 355, 356, 357
Filfia, 190
Filiki Atairia, 315
Flaubert, Gustave, 210, 215
  Salammbô, 214
France, 1–13, 19, 22, 86, 120, 165, 227, 261, 304, 340 see also French, the
Franciscans, 388
French, the, 18, 19, 89, 184, 201 see also France
Frendo, Julia, 166, 168, 171–2, 174, 175–86, 187, 188, 189, 190, 192, 195, 196
Frendo, Lizzie, 168, 189
Frendo, Natalino, 164–71, 173–5, 176, 177, 182, 185, 186, 188, 189–90, 194, 195, 196

Gaddafi, Mu'ammer ('the Leader'), 238, 246, 250–1, 251–2, 253, 256, 257, 258, 272
Gades (Cadiz), 40
Galata Bridge, Istanbul, 99, 101
Galen, 117
Gallipoli, 106
  Battle of, 106
Garden of Gethsemane, 387–8
Garden of Hesperides, 265
Gaza, 369, 370, 371, 383, 390
Gebel Escarpment, 246
George (oil worker in Libya), 245
Georgios (taverna owner in Lesvos), 298, 299, 311
Germans, 301, 315
Gethsemane, 387–8
Ghasri, 186
Gideon (acquaintance in Crete), 351, 352
Giorgio (olive farmer in Malta), 166–7
Glasgow, 8
Gokova, 132
Golan Heights, 67, 378, 380–1, 383
Golden Chain, 104
Golden Horn, 101
Gozo, 160, 163, 165, 174, 175, 186–7, 196
Grand Bazaar, Istanbul, 99
Grasse, 165

Great Man-Made River
Project, 257–8, 271
Great Mosque (Jami ez-
Zituna), Tunis, 201
Grecani, 329
Greece, 65, 86, 97, 102, 109, 214,
215, 216, 244, 288, 364
travels in, 289–333
see also Greeks, the
Greeks, 5, 10, 40, 51, 58, 79, 102,
107, 116, 118, 120, 123, 124,
180, 206, 207, 215, 221, 264–5,
274, 275, 276, 278, 284, 287,
302, 325–6, 417 see also
Greece
Green Book, The, 253
Green Line, Beirut, 34, 35
Green Mountain, 246, 264–5,
266, 274, 275, 330
Greene, Graham, 64
A Burnt-out Case, 273
Stamboul Train, 99
Ways of Escape, 273
Guaran, 260
Guellala, 224–9, 231
Gulf of Yera, 312

Hadrian, Emperor, 35,
369
Hagar Qim, 190
Haifa, 294
Halliburton, 256–7, 258
Hamas, 312
Hammamet, 212–14

Hani (driver in Lebanon), 15,
16, 24, 25, 28
Haredim, 364–5, 374
al-Hariri, Rafiq, 21, 31, 32, 33, 62
Harissa, 15
Hasdrubal, 209
Havuzbaşi, 128
Haz-Zebbug, 163, 186
Helen of Troy, 107
Hellespont, 106
Herodes Atticus theatre,
Athens, 292
Herodotus, 5, 39, 214–15
Hesperides, Garden of, 265
Hezbollah, 19–20, 43–4, 55, 62,
63, 65, 66, 229
Hiram, King of Tyre, 35, 40
Hittites, 147
Homer, 129, 221, 347, 348
Iliad, The, 107
Homs Pass, 355
Hotel Africa, Tunis, 200–1, 204
Houmt Souk, 220
Hussein, Saddam, 214
Hüyük, 139, 140, 142, 148

Ice Age, 25, 160
IDF see Israeli Defence Force
Idris, King, 253
Imittos, 291
India, 79, 214–15
Ionian Islands, 305
Iráklion, 335, 348, 357
Museum of, 357, 358

Iran, 7, 19, 44, 104, 254, 413

Iraq, 2, 3, 7, 31, 61, 67, 81–2, 86, 151, 214, 256, 285–6

Islam, 54, 55, 71, 74, 94–5, 105, 284, 285 *see also* Muslims

Israel, 19, 20, 40, 43, 44, 46, 55, 63, 67, 229, 288, 294, 312, 316, 362, 363
travels in, 364–414

Israeli Defence Force (IDF), 379, 391, 404, 408

Istanbul, 97–105, 106

Italians, 90, 94, 132, 184, 252, 253, 257, 265, 276 *see also* Italy

Italy, 131, 173, 181, 184, 193, 197, 208, 329 *see also* Italians

Izmir, 97, 128, 129

Jacob (acquaintance in Israel), 401, 403, 410, 411

Jaffa, 368–9

Jamel (driver in Libya), 269, 270–1, 272, 275, 277, 278, 281–3, 284, 285–6

Jami ez-Zituna (Great Mosque), Tunis, 201

Jarmo, 155

Jeblazzara, 179

Jericho, 49

Jerusalem, 374–5, 384, 385, 386–91, 398, 399
Temple of, 35, 40, 225

Jerusalem Post, 373, 390

Jews, 225, 228–9, 364–5, 369, 370, 376, 390, 399, 400, 405
see also Israel

John the Baptist, 71, 376

Jordan, 61, 67, 370, 377, 378, 383, 388

Judaea, 369, 370, 373, 383, 417, 418

Kalamata, 294, 319, 324, 325–7, 330, 333

Kalamata olives, 314, 319, 327

Kale, 133, 135

Karaman, 151, 152

Katris, Professor, 308–11

Kayseri, 97

Keenan, Brian, 44

Kekova (Tristomo), 145

Khalifa (acquaintance on flight to Libya), 240–1

Khan al-Sabun, Aleppo, 89–90

Khan al-Zait, Damascus, 73–4

Kidron Valley, 389

Kiniklis, Georgios, 313–16

Kissufim, 390–1

Knights of St John, 160, 162, 180, 181

Knossos, 348, 354, 355, 356, 357, 358

Koloves olives, 314

Kommos, 354

Konya, 140, 152

Koran, 94

Kuçuk Deniz, Old Foça, 123–4

Kupek, 217
Kurassi, 379
Kurds, 103

Lacydon, creek of, 5
Ladoelies olives, 314
Latakia, 94, 97
Laurent (French student in
    Turkey), 118
Lausanne, Treaty of, 102, 302
Lawrence, D.H., 207–8
Lawrence, T.E., 87
League of Nations, 369–70
Lebanon, 2, 3, 5, 7, 193, 194, 227,
    377, 378, 382, 383
    travels in, 14–60, 61–6
Lena (acquaintance in
    Lebanon), 53, 54–5
Leptis Magna, 243, 248–50, 252
Lesvos, 116, 178, 226–7,
    294–316, 319, 340, 356
Levant, 2, 18, 109, 146, 155, 355,
    356 see also names of
    countries
Leyla (maid in Lebanon), 16,
    18, 24
Libération, 7, 66
Libya, 55, 86, 215, 224, 237, 330,
    388
        travels in, 238–88
Limona, Monastery of, 307
Lipari, 118
London, 2, 8, 14, 15, 16, 30, 104,
    238, 264

London Illustrated News, 358
Loutra, 312–16
Love Valley, 158
Lower Galilee, 379
Lydians, 120
Lykavittos Hill, Athens, 290,
    291–2, 316–17

Ma'adi, 65
Ma'alula, 75–6
McCarthy, John, 44
Macedonians, 321
Magna Graecia, 329
Malida (acquaintance in
    Bethelehem), 394, 395, 397
Mallowan, Max, 87–8
Malta, 40, 97, 225, 276, 356
    travels in, 160–96
Maria (cleaner in Malta), 188
Marie (acquaintance in
    Lebanon), 52–4, 55
Mark Antony, 72, 322
Maronites, 18–19, 57
Marsa, 179
Marseille, 1–13, 22, 90, 120, 124,
    207, 304
Mary (mother of Christ), 376
Mary Magdalene, 388
Mary's Tomb, Jerusalem, 389
Maryam (friend in Lebanon),
    14–15, 16, 17, 18, 20, 21, 22,
    25, 27, 30, 52
Masada, 418
Matala, 349–52

Mauromati, 327, 328–31

Mdina, 163

Mea Shearim, Jerusalem, 374

Mehldau, Brad, 52

Menderes (Scamander) river, 109

Mesopotamia, 50, 64, 83, 84, 355

Messini, 265, 327–30

Metcalfe, Dr C.R., 192

Mexico, 22

Mgarr, 186

Michel (husband), 3, 54, 56, 77, 85, 87, 97, 127, 160, 213, 236, 273, 274, 276, 280, 315, 320, 349, 357, 362, 368, 412, 415, 416

  in Israel, 373, 374, 376, 377, 378, 381, 382, 383, 384, 385

  in Marseille, 1, 4–5, 7, 8, 9, 12

  in Turkey, 130, 131, 132, 134, 135, 137, 138, 139, 141, 142, 143, 145, 149, 151, 152, 157, 158, 159

Middle East, 2, 3, 155, 356, 383, 418 see also names of countries

Midnight Express, 103

Midoun, 230, 231–5

al-Mina, 41

Minoans, 29, 347–9, 354–7, 357–61, 362, 364, 417

Minos, King, 357

Minotaur, 347

Mireille (French student in Turkey), 118

Misir Çarşisi, Istanbul, 100–1

Mitchell, Joni, 350

Mnajdra, 190

Mohammed (Lebanese boy), 47, 48

Montreal, 53, 55

Moses, 103

Mosta, 184

Mount Lebanon range, 17, 19, 25, 26, 38, 50, 61, 64, 79

Mount of Beatitudes, 379

Mount of Olives, 387–9

Mount Olympus, 289, 322

Mount Tabor, 379

Mugla, 130, 132

Muhammad, Prophet, 89, 95, 103, 104, 219, 233

Muhammad (driver in Syria), 75, 77, 80, 88, 92

Muhammad (interpreter in Syria), 75, 77, 78, 80, 81, 83–4, 85–6, 87, 88, 89, 92

al-Mukhtar, Umar, 276

Munich, 351

Murat (driver in Turkey), 105, 106, 109–11, 112, 113, 114, 116, 117, 118, 119, 122, 128, 129, 130–1, 132

Muslims, 18–19, 34, 37, 38, 48, 70, 71, 95, 103, 104–5, 233, 388

see also Druze; Islam;
Shi'ites; Sunnis
Mustafa Kemal *see* Atatürk
Mut, 150
Mycenae, 347
Mycenaeans, 314, 360, 361
Myra, 135
Mytilene, 296–312, 313, 315

Nablus, 90
Nadia (hotel proprietress in
Tripoli), 56, 61
Naji (driver in Lebanon), 37–8
National Museum, Beirut, 34,
35
National Museum of
Archaeology, Valletta, 162
Nazareth, 384–5
Neolithic period, 29, 108,
155–6, 162, 182, 193–4, 277, 317
New Foça (Yeni Foça), 120–2
New Testament, 379
New Yorker, 256–7
Nice, 159
Nicholas, St, 135, 361
Nile, River, 214
Nile Valley, 50
Noah, 360
Notre Dame de la Garde
basilica, Marseille, 7–8
Nubia, 50, 65

O'Brien, Seamus, 266–8, 269,
272

Odeon of Herodes Atticus,
Athens, 292
Odysseus, 187, 220, 221, 222, 354
Oea, 243
Old Foça *see* Eski Foça
Old Testament, 360
Olive Castle hotel, Tripoli,
56
Olive Egg Tree, Midoun, 230,
231, 233, 234–5
Olivit, 272
Olympus, Mount, 289, 322
Omalos Plateau, 341, 344
Omayyad Mosque,
Damascus, 71
Orontes Valley, 92
Ottomans/Ottoman Empire,
18, 86, 89, 98, 101, 102–3, 107,
116, 253, 265, 298, 302, 304,
305, 307, 314–15, 369, 417
Our Lady of Lebanon statue,
Harissa, 15

Palestine, 29, 64, 75, 79, 86, 90,
109, 369–70, 380, 383, 390,
403, 412, 418
Palestinian Territories, 46, 369,
383
Palestinians, 45–6, 312, 369, 370,
371, 391–2, 395–6, 399, 400,
402, 403, 404, 405–6, 407,
408, 410, 411, 413
Palmyra, 76–9
Panathenaea, 293–4

Papadopoulos, Georgios, 292, 293
Paris, 4, 8, 236, 415
Parker, Alan, 103
Parnitha, 291
Pasiphae, 347
Paul, St, 72, 177, 187
Paul (friend in Lebanon), 14, 15, 17, 18, 19, 20, 22, 24, 25, 27, 28, 30, 52
Paulos (acquaintance in Greece), 343
Pavilion of Sacred Relics, Topkapi Palace, Istanbul, 103
Pelekani's bookshop, Chania, 336
Peloponnese, 265, 294, 305, 314, 318–33, 347, 356, 360, 361
People's Congress (Libya), 253
Pergamum, 117–18
Persia, 79, 84, 214, 215 see also Persians
Persians, 116, 120, 321 see also Persia
Pete (oil expert in Libya), 254, 255
Petros (shop-owner in Lesvos), 299, 300–3, 316
Philip II, King of Macedonia, 321
Phocaea, 5, 120, 123–4 see also Eski Foça

Phocaeans, 5, 120, 124, 207
Phoenician alphabet, 40
Phoenicians, 5, 21, 28, 29, 39, 40–1, 51, 52, 55–6, 58, 86, 124, 148, 150, 161, 162, 169, 171, 178, 179, 182, 183, 187, 193, 195, 205, 206, 207, 215, 217, 222, 225, 243, 249, 259, 275, 287, 289, 291, 321, 325–6, 349, 417
Pillars of Hercules, 41
Piraeus, 290, 295, 334
Pithos Garden, Troy, 107
Plant for Peace, 391
Pliny the Elder, 163, 173, 178
Pompey, 249
Porte de France (Bab el Bahr), Tunis, 203
Portugal, 41, 243
Poseidon, 289
Priapus, 127–8
Provençals, 10, 11
Provence, 120
Ptolemy, 274
Punic Wars, 178, 208

al-Qaeda, 44, 225
Qaffin, 401, 402, 404, 406, 408, 409, 411, 412
al-Qalamoon Mountains, 75
Qana, 45, 46–9, 229
Quashia (gardener), 11, 12, 77, 127, 144, 159, 160, 199–200, 273, 325, 415

Rabbis for Peace, 396
Ramadan (month of fasting), 199, 200, 201, 220, 228
Ramadan (olive mill owner in Libya), 261–2
Raqqa, 85
Reagan, President Ronald, 258
Red Beach, 350–1, 352
Red Cross, 406
Red Sea, 39, 103, 148, 155
Reporters Sans Frontières, 7
Republic of Greater Lebanon, 18–19
Rhodes, 162
Romans, 41, 65, 79, 101, 108, 109, 124, 170, 171, 178, 179, 180, 207–8, 209, 215, 217, 222, 224, 243, 249, 250, 259, 265, 274, 284, 287, 321–2, 369, 417, 418
Ross, Dr Douglas, 213, 215–16
Rothschild estates, 380
Roussos, Demis, 52

al-Saadi, Hussein Hanoun, 7
Sabratha, 243, 256, 257, 259–60
Saddam Hussein, 214
Sahara, 219, 222
Sahia, Madame, 43–4, 62
Saida see Sidon
St Julian's Bay, 175
St Paul's Bay, 164, 176, 177–8
St Paul's Chapel, Damascus, 72

St Pawl Milqi, Malta, 177–9
Salem, 391
Sally (acquaintance in Lesvos), 301, 302
Samaria, 370, 383
Samarian Gorge, 341
Samuel (acquaintance in Israel), 401
San Blas, 174, 186
Santorini (Thera), 265, 360
Sataf region, 373, 376–8, 385
Saudi Arabia, 55
Saul see Paul, St
Scamander (Menderes) river, 109
Schliemann, Heinrich, 107, 347–8
Sea of Galilee, 378, 379, 402
Sea of Marmara, 106
Selçuk, 125, 128
Sfax, 216, 217
Sharon, Ariel, 371, 390
Shi'ites, 19, 38, 43, 44, 45, 46, 47, 48–9, 63, 104
Sicily, 160, 161, 166, 167, 181, 184, 191, 193, 197, 261, 321, 329, 356
Sidi Bou Said, 210, 211–12
Sidi El Kalani, 217
Sidon (Saida), 19, 28, 37, 49, 51, 109
Silk Route, 79
Sirt, 251
Six Day War, 67, 378, 381
Skampanas, Professor, 307–8

Skorba, 191–4
Solomon, King, 35, 40
Solon, 216
Souk al Attarine, Tunis, 201
Sour see Tyre
Sousse, 216
South Africa, 247
Spain, 40, 51, 86, 120, 162, 181, 182, 206, 243
Sparta, 316, 319–24, 329–30 see also Spartans
Spartans, 265, 320–1, 322, 327, 330 see also Sparta
Spice Market, Istanbul, 100–1
Stark, Freya, 73
Stephanie (acquaintance in Libya), 267, 268, 269–70, 272–3
Stevens, Cat, 350
Stone Age, 30, 108, 135, 145, 151, 156, 162, 192, 193, 196, 221, 276–7, 417
Strabo, 179
Sunnis, 18–19, 44, 70, 104
Susa, 266, 277–84
Syria, 2, 5, 18, 19, 21, 29, 44, 55, 59, 61, 62, 63, 64, 66, 67, 97, 109, 155, 195, 355, 361, 377, 378, 380, 382, 383
    travels in, 67–96

Tabcha, 380
Tabor, Mount, 379
Tarsus, 72

Taurus Mountains, 148
    journey across, 149–51
Tavas, 133
Tel Aviv, 357, 364, 366–7, 369, 373, 378, 382, 400
Tent of Nations, 397
Thebes, 329
Thera (Santorini), 265, 360
Thermi, 308
Theseus, 347
Three Cities, 160
Tiberias, 379
Timothy, Chris, 175
Tishreen restaurant, Nazareth, 384–5
Tolmeta, 274, 281
Tonio (assistant at olive mill in Malta), 165, 166, 168
Topkapi Palace, Istanbul, 103
Tripoli, Greece, 319
Tripoli, Lebanon, 19, 28, 55–6, 90
Tripoli, Libya, 241–5, 250–4, 260
Tripolitania, 243, 349
Tristomo (Kekova), 145
Troas plains, 108, 109
Troy, 105, 107–9, 347, 355
Trump, David H.: Skorba, 192
Tu Bishvat, 371–3, 376, 378, 390, 418
Tunis, 197–205, 210, 216
Tunisia, 11, 41, 254, 261
    travels in, 197–237

Turkey, 5, 29, 50, 61, 67, 83, 86, 96, 276, 295, 302, 303, 313, 314, 347
        travels in, 97–159
Turkish War of Independence, 102
Twain, Mark, 72, 368
Tyre (Sour), 19, 28, 36, 37, 38–46, 49, 51, 109, 124, 161, 169, 171, 193, 206, 275

Ugarit, 94, 97
UN, 43, 44–5, 46, 47
UNESCO, 4, 45, 386
United States, 22, 31, 44, 81, 256, 257, 258
UNSCO (United Nations Special Coordinator), 390
Upper Barrakka Gardens, Valletta, 160
Ürgüp, 156
Uri (acquaintance in Israel), 400–1, 403–4
Utica, 208
Uzbekistan, 254

Valletta, 160, 162, 181, 190, 196, 197
Valley of Tears, 381
Venetians/Venice, 305
Versailles, Treaty of, 89
Victoria, Queen, 35–6
Vince (fisherman in Malta), 183

Wadi Kuf, 275
Wadi Lebda, 249
Waite, Terry, 44, 62
Wardija, 164
    residence and farm of Frendo family at, 164–9, 171–5, 176–7, 187–90, 194–6
Weitzlar, 376
West Bank, 90, 369, 370, 373, 374, 383, 384, 391, 395, 400, 402
White Mountains, 335, 336, 338–47
World War I (1914–18), 18, 89
World War II (1939–45), 301, 305, 315, 351

Xerxes, King of Persia, 106

Yeni Foça (New Foça), 120–2
Yiannis (taverna owner in Lesvos), 298, 299–300, 311
Yusef (street-seller in Jerusalem), 389, 397

Zabia (landlady in Crete), 353–4
Zawia, 260
Zebbug, 182
Zefat, 380
Zegtun, 163
Zenobia, Queen of Palmyra, 77, 79
Zgharta, 57–60
Zionists, 371, 372, 376